MECHANICS' INSTITUTE
❦ MECHANICS' ❧
MERCANTILE LIBRARY

PHILIP SIDNEY

Also by Alan Stewart

Close Readers: Humanism and Sodomy in Early Modern England

Hostage to Fortune: The Troubled Life of Francis Bacon 1561–1626
(coauthored with Lisa Jardine)

PHILIPS SYDNEY, RIDDER.
OVERSTE VAN VLISSINGE EN RAMMEKENS.

PHILIP SIDNEY
A Double Life

Alan Stewart

THOMAS DUNNE BOOKS
St. Martin's Press ❧ New York

THOMAS DUNNE BOOKS
An imprint of St. Martin's Press

www.stmartins.com

ISBN 0-312-28287-7

First published in Great Britain by Chatto & Windus
Random House U.K. Limited

First U.S. Edition: September 2001

10 9 8 7 6 5 4 3 2 1

For Andrew

Acknowledgements

Working on Philip Sidney left me in constant awe at the huge diversity of activities the man undertook in his short life – and at the knowledges that have to be reassembled to understand that life now. It took many friends and colleagues to explain to me everything from the Welsh wool trade to the Polish electoral system. My thanks go to Gavin Alexander, Peter Barber, Joseph Black, Warren Boutcher, Tricia Bracher, Alan Bray, Rebecca de Saintonge, Eliane Glaser, Lisa Jardine, Rachel Jardine, Roger Kuin, Elizabeth Lewis, Jeremy Maule, Andrew Penman. Gareth Roberts, Bill Sherman, Mark Taviner, Piotr Urbanski, Jonathan Woolfson and Sharon Zink. Especial thanks to Lorna Hutson, who first taught me to read Sidney; to my agent Maggie Pearlstine, for her belief in this book right from the start; and to Patricia Brewerton, for her constant support and for allowing me to draw on her important unpublished work. Mr James Lawson, the archivist of Shrewsbury School, provided expertise on sixteenth-century Shrewsbury. The first audience for this material was at Pennsylvania State University: Patrick Cheney, Marie Hojnacki, Guido Ruggiero, Garrett Sullivan and Linda Woodbridge made me welcome and provided thoughtful comments. As ever, I am indebted to the staff of various libraries and archives: the Rare Books and Manuscripts Room of the British Library at St Pancras; the University of London Library; the Institute of Historical Research; the Warburg Institute; Trinity College, Cambridge; Cambridge University Library; the Bodleian Library, Oxford; and Harvard College Library. I am grateful to the Viscount de L'Isle and Dudley for access to his family papers, now housed at the Centre for Kentish Studies in Maidstone. Joanne, Howard and Joshua Gorner lent me their home and gave me the chance to finish this book.

Most importantly, my editor at Chatto & Windus, Rebecca Carter, refused to let Philip lie in peace until I'd got him right. For that he, and I, are in her debt.

Contents

List of Illustrations

ILLUSTRATIONS APPEARING WITHIN THE TEXT

Title page: Sir Philip Sidney as Governor of Flushing and Ramekins. Reproduced courtesy of the Stedelijk Museum Zutphen, the Netherlands.

BLACK AND WHITE PLATES

Author's Note

Some translations of the correspondence between Sidney and Languet draw on previously published versions by Stueart Pears (1845), Malcolm William Wallace (1915) and James M. Osborn (1972). Translations of other passages are credited in the endnotes, or are my own.

The early modern English year began on 25 March. Throughout the book, I have silently 'modernised' dates so that the year begins on the preceding 1 January. A further complication arises when considering sources from 1581 when the continental calendar moved ten days ahead of the English, so that 25 December in the Low Countries was 15 December in England, and so on. Unless otherwise stated, the English calendar has been used; in some cases, however (as in chapter 11), it has been necessary, for reasons which will become obvious, to quote both versions of the date in the endnotes.

Introduction

O NE DAY IN 1635, Mr Richard Aubrey took his young son to visit Mr Singleton, a Gloucester alderman and wool-draper. Nine-year-old John was drawn to an intriguing sight over the chimney in Singleton's parlour: a pictorial representation of a funeral procession, engraved and printed on large sheets of paper pasted together, 'which in length was, I believe, the length of the room at least'. But he became truly fascinated when Mr Singleton 'contrived it to be turned upon two pins, that turning one of them made the figures march

all in order. It did make such a strong impression on my tender phantasy,' he recalled in old age, 'that I remember it as if it were but yesterday.'[1]

As John gazed on, a story unravelled. First he saw a gentleman look down as a ship, labelled the *Black Pinnace*, sailed across the chimney. Then he saw a coffin lying in a vaulted room, surrounded by hangings bearing coats of arms. And then a procession marched from right to left: poor men and soldiers, gentlemen and yeomen servants, chaplains, noblemen, aldermen, the Lord Mayor himself, 300 London citizens in arms, and a war horse splendidly adorned, ridden by a page scarcely older than John trailing a broken lance. In the midst of all the splendour came the coffin, borne by fourteen men. All in all, 344 figures processed across Mr Singleton's parlour chimney.

What John was seeing, fifty years after the event, was the funeral of Sir Philip Sidney, as his body made its slow way from the Low Countries, where he had died at Arnhem, to lie in state at the Minories Church just outside Aldgate, thence to be carried through the streets of London to St Paul's Cathedral, where he was buried on 16 February 1587. Every detail had been preserved on this thirty-eight-foot-long roll, engraved by Derick Theodor de Brii, with a narrative by Thomas Lant explaining each stage. According to Lant, Principal Secretary of State Sir Francis Walsingham, Sidney's father-in-law, had 'spared not any cost to have this funeral well performed'. The city streets 'were so thronged with people that the mourners had scarcely room to pass; the houses likewise were as full as they might be, of which great multitude there were few or none

that shed not some tears as the corpse passed by them'. Sidney was buried to the sound of a double volley, to 'give unto his famous life and death a martial "Vale"'.[2]

To boys of John Aubrey's generation, it seemed only natural that Sidney should have had such a splendid funeral. He was, after all, a legendary figure from the legendary age of the Virgin Queen Elizabeth: a great national hero, courtier, soldier and poet, who epitomised the ideals of Elizabethan chivalry, passionate Protestantism and an ineffable sense of Englishness. When the Bodleian Library put up a new frieze in the 1610s, memorialising the world's greatest authors, the portrait of Philip Sidney headed the modern 'greats', just as Homer headed the ancients.

John Aubrey's Philip Sidney is the same Philip Sidney I first encountered at school. That funeral procession has been marching across the English imagination for the last 400 years. But we have also known for a long time that the spectacular obsequies were strangely out of proportion to Sidney's status and reputation. Born into a respectable gentry family with an honourable history of royal service, Philip indeed showed early promise for a career in diplomacy, but his close identification with his uncle, the Earl of Leicester, and a series of court controversies blocked that path. Much of his adult life was spent in the country, strapped for cash, penning what he himself spoke of as literary trifles, none of which he actually published. Only in his final year did he win a prestigious military posting, as Governor of the Low Countries'

port of Flushing — and even that was linked to his uncle's appointment there as Governor General.

The funeral was, in fact, the last master-stroke of a major propaganda exercise initiated by Leicester after the battle of Zutphen, at which Sidney had received his fatal wounds. To show their respect, the Dutch authorities urged Leicester to allow them to bury Sidney at their expense, in return for which honour they would erect to his memory 'as fair a monument as any prince had in Christendom, even though it should cost half a ton of gold to build it'.[3] But Leicester had other plans for the memory of his young nephew. He needed to elevate the skirmish at Zutphen (which had in fact failed to achieve its military objective) into a glorious victory. A slew of young English gentlemen were knighted for their prowess on the field; Sidney bequeathed his best sword to the young Earl of Essex, symbolically passing on his role of English hero; and finally his body returned home in slow, pompous victory. By the time the funeral took place – delayed for four months until Walsingham could raise the funds to finance it – Sidney's reputation was assured.

And so the myth grew, bolstered by tribute volumes of verse from the Universities of Cambridge and Oxford, and from various individuals, all eager to tell the brave life and gallant death of this tragic young hero.[4] His unpublished writings, some of them mere fragments, were dragged into the light, with various pirated versions soon put out of business by the 'official' versions compiled by Sidney's sister Mary, Countess of Pembroke, and his old friend Fulke Greville. Eventually,

Sidney's prose romance *The Arcadia*, his sonnet sequence *Astrophil and Stella* and his critical work *The Defence of Poesie* became popular and acclaimed; an unparalleled seven separate editions of his *Works* were published in England during the seventeenth century; his writings were translated into French, Italian, German and Spanish, and were the subject of learned analyses in Latin.[5]

Fulke Greville and Thomas Moffet, servant to the Countess of Pembroke, contributed to the myth by writing the first, idealising lives of Sidney. As biographies, they leave much to be desired. Greville's piece, designed as a dedicatory preface to an edition of his own works, was written partially as an implied attack on the regime of James I, by lauding that of his predecessor Elizabeth – an approach that necessarily obscured the rather strained relationship between Elizabeth and Sidney. Moffet's biography was never intended for publication, but was written to provide Sidney's young nephew William with the model of a great man. Both accounts contain fascinating material, but the reader looking for hard historical fact may have difficulty discerning it among the thickets of eulogy.[6] Together the funeral, the publication of Sidney's works and the writing of his life created the figure who became the epitome of Elizabethan chivalry.

Embarking on this biography, I was ready to believe that this figure might be the enduring result of a brilliant piece of Renaissance hagiography. What I did not expect to find was that Philip Sidney *was* a hero — only not in England. As I moved away from the courtly poetry for

which he is best known, and towards which biographers inevitably tend to gravitate, I found Sidney's name in the oddest places: in university records in Padua, in Spanish intelligence reports, in learned correspondence sent from Prague, Cracow and Bratislava, in Latin verse tributes from Leiden and Heidelberg, in the dedicatory epistles of scholarly tomes printed in Geneva, Antwerp and Frankfurt. But, with hindsight, this should not have come as a surprise. A glance at his *curriculum vitae* dispels any notion of Sidney as the quintessential Englishman. Although born into the garden of England — Kent — he spent much of his childhood in the Welsh borderlands, watched his father rule Wales and attempt to rule Ireland, passed much of his adolescence and adult life in France, Germany, Austria, Czechoslovakia,

Hungary, Poland, Italy, Ireland, Holland and Flanders. Even when in England, he was often to be found looking back across the Channel, or north into Scotland, or even further, towards possibilities in the New World.

On the Continent, I soon discovered, Philip Sidney was a name to conjure with, long before his death. Outside England, to be the son of the Pro-rex of Ireland and Wales, and the heir of the Earls of Warwick and Leicester – the latter often mooted as a husband for Elizabeth – brought considerable attention and respect. Sidney corresponded with the leading European scholars of the day, and writers and publishers dedicated major academic works to him, seeing him as a natural route to English audiences. His perceived 'princely' status gave him direct access

to European leaders. He was made a French baron at the age of seventeen, considered marriage proposals from two princesses, and inspired an avalanche of panegyrical verse throughout the last ten years of his life. He was an acknowledged leader of men, who was asked by both Prince Johann Casimir and Prince William of Orange to head English troops on the Continent. The Dutch demanded that he should lead the garrison at their most important port, and at the time of his death he was being openly spoken of as the next ruler of the Low Countries.

And yet in England he remained just another courtier, often too impecunious even to *be* a courtier. It could be argued that, on 9 January 1583, Sidney did achieve English glory, when he was knighted *Sir* Philip

Sidney of Penshurst. But even this honour, the most substantial he ever received at home, was earned through success in Europe. Johann Casimir was about to be installed as a Knight of the Garter, the title having been conferred on him by Queen Elizabeth during an earlier visit to England. On that occasion, Casimir had named to serve as his proxy Philip Sidney, his close ally and friend. According to etiquette, however, the proxy had to have the status of a knight. In order to honour Casimir's wishes, the queen was therefore forced to dub Sidney.[7] Casimir chose Philip as his proxy precisely because, in his eyes, Sidney was already suitably elevated. But, as Sidney told his friend Fulke Greville, such outside recognition was unlikely to endear him to his own sovereign. 'Princes love not that foreign powers should have

extraordinary interest in their subjects, much less to be taught by them how they should place their own, as arguments either upbraiding ignorance or lack of large rewarding goodness in them.'[8] Elizabeth was a shrewd monarch, who knew that she had to keep control over her court, and in that cause, over the last decade of Sidney's life, she consistently belittled and embarrassed him. Philip was therefore forced to lead a double life: of fame and praise abroad, and of comparative – and deliberate – neglect at home.

Philip Sidney has shone through four centuries as England's hero, its shepherd-knight, its greatest courtier-poet. That reputation was dreamed up by a master-propagandist, striving to gain English imperial glory against all the odds in the most wretched and botched of wars. By tracking Sidney back into Europe, however, we find a man of real stature, magnetic charisma and immense political potential, who was recognised, loved and prized in his own lifetime – the Philip Sidney to whom European Protestantism looked as its greatest hope.

1. Some of De Brii's thirty-two plates for Thomas Lant's 'Funeral Procession of Sir Philip Sidney'.

CHAPTER ONE

A Dudley in Blood

WITH HIS FIRST breath, Philip Sidney was thrust into politics. An entry in the handsome Sidney family psalter proudly records the happy event at the family estate of Penshurst in Kent on 30 November 1554:

> The nativity of Philip Sidney son and heir of Sir Henry Sidney knight, and the Lady Mary his wife, eldest daughter of John, duke of Northumberland, was on Friday the last of November being St Andrew's Day, a quarter before five in the morning . . . anno domini Milessimo, Quingentessimo, Quinquagessimo quarto. His godfathers were the great king Philip, king of Spain, and the noble John Russell earl of Bedford. And his godmother, the most virtuous Lady Jane Duchess of Northumberland his grandmother.[1]

An ancient country house, a noble family tree, royal patronage: Philip was the ultimate silver-spoon baby. But that psalter entry records something more than just his pre-ordained entry into Tudor high society. It tells of a canny bit of political manoeuvring designed to drag Philip's family out of the mire.

Henry Sidney had married Lady Mary Dudley on 29 March 1551. To many, this match, of a mere gentleman to the eldest daughter of the ancient Dudley dynasty, was a serious piece of social climbing on Henry's part. But shrewder commentators saw that it would also pay dividends for Henry's father-in-law John Dudley, then Earl of Warwick. Henry Sidney had already gained a reputation for 'comeliness of person, gallantness and liveliness of spirit, virtue, quality, beauty and good composition of body, the only odd man and paragon of the court'.[2] More crucially, he was a trusted intimate of the young king Edward VI, who 'used him not only as a companion', according to a chronicler, 'but many times as a bedfellow'. 'While I was present with him,' Henry later recalled, 'he would always be cheerful and pleasant with me, and in my absence give me such words of praise as far exceeded my desert.' The king

9

THE DUDLEYS

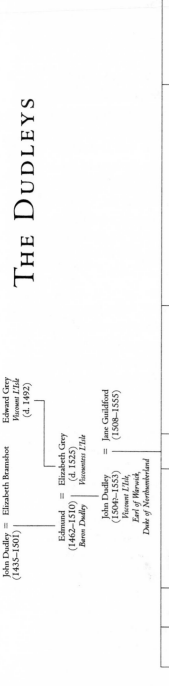
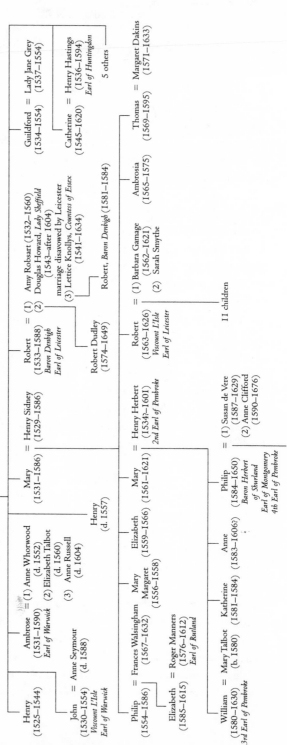

made good his verbal praise with rewards in the form of prestigious, lucrative posts: Chief Cupbearer to the king for life, Chief Cipherer to the king for life, Chief Steward of an array of royal manors, mansions and parks. 'Finally he always made too much of me,' Henry fondly remembered.[3]

No matter what he had achieved in his own right, from the moment he married, Henry Sidney's respectable but low-key identity was inevitably and totally subsumed by the glamorous Dudleys. At court, Henry was seen as part of an identifiable Dudley clique – indeed, he was knighted on the very day in October 1551 that his father-in-law was promoted to the duchy of Northumberland.[4] The newly knighted Sir Henry was given lands in Kent and Wiltshire, and was licensed to retain (in addition to his menial servants) fifty gentlemen, yeomen and others, who might wear his livery badge. As a sign of his identification with his in-laws, Sir Henry quartered the Sidney badge, a porcupine, with the Bear and Ragged Staff, badge of all the Earls of Warwick. Their device was said to have originated from the name of Arthgal, the first Earl of Warwick, a knight of King Arthur's Round Table ('Arthgal' deriving from 'Arth' or 'Naarth', signifying a bear). According to legend, one of Arthgal's descendants slew a knight, who had threatened him with a tree torn up at its roots – hence the bear and ragged staff.

Allying with the Dudleys, however, had its dangerous side. Northumberland, as an ardent Protestant, was part of the group of men firmly committed to the new Reformed agenda that Henry VIII had introduced in the 1530s, and which Edward VI was furthering now. As it became clear that the sickly Edward was not going to rule for long, these men looked towards his heir, Edward's half-sister Mary, with alarm. Mary, the daughter of Henry's rejected first wife Catherine of Aragon, was a passionate Catholic. No one could have any doubt that her accession would force England back into the hands of Rome – and Northumberland was determined that would never happen. He pushed Edward to reject Mary's claim, and instead to will the throne to a distant cousin named Lady Jane Grey, which he did on 21 June 1553.

But this was not merely Protestant ardour: Northumberland had exorbitant ambitions for his own family. On 21 May 1553, Lady Jane had married Northumberland's son, Guildford Dudley, privately at his London base, Durham House. Four days later the same venue saw Lady

Jane's younger sister Catherine Grey marry Henry Herbert, heir of the Earl of Pembroke; and the Earl of Huntingdon's heir Henry Hastings marry Katherine Dudley, Northumberland's daughter, who was all of seven. These hurried matches linked the Dudley–Grey axis to two more of England's most powerful families; even to the most dewy-eyed romantic, they stank of political manoeuvring. On 9 July 1553, three days after Edward died, Lady Jane Grey was declared Queen of England. The Dudleys had seized the throne.

The fate of this English queen is as well known as it is sad. In only two weeks Mary Tudor was safely installed on the throne, and Northumberland and his sons were imprisoned in the Tower of London. Sir Henry hastily abandoned Northumberland and swore allegiance to the new queen on the day after her accession, but the Sidneys (both husband and wife) were already heavily compromised by their part in Mary's father's plans. Sir Henry was among those who had allegedly filled Edward's head with 'continual discourses of Lady Jane [Grey], the high esteem in which she was for her zeal and piety' – a steady trickle of praise that persuaded Edward to name Lady Jane to succeed him;[5] Lady Jane had revealed under interrogation that the news that she was now queen had been brought to her by 'the Lady Sidney, my sister-in-law, daughter of the duchess of Northumberland'.[6] It seemed that, for all his personal popularity, Sir Henry was finished. Writing towards the end of 1554, a Marian supporter named Robert Wingfield bemoaned Sidney's mistakes in allying himself to Northumberland, referring to him as being 'of a good family and a young man of great promise, if he had not rashly thrown in his lot with this crew'.[7]

So when Lady Sidney realised she was carrying her first child early in 1554, she knew its prospects were bleak. Her father had already been beheaded, his last words being a scaffold speech that roundly denounced Protestantism – a recantation that was promptly printed and distributed all over the Continent, to the shame of his erstwhile allies. The February 1554 executions on Tower Green of Lady Sidney's brother Guildford and of Lady Jane herself were still fresh and painful in the mind; the death sentences hanging over her remaining brothers in the Tower, stripped of their estates and titles, were gruesome reminders of the dangerous future of the unborn child.

And yet they escaped. What saved the Sidneys was a bizarre mixture of pure luck and, strange as it may sound, a flair for modern languages. In June 1551, King Edward had appointed Henry to an embassy led by the Marquis of Northampton, carrying the habit of the Order of the Garter to the French king Henri II, as part of a campaign to win Henri's daughter Elizabeth as a bride for the English king. Sir Henry was entrusted with delivering a report on Northampton's reception, suggesting that the ambassador trusted Henry's verbal skills.[8] In December 1552, Sir Henry was selected as Edward's special envoy to France, to act as a mediator in the French king's wars with the emperor. The mission failed, but Sir Henry was 'very courteously used by the King and Constable' ('gaining a chain worth six hundred crowns and a fair courser of Naples') and impressed Englishmen on the ground: Sir William Pickering commended his 'dexterity and his discreet and wise handling of the matter confided with him', and informed Sir William Cecil that 'Sir Henry Sidney has accomplished his commission with so great wisdom and circumspection in all the contents thereof as in his mind more could not have been expected of any man'.[9] Northumberland had advised Cecil that Sir Henry 'should go to the emperor, having more means to express his mind in Italian than French', but evidently his French was more than adequate to the task.[10]

With this reputation for languages and diplomatic panache, Sir Henry was an obvious choice to accompany the Earl of Bedford on his mission to Spain in the early summer of 1554 to fetch Mary's intended husband, Philip of Spain.[11] It was a major embassy. The Spanish groom met the ambassadors at Santiago de Compostela, and signed the marriage contract carried by Bedford; on Sunday 24 June, Philip and the English embassy attended high mass in Compostela cathedral. Philip's train of seventy large vessels, covered by 4,000 troops with thirty armed ships defending the rear, sailed from La Coruña on 13 July, on stormy seas. It was met by English and Dutch armed vessels off the Isle of Wight, and brought into Southampton harbour during the afternoon of 20 July. Philip was determined – indeed required – to make a particular effort to forge friendly relations with the Englishmen sent to serve him. By the terms of the marriage treaty, he must 'receive and admit into the service of his household and court gentlemen and yeomen of the said realm of England in convenient number, and them as his proper subjects shall esteem, entertain and nourish';[12] he soon realised, as he wrote to the

Spanish ambassador in England, Simon Renard, that 'When I arrive I shall have to accept the services of natives in order to show them that I mean to trust myself to them, and favour them as much as if I were an Englishman born.'[13]

So, thanks to his prowess in continental languages, Sir Henry met the young Spanish king, who needed to be seen to befriend Englishmen. It was a mutually beneficial arrangement, which paid dividends when Philip Sidney was born. A sixteenth-century christening was inescapably political. When the new parents chose godparents to name the child, they were inviting their blessing on themselves as much as on the child. Using the infant boy as bait, the Sidneys lured the queen's husband into helping them revive the shattered fortunes of the Dudleys. Sir Henry called on Philip to name his son, inviting his embassy partner the Earl of Bedford to be the other godfather, just to hammer home the link. As godmother, they chose Lady Sidney's mother Jane, Northumberland's widow. Thus a baptism saved the skins of the Dudleys: and, for the rest of his life, Philip Sidney would carry the name of a Catholic Spanish king, the badge of his parents' self-serving politicking.

Philip spent his first years at the Sidneys' family seat, Penshurst, a fourteenth-century, stone-built house, nestled in the hop-filled valleys of Kent. It was the very image of medieval stability. At its heart lay the impressive Barons' Hall, with its heavy open-timbered chestnut roof (some sixty feet from the floor to its apex), an octagonal hearth in the middle of the room and a minstrels' gallery above the screens. A few hundred yards away, his paternal grandfather's body rested in the parish church of St John the Baptist. Years later, when Philip wanted to depict a worthy house in *The Arcadia*, it could have been Penshurst he was describing: 'built of fair and strong stone, not affecting so much any extraordinary fineness, as an honourable representing of a firm stateliness'. In the early seventeenth century, Ben Jonson eulogised Penshurst as a 'reverenced . . . ancient pile', an estate where feudal loyalties still ran deep. Unprompted, the locals trooped in, 'no one empty-handed, to salute thy lord, and lady', with capons, cakes, nuts, apples, cheeses, and 'ripe daughters' with baskets full of similarly ripe plums and pears.[14]

But Jonson's version of Penshurst was an idealistic mirage, the medieval stateliness of the Sidneys a clever illusion. Penshurst had been granted to Sir William Sidney, Philip's grandfather, as recently as April 1552. Certainly, the Sidneys were an old family, with an ancestry reaching back to one John de Sydenie, who had property in Chiddingfold on the Surrey–Sussex border in 1280. But Sir Henry preferred to trace his family tree back to a French 'William de Sidne', chamberlain to Henry II, and spent considerable funds 'researching' this spurious pedigree. In fact, the Sidneys' fortunes were not even half a century old. Sir William Sidney was related through his mother to Charles Brandon, who married Henry VIII's sister Mary. This had helped his own rise. As one of the esquires of the household in Henry VIII, he came to prominence in matters military, as part of an English force assisting Ferdinand, King of Aragon and Castile, against the Moors in 1510; commanding part of the English fleet, and receiving a knighthood at the burning of the town of Conquest in 1512; taking part in the sea-fight off Brest and in the battle of Flodden Field, in which he led the right wing of the Earl of Surrey's army, for which action he was made a knight banneret, with a royal annuity of fifty marks per annum for life. Flodden Field also provided Sir William with a wife: Anne, daughter of Sir Hugh Pagenham, who was widowed at the battle when her husband Thomas FitzWilliam was killed.

When Henry Sidney, born on 20 July 1529, was baptised, his father's status was such that Henry could boast as godparents Sir William Fitzwilliam, later the Earl of Southampton; Lady Kingston, wife of the king's household controller; and Henry VIII himself, for whom he was named.[15] But the Sidneys' greatest success came in the service of Henry's young heir, Prince Edward. Sir William became the first chamberlain of Edward's household, and later his steward. Indeed, Edward's welfare was something of a Sidney family business, with Henry's mother acting as royal governess and his maternal aunt Sybil Penne being appointed 'in such place as among meaner personages is called a dry nurse, for from the time he [Edward] left sucking, she continually lay in bed with him, so long as he remained in woman's government'.[16]

It was only natural that Henry would follow his father into the household and at the age of ten (as he recalled) he was 'put' by Henry VIII 'to his sweet son Prince Edward, my most dear master, prince, and sovereign, the first boy that ever he had'. In this rarefied environment Henry spent his formative years. Although already in full-time service, he was still only an adolescent and was subject to the intense educational training that produced (and probably hastened the demise of) his royal master. While Sir William dealt with Edward's domestic arrangements, his education was in the hands of former Eton headmaster Richard Cox, aided by the Cambridge Regius Professor of Greek, John Cheke, Sir Anthony Cooke, Roger Ascham and a French master named John Belmain. All were committed to the new humanist learning, with a definite Protestant – even Calvinist – stance, which they did not hesitate to instil in their charges. Edward shared his glittering tutors with an entourage of other boys, which included Ambrose and Robert Dudley, sons of the Earl of Warwick; Henry Hastings, son of the Earl of Huntingdon; and Henry Sidney. The result was that Henry 'profited very well, both in the Latin and French tongues, for he had a very good wit, and was very forward in all good actions, and whereof was conceived some good things would come of him'.[17] Here he gained his grounding in the languages that saw him through the Marian accession.

When his father died in 1554, Sir Henry inherited his estates and set about turning Penshurst into the perfect ancestral pile. He built a range of rooms that followed the line of the old wall along its northern aspect, including the King's Tower which became the new entrance to the house. He deliberately used traditional local sandstone and red brick, marking a departure from the ornate style of much contemporary building. As he planned, visitors approaching Penshurst now saw a long façade with the King's Tower in the middle, drawing their attention to the screens at the heart of the (genuinely) medieval building. Above the oak doors of the King's Tower, where the Sidney arms impaled the Dudley arms, Sir Henry eventually placed the following inscription:

The most religious and renowned Prince Edward the sixth, King of England, France and Ireland, gave this House of Pencester with the manors, lands and appertenances thereunto belonging unto his trusty, and well-beloved servant Sir William Sidney, knight banneret, serving him from the time of his birth unto his coronation in the offices of Chamberlain and Steward of his Household; in commemoration of which most worthy and famous King Sir Henry Sidney, Knight of the most Noble Order of the Garter, Lord President of the Council, established in the Marches of Wales, son and heir to the aforenamed Sir

William caused this Tower to be builded and that most excellent
Prince's arms to be erected. Anno Domini 1585.[18]

Sir Henry's confected stability also obscured the troubled fortunes of
Penshurst itself. The estate's recent owners had an alarmingly poor
record. Henry Stafford, second Duke of Buckingham, had been executed
in 1483 for his part in a plot to put the Earl of Richmond (later Henry
VII) on the throne. In time, his second son, Edward Stafford, was
restored as third Duke of Buckingham and lived a grand lifestyle at
Penshurst, entertaining King Henry VIII in 1519 at a sky-high cost of
£2,500. Buckingham was a proud man who insisted on his social
superiority to men he considered upstarts: when Henry VIII's Cardinal
Wolsey dared to dip his hands in the basin Buckingham was holding up
to the king, he emptied it over the cardinal's feet. However, Buckingham
went too far when he talked openly of his prospects of succeeding to the
throne: he was committed to the Tower, tried and found guilty of
treachery, and beheaded on Tower Hill on 17 May 1521. Penshurst was
seized by the Crown, and was later bestowed (ironically enough) on John
Dudley, although he never took residence. It was then given to Sir Ralph
Fane, a much-honoured soldier, but when Edward VI's 'Protector'
Somerset was convicted of treason in 1552, Fane went with him, also
ending his life on Tower Hill, although (as his lowly status befitted) he
was hanged rather than executed.[19] Only then was the estate given to Sir
William Sidney. Two Buckinghams, Northumberland and Fane –
Penshurst had an unsettled and bloody history. But for Philip,
deliberately sheltered from such things, Penshurst was the very image of
solid antiquity, filling his impressionable mind with chivalric images of
yore.

The Sidneys' ploy to use their baby son to ease the path of the Dudleys
was slowly successful. Sir Henry was befriended by the Spanish king's
counsellors, especially the Duke of Medina Celi and Don Diego de
Mendoza, and gradually began to use his Spanish connections at court to
intercede on behalf of his Dudley kinsmen. It helped that his sister
Mary's daughter Jane Dormer was an intimate of Queen Mary. When her
mother had died in 1542, Jane, only four years old, had been placed with
her Catholic grandmother: Jane, Lady Dormer. In time, she joined the
household of the then Princess Mary, and was now among her most

trusted servants: the carver of her meat, she slept in the queen's bedchamber, and at the end was entrusted with delivering the dying queen's jewels and last wishes to Elizabeth.[20]

Philip's godmother the dowager Duchess of Northumberland also found support among the Spanish party before she died in January 1555, aged forty-six. The terms of the duchess' will placed her estates in the hands of her executors, including Sir Henry, 'in consideration that they should have special regard to aiding her sons and daughters', and that request was reiterated in the various bequests to friendly Spaniards. She left to the Duchess of Alva 'her green parrot, having nothing for her else, praying her grace to continue a good lady to all her children, as she has before'. Other bequests went to Don Diego de Mendoza and the Dukes of Salvan and Mathenon, and 'to the Lords and Gentleman of the Privy Chamber, that did her sons good, beseeching them for God's sake to continue the good lords to her sons in their needs': these were links forged by her son-in-law.[21] King Philip showed his favour to the Dudley brothers Ambrose and Robert by including them in his Anglo-Spanish tournament during the winter of 1554–5,[22] and on 4 May 1555 Ambrose was allowed to inherit, despite the attainder hanging over him. The Dudley brothers distinguished themselves militarily under the king at the battle of St Quentin (Lord Henry Dudley died on the field), and eventually, by a 1558 Act of Parliament, Ambrose and Robert were restored to their knighthoods, and their sisters Lady Mary Sidney and Lady Katherine Hastings were restored and enabled in blood and name.[23]

Sir Henry also benefited personally from his Spanish connections, his name being added to the pension list by Philip. In the spring of 1555 Sir Henry was honoured by his appointment as an official envoy to the King of the Romans and the King of Bohemia, charged with announcing the happy news that the queen had been delivered of an heir – he even received advance expenses of 500 marks, an event almost unheard of in tight-fisted Tudor diplomacy. (It soon became clear, however, that Mary's pregnancy had been 'mere wind', and the mission was cancelled.)[24] Yet despite these prestigious honours, Sir Henry was not happy. Although his position appeared stable enough, he felt that continuing to be dependent on the patronage of a Spanish king was untenable. Eventually, he decided that the only option was to get away from the court – the only life he had ever known – and find himself a position where the personal pressures to satisfy both Dudley and Habsburg interests would be alleviated. 'After I had spent some months in Spain, neither liking nor liked as I had been,' he recalled, 'I fancied to live in Ireland, and to serve as Treasurer.'[25]

Ireland was not a random choice. In the spring of 1555, Sir Henry's sister Frances had married Thomas Radcliffe, who would later become Earl of Sussex; soon afterwards, Sussex was appointed Lord Deputy of Ireland, and it was relatively easy for Sir Henry to accompany him when he set out for Dublin in May 1556. In Ireland he 'had the leading both of horsemen and footmen, and served as ordinarily with them as any other private captain did there'. His Irish exploits provided good, bloodthirsty stories to tell his young son. Sussex's first foray into Ireland ('which was a long and great and an honourable one') was against James MacConnell, 'a mighty captain of Scots'. Sussex defeated MacConnell's forces, 'after a good fight', and 'chased him with slaughter of a great number of his best men'. But it was Sir Henry who proved most brave: 'I there fought and killed him with my own hand, who thought to have overmatched me. Some more blood I drew, though I cannot brag that I lost any.' In the summer of 1557, Sussex sent Sidney to the island of Raghlyns (Rathlin Island), where previously English forces had been imprisoned, hurt or killed. 'But we,' Sir Henry boasted proudly, 'landed more politickly and safely, and encamped in the isle until we had spoiled the same of all mankind, corn, and cattle in it.' His ability was soon recognised, and on four occasions he was appointed Lord Justice in Sussex's absence, 'thrice by commission out of England, and once by choice of that country; such was the great favour of that Queen to me, and good liking of the people of me'.[26]

Philip was eighteen months old when his father decided to pursue his career in Ireland; save for one brief visit, in July 1557, when he returned to court to obtain further funds and ammunition, Sir Henry was absent until Philip was almost five. During this posting, Sir Henry 'boarded together' with his wife, usually at Athlone Castle, while Philip stayed at Penshurst.[27] Like most young boys of his rank, Philip spent his early years mainly in the company of servants, probably starting with a wet nurse at birth. Such a distance between parents and children was not unusual, but Philip was further isolated by the lack of siblings to keep him company. A sister, Mary Margaret, was born two years after him (she was the god-daughter of Queen Mary) but she died at 'one year and three quarters old' in 1558. Another sister, Elizabeth, was born in 1559 or 1560, when Philip was about five, and would have been a young companion for him until he went to school (she also died young, in 1566). A third sister, Mary, was born on 27 October 1561. But his first brother, Robert, was not born until 19 November 1563, by which time Philip was almost nine.[28] So Philip's chief formative influences were the servants. Responsibility for his board lay with Anne Mantell, to whom Sir Henry paid £18 6s. 3d. in 1560, £12 of which was for that purpose.[29]

Even from the fragments of evidence that have survived, Philip emerges as a serious young boy with what his early biographer Thomas Moffet calls 'a character of his own'. He was a sickly child – the prerogative of the gentry, but in Philip's case the illnesses appear to have been serious and frequent. From a horoscope he had cast in 1570 we know that 'During the very first year in which you saw the light of day you were tormented by a most serious fever, so that scarcely anyone hoped for your life.'[30] Philip also suffered some ill health in 1560, when the considerable sum of £3 16s. was paid to the 'poticary' (apothecary) for his services.[31] This is supported by Moffet (who may have used Anne Mantell as his source): 'When he had scarce completed six years of life, measles and smallpox laid waste, as with little mines, the excellence and fashion of his beauty.'[32] His horoscope also records that 'In the course of the ninth year of your life you suffered from scabs and foul uncleanness throughout your body, just as if you had been poisoned.'[33] Such serious illnesses were not uncommon in young children at the time, but Philip was the eldest son and heir, and accordingly his health was closely scrutinised. Throughout his life, he continued to suffer from generally frail health: he could be relied upon to fall victim to the heat in Italy, or the damp in Ireland. Luckily, he never contracted the 'gout', which afflicted so many gentlemen of his generation: his ill health rarely hindered his career, although the excuse of ill health would later delay many a journey that Philip preferred not to undertake.

Philip soon eclipsed his peers. As an example of his piety and precocity, Moffet tells of when, at the age of three, 'he beheld the moon, with clean hands and head covered he used to pray to it and devoutly to worship – as if in his earliest years he had compassed the heavens with his mind, and wondered at the works of his Creator'. Books, even at this tender age, were his constant companions. 'He so held letters in his affection and care that he would scarce ever sleep, still less go forth, without a book. Nor did he direct his eyes so much to the coloured and gilded cover of the book as to the letters and meaning of it.' Moffet's is a beautiful image, and brings to mind the striking illustrations in the big vellum-bound Sidney family psalter. But the image is slightly spoiled when one realises that Moffet had it suggested to him by the eleventh sonnet in Sidney's *Astrophil and Stella*, in which Love is described as:

> . . . like a child that some fair book doth find,
> With gilded leaves or coloured vellum plays,
> Or at the most on some fine picture stays,
> But never heeds the fruit of writer's mind.

Moffet's version of the precociously unchildlike Philip is a perfect inversion of the adult Sidney's portrayal of the childlike child.[34] Like so many of the posthumous accounts of Philip's life, the facts are hopelessly confused with the images of his fiction.

The history books tell us that Elizabeth was a Protestant queen who saved England from the persecutions of the bloody Catholic Mary Tudor, and returned it to the Protestant path paved by her father, Henry VIII, and her brother Edward VI. They assure us that, among the agitators for this Protestant policy, one of the most vehement was her favourite Robert Dudley, later Earl of Leicester. And they are certain that it was this path that was followed by Leicester's nephew, Philip Sidney.

But these facts only become truisms with the hindsight of history. When Elizabeth acceded to the throne on 17 November 1558, no one was sure what her reign would bring. Certainly, she would have to deal with the myriad social evils of the country: internal dissent on political and religious grounds; a wavering foreign policy, which had only recently lost Calais; and a recent past that had seen five monarchs in scarcely twice as many years. Add to that the fact that Elizabeth was a woman, an unmarried woman at that, with no clear successor: the idea that she would reign for the next forty-five years, bringing England to a new dominance in international affairs, would have seemed hopelessly optimistic.

Although Philip was still two weeks shy of his fourth birthday at the time of her accession, the early years of Elizabeth's reign put in place many of the factors that were to help and hinder him for the rest of his life. In these years his parents, both Sir Henry and Lady Sidney, took on a significance at the heart of English politics, both domestic and foreign, which they would never repeat.

Elizabeth's first action on gaining power was to fill the prime political posts with men she felt she could trust. There were few innovations: most of these men were drawn from the circle close to her half-brother Edward VI, and the youngest, Sir William Cecil, was now thirty-eight. She cut Mary's unwieldly inner circle of advisers, the Privy Council, by one-third to a more manageable score of men. Only the regional magnates – men whose local power-bases were too strong to challenge – were allowed to stay. Intimates of her brother, such as Sir Edward Rogers and Sir Francis Knollys, were promoted, and Cecil (who had been knighted on the same day as Sir Henry) was restored as Secretary of State – as a friend remarked to him, he had returned to 'your old room'.[35] This inner circle was dominated by university-trained laymen rather than clerics, but only two (Francis, second Earl of Bedford, and Sir Francis Knollys) were outspoken Protestants. It was, in the final analysis, a moderate set of men.

There was one intriguing appointment. Three days before Mary's death, Philip of Spain's ambassador, the Count of Feria, had reported to his master that the inner circle of the new queen, Elizabeth, would include Lord Robert Dudley.[36] In Feria's estimation, Elizabeth was 'a very vain and clever woman. She must have been thoroughly schooled in the manner in which her father conducted his affairs, and I am very much afraid that she will not be well-disposed in matters of religion, for I see her inclined to govern through men who are believed to be heretics and I am told that all the women around her definitely are.' He identified as particularly influential 'the earl of Bedford, Throckmorton, Peter Carew and Harrington' – and 'Lord Robert'. Feria was well informed about Lord Robert Dudley – not surprisingly. His wife-to-be was Jane Dormer, Sir Henry's niece and Queen Mary's beloved confidante: she left England at Elizabeth's accession for life at the Spanish court. Now, as in years to come, she provided a vital conduit for intelligence between Spain and the Sidneys, their correspondence made permissible under the cover of familial ties.

By the time Elizabeth arrived at court from Hatfield on 22 November, Lord Robert Dudley was already installed as Master of the Horse, a position that his brother John had filled five years earlier. The post drew on Dudley's expertise with horses – he had to co-ordinate the court's transport, supervise the royal studs, train and equip the horses, and provide horses for officials and messengers, the queen's annual progresses and ceremonial journeys. Master of the Horse was a household position (bringing with it a suite of rooms), which put Dudley in frequent, intimate contact with the queen – in an age when intimacy was often read as influence. By this time Robert was twenty-five, the same age as the queen. He was tall (almost six feet), slender, athletic, and with ironic eyes, which inspired Elizabeth's nickname for him – 'Two eyes' – and the

3. Robert Dudley leads the royal charger in Elizabeth's coronation procession.

signature on his letters to her: o o. He had a taste for the good things of life: fine food, archery, tennis, gambling and expensive European fabrics, buying up thousands of crowns' worth of crimson and black velvet, and variously coloured silks and satins – in time his wardrobe would become immense. To those who disliked him – and his enemies were many and immediate – he was a dark, foreign, dangerous presence: 'The Gypsy'.[37]

Robert's promotion was accompanied by other favours for the surviving Dudleys: Ambrose was appointed Chief Pantler (an honorary household post) at the coronation, receiving the manor of Kibworth Beauchamp, and then granted the post of Master of the Ordnance (which his father had held as 'Master of the Tower Armouries').[38] Their sister, Lady Sidney, was quickly installed as Gentlewoman of the Privy

Chamber, one of the posts most intimate to the queen.[39] As such, she had regular access to Elizabeth, a position that it would be foolhardy to see as a 'female', 'domestic' and therefore apolitical space. Under a male monarch, such positions translated into political influence, such as Sir Henry had enjoyed with Edward VI. Under Elizabeth, formal power was focused in her Privy Council, but the political influence of her circle of intimate women was widely recognised. Clerk to the Privy Council Robert Beale spoke from experience when he gave advice on how best to approach the royal presence: 'Learn before your access her Majesty's disposition by some in the Privy Chamber with whom you must keep credit, for that will stand you in much stead; and yet yield not too much to their importunity for suits, for so you may be blamed – nevertheless pleasure them when conveniently you may.'[40]

Sir Henry's future was much less certain than that of his wife. Lord Deputy Sussex returned to England in December 1558, on hearing of Mary's death; he had no desire to return to Ireland and urged Elizabeth to create Sir Henry Lord Deputy in his stead. But the idea did not appeal. Perhaps Elizabeth was suspicious of a man who had so readily changed sides to support her sister, and who had acknowledged links with the Spanish court. So Sussex returned to Ireland in August 1559, and Sir Henry made his way to court to lobby for his future. Several possible roles were mooted. In November 1559, Westminster gossip was mentioning his name alongside 'Mr Poulett' as a possible Lord President of Wales.[41] The following month, Sir Thomas Challoner was advising Cecil that none was worthier than Sir Henry Sidney to be sent on an embassy to King Philip, although he was not sure whether Sidney's Spanish was up to the task of perfectly understanding the king, 'whose quick and soft speech is hard of [for] a young beginner in Spanish to be well at the first comprehended' (presumably he was unaware of Sir Henry's earlier attendance on Philip).[42] In February 1560, Sir Henry was among the men whom Elizabeth's ambassador at the French court, Sir Nicholas Throckmorton, suggested to the queen might replace him, arguing that Sir Henry was a man 'of whom the French have good opinion'.[43] In the meantime, the Sidneys became familiar figures at court and, as the reports of the Spanish envoys in London show, rather busy political operators in the prime political battle of the day – Elizabeth's marriage negotiations.

With the succession unsettled, everyone was looking for Elizabeth to marry, and to provide an heir. Philip II supplied a series of possible Catholic suitors, talked up by the Count of Feria, but Elizabeth was playing a different game. To her first Parliament, on 10 February 1559, she proclaimed famously that they need not fear that she would choose an unsuitable husband: 'Whensoever it may please God to incline my heart to another kind of life, ye may well assure yourselves my meaning is not to do or determine anything wherewith the realm may or shall have just cause to be discontented.' Personally, however, she expressed no desire to be married: 'In the end, this shall be for me sufficient, that a marble stone shall declare that a Queen, having reigned such a time, lived and died a virgin.'[44] As Elizabeth was to point out many times during the following years, she could not *say* that she desired to get married, because that would be too sexually forward: so we should not perhaps take her predictions of lifelong virginity too literally as representing her ambition. The public, however, saw her as a woman with desires of her own – and desires that were aimed fair and square at Lord Robert Dudley.

Lord Robert was safely married, to Amy Robsart, but his wife (like many a courtier's wife) preferred to spend her time away from court, usually visiting friends and relatives. Her absence at least spared her some of the scandalous stories circulating in court and in London, obscenely linking the queen and her horse-master. It was said that Lord Robert was only waiting for Amy to die so that he could become King of England – after all, his father and brother Guildford had almost achieved that. By April 1559, when Lord Robert was nominated as a Knight of the Garter, an award usually reserved for distinguished service, the Spanish ambassador the Count of Feria reported that:

> During the last few days Lord Robert has come so much into favour that he does whatever he likes with affairs and it is even said that her majesty visits him in his chamber day and night. People talk of this so freely that they go so far as to say that his wife has a malady in one of her breasts and the Queen is only waiting for her to die to marry Lord Robert. I can assure your Majesty that I have been brought to consider whether it would not be well to approach Lord Robert on your Majesty's behalf promising your help and favour and coming to terms with him.[45]

The rumours made Lord Robert a vulnerable target for envy and resentment, which sometimes spilled out into violent hatred. In December 1558, two brothers were arrested on charges of plotting against Lord Robert and held for almost two years.[46] As early as August 1559, Justices of the Peace in Essex were questioning a Brentwood woman who had gossiped that the queen was pregnant by Lord Robert.[47] In September of that year, Drue Drury was imprisoned 'for that it was suspected lest he would have slain the Lord Robert, whom he thought to be uncomely to be so great with the queen'.[48] More dangerous was England's most powerful peer, the young Thomas Howard, fourth Duke of Norfolk. Philip II's London representative de Quadra reported that 'The duke of Norfolk is the chief of Lord Robert's enemies, who are all the principal people in the kingdom . . . he said that if Lord Robert did not abandon his present pretensions and presumptions, he would not die in his bed . . . I think his hatred of Lord Robert will continue, as the duke and the rest of them cannot put up with his being king.'[49]

Others decided to take advantage of Lord Robert's new-found status with the queen. Begging letters were soon flooding in, asking him to use his influence – George Gilpin needing an overdue land grant executed; Sir James Croft appealing on behalf of a widowed gentlewoman; Lady Elizabeth Darcy wanting a court post for her son; the Earl of Ormond sending a servant to be groom of the stable; the Bishop of Worcester wanting Robert to continue with his 'honest and righteous causes'; a disgraced courtier named Thomas Benger hoping for intercession with the queen. And although his later reputation was one of militant Protestantism, it is clear that during the early Elizabethan years Lord Robert was a particularly attractive figure for disillusioned Catholics such as Sir Thomas Cornwallis, who had been deprived of his estates at Elizabeth's accession.[50]

Among the many prospective foreign suitors who tried their luck with Elizabeth, the most serious in these early days was the Archduke Charles, a younger brother of the Austrian Habsburg dynasty and a cousin of Philip II. In April 1559, Philip instructed his ambassador to forward this match to Elizabeth, and a month later an official imperial envoy arrived in London. At first, Elizabeth refused, but her refusal was seen as ambiguous and the two Habsburg ambassadors remained hopeful that the situation could be salvaged. Then, in September, Lady Sidney became involved.

On 7 September 1559, de Quadra, Bishop of Aquila, wrote to the Duchess of Parma. He told of how he and the emperor's ambassador had been 'advised by one of the ladies of the palace, a sister of Lord Robert, called Lady Sidney, that this was the best time to speak to the queen about the Archduke'. The Spaniard and the Englishwoman communicated with the help of an Italian translator 'although', as de Quadra remarked rather huffily, 'we can understand each other in Italian without him'. Lady Sidney informed de Quadra that Elizabeth wished the archduke to come at once, and that he should write to the emperor to send him, 'which he could do on her honour and word, and she (Lady Sidney) would never dare to say such a thing as she did in the presence of the Italian gentleman who was interpreting between us unless it were true'. De Quadra promised to write immediately, but Lady Sidney urged him to broach the matter directly with the queen, although 'the lady would not speak herself'.

Suspicious of this tip-off, the bishop did some investigating of his own. His sources told him that the queen had been thrown into a panic by news of an alleged plot against her and Lord Robert: they would be poisoned at a banquet thrown by the Earl of Arundel. This, in combination with the news that 3,000 French soldiers were about to invade Scotland, convinced Elizabeth that she had to marry. As de Quadra reported to Philip:

> Lady Sidney said that at all events I ought to be there and must not mind what the Queen said, as it is the custom of ladies here not to give their consent in such matters until they are teased into it. She said it would only take a few days, and the [Privy] Council would press her to marry. Lady Sidney said that if this were not true, I might be sure she would not say such a thing as it might cost her her life and she was acting now with the Queen's consent, but she (the Queen) would not speak to the Emperor's ambassador about it.

From the fuss being made of them, de Quadra determined that 'all London looks upon the affair as settled'.

Lady Sidney's message was backed up by Lord Robert and Elizabeth's Treasurer Parry, who confirmed that the queen had summoned both him and Lady Sidney the night before.[51] De Quadra wrote approvingly to the

Bishop of Arras: 'Lord Robert and his sister are certainly acting splendidly, and the King will have to reward them well.'[52] Lady Sidney then relayed to Elizabeth all that had transpired with de Quadra; Elizabeth approved of events, but cautioned that Lady Sidney should now leave the Spanish alone, so that she could observe what they would do. When Lady Sidney met the bishop again, 'she told me that she had been bidden to say no more than had been said in this business, and she was obliged to obey'. However, she added, 'she was sorry for it, as she knew that if she might speak she could say something that would please me; but this would suffice'. De Quadra should, she intimated, satisfy the queen that the archduke was indeed coming, but not 'try to draw her out any further, for we should never make her speak any more clearly than hitherto'. Matters should be left as they were. 'We have followed Lady Sidney's advice,' de Quadra wrote to the Duke of Alva, 'and have refrained from going to Hampton Court.' The queen, said Lady Sidney, felt it unfit for herself, as 'a queen and a maiden to summon anyone to marry her for her pleasure'. 'I might easily be deceived myself,' admitted de Quadra, 'but I do not believe that Lady Sidney and Lord Robert could be mistaken, and the latter says he never thought the Queen would go so far.'[53]

And then, in early November, the momentum ceased. De Quadra sensed that Lord Robert was favouring an alternative, Swedish match, and noted that he 'had had words with his sister because she was carrying the affair further than he desired'. There was evidently some communication breakdown between the Dudley siblings, which might suggest that the Sidneys' aspirations did not exactly match Lord Robert's. But a more dangerous rumour was out: one of de Quadra's reliable informers told him 'that Lord Robert has sent to poison his wife'. It all made sense. The queen had done all she ever would with the archduke and the Swede — her only objective was 'to keep Lord Robert's enemies and the country engaged with words until this wicked deed of killing his wife is consummated'. Then she would be able to marry him. Dudley's enemies in the Privy Council were making no secret of 'their evil opinion' of his intimacy with Elizabeth, about which de Quadra had now learned 'some extraordinary things'. And Lady Sidney was not her usual encouraging self when they met, but now seemed 'alarmed'. De Quadra knew he could not delay his audience with Elizabeth any longer.

The following day, Elizabeth met de Quadra and the emperor's ambassador. Sensing that she was merely going to trot out the same self-justification, de Quadra determined to tell her what 'some of the principal persons of her Court' – without mentioning any names – had told them, claiming that 'they took this step by her orders, as she had refrained from telling us herself from modesty'. Elizabeth was unfazed. She answered 'that some one had done this with good intentions, but without any commission from her'. The ambassadors showed themselves 'aggrieved' by this, and Lady Sidney got the blame for this turn of events. 'I am obliged to complain of somebody in this matter,' de Quadra wrote, 'and have complained of Lady Sidney only, although in good truth she is no more to blame than I am, as I have said privately.' In fact, it was Lady Sidney's changed demeanour that had tipped him off: 'when I found Lady Sidney was doubtful and complained of the Queen and her brother (Lord Robert), I thought best to put an end to uncertainty'.

Knowing that chief among Dudley's enemies ('who are all the principal people in the kingdom') was the powerful Duke of Norfolk, de Quadra and the ambassador wrote to Norfolk, and sent 'a gentleman interpreter of ours' to him along with Sir Henry, who was also allegedly 'a great adherent of the Duke [Norfolk]'. Norfolk sent word 'that he should rejoice greatly if the affair could be brought about'.[54] De Quadra reported that Lady Sidney 'is glad I should take this step, as she says she will make known to the Queen and everybody what has occurred if she is asked'. By now the Spanish ambassador shared the conviction of many that Elizabeth had no intention of going through with the marriage, but was merely planning to 'amuse the crowd with the hope of the match in order to save the life of Lord Robert', whose paranoia grew daily. However, de Quadra was quite ready to believe there was a plot against Dudley, 'for not a man in the realm can suffer the idea of his being king'. On 17 November, Sir Henry went to de Quadra to tell him that Elizabeth was to send two ambassadors: himself to the emperor and another presumably to Philip, said Quadra, 'to make me believe that he still thought the match with the Archduke would be brought about'. But de Quadra no longer believed the queen was interested.[55]

The affair made crystal clear the strengths of the Sidneys' position at court, and also their intense vulnerability. Thanks to their kinship and intimacy with Robert Dudley, Lady Sidney's access to the queen and their recognised position with the Spanish officials (particularly via the Countess of Feria), the Sidneys were regarded as valuable go-betweens. But their standing was entirely dependent on reflected glory: it was Dudley who actually possessed the power, not them. If they pursued a path different from Lord Robert's, they were quickly brought back into line. And when arrangements went sour it was the Sidneys, as go-betweens, who had to face the wrath of the ambassador.

But even Dudley's power was not assured. His influence, completely disproportionate to his official position, infuriated many of his peers. In early September 1560 the habitually cautious Cecil found himself blurting out his frustration to the Spanish ambassador and threatening to retire. The queen's intimacy with Dudley was bound to ruin the realm, he complained, urging de Quadra to use his influence to warn her of the ramifications of her actions. He declared that Lord Robert would be better off in paradise, and concluded by repeating the rumour that he would kill his wife, Amy Robsart. Only days later, Amy's lifeless body was found at the bottom of a staircase. In an age weaned on conspiracy theories, it was tempting to many to believe that Dudley had had her murdered, despite the fact that she had long been known to be ill. Elizabeth's vigorous defence of her favourite in the matter did nothing to ease suspicions.

With the widowed Dudley now back on the marriage market, he became a threat in an altogether more tangible way – as possible husband for the queen. Elizabeth's Paris ambassador urged Cecil 'to do all [in] your endeavour to hinder that marriage; for if it take place there is no counsel or advice that can help . . . God and religion will be out of estimation, the Queen discredited, condemned, and neglected, and the country ruined, and made prey'. Dudley's follower Henry Killigrew boasted that 'Lord Robert shall run away with the hare and have the Queen.' At the French court, the Queen Mother Cathérine de Médicis got considerable comic mileage from the notion that Elizabeth was going to marry the man in charge of the royal stud. As Elizabeth's credibility waned, potential successors crawled out of the woodwork – the Earl of Huntingdon, or Lady Margaret Lennox, daughter of Henry VIII's sister Margaret.

In January 1561, Dudley called on the Sidneys for help.[56] The moves of the next few weeks are among the most bewildering of these always unpredictable years. Lord Robert proposed to marry Elizabeth. Despite their earlier falling out, the Sidneys could hardly refuse to support his campaign, which stood to benefit them considerably. On the other hand, it involved a complete repudiation of their Protestant affiliations. If what follows was indeed genuinely acted out, then it suggests a fierce, almost ruthless ambition not only in Lord Robert, but in the Sidneys themselves.

This time it was Sir Henry who called on de Quadra, telling him that Elizabeth wanted to marry Lord Robert, but needed an assurance of support from the Spanish king. If de Quadra could obtain this, then Elizabeth and her new husband would act to reestablish the Roman Catholic religion in England. Despite Robert's insistence, de Quadra was (not surprisingly) suspicious, and warned that religious belief should not be mixed up with the sordid business of politics. None the less, he eventually raised the matter directly with Elizabeth, who admitted that she had a preference for Lord Robert, but had in fact decided not to marry anyone. However, she (and then Dudley) did ask de Quadra to ascertain what Philip's reaction would be if (hypothetically) she were to marry one of her servants; the bishop decided to wait for further instructions from home.

While this line of enquiry was continuing, Dudley produced another trump card – the Roman Catholic Church's Council of Trent, which was about to reconvene. Would it not be helpful, he put it to de Quadra, for England to send a delegation? It may have been this proposition that took him too far. Elizabeth suddenly asked Cecil to take over negotiations with de Quadra. Robert naturally saw this as a snub, and rumours soon circulated that he planned to give the queen an ultimatum, backed by the Earl of Pembroke and Sir Henry – either she must marry him or license him to leave the country to serve Spain. One courtier reported. 'I hear she hath answered him that marry him she will not but will not only not license him to go over according to his political desire but will make him able to withstand the malice of his enemy.'

De Quadra continued to make encouraging noises to Lord Robert, hoping to push Elizabeth into receiving a papal nuncio, and possibly guaranteeing an English presence at Trent. Cecil countered by arranging to have several Roman Catholics seized in Flanders, who, under interrogation, helpfully revealed what appeared to be a Catholic conspiracy. As Cecil explained to Throckmorton, he 'thought it necessary to dull the papists' expectation by discovering of certain mass-mongers and punishing them. I take God to record I mean no evil to any of them, but only for the rebating of the papists' humours which by the Queen's lenity grow too rank. I find it hath done much good.'[57] It certainly put paid to de Quadra's hopes of seeing a papal nuncio at the English court. The queen was told by her Privy Council that she should not admit him, and this time she took their advice.

It also spelled the end for Dudley's marriage plans. Just to make sure, Cecil arranged for Sir Henry to be sent to a usefully distant posting. In May 1561, de Quadra reported to Philip II that:

> They have sent Sidney to his government in Wales a month since, when they determined to vary their mode of proceeding, as they know he would not play me false or approve of their new departure. He told me when he was going, that the sudden orders he had received to depart, without any need therefore, made him suspect that the Queen had changed her intentions, and he was sorry, amongst other reasons, because he knew in the long run Robert would have to pay for it.[58]

De Quadra's despatches documenting this alleged exchange between Dudley, Sidney, Elizabeth and himself have been hotly debated by historians and biographers. Was de Quadra misinterpreting what was going on? Were Dudley and the Sidneys deluded in believing that Robert could ever marry Elizabeth? Or was de Quadra deliberately misled by Dudley or Sidney? Beyond any doubt, the marriage was considered by some at the time to be a possible outcome. More importantly, the *rumour* of such a marriage possibility (founded or not) rippled around Europe and did its work. A Burgundian diplomat named Hubert Languet wrote of the hostility felt by the English to the possibility of a match between the queen and Lord Robert Dudley, 'the man of whom we have heard so much':

> The English leaders have made it plain to her [Elizabeth] that her too great familiarity with my lord Robert Dudley displeases them and that they will by no means allow him to wed her ... The Queen replied ... that she had never thought of contracting a marriage with my lord

Robert; but she was more attached to him than to any of the others because when she was deserted by everybody in the reign of her sister not only did he never lessen in any degree his kindness and humble attention to her, but he even sold his possessions that he might assist her with money, and therefore she thought it just that she should make some return for his good faith and constancy.[59]

A decade later, Hubert Languet was to get closer to these issues than he could possibly have imagined.

The Dudley fortunes rose almost unchecked through the 1560s. Robert was given various estates, including Kenilworth in Warwickshire, which he adopted as his base, in 1563; the following year, he was elevated to the peerage as Earl of Leicester, and appointed Chancellor of the University of Oxford. When the Sidneys' second son was born on 19 November 1563, he was named for his uncle Robert. Dudley's elder brother Ambrose was raised to the peerage as Earl of Warwick in 1561. A skilled soldier, he was at the head of the English forces that captured Le Havre in 1563, but a leg wound from a poisoned bullet was to cause him trouble for the rest of his life (the amputation of his leg in 1590 led to his death). Nevertheless in 1569 he commanded the southern forces who succeeded in thwarting the rebellion of the northern earls. Warwick married three times (finally in 1565), but his only child, a son from his first marriage, died before Philip Sidney was born. So, by default, Philip stood heir presumptive to both the Earl of Warwick and the Earl of Leicester – indeed, to the entire Dudley dynasty.[60]

Sir Henry benefited considerably from his connection with the Dudleys. He was licensed in 1560 to retain forty liveried servants of his own.[61] After standing in for brother-in-law Warwick in 1563 at his installation as a Knight of the Order of the Garter during Warwick's absence in France, Sir Henry was installed in his own right, on 14 May 1564, in St George's Chapel at Windsor Castle, sharing the honour with the French king Charles IX (then only fourteen) and Francis Russell, second Earl of Bedford, the son of Philip's other godfather. Although these were personal honours, the Sidneys were still popularly perceived as Dudleys. When Geoffrey Fenton dedicated his *Certaine Tragical Discourses written out of Frenche and Latin* to Lady Sidney in 1567, for example, he listed her qualities, but also those of 'the house whereof you took your beginning', citing 'your worthy participation with the excellent gifts of temperance and wonderful modesty in the two most famous earls of Leicester and Warwick your brethren, and most virtuous and renowned lady the Countess of Huntington your sister, to whose glory and general love amongst all sorts of people in this land [France], I need not add further circumstance or increase of praise'.[62]

Such an identification, however, could also have an adverse effect on the Sidneys. In 1564, Cecil told an agent of the Duke of Württemberg that the English nobility feared that a husband drawn from their own numbers would 'favour his family and oppress others'.[63] He returned to the theme three years later while outlining why Archduke Charles of Styria would make a better husband for the queen than Leicester: Leicester, he argued, 'shall study nothing but to enhance his own particular friends to wealth, to offices, to lands, and to offend others'. The first name on Cecil's list of Leicester's 'own particular friends' – even before his brother Ambrose – was 'Sir H. Sidney'.[64] Even if their personal positions diverged significantly from those of Leicester, anxieties about Leicester's lust for power thus inevitably assailed the Sidneys.

Sir Henry's message to his children about their Dudley heritage was, understandably, inconsistent. On one occasion, he allegedly told his sons 'that if they meant to live in order, they should ever behold whose sons, and seldom whose nephews they were'.[65] At other times he fiercely encouraged Philip's identification with the glamorous Dudleys. 'Remember, my son, the noble blood you are descended of, by your mother's side; and think that only by virtuous life and good action you shall be an ornament to that illustre family; and otherwise, through vice and sloth, you may be counted *labes generis* [a spot on your family], one of the greatest curses that can happen to man.'[66] For Philip, as he grew up, the Dudleys provided precisely the ancient and noble ancestry that the Sidneys themselves lacked. The family had held the seigniory of Dudley Castle since the time of Richard the Lionheart. It was, Philip later wrote, 'a house now noble, long since noble, with a nobility never interrupted, seated in a place which they have each father and each son continually owned'. Moreover, through Northumberland's mother and grandmother, the Dudleys could lay claim to other noble descent. Northumberland, 'by right of blood, and so accepted, was the ancientest viscount of England, heir in blood and arms to the first or second earl of England [Warwick], in blood of inheritance a Gray, a Talbot, a Beauchamp, a Berkeley, a Lislay'. In short, Philip wrote:

> I am a Dudley in blood, that Duke's [Northumberland's] daughter's son, and do acknowledge, though in all truth I may justly affirm that I am by my father's side of ancient and always well esteemed gentry and well matched gentry, yet I do acknowledge, I say, that my chiefest honour is to be a Dudley, and truly am glad to have cause to set forth the nobility of that blood whereof I am descended.[67]

CHAPTER TWO

Your Son and My Scholar

F INANCIAL NECESSITY SOON dictated that Philip's eyes
were opened to life beyond Penshurst Park. With establishments
to maintain at court for Lady Sidney, and in Wales for Sir Henry,
it made sense for the Sidneys to move the children from Penshurst to the
Council's houses on the Welsh border, primarily Ludlow Castle in
Shropshire and Tickenhill Palace near Bewdley in Worcestershire, where
Philip's sister Mary was born in 1561.

For the first time, Philip became aware of the extent of his father's
importance in his own domain. Although Sir Henry's appointment as
Lord President of the Council in the Marches (or border regions) had
been seen by some as little more than a ruse to keep him away from court,
he threw himself into the job and reaped the rewards. The Council had
authority over the twelve shires of Wales, plus Monmouthshire,
Herefordshire, Gloucestershire, Worcester, Shropshire and Cheshire,
and the towns of Bristol, Gloucester, Chester and Haverfordwest. In 1562
Bristol was exempted, and Cheshire left in 1569, but otherwise – some
grumblings from Worcester aside – Sir Henry was in control of these
regions until his death in 1586. The Council's powers were far-reaching,
with the jurisdictions of the English Star Chamber, Chancery and Court
of Requests rolled into one; in addition, it had control over ecclesiastical
offences (which included sexual incontinency and recusancy) and could
even (unlike the Star Chamber) try the capital offences of treason,
murder and felony. Sir Henry only had to make an 'especial suit' and a
surgeon named Simon Hyddye was made a burgess of Ludlow. As far as
Wales and the Marches were concerned, the Council *was* government,
and 'Sir Harry' was the ultimate authority.[1]

From innumerable tributes, it becomes clear that Sir Henry was a
personable leader, well able to engage those with whom he came into
contact. According to Edmund Campion, who served Sir Henry before
joining the Jesuits on the Continent, he was:

> stately without disdain, familiar without contempt, very continent and
> chaste of body, no more than enough liberal, learned in many languages,

and a great lover of learning, perfect in blazoning of arms, skilful of antiquities, of wit fresh and lively, in consultations very temperate, in utterance happy, which his experience and wisdom hath made artificial, a preferrer of many, a father to his servants, both in war and peace of commendable courage.[2]

It was at Ludlow Castle, where the Sidneys lodged, that Sir Henry's influence was most keenly felt. As local poet Thomas Churchyard recalled in 1587: 'Sir Harry Sidney being Lord President, built twelve rooms in the said castle, which goodly buildings doth show a great beauty to the same. He made also a goodly wardrobe underneath the new parlour, and repaired an old tower, called Mortimer's Tower, to keep the ancient records in the same: and he repaired a fair room under the Court house, to the same intent and purpose.'[3] These records were collected for a reason: the Welsh scholar David Powel recalled to Philip how 'Your father, with his great expenses and labour, having procured and gotten to his hands the histories of Wales and Ireland . . . committed unto me this of Wales, to be set forth in print, with direction to proceed therein, and necessary books for the doing thereof', and Powel did just that, producing his *Historie of Cambria* in 1584. To Powel, this was typical of a man 'who always hath been and yet is more inclined and bent to do good to his country, than to benefit or enrich himself, as Wales and Ireland, beside his own can bear him witness'.[4] In addition, Sir Henry initiated a systematic mapping of his region,[5] attempted to boost the iron industry of south-east Wales by importing skilled labour from Germany, and backed experiments to extract copper by precipitation from Myndydd Parys on Anglesey.

He also had to deal with issues that, given his previous record, posed more knotty ethical problems. Wales was still largely Catholic in its allegiances, but Sir Henry was determined not to stir up resentment against Reformation impositions dictated from London, and was less than pro-active in pursuing the many Welsh recusants – even going so far as to patch up a quarrel about the forest of Snowdon between Leicester and Sir Richard Bukeley, who was supported by Catholic Caernarvonshire squires. His pragmatic attitude left him vulnerable to charges of tacitly supporting recusancy – a legacy he was to bequeath to Philip many years later.

Throughout the region he was not only a celebrity but — since the queen never deigned to visit — the biggest celebrity. Shrewsbury's town accounts testify to the impact of a visit by the Lord President. In 1562, £12 10s. 8d. were paid 'for wine, an ox, feeding of horses, and other necessaries, given to Sir Henry Sidney, knight, lord President in the Marches of Wales, while he was here in the town in the month of August on account of his favour to the town'. When he visited in the late summer of 1573, eighteen chamber pieces were shot off in a 'royalty' (triumph) and 'an excellent oration made unto him by one of the scholars of the Free School'. Perhaps the most lavish display of affection was reserved for 1581, when Sir Henry, as Knight of the Garter, kept the feast of St George (23 April) with great splendour. On 8 May, he departed down the river, and was treated to a pageant staged on an island a quarter of a mile downstream, in which scholars, garbed as green water-nymphs, deplored his departure in song:

> And will your honour needs depart,
> And must it needs be so?
> Would God we could like fishes swim,
> That we might with thee go!

According to eyewitnesses, this was 'done so pitifully that truly it made many to weep; and my lord himself to change countenance'.[6]

Although the presidency brought acclaim, it also meant financial hardships for the Sidneys. As early as November 1560, Sir Henry petitioned Elizabeth to 'extend her liberality' to him by increasing the allowance for the Lord President's diet, which currently stood at the same level as it had twenty years earlier, 'and now every thing treble the price that then it was'. Elizabeth characteristically turned a deaf ear to the plea,[7] and in the first three years of his presidency, Sir Henry paid out on Council expenses from his own pocket some '£782, fifteen shillings, ninepence ha'penny'.[8]

Philip also had glimpses of a more exotic life, when his father was called on to undertake delicate diplomatic missions. Twice in 1562 Sir Henry left Wales, going once to Paris and once to Edinburgh, where he had to break the news to Mary, Queen of Scots that Elizabeth would not meet with her that year.[9] In each case, Elizabeth had an able ambassador resident on the scene (Sir Nicholas Throckmorton in Paris, Thomas Randolph in Edinburgh), but she evidently believed that Sir Henry possessed a particular expertise for these missions. She may also have been aware of the happy effects of sending a man who was effectively the ruler of Wales. As Lord President, Sir Henry possessed a status and eminence that were much appreciated by those to whom he was sent: Randolph reported that 'Nothing was left undone by Sidney that appertained to his duty. The noblemen here esteem the honour great that such a man should be sent to treat of matters.'[10] When the names of Henry Sidney and Lord Montague were mentioned in connection with a rumoured embassy to Philip of Spain the following year, Elizabeth's ambassador in Madrid, Sir Thomas Challoner, wrote that Sir Henry would be more welcome than the socially superior Montague: 'If Sir Henry had come it would have been as though they had furnished the place with one, though not so great in appearance, yet perchance accounted nearer the prince's hand.'[11] The point is not that Sir Henry was in fact 'nearer the prince's hand' than Montague – indeed, Elizabeth kept him at arm's length all his career – but that he was *perceived* as being so: and, more importantly, that others behaved towards him as if that perception were true.

From his mother, Philip gained a more intimate picture of royal service. The young queen was a demanding, often intemperate mistress whose whims had to be satisfied. Lady Sidney even had to be careful what she wore: on one occasion, when she had donned a particularly fine velvet gown, she ended up having to pay for one for the queen. To her servant John Cockeram, she wrote hurriedly: 'Her majesty likes so well of the velvet that my lord gave me last for a gown as she hath very earnestly willed me to send her so much of it as will make her a loose gown ... If there be twelve yards it is enough. You may not slack the care hereof, for she will take it ill and it is now in the worst time for my lord for divers considerations to dislike her for such a trifle ... There is no remedy but it must be had.'[12]

The devotion of Elizabeth's servants had to be absolute, whatever the consequences. When Philip was seven, Lady Sidney was among the trusted women who nursed the queen through a bout of smallpox that swept through the court. Elizabeth made a good recovery, but Lady Sidney's reward was to contract the disease herself. She survived, but with terrible facial scarring. Sir Henry, away from court on his French diplomatic mission to Le Havre, recalled bluntly: 'When I went to Newhaven [Le Havre] I left her a full fair lady, in mine eye at least the fairest, and when I returned I found her as foul a lady as the smallpox could make her.' The scars, he alleged, 'to her resolute discomfort ever since hath done and doth remain in her face'. As a result, Lady Sidney spent much of her time alone, away from the family, 'solitarily *sicut nicticorax in domicilio suo* [like an owl of the desert in her house], more to my charge than if we had boarded together, as we did before that evil accident happened'.[13] Sir Henry's claims, made in 1583, rather overstate the case. Although Lady Sidney kept a residence in Limehouse, far from receding from the world she supported her husband at court, even accompanying him to Ireland[14] – indeed, several letters exist from Sir Henry begging for his wife to be allowed to come to him.[15]

Philip's education started young. First-born boys of his class were commonly raised with just enough education, most of it instilled at home, to oversee the financial and legal demands of their properties and their children's marriage negotiations. Anything else would have been an accomplishment rather than a necessity. Sir Henry and Lady Sidney, however, had educational standards higher than the average. Sir Henry, as we have seen, was a product of Edward VI's fabled schoolroom. Lady Sidney's mother had been a learned woman, taught by the famed Spanish humanist Juan Luis Vives. In 1553 she commissioned two tracts by the scientist John Dee: 'The Philosophical & Poetical Original occasions of the Configurations, & names of the heavenly Asterisms', and 'The true cause, & account (not vulgar) of Floods & Ebbs'. Evidently encouraged by her mother, the young Mary Dudley was taught penmanship and learned Latin and French (as witnessed by her annotations on her copy of Hall's *Chronicles*). She also spoke fluent Italian and, like her mother, corresponded with Dee.[16]

Thomas Moffet records that when Philip turned seven (the age that most classical authorities recommended for the beginning of formal education) his parents appointed 'a tutor of suitable manners and morals', to instruct him in languages, veneration of God, literature, public affairs and virtuous action, in that order. Philip proved an avid student; when his parents allowed him 'entire liberty' with his learning, he chose to spend 'the largest part of the day in studies, so that scarcely was he unoccupied at breakfast, and still more rarely at luncheon'. Philip later wrote in one of his sonnets of the rigours of being drilled in Latin grammar: 'O Grammar rules, o now your virtues show;/So children still read you with awful eyes'.[17] But in truth, he enjoyed the hard work. The Philip whom Moffet depicts is precociously scholarly, a serious boy who joined in the games of servants only when absolutely forced to, and would leave them in a moment to return to his literary studies.[18]

In later years there was a series of tutors in the Sidney household, some with specialisms. We can glean the presence of a 'Mistress Maria, the Italian', who perhaps imparted knowledge of her native tongue, in 1572 and 1573; of 'Mr Lodwicke', who was 'skolemaster' to Philip's sister Ambrosia – probably Lodowick Bryskett, who later attended Philip in Europe. There was a 'Mr Thornton', who fulfilled that function in 1573 and 1574, in whom it is tempting to see Philip's Oxford tutor Thomas Thornton.[19] Whether any of these taught Philip at Penshurst remains uncertain. There are also traces of a French tutor named Johan or Jean Tessel or Tassel, although at what stage he entered Philip's life is unknown: in 1569, Sir Henry would send Tassel to Secretary of State Sir William Cecil to teach French to his daughter Anne: 'he can do it well and doubtless is very honest, he hath served me a long time'.[20]

However, in November 1564, Sir Henry broke with the conventions of his class and sent Philip away to school – to Shrewsbury, in the Marches of Wales. The antiquarian William Camden wrote of Shrewsbury as 'a fair and goodly city . . . well frequented and traded, full of good merchandise, and by reason of the citizens' painful diligence, with cloth-making and traffic with Welshmen, rich and wealthy. For hither, almost all the commodities of Wales, do conflow as it were to a common mart of all nations, whereupon it is inhabited both with Welsh and English speaking both languages.'[21]

The choice of Shrewsbury provided more than simply a grammar-school education in a prosperous town. First, it placed Philip physically within Sir Henry's political stronghold, and suggested the possibility of dynastic continuity in the region. As such, it was the latest step in a long-term campaign by Sir Henry to integrate his son into life in the Marches. In May of that year, aged just nine, Philip had been instituted as incumbent of the parsonage of Whitford in the parish of Skyveog by

Thomas, Bishop of St Asaph, and soon afterwards induced as Prebend of Llangunlo in the diocese of St Davids, and as Prebend of Hereford.[22] Second, and more importantly, the choice of town and school was politically and doctrinally loaded. Sir Henry was determined that no one should doubt the Protestant credentials of his eldest son. He placed Philip in an environment untainted by the political manoeuvring of his parents and relatives. In one brilliant move, Philip became the product of an ardently Calvinist school, on the margins of English life far from court.

The Marches were generally considered a doctrinally conservative area, which is to say that they remained a Catholic stronghold for years into the Reformation. Early in 1564, when a national survey was carried out to assess levels of religious conformity, tabulating the results into 'godly' Protestants (marked with a 'G'), 'moderates' and 'Catholics', Sir Henry quipped that 'if they wished to put into the provincial governments men of the new religion, they must send them' from London, since there were 'none in the Marches of Wales'.[23] However, the report for Shrewsbury proved an exception. There, a small élite of Protestant landowners and merchants was identified, centring on a few prominent local families, most notably the Corbetts and Newports.[24]

Another focal point was the school, and its headmaster: 'Thomas Ashton, schoolmaster, and a worthy man amongst them'.[25] Ashton was a recent addition to Shrewsbury's civic life. Although a charter had been passed as early as 1552 to establish a school to advance the youth 'in good learning and godly education' – that epithet 'godly' signalling its adherence to Protestant principles – it was not until 1561 that Ashton had become involved: in that year, he was praised by the Bishop of Coventry and Lichfield as the only 'godly preacher within these parties of my diocese', having begun 'a good work to the furtherance of a school in Shrewsbury'.[26] Ashton was a veteran pedagogue, elected in 1524 a Fellow of St John's College, Cambridge, the college that also produced Roger Ascham, John Cheke and William Cecil.[27] He was quickly adopted by the local Protestant community: in the same month (June 1561) he acted as a sponsor at a Corbett family baptism, and his appointment as schoolmaster was confirmed by the Shrewsbury bailiffs, with a generous stipend of forty pounds per annum.[28]

Under Ashton, Shrewsbury School flourished – by the end of 1561,

260 boys had been entered on the school's register book, and William Camden claimed in 1586 that the school had 'more scholars in number ... than in any one school throughout all England again'.[29] Still, Philip's entry was a major event in Ashton's headmastership. Shrewsbury School traditionally drew its pupils, both poor and gentle, from Shrewsbury's townsmen and 'strangers' from the surrounding countryside, indicated in the admissions register as *oppidani* and *alieni*. In November 1564, however, the register (usually the most perfunctory of records) bursts into life, detailing elaborately the ancestry and nobility of three new charges:

Philippus Sidney filius et heres Henrici Sidney militis de pensarst in comit. Cantie et domini presidis confinium Cambriæ nec non serenissimi ordinis garterii militis [Philip Sidney, son of Sir Henry Sidney of Penhurst in the county of Kent, Lord President of the Marches of Wales, and Knight of the Order of the Garter]

foulkus gryuell filius et heres foulki gryvell armigeri de beachams courte in comit. Warvici [Fulke Greville, son and heir of Sir Fulke Greville of Beachamps Court in the county of Warwick]

Jacobus harington filius Jacobi harington armigeri de Exton in comit. Rutlandiæ [James Harrington, son of Sir James Harrington of Exton in the county of Rutland][30]

Placing his eldest son in the leading school of the region signalled Sir Henry's investment in his post. Surrounding Philip with other 'alien' gentry (Harrington was the son of Sir Henry's sister Lucy, and Greville a distant kinsman of the Dudleys) put the hitherto parochial Shrewsbury School on the national map.

School life meant a complete revolution in Philip's personal circumstances. Shrewsbury School was still three decades away from the fine stone building that remains today as the Old Schools. When Philip entered, it was a single-storey timber-framed building built next to the town gaol on the evocatively named Ratonyslane (Rats' or Rotten Lane), lacking even dormitories for its charges, since of course most of them were local; it also lacked privies, forcing the boys out into a neighbouring field, although Philip was promptly provided with his own personal close-stool.[31]

During term-time, all the *alieni* had to board, or 'table', in town, boosting the town's population by some 5 per cent and artificially inflating rents. (In 1586, residents of Knockyn Street complained that rooms were being let to School boys at 'an exceeding great rent as thereby it is that no poor man can have any house at a reasonable rent'.)[32] Greville's and Harrington's lodgings are unknown, but Philip tabled, on the charmingly named 'Dogpole', in the household of George Leigh, a merchant who also figured prominently in the 1564 'godly' return.[33] A leading light in Shrewsbury's wool trade, Leigh sold local wools to cloth-making towns as far afield as Coggeshall and Dedham in Essex, via a middleman at the Maidenhead Inn in St Giles in the Field, Middlesex.[34] As a result of his commercial acumen, Leigh had become one of Shrewsbury's leading politicians, a freeman since March 1551, member of the Drapers' Company since 1553, burgess since 1555, and twice MP for the town. Earlier in 1564, he had become a bailiff, and the following year would become an alderman. Boasting the Lord President's son in his household was the final coup that confirmed Leigh's standing among Shrewsbury's civic élite.

Although Philip spent long days at school (7 a.m. to 4.30 p.m. from November to January, 6 a.m. to 5.30 p.m. from February to October), he was effectively living for three years in the house of a border-town wool merchant – a rare chance for a boy of his rank to see the inner domestic workings of the merchant classes. He took his meals with the Leigh family, including dinner (between 11 a.m. and 12.45 p.m.), and went to one of the town's four churches with them, probably St Mary's, which had close connections with both the Drapers' Company and the School. Being a schoolboy in Shrewsbury meant full involvement in the town's life, since Free School boys were regarded as something of a communal resource. One of Philip's peers, a tailor's son named Richard Langley, later recalled being asked by an illiterate cooper in 1566 to travel to Alberbury to witness a bond, 'at what time he was a scholar in the free school of Shrewsbury'.[35]

Philip and Fulke were immediately assigned to form three, James to the lower form five. This gives us some idea of Philip's academic prowess to date. By the time he went to school (aged almost ten) Philip's mastery of Latin must have been sufficient to enable him 'to write his own name with his own hand . . . read English perfectly and have his *accidens* without the book, . . . give any case of any number of a noun substantive or adjective and any person of any number of a verb active and passive, and . . . make a Latin by any of the concords, the Latin words being first given him'.[36] It was a necessary basis, since the curriculum was based on Latin and Greek texts.

For the first time, Philip had to be provided with his own personal retinue, separate from the family servants. Throughout his life, daily chores would be undertaken by one or more serving men who got to know their master intimately, sharing with him a suite of rooms, or even the same room. In Shrewsbury, Philip's retinue was restricted to a steward named Thomas Marshall, and at a later date to one Randall Calcott. Marshall's accounts, combined with the school ordinances,[37] allow us to reconstruct both the syllabus and the material demands of Philip's school education, led by Ashton and two undermasters, Thomas Wylton and Richard Atyks. He probably started with Cicero's letters, the plays of Terence, and the moral saws of Cato (a replacement Cato, 'his former being lost', was bought in September 1566), before moving on to Sallust (purchased for fourteen pence in June 1566). Ashton eased the boys into their Latin learning by making an abstract of phrases from Cicero's *De officiis* and a work by Juan Luis Vives: Marshall records a payment for three shillings on 16 January 1566 'for a written book being an abstract of Mr Ashton's doing of Tully's Offices and Lodovicus dialogue wise'. Around the same time, a copy of Radulphus Gualterius Tigurinus' technical manual on syllables and quantities in Latin verse was purchased for eightpence, presumably to facilitate Philip's study of Virgil (costing twenty pence): this work, unpublished in England until 1573, would have to have been imported. Caesar, Livy, Ovid and Horace would follow later. It was also only after reading Virgil that a small amount of Greek would be introduced, probably restricted to Greek grammar, the New Testament (perhaps studied alongside an English translation), Isocrates (probably studied alongside Cicero's orations) and Xenophon's *Cyropædeia*. Penmanship was also taught: Marshall spent twelvepence on 'three example books for the secretary hand for the young gentlemen'. Religious devotion was written into the timetable, as recorded in the school ordinances: 'Prayers now usually had in the said school shall be sung and said every morning devoutly upon their knees immediately after the school bell doth cease ringing, and likewise before they depart from school in the evening.'

All this amounted to a fairly standard grammar-school education for the period, but there are clear signs of Ashton's particular influence. Religious instruction came firmly from 'Calvin's catechism', costing fourpence in February 1566, providing Philip with a doctrinal model that owed more to Geneva than to the Church of England. Ashton was particularly interested in theatrical productions, following the lead of Martin Bucer that drama could benefit the Protestant cause. His ordinances state: 'Every Thursday the scholars of the first form before they go to play, shall for exercise declaim and play one act of a comedy, and every Saturday versify, and against Monday morning ensuing give up their themes or epistles, and all other exercises of writing or speaking shall be used in Latin.' Each Whitsuntide Ashton staged a religious play throughout the holiday period in the 'Quarry', an old dry quarry beyond the city walls, which had once formed part of the local monastery. It was Ashton's idea to take a staple of popular local culture – the Catholic 'mysteries', which had been banned – and turn it into an occasion for spreading the Protestant gospel. Whereas once the town's guildsmen had taken the parts, now the School's boys did; but Ashton ensured that the local guilds still paid for the privilege. In 1566, the Quarry saw *Julian the Apostate*, and in 1569 the *Play of the Passion*, which was enthusiastically received by the anonymous chronicler who recorded that it drew into Shrewsbury a 'great number of people of noblemen and others', who praised it 'greatly . . . The chief author thereof was one master Astoon [Ashton] being the head schoolmaster of the Free School there, a godly and learned man who took marvellous great pains therein.'[38] It may have been in one of these plays that Philip made his first public appearance. What this educational model meant in practice was that Philip's academic knowledge was filtered through a Calvinist glass.

Beyond the curriculum, there are signs of Sir Henry's influence. Philip continued to keep up his French: Marshall records the purchase of 'a French grammar' in September 1566, and eightpence was paid out 'for two quires of paper for example books, phrases, and sentences in Latin and French'. Remarkably, Philip's copy of François de Belleforest's French translation of Matteo Bandello's *Histoires Tragiques* (printed in

1561) survives with its inscription, '*Je suis apartenant a monsieur Philipe Sidnaie qui me trouve cy me rende a qui je suis*' (I belong to Master Philip Sidney; let anyone who finds me return me to my owner). Fulke Greville wanted to make his mark as well: in a much neater hand is written 'foulke grivell' and, sideways, 'foulke grivell is a good boy witness . . .' Sadly, the name of the 'witness' is now illegible.[39]

Belleforest seems at first sight a strange choice for a serious young boy, and his romance tales (the stuff Shakespeare's comedies were made on) hardly the moral fare to stand beside Calvin and Xenophon on his bookshelf. But a clue as to how Philip was encouraged to read such fictions may be found in Geoffrey Fenton's 1569 translation of *Tragicall Discourses*, dedicated to Lady Sidney. Drawing on similar romance material, Fenton claims that reading such fiction can have a moral and practical value: 'And truly,' he asks, 'may a man put to the view of the world any ancient report whose profession is to declare a truth, than to prefer the feigned tales of poets, which yet we see for diverse good respects tolerated to be read in all ages.' Although Fenton's argument here – that through fiction one may better provide the moral and political lessons of history – has been seen as naïve or ironic, it was one that Philip took to heart.[40]

While Philip was at Shrewsbury he received a formal letter of advice from his father[41] ('my first letter that ever I did write to you'), a gesture that was to become *de rigueur* for any well-meaning humanist father to send to his scholarly son – fourteen years later, Philip was to send one to his younger brother, Robert, and Shakespeare parodied the genre in Polonius' advice to Laertes in *Hamlet*. (Following Philip's death, this letter was printed; only one copy now exists, in Shrewsbury School Library.)[42] Sir Henry acknowledged receipt of two letters from Philip, one in Latin, one in French – suggesting that even in the personal correspondence of father and son there was an expectation of academic endeavour – and willed Philip 'to exercise that practice of learning often, for it will stand you in most stead in that profession of life that you are born to live in'. Sir Henry recognised the need for the myriad skills involved in letter-writing, and was determined that Philip would be properly prepared.

Much of the letter comprised standard advice, recommending hearty prayer; the importance of marking 'the sense and the matter' of what he read, 'as well as the words'; showing obedience towards his masters and courtesy to all men; being a listener rather than a speaker; and, when he spoke, keeping his speech clean and modest. In a sudden flash of vivid imagery, Sir Henry advised his son to 'Think upon every word that you will speak before you utter it, and remember how nature hath ramparted up, as it were, the tongue with teeth, lips – yea, and hair without [outside] the lips, and all betokening reins and bridles for the loose use of that member. Above all things,' he concluded, 'tell no untruth.'

Through the moral platitudes comes one *ad hominem* concern: for Philip's health, which was clearly a source of parental anxiety. Philip's passion for studying could be dangerous, as Moffet relates: 'Nights and days in ceaseless and related studies he worked upon the anvil of wit, reason and memory, at some harm to his welfare; yet he did not wish on this account to give over literary studies, which lie in wait against health.'[43] In addition to his exhortation to 'moderate diet', the occasional glass of wine, and cleanliness, Sir Henry therefore advised Philip to 'use exercise of body, yet such as is without peril to your bones and joints; it will increase your force and enlarge your breath'. He should study during 'such hours as your discreet master doth assign you earnestly, and the time I know he will so limit as shall be both sufficient for your learning and safe for your health'.

Even at this early stage, Philip had developed a reputation for a seriousness that sometimes threatened to topple into melancholy. According to Moffet, he participated in schoolboy games only 'negligently . . . among those whom he could have excelled, he desired only to be an equal'. His schoolfellow Greville provides a not dissimilar portrait: 'Though I lived with him and knew him from a child, yet I never knew him other than a man, with such staidness of mind, lovely and familiar gravity, as carried grace and reverence above his years.'[44] Sir Henry felt that his eldest son might be letting down what he clearly saw as a Sidney tradition. 'Give yourself to be merry; for you degenerate from your father if you find not yourself most able in wit and body to do anything when you are most merry.'

His mother added a touching postscript, saying that she would not write him a letter while he had such good advice to study, and urging him 'to have always before the eyes of your mind these excellent counsels of my lord, your dear father, and that you fail not continually, once in four or five days, to read them over'. She concluded: 'Farewell, my little Philip, and once again the Lord bless you! Your loving mother, Mary Sidney.'

Philip's presence in Shrewsbury took on a new significance in December 1565, when his parents sailed to Ireland so that Sir Henry could take up his new post as Lord Deputy of Ireland. Thomas Marshall's surviving accounts start as Sir Henry and Lady Mary departed from Westchester bound for Ireland on 3 December 1565, when Sir Henry handed Marshall 'the sum of twenty nobles a month', totalling £6 13s. and 4d.[45] In his first day (Tuesday 4th) at Westchester, Marshall had to find considerable funds to cover his charges' travel expenses:

> Washing the linen of Philip and his companions: 3s. 4d. Wiping and making clean their boots, 6d. A yard of cloth to make Mr Philip a pair of boothose [overstockings] having none but a pair of linen which were too thin to ride in after his disease. 3s. 4d. Making these boothose and for stitching silk. 18d. A dozen of silk points. 6d. Mending his hose and setting boots on the last. 4d. A false scabbard for his rapier. 4d. Horsemeat for the three little nags that were left for us two days and a half after your lordship's departure. 3s. 6d. Showing the nags. 12d. Two collars for them. 2d. On Wednesday 4th, staying overnight at Chirk at the home of one Mr Edwards, the boots needed cleaning again. 4d.

Sir Henry's departure had been public knowledge as early as September, but was delayed 'for want of money', when funds earmarked for Ireland were diverted to support the rebels in Scotland.[46] The honour he felt at being appointed Lord Deputy of Ireland was tinged with regret that he had to leave Wales (although he would remain Lord President). He later wrote of Wales: 'A happy place of government it is, for a better people to govern, or better subjects to their sovereign, Europe holdeth not. But yet hath not my life been so domestically spent in Wales, and the sweet marches of the same, but that I have been employed in other foreign actions.'[47] He was not exaggerating. Since becoming Lord President in 1560, Sir Henry had been ordered away on missions to France and Scotland; now Ireland would take up all his time until 1571, save for a brief interlude in 1567–8 when he returned to court. More Sidney domestic outposts were created in Drogheda, and at the Queen's Castle in Dublin, where the younger Sidney children visited their father – the Penshurst accounts include entries for moving the Sidney household from Dublin Castle to London; Philip's sister Elizabeth died while living with her father in Dublin in 1567, and was buried in its cathedral.[48] Philip was thus even further isolated from his family than he had been previously.

Sir Henry's duties in Welsh government were now undertaken by a succession of vice-presidents. Philip, however, served another function, physically representing the Sidneys in the Marches. It was quite a responsibility. During the school vacations Philip had to pay courtesy calls to his father's allies in the border country. At New Year 1566, for example, he spent time with Sir Richard and Lady Newport at Eyton-on-Severn, near Wroxeter. Illness in the School forced a brief return visit in May, when, as Thomas Marshall recounts, Philip and his retinue 'went to visit at the house of Sir Andrew Corbett and that of Sir Richard Newport when the scholars were sick'; in June, Marshall paid twelvepence 'for perfumes to air the chamber with when we came forth of the country after the young gentlemen were recovered'.[49] Philip's presence at these houses helpfully endorsed Sir Henry's continuing support and patronage. On occasions, Philip, embodying his father, must have presented a vaguely comical sight: when Mary, wife of his host George Leigh, gave birth to another son in the summer of 1566, Lady Newport stood as godmother and Philip Sidney stood as godfather, giving the baby boy his name and making the customary gifts of cash to the midwife and the nurse (Mrs Leigh refused any gift for herself). Lady Newport was an important local figure in her mid-forties; Master Philip was all of eleven.[50]

Now that his parents were away in Ireland, responsibility for Philip during the school vacations fell to his uncle Robert Dudley, now Earl of Leicester, who called him to Kenilworth, from where they would travel to Oxford, to await the queen. Keen to share in the glory of his most prominent student, Thomas Ashton joined Philip and his servants Marshall and Calcott, when they set out on 14 August 1566.[51] From the gifts to Philip that Marshall recorded, we know that Philip met Walter Devereux, Viscount Hereford (and later Earl of Essex) on this journey; Devereux made Philip a gift of a 'red horse', for which a saddle with a fringe of black silk was made, and at Kenilworth the gifts continued.

Leicester, dismayed at Philip's much-patched wardrobe, replaced it with a completely new one, which included doublets in crimson satin and green taffeta, a damask gown with lace trim, hose of crimson velvet and three leather jerkins – the most beautiful of which was white with an edge of 'parchment gold lace'.[52]

This was perhaps the first occasion on which Philip had spent time being introduced as Leicester's nephew, rather than as his father's son. By 1566, Leicester had taken on a powerful new persona. After the messy politicking of the early 1560s, the earl had deliberately aligned himself with a Protestant agenda, denying that his Reformist faith had ever failed: 'I take Almighty God to my record, I never altered my mind or thought from my youth touching my religion, and you know I was from my cradle ever brought up in it.'[53] Leicester's emphatic stand destroyed Spanish hopes that they could use him: later in 1566, the Spanish ambassador Guzmán de Silva would write gloomily to his king that 'Leicester has gone over to the heretics'.[54] By 1568, he would be taking communion in the French Huguenot church in London, and he started to provide 'secret' support to Huguenots in La Rochelle. Such moves were designed to give him an international profile of radical Protestantism. An expatriate in Frankfurt named William Rowe read the signs and wrote to Leicester, exhorting him 'to build with both hands the church of God in England, to the rooting out of all tyranny'.[55]

At the same time, a new focus for Leicester's ambitions was revealed. During 1566, a series of popular uprisings in the Low Countries swayed the rule of Philip II, who had inherited them from his father Charles V. On the ground three local rulers, William of Orange and the Counts of Egmont and Horne, managed to impose some sort of order, but were forced to make some concessions to the rebels' Protestant demands. Philip reacted to the situation harshly, sending in the hardline Duke of Alva, who restored order, executing Horne and Egmont (Orange fled the country, and failed in his bid to stir up popular revolt). As Alva started to clamp down on what he regarded as heretical practices, there was a mass exodus of Dutch Protestants, to England among other places: it was estimated that 6,000 refugees reached London, with 4,000 more in Norwich.[56] Leicester was seen as a popular beacon for the dispossessed Netherlanders.

While he consolidated this new reputation in Europe, however,

Leicester knew that his personal prospects at home were being severely curtailed by the queen's continued interest in him as her favourite. Although Amy Robsart's tragic death was long in the past, he was effectively barred from remarrying: Elizabeth may have ruled him out as *her* husband, but she was not going to let him marry elsewhere. For Philip, this had far-reaching implications. If his uncle Warwick remained childless, as seemed increasingly likely, then Philip would remain heir presumptive to Leicester, who was widely perceived as favourite to – and the only possible English husband for – Elizabeth. This role now came with important doctrinal expectations, but with Thomas Ashton's schooling preparing him, Philip was the impeccable heir to his uncle's new-found continental status as Protestant icon.

It was as such that Leicester first paraded his nephew in the summer of 1566. In late August, Philip travelled to Oxford, lodging in Lincoln College with its rector John Bridgwater, who was also one of Leicester's chaplains. The royal party entered the town from Woodstock on 31 August, in great finery, the queen herself on an open chariot. The visit progressed until 8 September with the dramas, disputations and sermon that characterised Elizabeth's visit to the universities. Philip and Thomas Ashton were joined at Oxford by Thomas Wilson, author of the influential tract *The Arte of Rhetorike*; if they shadowed Leicester, as presumably they did, they would have attended, in addition to the formal disputations, three plays – during one of which, Richard Edwards' *Palamon and Arcite*, the scaffolding erected to hold the audience gave way, resulting in several casualties.[57] According to his 1570 horoscope, this summer witnessed the first occasion that Philip appeared before the sovereign who would influence his life so radically: he was an 'orator . . . before that most serene prince Elizabeth'.[58] Perhaps this occurred at Oxford, or possibly at Woodstock, where the queen returned after her visit: the Spanish ambassador had alleged that without practice English boys could not perform well so Elizabeth summoned some of them to debate in Latin before her. Whatever the occasion, it must have been a milestone for Philip, a proud moment for Leicester, and a taste of what the boy would be expected to do over the next years.

When Philip returned to Shrewsbury, it was with a new saddle and trunk embossed with the bear and ragged staff – the Dudley family crest

– and with a Frenchman named Oliver from the Earl of Warwick's retinue. He was indeed a Dudley.

Most boys stayed at Shrewsbury for no more than five years: Philip would have reached the top of the school by 1568, and he may have left slightly earlier. On 2 February 1568 his name appears in the Admissions Register of Gray's Inn in Holborn.[59] This does not necessarily indicate that he was long resident there, or that he studied law to any degree. Many young gentlemen were on the books at Gray's Inn, often just to provide themselves with a usefully located place to dine close to London and Westminster. Philip's name does not occur elsewhere in the surviving Gray's Inn records, and we know that soon thereafter he was resident at the university in Oxford.

Shrewsbury School had strong links with St John's College in Cambridge – and Greville and Harrington ended up in Cambridge colleges – but since Leicester had assumed responsibility for Philip's well-being in Sir Henry's absence, the choice ultimately had to be Oxford, of which Leicester was Chancellor. He lodged his nephew with his Vice-Chancellor, Dr Thomas Cooper, who was also Dean of Christ Church. Like Ashton, Cooper came with faultless Protestant credentials. He had interrupted his Oxford career when Mary came to the throne, joining the Protestant polemicists John Foxe and Robert Crowley in a principled walk-out. Since the accession of Elizabeth he had returned to Oxford, and had recently dedicated his English/Latin dictionary, *Thesavrvs Lingvæ Romanæ et Britannicæ*, to Leicester.[60] Cooper was universally admired for 'his learning and sanctity of life', but was dogged by scurrilous libels about his wife, an Oxford woman who allegedly 'proved too light for his gravity'.[61]

The tutor looked after his charge both pastorally and pedagogically, usually being responsible for purchasing the student's books and other necessaries (in the hope that the family would reimburse him quarterly), and for the student's debts. A payment of forty-eight pounds to Cooper for seventy-two weeks' 'diets' ending on Midsummer Day 1569 indicates that Philip was resident in Oxford from February 1568, when he was thirteen years old. While there is no record of Philip's matriculation or graduation from Christ Church, he was presumably living in the college (a letter he sent in February 1570 refers to 'this college of Christ

Church').[62] Leicester applied in March 1570 to Matthew Parker, the Archbishop of Canterbury, 'for licence to be granted to my boy Philip Sidney, who is somewhat subject to sickness, for eating flesh this Lent', this licence, 'in whatsoever form may seem best unto you so as he may have with him Mr Doctor Cooper, who is his tutor'.[63] According to Thomas Moffet, funds were 'provided by the kindness of his uncles' as well as by 'the affection of his parents'. Predictably, just as Philip 'did not very willingly join in conversation, whether in light or serious vein, with the reprobate', these funds were spent 'not upon pleasures . . . but he distributed them either frugally for his own use or more generously for the alleviation of learned men'.[64]

While Cooper was his 'tutor', the man whom Philip described as 'my reader' was Thomas Thornton, then in his late twenties and at the beginning of a career that would later find him Vice-Chancellor of Oxford and Master of Ledbury Hospital in Herefordshire. In Thornton's case, the appointment worked to his benefit as well as Philip's.[65] Philip's respect for 'the worthiness of his life and learning', added to Thornton's 'desert towards me', prompted him to gain high-level support from Cecil and Leicester for Thornton's bid for a canonry in Christ Church. When one came free at the death of Thomas Day, a rival candidate appeared in the form of Toby Matthew, a precocious young man who already at twenty-three had been unanimously elected Public Orator of the University. Philip was 'forced for better expedition to use an unaccustomed manner of writing', and petition Cecil directly to counter some rumours against Thornton, which had been spread through Oxford: Thornton gained Day's stall.[66] This was Philip's first known intervention into public affairs, and Thornton never forgot the gesture: his monument records 'that he was a common refuge for young poor scholars of great hopes and parts, and tutor to Sir Philip Sidney when he was of Christ Church'.[67]

Philip encountered an Oxford curriculum based on grammar, rhetoric and dialectic. For grammar, he probably read Priscian or Linacre as well as Cicero, Horace and Virgil; for rhetoric, Cicero and Aristotle; and for dialectic, Porphyry or Aristotle. It was from these years that he gained his abiding interest in Aristotle, allegedly translating the first two books of his *Rhetoric* into English.[68] In his only recorded comment on his time at Oxford, Philip evinced a distaste for the voguish but empty imitation of classical style: 'Ciceronianism', he told his brother Robert in 1580, was 'the chief abuse of Oxford'.[69]

A more important training came from outside the curriculum: from his peer group. The young men who surrounded Philip at university took different paths in their lives, but at Oxford they were united by a passion for both classical and contemporary learning, and a belief that reading could best equip them to deal with the demands of a rapidly changing world – indeed, a world whose limits were constantly being called into question. Walter Ralegh at Oriel, and Richard Hakluyt at Christ Church, would use their knowledge to illuminate their voyages of discovery: Hakluyt dedicated his *Divers voyages touching the discouerie of America* to Philip in 1582.[70] Merton alumnus Thomas Bodley would be a crucial figure in English intelligence networks on the Continent, before using his sources to supply the books with which he would re-establish Oxford's university library as the Bodleian. Henry Savile, also at Merton, would specialise in mathematics, providing a useful companion for Philip's brother Robert on his continental travels a decade later. At Magdalen was the writer and playwright John Lyly, whose *Euphues* would be the book *du jour* in 1578; the future theologian Richard Hooker studied at Corpus. Across the road at Broadgates Hall was a poor scholar named William Camden whom Thornton rescued and took into his own lodgings at Christ Church: Camden went on to become one of England's leading antiquarians and historians. His 1568 notebook, now in the British Library's Cotton collection, includes a Latin epigram with the title 'Ad P.S. cum Horat.' – perhaps a verse given to Philip with a copy of Horace?[71]

Philip also met Thomas Allen, a Catholic who in 1570 was forced to leave Trinity College for refusing to take orders, but joined Gloucester Hall, then just outside Oxford. Allen was something of an inside secret, a brilliant mathematician who inspired many outstanding students, but never published his work. Keenly interested, like his friend John Dee, in the more arcane aspects of science, it may well have been Allen who cast Philip's horoscope in 1570 or 1571. If so, Allen recognised early on Philip's potential, for he notes regretfully: 'I myself would have got to know your natural talent, so truly open and abundant, in the study and discipline of mathematics, had not the malice of time snatched me away from you, or rather had not the unjust demands of fate kept you from me' (perhaps a reference to Allen's move from Trinity?). 'I grieve to have lost a youth of so much promise, designed by Nature for the study of mathematics and by birth for that of the celestial philosophy, endowed with a happy keenness of mind, godlike talents, and a spirit looking continually upwards towards whatever is furthest removed from earthly matters.' He recalls particularly 'how zealous and eager your propensity for the study of the stars was when I went to visit you and there would be considerable discussion back and forth between us about astrology'.[72]

Philip seems to have treated his tutors as equals, entering into serious academic debate with them. Moffet tells of his 'affability of speech' in chance encounters with learned men in Oxford streets, 'not by hands alone were they joined, but even by heart's desire . . . He was never seen going to church, to the exercise ground, or to the public assembly hall (where he frequently employed himself) except as distinguished among the company of all the learned men.'[73] Philip, at least in Moffet's depiction, resembles less an Oxford undergraduate with a life bounded by college gates, than an independent intellectual.

For Leicester as Chancellor, Philip's presence at Oxford was highly useful. Just as he had been called on by his uncle to speak in front of the queen during his summer visit in 1566, now Philip was regularly summoned to perform. Richard Carew, a Cornish boy at Broadgates Hall who went on to become a noted translator and topographer, later recalled 'being a scholar in Oxford, of fourteen years' age, and three years' standing, upon a wrong conceived opinion touching my sufficiency, I was there called to dispute *ex tempore* with the matchless Sir Ph. Sidney, in presence of the earls, Leicester, Warwick, and divers other great personages'.[74] Similarly, Philip's horoscope records another oration before the queen, late in 1567 or early in 1568: 'Every member of our University of Oxford knows what wonderful potential was implanted in you by Nature for engaging in the noble arts, and how much progress you have made, to the great admiration of your generation and the applause of all who heard you, when you delivered an oration before her most serene Highness that was both eloquent and elegant, and this when you scarcely had passed your thirteenth year.'[75] Since Elizabeth did not visit Oxford in this time, it may well be that Leicester produced Philip for his party trick elsewhere – perhaps even at court.

It was not only Leicester and Warwick who expected Philip to perform. At some point Philip caught the eye of the Principal Secretary of State, Sir William Cecil, who saw in him a charming young man who might be wheeled out to delight, on Cecil's behalf, whenever required. Philip entered, somewhat grudgingly, into a correspondence with Cecil, in which the two men exchanged compliments in formal, rather flat Latin. Cecil's side of the correspondence has not survived, but two of Philip's letters display a Latin style dictated by textbook examples rather than personal flair. For instance, when Cecil accuses Philip of ingratitude, it is clearly designed as – and understood as – the cue for a copious discourse on a standard topic:

> This may have given rise in you to some natural suspicion of ingratitude on my part, than which I have always thought there is no vice more detestable, no offence more unworthy, and no crime more heinous; in a youth it betrays rudeness of manners, in a mature man it is worthy of the deepest censure, in old age it is positively wicked. Therefore I beseech your honour to believe that nothing is farther from me, that there is nothing I would more carefully avoid.[76]

Sir Henry played along with Cecil's perception of his son as a bookworm, begging Cecil's wife to ensure that her son (by which he meant Philip) should limit his studying 'for I fear he will be too much given to his book, and yet I have heard of few wise fathers doubt that in their children'.[77]

However, the pressure of being a son to multiple 'fathers' proved logistically difficult. On one unfortunate occasion Philip was not available when Cecil wanted him, having been spirited away to Wales by his father on his brief visit home. Cecil dashed off a missive to Sir Henry:

> Now I have not many things of weight saving one, and that is heavy for you to hear, considering you have therein offended many. And not to detain you in longer expectation this it is: you carried away your son and my scholar from Oxford, not only from his book, but from the commodity to have been seen, of my lordships his uncles, and to have been opposed by me [in debate?] and to have pleasured both me and my wife. I think indeed either you forgat the Queen's progress to be so near Oxford or else you have some matter of necessity to allege, which for your taking him from Oxford, and for delaying of him so long in wild

Wales, I think my lord of Leicester will challenge you earnestly and therefore I will say Dixi [I have spoken].[78]

Cecil's use of the word 'commodity' begs the question: to whom was Philip's appearance commodious?

Philip was soon assured of the affections of the Cecil household. By the summer of 1568, Cecil was ending his letters to Sir Henry with elaborate displays of family bonding: 'as you have gently and courteously remembered in your commendations my wife and your little maid my daughter, so I wish health to my good lady your wife, and increase of all goodness to your son my darling Mr Philip'.[79] The specificity of the commendations – to Cecil's daughter Anne and Sidney's eldest son – suggests that moves were already under way to consolidate the families' connections by a marriage. In August, Sir Henry was temporarily back in Shropshire with Philip, and wrote to Cecil recommending 'unto you my wife myself and my boy'.[80] By November of that year, Sir Henry was referring to 'my sweet jewel, your daughter', while Cecil made a 'courteous visitation' of Lady Sidney, and Sir Henry begged him 'sometime hearken of our boy'.[81]

In January 1569, Philip, now fourteen, was at court with Cecil. 'Your Philip is here,' reported the Secretary to Sir Henry, 'in whom I take more comfort than I do openly utter for avoiding of wrong interpretation he is wordy [worthy] to be loved and so I do love him as he were mine own'.[82] But there was a world of difference between loving Philip as if he were his own, and actually making him his own. As Sir Henry forced the marriage question more assertively, Cecil's enthusiasm suddenly cooled:

My good Lord, if my power for doing, or my leisure for writing were as some portion of my desire is to testify to you my goodwill, you should have as good proof thereof, as I see you have in hope an assurance. I thank you for your free offer made to me by your letters ... concerning your son, whom truly I do so like for his own conditions and singular towardness in all good things, as I think you a happy father for so joyful a son. And as for the interest that it pleaseth you to offer me in him, I must confess if the child alone were valued, without the natural good that dependeth of you his father, I could not but think him wordy the love I bear him, which certainly is more than I do express outwardly,

for avoiding of sinister interpretation for as for the accompt to have
him my son, I see so many incidenties, as it sufficeth me to love the
child for himself, without regard therein of my daughter whom surely I
love so well, as so it be within my degree or not much above, I shall
think none too good for her. Thus you see a father's fondness which to
a father I dare discover, and so for this time it sufficeth.[83]

This cooling was the knee-jerk strategy of a man moving from courtly
pleasantries to the hard-headed business of marriage negotiations. Sir
Henry, suddenly out of his depth, sent his trusted servant Edward
Waterhouse to negotiate with Cecil:

Let me know what you would have me do, and you shall find me ready.
For before God in these matters I am utterly ignorant as one that never
made a marriage in his life. But I mean truly and sincerely loving your
daughter as one of my own, regarding her virtue above any other dot
[dowry], and your friendship more than all the money you will give.
And for my boy I confess that if I might have every week a boy I should
never have none like him, and accordingly I have dealt with him, for I
do not know above a hundred a year of mine that I have not already
assured to him.[84]

As early as 1568, Sir Henry had ordered the drawing up of a statement of
the yearly value of his lands and other holdings in the counties of Kent,
Lincoln, Rutland and Surrey: the resulting figure (£1,140 4s. 2d.) was now
used as the basis for a tentative marriage settlement between the Cecils
and the Sidneys, dated 6 August 1569.[85] Cecil first worked out terms,
tellingly enough, with Leicester, and sent them to Sir Henry in Dublin.
His messenger reported that the Lord Deputy 'doth very well like every
of them, and is ready to perform it, in such sort as by yourself shall be
thought meet', and was content to let the marriage money go to Philip
and Anne rather than to himself.[86] Cecil asked his agent in Ireland,
Nicholas White, to look into the terms of the agreement, and White
reported back that he had had 'a doubt' [suspicion] of the articles,
discovering that the land was worth less than previously believed, and
there was some question of what assurances there were for Anne, should
Philip refuse to marry her.[87]

Perhaps because of White's 'doubt', the negotiations trailed off in some (possibly deliberate) confusion. When Cecil sent a marriage contract to Sir Henry in Ireland, it somehow went missing. Cecil complained of Sir Henry's coldness, to which Sir Henry replied:

> Now for our particular, and for our children, I am sorry that you find coldness anywhere in proceeding, where such good liking appeared in the beginning, but for my part, I was never more ready to perfect that matter, than presently I am, assuring you for my part, if I might have the greatest prince's daughter in Christendom for him, the match spoken of between us on my part should not be broken. Sureties I confess I received signed as I remember by my lord of Leicester and you, and well allowed by me, but where they be God knoweth, for Waterhouse is weaned from me, and John Thomas is sick, the paper I cannot find, but this for truth Sir I was never more joyous of the match than now I am; but how and which way never confer with me while I am here, without special direction, for I neither can care, nor consider while I here dwell, for wife child or my self.

However, despite Sir Henry's optimistic references to 'our daughter Anne', it was clear to all concerned that the likelihood of the match was fast receding.[88]

All hope was lost when Sir William was created Lord Burghley on 25 February 1571, instantly rendering his daughter a far more valuable catch for prospective suitors. Indeed, less than six months later, in July 1571, Edward de Vere, Earl of Oxford, publicly declared to the queen at Hampton Court his desire to marry Anne Cecil, to which Elizabeth assented. Despite being Cecil's ward, Oxford was hardly an ideal choice. His main claim to fame thus far lay in killing one of Cecil's servants at Cecil House; he had escaped charges by having the death judged a *felo de se* (suicide), caused by the unfortunate servant's 'running upon a point of a fence sword of the said earl'.[89] It was not a popular match. There were reports of 'great weeping, wailing and sorrowful cheer, of these that hoped to have had that golden day'.[90]

Even as he congratulated the new Lord Burghley on the match, Sir William Fitzwilliam let slip that he would rather have seen Philip (his nephew) as the groom.[91] Burghley himself admitted to the Earl of

Rutland, another suitor, that before Oxford proposed the marriage, he might have thought it 'strange'. He could only claim lamely that the impetus had come from Oxford, and 'there is much more of him of understanding than any stranger to him would think'. In the same letter, Burghley intimated that he had not been disposed to consider further marriage proposals after 'the former intention of a marriage with Mr Philip Sidney', implying that the Sidney prospect was dead even *before* Oxford entered the fray.[92] Despite widespread reservations, Oxford married Anne in November 1571; it was, as all predicted, an unhappy match, which saw Oxford mistreat his wife appallingly, and eventually abandon her for a string of other women and servant boys.

The whole affair was a useful lesson for Philip. He had played by the rules, embodying the young humanist scholar whom Burghley saw as the perfect son-in-law. Sir Henry had made all the right moves, entwining the two families as he provided intelligence for his son's future father-in-law. But the bottom line for Burghley was money and status, and the Sidney family simply did not have enough. Oxford was fabulously wealthy, as was the Earl of Derby, to whom Burghley arranged a match for his daughter Elizabeth. Even from the grave, he controlled his two remaining daughters' marriages: each should receive £4,000 – but only if they married an earl. Bequests then dropped according to their married rank: £3,000 for a baron, £2,000 for any other rank. Not surprisingly, both daughters chose earls.[93] The distance between rhetoric and reality was vast: no matter how elaborate the compliments paid to his 'young scholar', Master Philip Sidney was never going to be a match on English soil for Edward de Vere, seventeenth Earl of Oxford.

At the age of fifteen, then, Philip found his marriage prospects closed off, at least temporarily. During the summer of 1570, Sir Henry decided that his son's best bet was to join him in Ireland. Since the only surviving letter from Sir Henry to Philip is his advice letter of 1566, we do not know how much Philip knew of his father's exploits in Ireland, or whether Philip was responsible for this initiative, but by now the Lord Deputy's experience in Ireland had made clear the problems that a Sidney was likely to have in serving Elizabeth.[94]

Sir Henry had not at first relished his Irish posting. On their maiden voyage, one of the ships carrying the Sidneys' goods was wrecked. The political situation that he discovered on his arrival was less than heartening: 'Never saw I a more waste and desolate land,' he told the queen:

> There heard I such lamentable cries and doleful complaints, made by that small remain of poor people which yet are left . . . Besides this, such horrible and lamentable spectacles there are to behold, as the burning of villages, the ruin of churches . . . the view of the bones and skulls of the dead subjects, who partly by murder, partly by famine, have died in the fields; as, in truth, hardly any Christian with dry eyes could behold.[95]

There was little he could do to remedy Ireland's plight – or his own. 'This realm will ruin under my rule, haply to my shame,' he complained to Leicester, 'but undoubtedly to England's harm. Yea, and will under any man, whom the Queen shall send, though he have the force of Hercules, the magnanimity of Caesar, the diligence of Alexander, and the eloquence of Tully: her highness withdrawing her gracious countenance.' Clearly, the new Lord Deputy had his work cut out.[96]

Sir Henry had his military and political victories in Ireland, but his life was costly, and his strategy often only reactive. While Philip was enjoying the glories of Kenilworth and Oxford in September 1566, Sir Henry was writing to Leicester from Drogheda: 'Ah! my dearest lord that you could find in your heart to lose one of your fingers to have me at home; God defend that you should lose any one joint from me, but I would that I had lost a hand that I were delivered of this cursed charge.' Despite all his work, he was the victim of slanderous charges, and in disgrace with the queen. 'Help me home speedily, or Almighty God dissolve my troubled spirit from my overtoiled body . . . As you love me and the issue of your worthy spirit help me out of this wretched land or I shall shortly die, for, before God, I am myself half dead already of very grief and toil . . . Pardon my shaking hand; I fear I am entered into a palsy.'[97]

Lady Sidney was also affected detrimentally by her time in Ireland. She remained at Drogheda when Sir Henry returned briefly to London in 1567. As Edmund Campion relates in his history of Ireland, Drogheda came under attack by the rebels: it was Lady Sidney who commanded the Mayor of Dublin to come to the town's aid to 'brake the rage of the enemies', which he successfully did. Not all her interventions were so happy, however: Sir Henry recalled how a bitter letter to him from the queen 'so perplexed my most dear wife, as she fell most grievously sick upon the same, and in that sickness remained once in trance above fifty-two hours.' After she recovered, Sir Henry despatched his wife back to England, 'where she lived till my coming over, somewhat to my charges'.[98] When he eventually followed his wife home, Sir Henry found his reception cold; Elizabeth started to dismantle the programme of reforms he had set in motion; and, to cap it all, he fell ill with the gallstones that periodically troubled him: according to his physician, Sir Henry had to return to Penshurst, where he finally passed a stone 'the quantity of a nutmeg'.[99]

When Sir Henry returned to Ireland in 1568, he found that his best efforts had been systematically sabotaged by Thomas Butler, the tenth Earl of Ormond, an Irish magnate who had established himself at court as one of Elizabeth's favourites. A deadly rival of Leicester, Ormond did his utmost to make life difficult for Leicester's brother-in-law by advising Elizabeth against the Lord Deputy's policies, as reported to him by agents in Ireland. In February 1569, Sir Henry moaned to Cecil:

> I dare affirm, there is no servant in Christendom, that endureth greater
> toil of mind and body than I do, nor that with so little assistance
> wieldeth so weighty matters and meeteth with so many and variable
> accidents . . . Herewith I have such a familiar of penury, as I think never
> none endured as a prince deputy; what should I in particular dilate it,
> when I am forced to borrow, yea almost to beg for my dinner? How
> then doth my servants, how then my soldiers, but most of all, how doth
> the poor country, which hath borne all, without receiving any thing, this
> ten years past.[100]

In early 1569, Sir Henry came under violent attack in the Irish Parliament from the leader of the old settlers, Sir Edmund Butler. Once again, it was his Dudley connection that made Sidney vulnerable. Butler, Sir Henry alleged, claimed to his fellow rebels 'that the cause of his stir was, that the Earl of Leicester, enemy to his brother and house, should marry the Queen, and be king of England, and that I should be king of Ireland; their mortal foe and brother to the Earl of Leicester, of whom I should hold Ireland (as might appear) by bearing the ragged staff continually in my pencel [a pennon or streamer] before, which indeed I did'.[101]

The claim might sound ridiculous, but Butler's scaremongering had its roots in political reality. Since the reign of Henry II, the English sovereign had claimed lordship over Ireland (*dominus Hibernia*), but in recent decades the vocabulary had shifted significantly. According to an Act passed by the Irish Parliament on 18 June 1541, Ireland was now a *kingdom* 'united and knit to the imperial crown of the realm of England', and the King of England was also the King of Ireland. Of course, the 'King of Ireland' amounted in practice to little more than a legal fiction: as the Irish historian Ciaran Brady has written, 'neither a colony nor yet an independent sovereign entity, Ireland was a curious hybrid, a kingdom whose own sovereign denied its autonomy'. But on the European mainland the image of the Lord Deputy of Ireland remained that of an official with power unparalleled in European politics. Even the translation of the job title into European languages helped. By a useful semantic slip, the English 'Lord Deputy' became the Latin 'Pro-rex' (Viceroy), and continental observers insisted on regarding the Lord Deputy as a person with royal powers, and at least quasi-royal status.[102]

Sir Henry's supporters made good use of this loophole in representation. A woodcut in John Derricke's 1581 publication, *The Image of Irelande*, which was dedicated to Philip, depicts Sir Henry Sidney sitting on a throne, wearing a crown and full regalia, as Turlough Luineach

4. John Derricke's woodcut of Sir Henry Sidney as pro-rex of Ireland.

O'Neill submits to him. The accompanying text makes clear the implications of the picture:

> Lo where he sits in honour's seat, most comely to be seen,
> As worthier to represent, the person of a queen.[103]

That final line contains the crucial ambiguity that would help in later years to fuel Philip's political life in Europe: in 'representing' the person of the monarch, was the Lord Deputy physically embodying an absent queen or physically replacing an absent queen? To many in Ireland, and to many in Europe, the Lord Deputy *was* the ruler of Ireland.

But the image could also be exploited by his enemies. Butler drew on this anomaly, planting in Elizabeth's mind new seeds of doubt to complement those she already had regarding Sir Henry. Her doubt was enough to sabotage his plans for Philip. The one thing that could boost his morale was to have his son and heir by his side. Sir Henry was hugely proud of Philip. Fulke Greville recalled how Sir Henry had called Philip 'in my hearing (though I unseen) *lumen familiae suae* [light of his family]'.[104] Now he wanted that light to shine on Ireland. Philip readily agreed to the proposal, and plans were put in place – until something, or someone, intervened to keep him in England. A letter from the queen herself to Sir Henry, dated 19 August 1570, sketches the situation:

> Where we perceive that you have commanded that your eldest son
> Philip should now come over thither to you into Ireland, we find him
> thereto willing but considering the universality of sickness partly of
> agues, partly by plague dispersed in the countries betwixt this and the
> passage into Ireland, we think it not safe for him and therefore we have
> taken upon us to license you to come hither to us before winter except
> there be great cause to the contrary.[105]

What this letter makes clear is that Sir Henry's word on the future of his son could easily be overruled. Who decided against Philip's going to Ireland? Was it Cecil or Leicester, wanting him for their own purposes? Or was the queen suspicious of Sir Henry building up a dynasty in Ireland?

Whatever the case, Elizabeth's refusal to allow Philip to join him was the last straw for Sir Henry. Ormond, he alleged, 'sometime with clamour, but oftener with whispering, did bitterly backbite me, saying that his brethren were driven by my cruelty to rebel, and that he nor his could never have any justice of me'. This produced 'sour letters' from the queen, which he found 'torturous'. Ultimately, 'tired with toil of mind and body in that cursed country', he insisted on – and received – his recall.

On 25 March 1571, leaving the country in the hands of brother-in-law Fitzwilliam, Sir Henry left Dublin quay and, as Edmund Campion recorded, 'He was honoured at the point of his going, with such recourse, pomp, music, shows and interludes, as no man remembereth the like.' It was a different story when he returned to court, where he encountered 'more cold acceptation than I hoped for', and constant rumours that the war with the Butlers had been provoked 'by my malice borne to them, and that else there was little or nothing done' during his time there.[106]

Philip's time at Oxford came to an abrupt end in April 1571 when an outbreak of plague shut down university operations for nearly a year. Many Christ Church members decamped to nearby Wallingford, where the college had property; Blunt's account books for the year beginning 31 May 1571, however, reveal that £38 11s. 6d. was paid out for 'expenses of Mr Philip Sidney, in time of sickness at Reading, and other'.[107] The 'sickness' might indicate that Philip himself was ill at Reading, or might merely record that he was at Reading 'in time of sickness'. Otherwise, no trace remains of Philip's movements during this year, which has left biographers free to speculate that he spent time at the university of Cambridge. The inspiration for this comes from a marginal note (probably by printer Thomas Cadman) in a 1587 tribute by George Whetstone, that 'He was in his time and for his continuance reputed the best scholar in Cambridge.' Another posthumous tribute, by Lawrence Humphreys, Vice Chancellor of Oxford, has Philip's shade addressing Cambridge, and referring to himself there as 'a guest' (*hospes*), so it may be that he did indeed at least pay a visit there.[108]

One tantalising scrap of evidence points in another direction. In the papers of the magus, scholar and collector Dr John Dee there is a list of documents that demonstrate his service to prominent English personages. They include letters from Lady Sidney written in 1571, asking him to come to her at court.[109] Could it be that John Dee was providing the kind of intellectual stimulation for Philip that Thomas Allen had provided at Oxford? Whatever the case, the most likely scenario is that sometime in 1571 Philip was drawn to court, where now his father, mother and uncle were all in full-time attendance on the queen.

CHAPTER THREE

Young and Raw

P HILIP OWED THE next move in his life to the jealousy of a queen. By the early 1570s, Elizabeth's continued affection for the Earl of Leicester had turned him into an important political figure not only at home, but across northern Europe. But Elizabeth was suspicious of the man she had raised. She had no intention of letting Leicester out of the country to capitalise on his new-found *cachet*, and even less of letting him remarry. Elizabeth liked to keep alive the notion that her courtiers were in romantic – as well as political – thrall to her. At forty-two, Leicester, a widower for over a decade, knew that his continued influence with the queen depended on his remaining so. Denied a second wife and the legitimate son she might provide, Leicester therefore looked to his nephew Philip Sidney as both his heir and a possible representative abroad. Philip was now seventeen, educated, articulate and generally prized for his presentability; helpfully, Elizabeth was not so concerned to keep Philip close to home. And when, in early 1572, Leicester saw a way he might consolidate his position over the Channel, he called for the charms of Philip Sidney.

Elizabethan England's relationship with France encapsulated all the bewildering contradictions of European Renaissance politics, always teetering between doctrinal, economic and political loyalties. As a Protestant, Elizabeth was in one sense opposed to the rule of the Valois family in France, *tout court*. But in practice, she had to remain open to negotiation with the French king, sometimes in support of the Huguenots, France's embattled Protestants; sometimes to prevent the French entering into pacts with other powers – particularly Spain – which might threaten England further.

The French king, Charles IX, was young, and it was popularly believed that the reins of power were firmly held by his widowed mother, the Florentine Cathérine de Médicis. Cathérine was an incorrigible matchmaker, who saw an Anglo-French match as a solution to the two countries' costly bickering. In 1570–1, Elizabeth had explored the possibility of marrying the king's younger brother Henri, Duc d'Anjou, but negotiations had been halted when Anjou drifted dangerously closer to the Duc de Guise, an arch-Catholic who disapproved intensely of the Valois family's more flexible religiosity.

At the same time, Cathérine successfully negotiated the marriage of her daughter, Marguerite de Valois, to the Huguenot Henri, Prince of Navarre and heir to that throne. The announcement of this marriage had refuelled Huguenot hopes that the promises of the Edict of Toleration (1562) might finally come into force, and that their presence in France might indeed be tolerated. Protestant hopes were given a further boost in September 1571, when King Charles invited to court the Huguenot leader Admiral Gaspard de Coligny. Swept along by the impetus of the Navarre marriage, Coligny insisted to the king that now was the ideal time for France to launch an attack on the Spanish in Flanders – a successful assault would not only liberate the Low Countries from repression, but would free France from the prospect of Spanish forces on both its northern and southern borders. Charles was quietly supportive. In April 1572, the pace was forced when a rebel group of Dutch noblemen known as the Sea Beggars captured the vital island port of Brill, which controlled the passage of trade entering the North Sea from the Rhine. As the rebels seized other ports, the possibility of a Dutch Republic came into view.

For Leicester, mired in England, it became increasingly crucial to have a personal representative on the ground in Paris. His opportunity to send Philip to the Continent came with the announcement of a new special embassy to France, headed by Edward Fiennes de Clinton, created Earl of Lincoln for the occasion. The mission's purpose was merely to ratify the Treaty of Blois, a somewhat half-hearted defence pact, which agreed that neither England nor France would aid the enemies of the other – by which they meant Spain. The fine detail of the pact was hammered out in March 1572, and it was agreed that it would be signed and sealed simultaneously at the French and English courts by special embassies. As luck would have it, Lincoln's second wife had been a cousin of Leicester and Lady Sidney, and Lincoln was easily prevailed upon (presumably by Leicester) to include Philip among his charges.

What choice Philip was given in the matter is unclear, but he seems to have jumped at the opportunity. Tales told by his father and uncles of diplomatic and military missions to France and Spain must have given Europe a veneer of adventure that England sadly lacked. It was time to move on. Although he took academic life seriously, Philip was of too high a status to capitalise on his prowess by pursuing a career at the university or the Inns of Court. A life spent solely at court would be rendered something of an uphill struggle, thanks to Leicester's fluctuating fortunes and his father's almost constant lack of favour with the queen. The prospect of Philip following his father to Ireland had already been blocked by Elizabeth, perhaps anxious to avoid the threat of a dynastic power-base. With Anne Cecil off the market, no other bride had presented herself. And Europe provided an opportunity to see things that England could not offer – real wars, good-quality horses, decent wines, and a breath of freedom away from constant monitoring by parents, relatives and well-meaning but intrusive guardians.

Philip received his passport on 25 May 1572, the same day Lincoln was presented with his instructions.[1] It is clear from the wording of the passport that the embassy was a starting point, a handy launching pad for a far lengthier stay on the Continent. Elizabeth licensed 'our trusty and well beloved Philip Sidney esquire to go out of this our realm of England into the parts of beyond the seas, and there for his attaining to the knowledge of foreign languages to remain the space of [two] years next and immediately following after his departing out of our realm'. The reference to attaining foreign languages was standard phrasing in such instructions, although given Sir Henry's regard for modern vernaculars, quite to the point in Philip's case. The licence concluded with the proviso 'that the said Philip Sidney doth not haunt nor repair into the territories or countries of any prince or potentate not being with us in amity or league, nor do wittingly haunt and keep with any person our subject born, that is departed out of our realm without our licence or that contrary to our licence doth remain in the parts of beyond the seas, and doth not return into our realm as he ought to'. In effect, Philip was barred from visiting Italy or Spain, and from consorting with Englishmen in exile, who were usually perforce recusant Catholics.

Philip was also licensed to have 'three servants, four horses or geldings, and one hundred pounds in money or under and all other his and their bags, baggages and necessaries'. Sir Henry Sidney's hand is evident in the choice of servants. The three named servants were the Welshman Griffin Madox, who had served Sir Henry, and spoke and wrote Welsh; a long-term Sidney retainer named Harry White; and one John Fisher, about whom we know nothing more. Philip was also accompanied by Lodowick Bryskett, whose capacity hovered between friend and servant.[2] Bryskett, seven or eight years Philip's senior, had multiple links with the Sidney family. His father was a Genoese-born merchant named Antonio Bruschetto, who came to England in 1523 and was 'denized' on 4 December 1536 as Anthony Bryskett. Anthony soon established himself as one of London's most successful merchants (with large houses in St Gabriel Fenchurch and suburban Hackney), a recognisable face at court, and friend of the great London merchant Sir Thomas Gresham and the famed Italian, Benedict Spinola. Bryskett also had useful connections on the Continent: his elder sister Lucrece had married Vincent Guicciardini, part of the powerful Florentine merchant clan, which had links across Europe.

Lodowick, the third of five sons, was born in the family home at Hackney, but sent to school at Tunbridge in Kent, a few miles from Penshurst. There he contracted a 'quartain ague', and his education had to be completed at home. His father wanted him to specialise in physic and, as Lodowick recalled, 'all the time I spent by his direction in study, I employed in the knowledge of the principles thereof'. These studies were followed by time at Trinity College, Cambridge. However, 'higher providence', as Bryskett put it ironically, 'made me of a scholar to become a servant'.[3] He worked for his father, taking despatches to Sir William Cecil in February 1564 and, perhaps with Cecil's intervention, ended up in the Sidneys' Penshurst household. From 1565, Bryskett served the Lord Deputy in Ireland. Sir Henry used Lodowick's Italian connections to good effect: the Penshurst accounts include a payment to Bryskett of three pounds during a business mission he undertook to Italy, on 22 November 1569.[4] Bryskett soon earned the complete trust of the Lord Deputy, so that when Edmund Molyneux, the Clerk of the Council, travelled to Ireland with Sir Henry in the spring of 1571, he left Bryskett to 'serve in his room [i.e. in his place]' as clerk – as Lord Justice Fitzwilliam remarked to Lord Burghley, it was a rare honour: 'I have not seen a clerk of the Council so do afore this.'[5] So Bryskett, an accomplished, well-travelled linguist, was an obvious choice to accompany Philip when he set out in the summer of 1572: a natural language teacher, and the kind of companion with whom Philip could discuss literature and politics.

Lincoln's was to be a short mission, since the treaty had already been worked out to the last letter. The 'duties' of the embassy members lay largely in making up numbers at a series of banquets and entertainments. As a result, Lincoln's retinue was hardly high-powered, filled with as many freeloading family members as distinguished diplomats.[6] Even before the party boarded its convoy of ships, Philip witnessed at first hand the highly nuanced game of diplomatic etiquette they were playing with the French. Each party was to cross the Channel in ships belonging to the other country; however, each wanted to see the other set out first. For much of May, both Lincoln and his French counterpart Montmorency stalled — indeed, Elizabeth refused to issue instructions or passports until she was informed that Montmorency was indeed *en route*.

Finally leaving England on 27 May, Lincoln and his entourage arrived in Paris on Sunday 8 June. Like most sixteenth-century Englishmen, Philip was probably shocked by the French capital. Although London was a teeming, cosmopolitan city, nothing prepared visitors for the dense, overcrowded streets of Paris. Still a walled city with a distinctly medieval feel, Paris in the summer of 1572 was notably hotter than usual and suffering from what the English ambassador called 'the dearth': a shortage of produce bequeathed by failed harvests and almost constant war over a period of years. As the summer drew on, the temperature rose, the population increased and the dearth worsened. Philip was lucky enough, for the first few weeks at least, to be housed in rooms at the royal palace, the Louvre, along with the rest of Lincoln's embassy.[7]

Once installed, Philip promptly set off for the English embassy in the Faubourg St-Germain bearing a letter from Leicester to the resident ambassador in Paris, Francis Walsingham. Once again, responsibility was being passed on, and the appointment of Walsingham *in loco parentis* was perhaps the most significant to date in influencing Philip's adult life.[8] In 1572, Walsingham was in his early forties, and at the beginning of his high-profile political career (the following year he would replace Burghley as Principal Secretary of State). Born the son of a London lawyer, he was educated at King's College, Cambridge, and Gray's Inn, but his ardent Protestantism forced him into exile during the reign of Mary Tudor. When he returned to England after Elizabeth's accession, he steadily won the confidence of some of her leading counsellors, among them Cecil and Leicester. His particular gift, honed during his time on the Continent, was in intelligence-gathering. In August 1568, for example, he managed to provide Cecil with a list of new English arrivals in Italy over the preceding three months. The following year, it was his personal sources that unmasked the plot of the Italian merchant Roberto di Ridolfi to kill the queen. While England's official intelligence was based on paid correspondents and embassy contacts, Walsingham was happy to tap less reputable sources if they could provide better information.

The combination of unassailable Protestant credentials and a highly effective intelligence network made Walsingham the perfect choice to handle the tangled Anglo-French negotiations of the early 1570s. In autumn 1570, he was sent to Paris as a second to Elizabeth's ambassador Sir Henry Norris, in an attempt to persuade the French king to practise toleration towards his Huguenot subjects. His performance there guaranteed that, when Elizabeth decided to pursue the prospect of marriage with Anjou, Walsingham quietly replaced Norris. He possessed a political astuteness and realism that tempered his sincere Protestantism and enabled him to reconcile the contradictions thrown up by conflicting national and religious concerns. Although on principle opposed to a Catholic marriage for his queen, Walsingham realised that it might be used to force French intervention in the Low Countries against the Spanish – a small price to pay for the greater good.

Now, in the summer of 1572, with the Protestant cause in France at its highest ebb, Walsingham was facing his greatest diplomatic challenge. The letter of recommendation with which Leicester entrusted his nephew Philip has survived and is worth quoting at length:

Mr Walsingham, Forasmuch as my nephew Philip Sidney is licensed to travel and doth presently repair to those parts with my Lord Admiral, I have thought good to commend him by these my letters friendly unto you, as to one I am well assured will have a special care of him during his abode there. He is young and raw and no doubt shall find those countries and the demeanours of the people somewhat strange unto him. And therefore your good advice and counsel shall greatly behove him for his better direction which I do most heartily pray you to vouchsafe him, with any friendly assurance you shall think needful for him. His father and I do intend his further travel if the world be quiet and you shall think it convenient for him, otherwise we pray you we may be advertised thereof to th'end the same his travel may be thereupon directed accordingly.[9]

'Young and raw' – a strong reminder that at this point Philip was just seventeen, and the product of a somewhat rarefied intellectual life at Shrewsbury and Oxford. Leicester and Sir Henry were anxious as to how Philip would react to the strangeness of European culture, but in describing him as 'young and raw' they were signalling less his ignorance or naïvety than his malleability. Philip was vulnerable to being seduced by evil influences, hence the need for the appointment of Walsingham as a third parent.

Walsingham took his new parental duties seriously. He watched Philip with his servants, and did not like what he saw. He wrote to Leicester complaining of 'the evil practice of your said nephew's servants', and worrying that unless steps were taken, 'the young gentleman your nephew shall be in danger of a very lewd practice, which were great pity in respect of the rare gifts that are in him'.[10] What was the 'evil practice' of the servants? With the ambiguity of sixteenth-century English syntax, it is not clear whether Philip was in danger of being the victim of a 'lewd practice', or of being drawn into practising a 'lewd practice'. The phrase itself could feasibly refer to a whole range of dubious practices of which Walsingham might disapprove – financial, sexual or indeed religious. Perhaps Walsingham instinctively distrusted the Italian heritage of Lodowick Bryskett, or the evident Welshness of Griffin Madox. It was an early sign that Philip might not always be exactly what his mentors wished.

From the despatches of Sir Thomas Smith, who had been in Paris some months finalising the treaty, we can reconstruct the formal events of the embassy: a series of audiences, dinners and lavish entertainments. For Philip, it was his first glimpse of a political regime other than the one in which he had been raised, and the large Valois royal family must have provided an interesting contrast to Elizabeth's solitary rule: this court had complex manoeuvrings, with no single, certain locus of power.

A day after the English arrived, sad news put something of a pall on proceedings before they had begun. On 9 June, Jeanne d'Albret, Queen of Navarre, and mother of the prospective bridegroom Henri, died suddenly at the age of forty-three. The French court immediately assumed the proper black mourning apparel, and no activities took place until the end of the week. But then, on Friday 13 June, the programme swung into action. That morning, King Charles received Lincoln's embassy at the Château de Madrid in the Bois de Boulogne, and they all dined there that afternoon, and again on the Saturday. Sunday 15th, the day chosen for the ratification of the Treaty on both sides of the Channel, saw the whole party move first to the Louvre, and then to the church of St-Germain, where oaths were exchanged, before supper at the queen mother's building in the Tuilleries. On Monday, according to Sir Thomas Smith's account, the Huguenot leader Coligny showed 'a loving, free, and liberal heart' by providing supper for the English. The following day, the Duc d'Anjou entertained at his own lodgings, providing 'excellent music (as they said, that could skill of it) first of the voice with virginals, then of Voninis' school, with the voice, viols, and lutes; after that an Italian comedy, which ended, vaulting with notable supersalts [somersaults] and through hoops, and last all the antics, of carrying men one upon another which some men call *labores Herculis* [the labours of Hercules]'. Anjou's younger brother François, Duc d'Alençon was the host on Wednesday, although he had to borrow the Count de Retz's house, since his own was too small. Even so, his entertainments had to be cut short because the weather was too hot, and everyone was cramped, but he redeemed himself: as his guests departed, spouts of 'damask and fine water' rained down, 'and then a mad fellow [blew] damask and fine smelling powder all about'. On Thursday, the guests gratefully dined *al fresco*, 'abroad amongst trees as in an arbour' at the invitation of the Duc de Nevers; and on Friday 20 June, formal farewells were made and lavish gifts exchanged.

There was a serious side to all the wining and dining, the tumblers and the showers of scented powder. The scale and quality of the entertainment were crucially monitored, as senior ministers on one side of the Channel waited for information on how their representatives were being treated on the other. In England, the French ambassador Montmorency made much of how lavishly Paris was treating Lincoln; Burghley wrote to Walsingham to find out exactly 'how my lord and you have been feasted and entertained, which they [the French] do here give out with large speeches, but how indeed the same is warranted I know not; sure I am, that they [the French in England] have been so feasted and entreated, as none in my memory hath been greater'. The only way in which the English treatment of the French fell short, according to Burghley, was that no lord entertained them – except Leicester, and Burghley himself, who, 'to observe their manner', thoughtfully provided a flesh-free 'collation of all things I could procure'.[11] Even the gifts were instantly valued, Lincoln's gilt plate weighing 2,800 ounces 'which may be valued at 10s. the ounce, considering the workmanship, and that the silver is finer than in England'.[12]

Much of the embassy's energy was spent on observing who said what to whom, where, when, in whose company – and what all that meant. On the first day, the queen mother was too ill to meet the English embassy, so they were kept waiting for a day at the Louvre: this must either be a snub or a delaying tactic. At the Louvre, Lincoln was treated to a private tour of the king's 'closets and chambers': a welcome sign of personal favour. In church, the English were placed in a side-chapel so that they could hear evensong, rather than attend the Catholic mass: a nice, sensitive touch, it was agreed. In the Tuilleries, Charles showed Lincoln around the large gardens, but attention was truly piqued when the king and Anjou were joined by the Huguenot leader Coligny for almost an hour's intense conversation – Smith noted how some of the French seemed pleased, while others were openly suspicious and annoyed.

Even dress was important. On the day of ratification, the king came to fetch Lincoln 'richly appareled', having shed his mourning garb for the Queen of Navarre. He explained that 'although he had cause to mourn' – and it was indeed standard practice to mourn for a month at the death of one of royal blood – 'yet he did so rejoice of my Lord Admiral's coming, and at this amity that he could not mourn indeed, and therefore he would use no hypocrisy but dispense with himself and all the other, to show in their apparel the joy they had in their hearts'. It was a cunning move: ostensibly flattering the English, while backhandedly insulting Huguenot sensibilities, it effectively forced the English Protestants to choose between being English (and pleased) or Protestant (and offended). For the first time in his life, Philip realised that, outside the safe certainties of Elizabeth's Protestant England, being English and being Protestant were not necessarily synonymous.

Philip Sidney's name does not appear in Sir Thomas Smith's lengthy despatches. This in itself is not surprising. Smith was only interested in the way the key figures of the French court – the king, the queen mother, Anjou and Alençon, Guise and Coligny – interacted with the leading English officials, by which he meant Lincoln, Walsingham and himself. Throughout his account, there are passing comments that 'the lords and the rest of the train were feasted in another place'. Philip was always in this other place, lacking any official function in the embassy. There is no evidence to suggest that Philip made any impact whatsoever on the French court in the overcrowded, overheated days of the Lincoln embassy. What it could have taught him, however, were the skills to observe and absorb the highly nuanced games of diplomatic etiquette, perhaps with the guidance of a master of the game, Walsingham. These would be lessons well learned.

After Lincoln and his embassy had made their farewells and started on their way back to England, Philip entered into a different Paris. His lodgings are unknown, but it seems likely that he and his small retinue stayed with Walsingham in the Faubourg St-Germain, although the ambassador was pushed for funds. Indeed, Lincoln had promised Walsingham that he would consult with Burghley about the resident ambassador's 'intolerable charges', caused 'through the daily increase of dearth', in the hope of increasing his 'diet', or daily allowance. 'Otherwise,' Walsingham warned Burghley, 'I shall not be able to hold out, my monthly charges drawing now to two hundred pounds the month, notwithstanding my diet is thin, my family reduced to as small a proportion as may be, and my horse being only twelve.'[13]

Financial worries notwithstanding, Walsingham was pledged to keep a watchful eye on Philip, and so he provided him with an entrée into his own social and professional circles – circles that were to influence Philip's life immeasurably. Philip carried with him not only the personal endorsement of Walsingham but his birthright as son of Sir Henry Sidney and nephew of the Earls of Leicester and Warwick, and that was enough to guarantee that attention was paid to him.

From the surviving pages of Walsingham's diary we know that one of his most frequent dining companions was the Saxony ambassador, the Burgundian Hubert Languet, whom he probably met through his brother-in-law and sometime secretary Robert Beale, who was at the

University of Wittenberg alongside Languet in 1560.[14] When Walsingham arrived back in Paris in mid-January 1571, after a brief return home, Languet was his first dinner guest.[15] This was not merely a matter of personal fondness: Languet was one of the most important diplomats in Paris, by the summer of 1572 representing not only Augustus of Saxony, but also tacitly the concerns of other German states.[16] We also know, from a chance reference in a letter, that Philip became acquainted with Gaspard de Schomberg, a German-born but naturalised French citizen, who was Charles' ambassador to the German states (effectively Languet's counterpart): Philip later wrote to Leicester about 'one Schomberg, an Almain . . . a gentleman whom I knew in the court of France, always very affectionate to the king's service'.[17]

From Walsingham's diary, there is evidence that the ambassador invited into his house 'Monsieur Ramus', the famed logician and humanist Pierre de la Ramée.[18] Petrus Ramus' notoriety sprang initially from his stunning iconoclastic defence of his thesis at the University of Paris: '*quaecunque ab Aristotele dicta sint falsa*' (whatever Aristotle has advanced is false). His fame spread not only for his scholarly work (for which he became Regius Professor at the Collège de France) but also for his strident Huguenot views. In his enemies' minds the two were conflated, his attack on Aristotelian logic somehow becoming an attack on theological tenets of the Roman Catholic Church. His posthumous editor, Théophile de Banos, recorded that Philip 'not only loved Ramus as a father when alive, but esteemed and reverenced him after death',[19] so it seems that Walsingham introduced Philip to the great French scholar, and that the two developed a friendship during the summer of 1572.

In the same circle was Ramus' preferred printer, the Huguenot André Wechel, who maintained the reputation of his father, Chrétien Wechel, for high-quality scholarly volumes.[20] Languet was currently acting as an intermediary between Wechel and another friend, Joachim Camerarius in Nuremberg, while Wechel was printing Camerarius' edition of Xenophon.[21] In Wechel, Philip saw a living example of the dangers of propagating Huguenot beliefs in France: Wechel had been driven out of Paris in 1568 by a mob who had attacked his printing works, burned his books and confiscated his property. After some months in Germany and the Rhineland, Wechel had returned to Paris and re-established his business in June of 1571, but he remained nervous of a repeat performance. Wechel's importance to the Huguenot cause lay not merely in his printing of Protestant texts, but in his sheltering of a succession of Protestant men whom he allowed to stay, at peppercorn rates, in his large house on the west side of St-Jean de Beauvais. These men were usually young and German: one such, Lucas Geizkofler, recorded in his journal that Wechel 'loved Germans and treated them so well for a derisory sum'.[22]

Other new friends included Dr Felix Platter from the University of Basle and the young German student Johann Conrad Brüning, who later reminded Philip of their friendship in Paris when he needed Philip's help after accidentally killing a man.[23] Philip also established a friendship with the Strasburg jurist Dr Jean Lobbet (Lobbetius), who acted as an agent for the French court at various imperial cities — 'an experienced and good hearted man' according to Geizkofler,[24] with whom Philip pursued a long, full correspondence over several years: it was Lobbet who was later entrusted with arranging a suitable education in Strasburg for Philip's younger brother Robert.[25]

These men — Languet, Ramus, de Banos, Wechel, Lobbet — were all intellectuals, whose intellectual work was done in the name of a particular religious and political cause: to support the fight of the Huguenots and oppressed Protestants throughout Europe. It was this milieu that quickly drew Philip in, and among which he was to live for the rest of his life. As Philip cemented his new-found friendships in July, Sir Humphrey Gilbert and a large company of English volunteers were crossing the Channel, ostensibly without royal consent, but in fact with detailed instructions to occupy Flushing and Sluys, to prevent the French possessing them. This rare show of support from Elizabeth for the embattled Dutch Protestants boosted the hopes of Coligny and Walsingham. Just as Leicester had hoped, Philip was plunged directly into Protestant Europe's most politically active circles at precisely the moment when their shared cause appeared to be at its apex.

All Protestant eyes were turned to Paris for the wedding of Henri de Navarre and Marguerite de Valois in August. On his mother's death, Henri had become King of Navarre and the marriage, already politically important, was now even more significant. Shortly after the funeral, Navarre set out for the capital; Charles, fearing that the Parisians would not welcome this Huguenot husband for their Valois princess, issued a royal proclamation on 30 June forbidding them to molest any foreigner, Navarre follower or Protestant. All over Europe Protestants took this as an open invitation to the wedding and started to flood in – some 1,500 German students were said to be lodging in Paris by the wedding day, causing considerable tension.[26]

Charles was forced to issue another edict on 7 July, forbidding the bearing of arms within the city walls. This came just in time to protect Navarre's entourage, numbering some 800 gentlemen, which reached the Porte St-Jacques the following day. Henri was formally greeted by Anjou and Alençon and a suitable array of nobles and court officials, but no word could mend the damage caused by the appearance of the Valois court: the Navarre men were still all in mourning black, while their hosts had long since returned to their usual scarlet robes. It was a tense journey as 1,500 horsemen in total rode to the Louvre through silent crowds.

The true mood of the Parisians was made plain a week later, when one of Coligny's military initiatives went horribly wrong. The French Huguenot Seigneur de Genlis, with Charles' support, was sent in early July to relieve Mons in Flanders, which was being besieged by Spanish forces. On 17 July, Genlis' attempts were ended by a complete rout. When Parisian citizens heard of his failure, according to a contemporary newsletter, they 'conceived such joy thereof as that they spared not to make open declaration of the same by general procession, banquets and such like congratulations'.[27] Embarrassed by this public glee at the failure of a plan he had backed, King Charles sought to obscure his own involvement and disowned Genlis. The queen mother immediately seized the initiative, and secured a decision on 9 August from the Council of State to oppose any further aggressive action. Coligny's policy of French intervention in the Low Countries was dead.

A true believer in the divine rightness of the Protestant cause, Walsingham refused to become despondent. To a cousin, Mr Brocket, he wrote on 10 August: 'Touching matters of Flanders which toucheth us most, there is neither cause of hope nor of despair. When I look upon the coldness of those whom it behoveth us to assist, then do I fear. When I consider how God is then readiest to show his omnipotency when things to the eye of the world seem most desperate, then I hope. And surely such is the state of this cause.'[28] But he also had forebodings of possible ramifications within France, sparked by Huguenot insistence that civil war would ensue if Coligny's plans failed: 'I fear,' he wrote to Burghley, 'there will follow fearful effects unless God put to His helping hand.'[29]

Meanwhile, Philip was being welcomed with open arms at the French court. For the first time, he appreciated what being Leicester's heir might mean. Doors flew open to rooms that were completely inaccessible to most Englishmen. Philip's fluent French was a source of great admiration, as Lodowick Bryskett later recalled: 'He was so admired among the graver sort of courtiers that when they could at any time have him in their company and conversation they would be very joyful, and no less delighted with his ready and witty answers than astonished to hear him speak the French language so well and aptly having been so short a while in the country.'[30]

The most lasting expression of his success in Paris, however, came on 9 August, when King Charles signed a patent addressed to 'le Grande Chambellan de France', which created Philip a gentleman of the royal bedchamber (*gentilhomme ordinaire de notre chambre*). The document survives among the Penshurst papers: although now badly damaged, it is still impressively grand and bears the traces of having been folded and produced many times during Philip's travels. Philip took on the title of 'Baron de Sidenay', entitling him 'to receive the honours, authorities, wages, rights, hostellages, profits and customary emoluments thereunto appertaining, during pleasure'.

How did a seventeen-year-old English boy come to be a gentleman of the French king's bedchamber, and a baron? Interestingly, the patent gives three reasons for honouring Philip: (a) the greatness of the house of Sidney, which has long since been close to the sovereign; (b) Philip's personal qualities; and (c) the friendship between Elizabeth and Charles. Certainly, Sir Henry's position as Lord Deputy of Ireland gave Philip a quasi-princely status, which would in itself make this honour reasonable. However, the name that is missing here is Leicester. It seems, from other sources, that Charles was using Philip as a means to get to the man he believed could influence Elizabeth. In the words of the sixteenth-century French historian Jacques-Auguste de Thou, 'the treaty of alliance which the king had just made with the queen of England, and the one which he was negotiating now with the Protestant princes of the Empire, made well known the favourable disposition of that prince towards the Protestants, because he wanted to have at his court one of the sons of the Elector Palatine, and one of the English lords who was the most zealous for that religion, like the Earl of Leicester, or the Baron Burghley'.[31] This is amplified in the account by Huguenot propagandist Simon Goulart, who recorded that Coligny had asserted that King Charles 'also desired to have from England, milord Leicester, and milord Burghley, or one of them, to feast them and to entertain them, as he desires to make much of all the loyal servants of his sister the Queen of England, as a sign of true alliance'.[32] In William Camden's account, however, the French had more malicious motives: 'There were also invited out of England, under colour of doing them honour Leicester and Burghley; and out of Germany the Palatine Elector['s] sons, that being brought into the net, both they and with them the Evangelical Religion, might with one stroke, if not have their throats cut, yet at leastwise receive a mortal wound.'[33]

As the physical representative of his uncle Leicester, Philip once again became a pawn between politicians, just as he had been at Shrewsbury and Oxford. This time, however, there was a personal pay-off. It was Philip himself who received the honours and became a French baron: now he had prestige of his own. In the short term, the patent and the honours meant that Philip had a ringside seat for the lavish celebrations that accompanied the Navarre–Valois marriage. According to Fulke Greville, who had only second-hand knowledge of this period of Philip's life, he met the young Navarre king at this time – Greville notes that Henri, 'having measured and mastered all the spirits in his own nation, found out this master-spirit among us, and used him like an equal in nature and, so, fit for friendship with a king'.[34] Philip may have been present at the secular ceremony of betrothal, in the Louvre on Sunday 17 August, and no doubt the next day witnessed the ceremony itself outside the cathedral of Notre-Dame: he would have been one of the 'noble counts and gentlemen who were not papists [who] remained outside the cathedral', whom Lucas Geizkofler observed 'walking up and down' until the bride and her entourage emerged from the Catholic blessing inside.[35]

Over the next few days, Philip enjoyed the celebrations laid on by the king, the groom and the Cardinal de Bourbon. Charles gave full rein to his passion for interludes, spectacles and bear-baiting. At Bourbon's palace on the Wednesday, a huge allegorical spectacle placed the king and his followers in heaven with Navarre and the Huguenots as Knights Errant trying to gain admittance, only to be repulsed by the Valois and sent to hell. Their release was permitted only after an hour of dancing nymphs. The subtext was blatant enough. The Huguenot historian Jean de Serres noted, 'This show was variously interpreted, for that the assailants who were most of them Protestants, did in vain attempt to get into the seats of the blessed, and were thrust down into Hell: for so they put a mockery upon the Protestants, and others did bode that it portended some mischief.'[36]

Worse was to come during the following day's tilting in the Louvre courtyard, as Walsingham and the other ambassadors looked on from their windowseats. Charles, his brothers Anjou and Alençon, the Duc de Guise and his kinsman the Duc d'Aumale were dressed as Amazons; Henri and his Huguenot followers as infidel Turks, complete with robes and turbans. Unsurprisingly in this clash Christian virtue triumphed, and heresy (for Islamic, read Huguenot) was defeated. Some commentators felt that matters were getting out of control. Jean de Serres complained that:

> so great was the magnificence of banquets and shows, and the king so
> earnestly bent to those matters, that he had no leisure, not only for
> weighty affairs but also not so much as to take his natural sleep. For in
> the French Court, dancings, maskings, stage-plays (wherein the king
> exceedingly delighteth) are commonly used in the night time: and so the
> time that is fittest for counsel and matters of governance, is by reason of
> nightly riotous sitting up of necessity continued in sleep.

De Serres took great exception to 'the familiarity of men and the women of the Queen Mother's train, and so great liberty of sporting, entertainment and talking together, as to foreign nations may seem incredible, and be thought of all honest persons a matter not very convenient for preservation of noble young ladies' chastity'.[37]

De Serres' dig at the queen mother's train was echoed in a great deal of anti-Cathérine sentiment, which focused on her Italian birth. Everywhere he looked de Serres saw Italians – and many now proclaimed that Paris was 'a colony and some a common sink of Italy'. But where de Serres saw Italians, others saw too many provincial Huguenots. Word on the street was that the queen mother was determined to curtail Coligny's influence; the implication was that Protestants were in danger. The Duc de Sully's father had prophesied that 'if the nuptials were celebrated at Paris, the bridal favours would be crimson'.[38] Lucas Geizkofler was warned by the Count of Hanau's *Hofmeister*, Paul von Welsperg, who had access to court gossip, that he should move out of the house of the vulnerable André Wechel and seek shelter with a priest named Blandis.[39] Coligny too was told that his life was in danger. And while the Huguenots were being humiliated in their Turkish turbans, a man named Maurevert was setting up a large harquebus on a tripod in a house on the narrow rue de Béthisy, down which Coligny walked every day from the Louvre to his lodgings.

On the morning of Friday 22 August, the Admiral de Coligny and his men returned to his lodgings after watching the king play tennis against Guise at the Louvre.[40] From his window, Maurevert fired three shots. As luck would have it, Coligny bent down to adjust his slipper at precisely the moment the bullets hit him, and so missed their full force. One blew off much of his right-hand index finger, and another lodged in his left arm. The king sent his own physician, the famed Ambroise Paré, to Coligny's lodgings: the amputation of the severed finger, and the three cuts with blunt scissors to remove the bullet, performed without anaesthetic, were excruciating but not life-threatening. A Huguenot summit meeting at Coligny's bedside that afternoon urged him to flee, but he determined to stay.[41]

While rumour raced through the city, Walsingham received official confirmation of the attack only between nine and ten in the evening, when the Count of Montgomery came to his house. Montgomery was surprisingly upbeat, saying that although 'he and those of the Religion [i.e. Huguenots] had just occasion to be right sorry for the admiral's hurt, so they had no less cause to rejoice to see the king so careful [full of care], as well for the curing of the admiral, as also for the searching out of the party that hurt him'. This, he claimed, was 'no small argument of the king's sincerity'; Walsingham judged that Montgomery's speech 'seemed to be void of all conspiracy and miscontentment', and saw no reason to disbelieve him.[42]

Indeed, at Coligny's personal request, King Charles visited the admiral in his lodgings; the queen mother and his brothers came along as escorts.

While upstairs they pledged their support for Coligny, downstairs Huguenot leaders, including Henri de Navarre and the Prince of Condé, were considering their options. The first impulse of many was to flee the city, but they were seduced by the king's vow: 'By God's death, I protest and promise to you that I will have justice done for this outrage.' As their leaders vacillated, Huguenots started to take to the streets, openly bearing weapons and looking for action. Parisian life ground to a halt as shopkeepers closed their businesses, the city gates were put under watch and the city's harquebusiers and archers were called to the place de Grève in anticipation of rioting.

As Saturday dawned, the reactions of the previous day seemed rather extreme. Coligny was pronounced out of danger; he would even regain the use of his arm, said his physicians. The rue de Béthisy was packed with Protestant well-wishers and the merely curious, well satisfied when the new bride Marguerite appeared to pay her respects. Coligny was endlessly patient and gracious to the stream of callers: to the German student Lucas Geizkofler, he 'spoke in a very friendly fashion, while consoling himself and saying that nothing had occurred or would happen to him without God's special providence; that he would leave revenge to the omnipotent, omniscient and just Judge. This consolation he supported with many *argumenta* and *exempla*.'[43] Philip may well have been among the crowds of Saturday callers.

The calm proved false. In quick succession it became known that Maurevert was the would-be assassin; that the man who held his getaway horse was an employee of the Duc de Guise; and that Maurevert's harquebus was from Anjou's armoury. These revelations set things in a new light. If Guise were arrested and interrogated, he might well implicate the queen mother, Anjou and Alençon. These three quickly concluded that they had to take immediate action, and only one option seemed feasible: extermination of the Huguenots. The Guise leaders had already set up the city constabulary and the royal forces in strategic locations; boats on the Rive Droite were chained to their moorings to prevent flight; a comprehensive survey of Huguenot dwellings was produced, by 'quartermen' (undermasters of the streets), who 'surveyed all the victualling houses and inns from house to house, and all the names of those of the Religion, together with the place of every of their lodgings they put in books, and with speed delivered over the same books to those of whom they had received that commandment'.[44] The city's organised underworld was tipped off by Marcel, provost of the Merchants of Paris, that the Huguenots and their belongings were about to become fair game. The sign would be the dawn bell of the Palais de Justice. Only one person still needed to be informed. After supper, Cathérine took Charles to one side. The Huguenots had a conspiracy to seize Paris and take the throne, she told him. It was his duty to save the city, the country, the throne and his family. He must slaughter the Huguenots.

Dawn was a long time to wait. Charles, Cathérine and Anjou were awake and dressed by 2 a.m., as guards assembled in the courtyard beneath. But the guards were too noisy: a handful of Protestant noblemen, their senses heightened by recent events, came to investigate. After a brief altercation, the guard opened fire, killing most of them. They could no longer wait until dawn. Cathérine, taking charge, ordered the tolling of the palace bells of St-Germain-l'Auxerrois: usually reserved for royal occasions, their ringing would signal that something was awry. She was right: within minutes other church bells rang out across the city.

The first target was obvious. At 4 a.m. the Duc de Guise, accompanied by his Swiss mercenaries, rode to the rue de Béthisy and forced his way into Coligny's lodgings. The admiral was already on his knees, praying: as he knelt, the mercenaries stabbed him repeatedly, then threw his body out of the window. The speed, brutality and exhibitionistic impulse of Coligny's murder set the tone for what was to come. Throughout the city Huguenot houses were attacked, their inhabitants – men, women, children – killed, and their bodies thrown into the street or the Seine. Conservative estimates put the total killed in the first orgy of Paris violence at 2,000.

Chaos overtook the capital. Nowhere seemed to be safe. Charles watched as the corpses of 200 Huguenots, whom he had housed in the Louvre 'for protection', were piled high in his courtyard. But Cathérine was too canny to allow the slaughter to be totally indiscriminate. She still had dreams of a marriage between Elizabeth and her son (if not Anjou, then perhaps Alençon), and needed to keep the English queen sweet. A royal guard was posted at Walsingham's house: Charles wrote to his London ambassador La Mothe Fénélon a few days later to assure him (and through him, Elizabeth) that 'Lord Walsingham was carefully protected during the trouble in his lodgings'.[45] However, the royal guard arrived slightly late. The Spanish ambassador Zuñiga reported that a mob led by a fanatic had besieged Walsingham's house, and that it was only when the Duc de Nevers arrived to station troops of the Royal Guard that the danger passed. Zuñiga also claimed that the mob invaded the embassy, killed two servants and forced Walsingham to hide. This explained why, when Zuñiga tried to call on his English counterpart, he found the house utterly locked and barred – not even a small wicker gate was open.[46]

There may be some truth in this report. Walsingham reported to Sir Thomas Smith, now returned home, that 'The duc of Nevers hath showed himself much addicted to our nation, having not spared to come and visit me in his own person, with offer of all kind of courtesy, not only to me, but also to divers of our English gentlemen. Besides that, he did very honourably entertain three English gentlemen, who otherwise had been in great jeopardy of their lives.'[47] Not all the English contingent were so lucky. Walsingham complained to the king 'that three of our nation were slain, and that divers were spoiled'.[48] An Englishman who was sent by the Lord Chamberlain to act as schoolmaster to the young Lord Wharton arrived only the day before the massacre, yet was killed: 'Alas,' lamented Sir Thomas Smith, 'he was acquainted with nobody, nor could be partaker of any evil dealing.'[49]

Protestants of all kinds – English, Dutch, German, even French and Italian – fled to the comparative safety of Walsingham's embassy. There they cowered in fear alongside the Walsinghams and their five-year-old daughter Frances. The Perugian historian Pietro Bizari, a convert to Protestantism, had left England on 12 August, heading for Venice. But on the 24th, he found himself in Paris. He later wrote of Walsingham that 'I owe my life to him because when in that bloody Parisian massacre I was exposed to the swords of a rabid mob and surrounded and entrapped by armed men, he, at that time ambassador to the Queen, freed me from the brink of death and benignly restored me to life.'[50] Another refugee was Timothy Bright, a Cambridge scholar now pursuing a career in medicine, which would ultimately see him appointed physician at St Bartholomew's Hospital. Even seventeen years later, he told Walsingham, the events were 'fresh with me in memory': 'your honour's house at that time was a very sanctuary, not only for all of our nation, but even to many strangers then in peril and virtuously disposed'. Bright rejoiced, 'not only for mine own safety, but for so many of my countrymen, partly of acquaintance and partly of the noble houses of this realm, who had all tasted of the rage of that furious tragedy, had not your honour shrouded them, and now are witnesses with me of that right noble act and companions of like obligation'.[51]

And where was Philip Sidney in all this chaos? There is no supporting evidence, but it is tempting to speculate that he was one of the 'three English gentlemen . . . in great jeopardy of their lives' whom Nevers saved. Another source tells us that Nevers decided to have some fun with these English gents. Allegedly, on Sunday, Nevers went riding with some of his retainers, four or five of whom had, sitting pillion behind them, 'tall bewildered-looking men', who turned out to be English noblemen. Nevers had spared their lives, by driving away the mob besieging their house – presumably Walsingham's embassy – which they were defending. But Nevers was not entirely altruistic: he thought it would be diverting to hold them captive for the whole day and force them to view the horrors at first hand, starting of course with Coligny's mangled body, which had become an instant attraction in the rue de Béthisy. When they reached the site, Nevers asked one of the Englishmen if he recognised the body. Despite the fact that he had commanded a party of English volunteers under the admiral during the last war, the Englishman knew better than to admit it. 'I have never seen him,' he declared.[52]

If Philip was indeed among these gentlemen, then he would have been forced to witness the horrors of the massacre. If he was not, he may have escaped seeing the worst. For we know from Timothy Bright that, alongside himself, the Walsinghams and Bizari, Philip Sidney was in the embassy building. As Bright recalled to Philip in 1584, 'I once had the good fortune to see you, viz. during the fateful storm of the Church in France, the St Bartholomew's Massacre (in which I was involved, and which my mind shudders to recall, and flees from in grief).'[53] He praised Walsingham:

> whose immense and honourable kindness saved my life during those days of terror in France, when the blood of the godly was everywhere being shed by fiendish killers. But why do I say 'saved *my* life'? For the most noble Francis Walsingham's house stood open, as asylum, to all those of our nation – as long as they were free from papist superstition

— who happened to be in Paris at that time. You yourself, Philip, had precisely that experience, and can thus vouch for [Walsingham's] nobility.[54]

The slaughter went on for days; Philip's new Paris acquaintances were all in danger. Petrus Ramus went into hiding as soon as he sensed danger: from the cellar of a bookshop on the rue St-Jean de Beauvais — perhaps Wechel's second bookshop — he listened as the looters destroyed its contents. By the Monday, however, he felt that the danger had passed and returned to his fifth-floor rooms at the Collège de Presles. But his confidence was misplaced. On Tuesday 26th, Ramus was disturbed by a gang as he was praying in his rooms. His despatch followed the now familiar ritual visited on Coligny: Ramus was stabbed and his body thrown out of the window. There, it was assaulted by students, who dragged his entrails through the Paris streets; they decapitated it, and threw what remained of the corpse into the Seine, by now visibly discoloured by the thousands of corpses deposited there.[55]

The Saxon ambassador Hubert Languet assumed that his diplomatic status would protect him from reprisals, and set out to track down his young friend Philippe Du Plessis-Mornay, an intimate of Navarre's, whom he feared was in danger. As Du Plessis' wife recalled, 'M. Languet, counting on his immunity as an ambassador in the midst of the fury of the massacre, set out, in danger of his life, to save M. Du Plessis and to furnish him with means to escape to Germany. Whilst on his way he [Languet] was seized by the mob and taken to the Madeleine, whence he was released by M. de Morvillier, chief Councillor of State, though not before he stood in fear of his life.' Ultimately, Du Plessis fled Paris disguised in clerk's clothing.[56]

The St Bartholomew's Day Massacre of August 1572 imprinted itself on the memory of every person who witnessed it. For many strangers, it created a shared experience to which they referred constantly, almost compulsively, for the rest of their lives. Hubert Languet and Philippe Du Plessis-Mornay saw the bloodshed as a personal and political watershed. The hours spent in the cramped English embassy were invoked again and again by men like Timothy Bright and Pietro Bizari. And yet Philip Sidney never wrote of the massacre. The nearest he came was seven years later, when he referred to the French queen mother, Cathérine de

Médicis, as 'the Jezebel of our age' and blamed the king for the bloodshed: Charles, he claimed, 'made oblation of his own sister's marriage, the easier to make massacres of all sexes'.[57] These comments imply suspicion of the Valois family, rather than of French Catholics more generally. There is nothing in his statement that would indicate that he had even been in Paris at the time – indeed, some critics have gone so far as to argue that he had already left.[58] But the words of Timothy Bright make it clear that Philip was indeed in Paris, and that he felt the full horror of those August days.

It did not take long before rumours of the atrocity began to reach England. By the time Walsingham's men arrived at Woodstock on 11 September to give the story a first-person reality, the court was already in a panic. The eyewitness accounts of the massacre 'did so amplify the cruel disorders there,' reported Sir Thomas Smith to Walsingham, 'and thereupon your dangers in every man's ears, whereof your friends made relation to her Highness, that finally her Majesty was content to write this letter for your return hither, to the French king'.[59] There was relief that most of the English contingent was safe. Smith commented to Walsingham:

> I am glad yet, that in those tumults and bloody proscriptions you did escape, and the young gentlemen that be there with you, and that the king had so great care and pity of our Nation so lately with strait amity confederate with him . . . How fearful and careful the mothers and parents be here of such young gentlemen as be there, you may easily guess by my Lady Lane, who prayeth earnestly that her son may be sent home with as much speed as may be.

Indeed, Lady Lane sent Walsingham's man back with thirty pounds in cash to ensure that her son's debts were paid off, so that he could leave Paris.[60]

Other young gentlemen were of more official concern. On 9 September, the Privy Council wrote to Walsingham:

> While we understand, that the English gentlemen that were in Paris at the time of the execution of the murder, were forced to retire to your house, where they did wisely; for your care of them, we and their friends

are beholding to you, and now we think good that they be advised to
return home; and namely, we desire you to procure for the Lord
Wharton and Mr Philip Sidney, the King's license and safe conduct to
come thence, and so we do require you to give them true knowledge of
our minds herein.[61]

Leicester compounded the official demand with an emotive personal plea
to Walsingham, 'trusting you will be a means for my nephew Sidney that
he may repair home considering the present state there'.[62]

But it was too late. By the time the official recall letters reached Paris,
Philip was long gone.

CHAPTER FOUR

An Extraordinary Young Man

B Y RIGHTS, PHILIP should have been on the first boat back to England. Walsingham made sure that his wife and daughter left town as soon as it was safe, and pleaded with Elizabeth for his own recall. But Philip's passport had another eighteen months to run, and it was too good to waste. Many of the Protestants fleeing Paris saw it as their duty to spread the word of the Massacre, to make something positive of the appalling bloodshed. Walsingham's friend Hubert Languet, for example, made his way directly to Strasburg and regaled the City Council there on 21 September 1572 with a harrowing account of the Massacre, although he toned down the dangers he himself had faced.[1] But Philip did not exploit his experiences in Paris in this way.

It seems that Philip's initial path was dictated by Francis Walsingham, who thought only of getting his young charge to somewhere safe, namely Heidelberg, the Calvinist capital of the Palatinate. The Elector, Frederick III 'the Pious', had been educated in Nancy, Paris, Liège and Brussels, and had close connections with France and the Low Countries. Raised a Catholic, he had converted to Lutheranism and then, in 1562, to Calvinism, taking Heidelberg with him. The Palatine's policy demanded complete religious liberty for Protestants in Catholic territories – although, it must be said, without granting those liberties to Roman Catholic subjects of Protestant princes. The city was thus a rare oasis for Protestants, its palatial yet heavily fortified *Schloss* a reassuring image of security. Its university was an acknowledged centre of humanism – it must have seemed to Walsingham the ideal location for the pious, Calvinist-educated young man.[2]

Philip's exact route to Heidelberg has never until now been clear. Our information comes from a single letter from Walsingham to Leicester, in which the ambassador tells how in mid-October he received word in Paris from messengers returning from Frankfurt that one of the gentlemen who were accompanying Philip to Heidelberg 'died by the way at a place called Balduc in Lorraine'. Working from a seventeenth-century printed version of the letter, which misread the manuscripts, scholars have previously been bemused by the place name of 'Bladin', which does not in fact exist. However, the original letter, which survives in the British Library's Cotton manuscripts collection, clearly reads 'Balduc', presumably referring to the town now known as Bar-le-Duc, due south of Verdun.[3]

The unfortunate dead gentleman has also confused scholars. 'By divers conjectures', Walsingham guessed that he must be 'the dean of Winchester'. Again, this figure has traditionally been misidentified as John Watson, who did become Dean of Winchester, but in fact lived on until 1584. The man to whom Walsingham is referring – and who indeed died in late 1572 – was Watson's predecessor, Francis Newton.[4] This fresh identification throws light on Walsingham's worries about Philip. The Gloucester-born Newton was a highly learned man, with four degrees from Cambridge colleges and fellowships at Trinity and Jesus. He had served as Vice-Chancellor of the University in 1562–3, and was ordained Deacon of Ely and university preacher (1560), holding a prebendary at York from 1560, before being promoted to the deanery at Winchester in 1565. His death was a particular blow to Walsingham for, as he told Leicester, Newton was the man he had 'employed to encounter the evil practices of your said nephew's servants'. Now, 'he being dead', Philip was in ever graver danger; Walsingham urged Leicester 'speedily [to] take order in that behalf, if already it be not done'. The combination of location (Heidelberg) and companion (Newton) suggests that Walsingham was highly concerned for Philip's moral, and doctrinal, welfare.

But for Walsingham his duties *in loco parentis* for Philip were now a fading priority. The Massacre had forced him to rethink his political position, and he no longer believed that English union with France was feasible or, indeed, desirable: 'I think [it] less peril to live with them as enemies than as friends,' he concluded sadly.[5] Elizabeth, however, was less certain. In October, less than two months after the bloodbath, she agreed to stand as godmother to King Charles' new daughter and sent an embassy, strategically headed by the Catholic Earl of Worcester, that would not reopen the wounds of the Massacre. It was only in November that she finally gave in to Walsingham's pleas for his recall; his departure from Paris spelled the end for Huguenot hopes of an alliance with England.

For Philip, however, as he turned eighteen, Walsingham's recall meant that he was free of direct control. The first thing he did when he heard the news was to leave Heidelberg. After what Philip had witnessed in Paris, perhaps its complacent Calvinism could not satisfy him.

Travel, for the properly educated young man, was always an educational experience. As Philip later advised his brother Robert, when he was about to set out on a similar journey, 'Your purpose is, being a gentleman born, to furnish yourself with the knowledge of such things, as may be serviceable to your country, and fit for your calling.' This meant acquiring 'the knowledge of all leagues, betwixt prince and prince, the topographical description of each country', and more specifically how each place was 'stored with ships, how with revenue, how with fortifications and garrisons, how the people warlikely trained or kept under', as well as 'their religions, policies, laws, bringing up of their children, discipline both for war, and peace'.[6]

This meant, in practice, that every itinerant educated Englishman was a potential intelligencer for whoever could make use of him. Information about Philip's first months in Germany is very sparse, but from the odd letters that have survived, we can tell that Philip was used on at least one occasion by Burghley (now Lord Treasurer) to undertake government-related business, and at least twice by Leicester regarding less official concerns. It may be that it was either Burghley or Leicester who suggested Philip's itinerary after Heidelberg: neither, however, had complete control over the young man.

There is only one extant reference to Philip's time in Heidelberg: according to a 1581 dedicatory epistle, he there first met the famed scholar and printer Henri Estienne, whose phenomenal five-volume *Thesaurus Græcae linguae* had just been published. Their friendship would ripen elsewhere.[7] From Heidelberg, Philip, Lodowick Bryskett and the servants travelled north past Mannheim and Darmstadt to Frankfurt. Frankfurt's position of natural strength, just a little way up the Main from where this river joined the Rhine, combined with its good harbour and excellent road connections, made it the central point not only for the Rhine Valley and for trade between the west and the north, but also for Bohemia, Austria, Switzerland, Italy and France. Twice a year, its Fair provided a focus for northern Europe's cloth trade, as well as the spice trade to the east, the wine trade to the south, and the manufacturing industries of several German cities. For merchants from Antwerp to Vienna, Frankfurt was the commercial heart of Europe. To Henri Estienne, whom Philip had just met in Heidelberg, the Fair – to which he penned a Latin encomium – was 'an epitome of all the emporia of the whole world'.[8]

At the Frankfurt Fair, Philip would have seen wines from Alsace, fine cloth from Strasburg, tapestries and sausages from Switzerland, eastern luxuries from Italy, fish from the Hanse towns, glass from Bohemia, iron from Styria, silver and tin from Saxony, copper from Thuringia – and cloth from the many Dutch traders who had made Frankfurt their permanent home. As Estienne put it, 'from each market there comes forth some new product, as once from Africa there was continually appearing some new sort of wild animal . . . All these places seem to have awaited the time of the Fair and to have reserved for it a sort of *cornucopia.*' There were sideshows too: a live elephant, a pelican, a rope dancer, a woman without hands who worked wonders with her feet, a *Meistersinger* competition. And on the sidelines were the inevitable quacks, dentists, fortune-tellers, drug-dealers, prostitutes, and the entire range of petty criminals drawn to a busy gathering where money flowed freely.

But most of the money changed hands in two markets – arms and horses. 'Is some prince equipping himself for carrying on a war?' advertised Estienne. 'Then he will find the Frankfurt Fair a veritable workshop of war . . . There he will find horses, there the various kinds of arms, there the other instruments of war, and so great a number indeed of each thing, that the time which he would spend elsewhere in seeking he would spend here in choosing.' As for the number of horses, exercised in an immense hippodrome, and stabled in every conceivable nook, 'who could not suppose that all the horses which Germany ever produced (to say nothing of the Hungarian, the Dacian, the Polish, the Danish, and others), had been brought together at this one time and place, and that the fodder of the whole country would be needed to feed them?'

Philip also found commerce nearer his own training. Since the late fifteenth century Frankfurt's Fair had been shadowed by a book fair, which had established itself as the Mecca of the booktrade, attracting printers from France, the Low Countries, French Switzerland and Italy, as well as Germany. It could be called 'the Frankfurt Athens', Estienne enthused. 'The Muses assemble their printers and booksellers in the city at the time of the Fair, and order them to bring with them the poets, the orators, the historians, the philosophers, and not only those whom Greece and Italy once had, but also those whom every day those lands gave birth to which are visited by the nine Sisters.' Thus Frankfurt offered something

> which can not be secured from mere libraries. For here all may enjoy the living voice of many honoured persons, who gather here from many different academies. Here very often right in the shops of the booksellers you can hear them discussing philosophy no less seriously than once the Socrateses and the Platos discussed it in the Lyceum. And not only the philosophers; those celebrated universities of Vienna, of Wittenberg, of Leipzig, of Heidelberg, of Strasburg, and, among other nations, those of Louvain, of Padua, of Oxford, of Cambridge . . . send to the Fair not only their philosophers, but also poets, representatives of oratory, of history, of the mathematical sciences, some even skilled in all these branches at once – those, in short, who profess to compass the whole circle of knowledge, which the Greeks profess to call *encyclopædia*.

From the time it was declared open by the firing of piece-shots from the bridge and the mill-dike at the lower end of the City, the Fair was a free market, with no restraints on buying and selling, even by foreigners, and no recognition of feuds. Citizens were allowed to take lodgers (the one exception being that Christians could not host Jews) and contingents from other cities congregated in particular boarding houses, which took the city's name – hence the Augsburger Hof, the Stadt Heidelberg and the Nueruberger Hof, the last of which alone fed over 125 strangers. This lifting of commercial restrictions on arms and horse trading also led to a measure of religious toleration (ironically, since those arms and horses were usually employed in religious wars) and the Fair became a magnet for the beleaguered Protestant communities of northern Europe. For the men with whom Philip had become friendly in Paris, Frankfurt was a home from home. He may have boarded with other English visitors to the Fair. However, according to his schoolfriend Fulke Greville, Philip stayed in Frankfurt with the Huguenot printer André Wechel.[9] Greville does not cite the source of his information, but it is an interesting and quite plausible suggestion. If Greville is right, Philip would have been lodged in '*das weisse Haus*', newly purchased by Wechel on the Zeil, right at the heart of Frankfurt's printing trade.[10] Wechel had been forced into Germany temporarily in 1569, but his flight to Frankfurt after the Massacre was for good. His sons-in-law Claude de Marne and Jean Aubri, both Frenchmen, were strategically placed in Vienna and Prague to facilitate the wide dissemination of his works. Since Wechel, like most other printers, resided on his own premises, Philip would have lived amid the typesetting, printing, proofreading and correcting that formed the daily business of a printer's house.

All this might be enough to explain Philip's eagerness to get to Frankfurt. Yet his true reason is probably contained in letters that he sent from the Fair to Leicester. It seems that he was acting in some capacity for his uncle, and the logical conclusion must be that Leicester suggested or commanded that Philip go to Frankfurt, perhaps to meet the leading political players who were attending various summit meetings there. Philip reported excitedly to Leicester on 23 March 1573:

> I was upon Thursday last with Count Lodowick [Louis of Nassau], the prince of Orange's second brother, whose honourable usage was such towards me, and such goodwill he seems to bear unto your lordship, that for want of furder hability [greater ability], I cannot but wish him

5. A printing shop in the late sixteenth century.

prosperous success to such noble enterprises, as I doubt not he will shortly (with the help of God) put into execution.

The letter is highly cryptic, but Roy Strong and Jan van Dorsten have suggested a possible reading. Before the Massacre, Louis of Nassau, younger brother of William of Orange, had a pet plan for the Low Countries, which he had been trying to sell to England and France. Louis suggested (according to Walsingham, who knew about the plan) that the provinces ought to be divided — England would get Holland and Zeeland, France would get Flanders and Artois; and the remaining provinces would go to an unnamed prince (presumably his brother). Since Walsingham knew of this scheme, it may be that Philip did too, and that this letter shows him approving of the project.[11] More certainly, this letter is another sign that Philip was recognised by Louis as being Leicester's nephew, and hence in some way his representative, but it also signals Philip's political impotence: he lacked 'furder hability', and could not see any way to help Louis in his campaign. The letter also suggests that, at this moment, Philip was unsure of *how* he was supposed to act for his uncle. He begins his letter by begging Leicester to give him fuller instructions:

> There being nothing of which I am so desirous (right honourable and my singular good lord and uncle) as to have continual and certain knowledge what your pleasure is, by which I may govern my little actions: I cannot be without some grief, that never since I came into Germany I could by any means understand it. Wherefore I have most humbly to beseech your lordship that if in any of my proceedings I have erred, you will vouchsafe to impute that to the not knowing your lordship's and their pleasure, by whose commandment I am likewise to be directed.[12]

Clearly, Philip was keen to please not only Leicester but those 'by whose commandment I am likewise to be directed' — his parents? the Privy Council? Walsingham? But this simple desire was not so simply met. Philip's travelling, outside those large cities with English embassies, often took him to areas where the postal service to England was a largely *ad hoc* affair. We know that Philip wrote to Leicester, and we may assume that he wrote to his father (who was often distant from court), but very few of these letters have survived. We can imagine that, for much of his time abroad, Philip was second-guessing what his sponsors wanted him to do.

In the meantime, he had more immediately pressing problems: he was short of cash. While Walsingham's quasi-parental care had kept him solvent in Paris, further afield Philip had to turn to money-lenders and credit-brokers. In Frankfurt, he raised the local equivalent of £120 from one Christian Rolgin; on 20 March 1573, he had to send a bill of exchange to his family's London banker William Blunt ('Master of the Counter in Wood Street') to raise the funds to pay back Rolgin's loan.[13] Further funds had to be raised from a Mr Culverwell, 'employing his credit for me, being driven into some necessity'; Culverwell was despatched with letters to Leicester who, Philip trusted, would reimburse him.[14] Philip's travelling life – with the costs of four men, horses and accommodation all to be found – was expensive, as the Penshurst accounts for the first year of his travel bear witness:

> For the use of Mr Philip Sidney – his fee for half year, £40; his entertainment in France until All Hallow-tide [i.e. the day of the Massacre], £100; to his man [Bryskett] the same time, £33 6s. 8d.; Acerbo Vitello for money paid to Mr Philip beyond the seas, £161 15s. od.; to John Ponton on Mr Philip's letter at his [Ponton's] return from France, £7; with sundry bills for clothing, £75 10s. od. -- £427 11s. 8d.[15]

After Frankfurt, Philip turned back on himself, and travelled south past Heidelberg to Strasburg – a manoeuvre that strongly suggests he had been commissioned to go there. Strasburg's Protestantism was centred on its recently built church of St Thomas, where Martin Bucer had preached, and on its educational institutions. Like the good humanist he had been trained to be, Philip was drawn to Strasburg's Gymnasium and its rector Jean Sturm ('Sturmius'), in his lifetime a legend of European humanist pedagogy. In England, Sturm's ideas had been aggressively marketed by Roger Ascham, the Cambridge scholar who taught Edward VI and Henry Sidney, and who tutored the young Princess Elizabeth, later becoming Latin secretary to her as queen. Ascham and Sturm never met, but they concocted and published a correspondence in which they established a self-serving mutual admiration society, praising and promoting their own educational ideals. Sturm's influence could be felt on every page of Ascham's English language pedagogical masterpiece *The Scholemaster*, which had been published posthumously just three years earlier, in 1570. Philip was an ardent proponent of Ascham and Sturm's preferred language learning technique of double translation: translating a passage from Latin into English, and then from the English back into Latin.[16]

In Strasburg Philip found lodgings with one Hubert de la Rose. He probably attended lectures at the Academy and classes at the Gymnasium, and he certainly visited Strasburg's Professor of Law, Dr Jean Lobbet, whom he had met in Paris. Keen to improve his knowledge on different fronts, Philip also travelled twenty-five miles out of Strasburg to inspect the fortifications being constructed on a 1,000-foot-high plateau at Phalsbourg, which would control the passes of the Vosges mountains – the kind of military preparations that he had never been able to observe in peacetime England.[17]

The influence of both Burghley and Leicester can be detected in Philip's dealings in Strasburg. When Philip met Sturm, the veteran pedagogue was sixty-five years old, exhausted from fighting a war of attrition against Strasburg's Lutheran opposition, and financially in trouble. His habit of making generous loans to embattled Huguenots had seen few returns; in recent months, financial stringency had forced him – against all his better instincts – to give his support to the campaign of Henry Duc d'Anjou to gain the Polish throne, in return for the writing off of his own considerable debts.[18]

Philip's arrival in Strasburg signalled a new job opportunity for Sturm. Since the beginning of her reign Elizabeth had relied on Dr Christopher Mont as her Strasburg correspondent, providing regular intelligence reports on local matters, attending events such as the Augsburg Diets, liaising with sympathetic German nobility, and acting as a knowledgeable escort for her envoys. Mont performed this service well into his seventies. When he died in October 1572,[19] Sturm saw an opening for a strong, sanctioned correspondence with England's political élite and promptly put in his bid for the job and the accompanying salary. Philip's visit allowed the exchange of correspondence with Burghley finalising the arrangement: one of his servants was sent back to England with a package of letters, and by return Burghley thanked Sturm 'for your kind reception of Philip Sidney'.

But a comment in Burghley's letter reveals another agenda, of which the Lord Treasurer was well aware. 'I know,' he wrote to Sturm, 'that his most honoured relatives [*parentes*] will thank you a great deal more.'[20] For it was not only Burghley who was using Philip to establish links with Jean Sturm. Sir John Wolley, Ascham's replacement as Elizabeth's French and Latin secretary, contacted Sturm offering himself as a replacement in the Ascham–Sturm friendship. It was an elegant conceit, but the pragmatic impetus was quite clear. 'I have been induced, accomplished Sturmius,' Wolley opened, 'to write to you at this present time at the desire of my singular good patron, the Earl of Leicester; who, as he himself was writing to you about other matters, wished me also to open the way to your friendship and correspondence by a letter of my own.'[21] Leicester, Wolley claimed, was keen that Sturm should intervene in a long-running English religious controversy by procuring the opinions of learned German divines, and relaying them to the English universities. Philip was stuck in the middle of these different agendas. He facilitated the 'official' link between Sturm and the English crown (via Burghley), but simultaneously promoted a parallel correspondence between Sturm and his 'most honoured relatives'.

Before he left Strasburg, Philip met up again with Henri Estienne who had followed Philip specifically, he later claimed, 'in order to see him and present a small manuscript of Greek maxims, in anticipation of later dedications of scholarly productions from his own press'.[22] The book, Estienne later recalled to Philip, which was 'written by the same hand that gave it into yours, pleased you very well: the novelty of the minute and elegant writing – which provided a sort of challenge to keenness of sight – seemed to make it acceptable'. The gift seems to have been inspired by Estienne's genuine passion for Philip's virtue:

> Somehow or other every time I see you and enjoy your company I feel more and more affection towards you. I first chanced to see you at Heidelberg, and a little afterwards at Strasburg, and then again, after a long time at Vienna; but at Strasburg the love which I had felt for you at Heidelberg greatly increased, and at Vienna the love I felt for you at Strasburg grew still more. Not that it is at all surprising that my love

for you should have grown in this way, since your gifts of mind, which had aroused it, seemed also to have grown.[23]

Coming on top of the success with Sturm, Philip must gradually have realised that forward-looking individuals – Sturm, Estienne, Lobbet – were seeing in him a young man of great potential.

Philip left Strasburg in late May of 1573, and started on the long journey east to Vienna, home to the court of the Holy Roman Emperor Maximilian. Here he soon renewed his acquaintance with another man who saw his potential. Hubert Languet was now fifty-five years old, older than Philip's father. Born in Burgundy, son of the Governor of Vitteaux, Languet was raised a Catholic and educated at the universities of Poitiers, Bologna and Padua, from where he proceeded as doctor of law in 1548. It was also in Padua that he read the book that changed his life: Philip Melanchthon's *Loci communes*, which used scriptural examples to promote a rationalist political doctrine. Inspired by this novel melding of religion and politics, Languet travelled to the university of Wittenberg in Saxony to meet Melanchthon, and there converted to Protestantism. In time, he was engaged by Saxony's elector Augustus to serve as his ambassador at the French court.

As one of the leading economic states in Germany, Saxony exercised considerable influence on its neighbours. Thus, when Languet made a formal address to the court of the French king Charles IX on 23 December 1570, it was made on behalf not only of Augustus, but of the combined Protestant German rulers. He was given remarkable leeway in his embassy, and in concert with de Schomberg (the French agent to the German states, with whom Philip struck up a friendship in Paris) was by 1572 orchestrating much of the international dealings between the German states and France. In May 1572, Languet had been in Paris with the specific goal of pulling off a deal between Augustus and King Charles, which was welcomed by the latter as part of the hoped-for league against Spain. Augustus, however, had been more reticent, well aware of France's shaky finances, and limited the resources he was willing to commit. The Massacre had destroyed any possibility of such a pact, and Augustus instead turned his attentions to the Holy Roman Emperor Maximilian who, although nominally a Roman Catholic, had a reputation for toleration. The summer of 1572 had also seen a vacancy arise on the Polish throne, and Augustus and Languet thought it wise to witness the emperor's manoeuvring on that subject at first hand: hence Languet's presence in Vienna.

Languet and Philip had almost certainly crossed paths earlier, in Paris the previous summer through Walsingham, or in Frankfurt in March through Wechel, but it was in Vienna that the relationship was cemented. From his lodgings in the house of Dr Michael Lingelsheim, a Strasburg-born reformer who had studied at Heidelberg and Basle,[24] Languet wrote to his longtime English friend Robert Beale, now clerk of Elizabeth's privy council, on 7 September 1573: 'We have with us Philip Sidney, an extraordinary young man, whom I greatly admire for his charming manners, his witty mind, and really a wisdom that generally exceeds what his age would lead one to expect. In one word, I think he is full-sail pursuing virtue, and I tell you, happy the parents who gave birth to a son of such exceptional talents.'[25]

It seems, from Languet's excited words, that his regard and respect for Philip were immediate. As Languet later wrote to Philip:

As long as I live, I shall consider the day when I first laid eyes on you a most happy one: the inner virtue which shines through your face, in your conversation, and in your every act, immediately compelled me to make you my friend. And opportunity knocked when you turned up here [in Vienna]. I do not know how destiny made this happen, but it was my very good fortune, and, thanks to your kindness, I then easily achieved that which I had decided to fight for with all my might. When I grew closer to you, I discovered that you were naturally inclined to virtue, and desired it so intensely, that I then considered myself so fortunate to have your friendship, and it was only the thought of you which brought me joy amidst the great misfortunes of my homeland.[26]

The friendship of Hubert Languet and Philip Sidney endured until Languet's death eight years later and produced a celebrated Latin correspondence; Philip himself realised the importance of Languet's letters and preserved them, passing them to his secretary Stephen LeSieur, who eventually procured their publication in 1633. Languet's letters have fascinated readers for 400 years (Philip's own have survived less well, and come to light only sporadically). On the surface, the relationship they reveal is a textbook example of Renaissance *amicitia*, that classically derived, intellectual bonding between two men. But there are hints throughout of more pragmatic concerns. To understand these letters we have to enter into a world where education, religion and politics were never separate issues; where personal friendship and political advantage could not be prised apart. Philip and Hubert Languet enjoyed a sincere, intimate friendship; at the same time they consciously assessed how they might take advantage of the benefits of this friendship. There was no contradiction in this, nothing pejoratively cynical. Just as marriage was openly recognised as a financial arrangement and hopefully an emotionally fulfilling attachment, so friendship could also be celebrated for its pragmatism, its practical benefits, so long as both partners were good men – and Languet constantly stressed Philip's innate virtue.

Philip's social life in Vienna was neatly tied to the milieu of his new friend. The presence of the highly educated Maximilian in Vienna encouraged cultural life both at the court and at the university, and Languet moved easily between the two. Philip soon adopted Languet's circle of diplomats, secretaries, printers, academics, writers and artists, and established friendships that would last beyond Vienna. He got to know the French king's Viennese ambassador Jean de Vulcob, Sieur de Sassy, and became very friendly with a young man in his entourage, Jacques Bochetel, Sieur de la Forêt; it was to Vulcob that Pietro Bizari, now in Augusta, wrote in October 1573, hoping that Philip might still be in Vienna.[27] An Italian medallist and sculptor named Antonio Abondio helped Philip with his language learning, and made a medal-sized portrait of him.[28] Philip even had a meeting with the great military commander General Lazarus von Schwendi.

Both Maximilian's physician, Johannes Crato von Crafftheim, and the curator of his gardens, botanist Charles de l'Écluse, were former students of Melanchthon alongside Languet at Wittenberg. Philip came to know them well, continuing to correspond with both men when he left Vienna. Although he maintained some distance by lodging, with a fellow Englishman named Thomas Coningsby, with one 'Raichel',[29] Philip was very much drawn into Languet's world.

Ironically, although there is a wealth of surviving correspondence between Languet and Philip detailing beautifully the periods during which the two were apart, we can glimpse them together on only a couple of occasions. One is a published account of table-talk at a dinner at which both were present; the other is a poetic representation of Languet by Philip. Neither is particularly useful as a naturalistic depiction of their friendship, but each contains some hints of the context in which they viewed it.

The table-talk comes from a meal where the company included Languet and the Camerarius brothers, Joachim and Philip.[30] Conversation turned to the question of 'Whether it was true (as the ancients say, and the moderns believe) that England cannot endure wolves, either bred in the country, or brought thither out of other places; and whether the same proceed of some hidden property and natural antipathy'. Philip made an extended oration, wittily describing how an English king had passed laws to banish wolves, in order to protect English sheep, but he admitted that wolves could still be 'seen in parks of great lords, who send for them out of Ireland and other places'. Philip's tale was not the concerned expression of the average Englishman for his country's animal life. Instead, it was a fairly simple beast fable, in which the wolves were Roman Catholics, banished from England by the king during the Reformation of the 1530s. Interestingly, there is definite criticism in Philip's description of the vicious campaigns to extirpate the wolves, especially in the official amnesty granted to offenders who could prove themselves to be ardent wolf-hunters. The programme had been so successful, he said, that wolves now lived only on private estates, in Scotland and across the seas.

According to Philip Camerarius, Philip's speech proved 'very pleasing to the company that sat at table with him, and no man would make any question thereof, especially when we saw it approved by Hubert Languet, a man of most exquisite judgement, and exceeding well travelled in the knowledge of things, and in the affairs of the world.'[31] It is difficult to imagine a modern forum that would appreciate this kind of table-talk. Its members would need to be academically highly trained, intellectually astute, politically involved, and able to render all those knowledges into a persuasive fictional form, in a classical language, and present it with considerable oratorical flair. But this is precisely the milieu into which Philip moved when he encountered Languet, and within which he would be lauded.

The second portrait of them together comes in Philip's poem 'As I my little flock on Ister bank', probably written after Languet's death, and inserted into *The Arcadia*.[32] The shepherd-poet Philisides (playing on Philip's own name) pipes to his flock on the banks of the Ister (Danube) as night comes on. The song he sings so that the flock will not stray is the song 'old Languet had me taught,/Languet, the shepherd best swift Ister knew', praising Languet's 'clerkly rede [advice]'. While this portrait of a pious, innately good teacher is fairly banal, there may be a significant detail in the idea of Languet teaching Philisides through 'old true tales . . . How shepherds did of yore, how now they thrive'. A mutual friend, Daniel Rogers, later described Languet to Philip as one who 'guided you through the histories and origins of states'.[33] The tale Languet tells here is another beast fable, describing a world populated solely by beasts, who chose to have a king. But by giving him too many powers, the beasts end up in painful thrall to their freely elected tyrant. The story ends with an exhortation: 'you, poor beasts, in patience bide your hell,/Or know your strengths, and then you shall do well'.

It is significant that these two glimpses of Languet and Philip together both concern gentle, but politically loaded, beast fables, because they point to two central aspects of their relationship. Philip's pen-portrait tallies with other contemporary attempts to capture Languet's gifts. His friend Joachim Camerarius, Professor of Humanities at Leipzig, recalled Languet as a superb conversationalist, blessed with a strong memory and powers of analysis, and an encyclopaedic knowledge of kings, courts and the lives of famous men. Most strikingly, wrote Camerarius, Languet habitually brought these skills and knowledges to bear on the contemporary political scene:

> I never heard a man, who could expound with so much prudence, certainty, plainness, evidence, and eloquence, whatever he undertook to relate; he never mistook the names of men; he was never wrong in the circumstances of time; nor did he ever confound the order and series of things and events. He had also a wonderful sagacity to discover the characters of men, and to conjecture which way men's tempers would lead them, and what was the inclination of their minds. He judged almost with certainty of their designs, and could most wonderfully foresee the event of things.[34]

Similarly, the great French historian Jacques Auguste de Thou, on meeting Languet in Baden in 1579, pronounced himself pleased 'with this man's eminent probity, and with his great judgment not only in the sciences, but also in public affairs, in which he had been engaged all his lifetime, having served several princes very faithfully: he was so well acquainted with the affairs of Germany, that he could instruct the Germans themselves in the affairs of their own country'.[35]

Languet's interest in contemporary politics had a cause. He was an anomaly, a French Huguenot who spent most of his life in German politics. During the early part of his diplomatic career he had been able to influence French politics while still working for Augustus. But after the Massacre, physically cut off from his roots, he – like Leicester and Walsingham in England – realised that oppressed Huguenots had to be supported by active intervention by external forces. The first step had to be bolstering Protestant resistance to Spanish domination in the Low Countries, and what he now perceived as Valois tyranny in France.

Languet has long been identified as the author of the tract *Vindiciae, contra tyrannos*, published in 1579 under the pseudonym 'Stephanus Junius Brutus'.[36] While nothing in his letters or other writings can be cited as evidence of his authorship, it can safely be stated that Languet belonged – politically, doctrinally and intellectually – to the circles that produced this work. Although clearly Huguenot-identified, the text itself is specifically directed not to 'either of the parties', but to anyone who professes Christian religion, 'whether they call it papal or reformed'. The call for a single united church is placed against an analysis of the current 'calamities and destruction in Gaul', which puts the blame, not on religious factions, but on 'evil arts, vicious counsels, and false and pestiferous doctrines of Niccolò Macchiavelli the Florentine', drawing on the commonplace identification of Florentine Cathérine de Médicis as a Machiavellian.[37] The book went on to discuss the circumstances under which resistance was justifiable, and concluded that certain sorts of tyranny warranted extreme measures. Read in the context of these ideas, the beast fable told by Languet on Ister bank becomes far more trenchant.

But the genre itself is also telling. The two men certainly discussed some heavy political and philosophical issues, but their tone is often light-hearted, even humorous. This should not be misread as levity, or dismissive irony. It is what the Renaissance called *ioco-serio*: a deliberate attempt to tackle grave issues in a playful manner, but to serious ends. Philip's English wolves and Languet's foolish beasts are prime examples of the genre – and beautiful illustrations of a friendship that was not afraid to take on the weightiest issues, albeit often disguised in the lightest of banter.

When the two friends were apart, Languet threw himself wholeheartedly into the role of tutor. He fashioned a programme of study to be continued when they were physically separated, with Languet providing an early form of distance learning. His philosophy was quite simple: education should be provided pragmatically to fit the student's position in life, devoting what was only a 'brief time' to 'the most necessary studies', by which he meant those things 'which it is improper for men of high degree not to know, and which may both adorn and shield you in the future'. Geometry, for example, might be of use to highborn men when they came to fortify and besiege cities, pitch camp and for the purposes of architecture – but at the advanced age of eighteen Philip no longer had time to master the subject, and it was, Languet opined, 'absurd to learn the elements of many skills for the sake of display rather than use'.[38]

Any pursuit of knowledge had to start with the Scriptures, followed by 'that branch of moral philosophy which teaches right and wrong'. Philip did not need to be persuaded to read history: 'you incline towards it of your own accord, and have already made great progress in it'.[39] This was indeed true: Philip excitedly recommended to Languet vernacular Italian histories that he thought he should read: 'in your next letter please tell me whether you own *L'Historia del Mondo* of Tarcagnota, the *Lettere de Prencipi*, *Lettere de Tredici Illustri Homini*, and *Imprese* of Girolamo Ruscelli, and *Il Stato di Vinegia* written by Contarini and Donato Giannotti, which are really choice books'.[40] Of concern next were languages, which were the declared reason for Philip's travel abroad. Begging for help, Philip lamented his Latin style: 'truly I am discovering that all I learn by writing badly is how to write badly'.[41] Languet predictably enough prescribed studying Cicero's letters and employing the technique of double translation; Philip vowed to take this advice a step further, by using Paolo Manuzio's Italian and French translations of Cicero (which he already possessed) to improve his skill in those languages.[42] Tellingly, while Languet was speaking only of classical languages, Philip, as his father's son, also raised the question of modern tongues.

Philip declared that he wanted enough Greek to read Aristotle in the original, particularly the *Politics*, 'for although translations appear virtually every day, I still suspect that they do not convey the author's meaning clearly or precisely enough'.[43] Languet was unconvinced, finding Aristotle 'for the most part so concise and pointed that he seems obscure even to those who have spent whole lifetimes reading him'. Indeed, Languet had mixed feelings on the question of Greek altogether – 'an excellent study' but time-consuming, when Latin was far more useful. 'I do urge you to learn first the things that are most essential and suit your position in life. You already know four languages [presumably English, French, Latin and Italian]. If, in the course of amusing yourself, you learned enough German to understand it more or less you would not, in my opinion, be wasting your effort.' German's allure lay purely in its practical use: 'You English have more trade with the Germans than with anyone else; their influence and power is already unparalleled in Christendom, and no doubt will increase even further, thanks to the stupidity of my people [the French] and their other neighbours.'[44] However, Philip despaired of ever mastering German, which had, he thought, 'a certain harshness' that made it hard to pick up at his age.[45]

Philip's energies in astronomy needed to be reconsidered. Languet considered astronomy a prerequisite for geography, 'and those who read history without knowing geography seem to me very like men who make journeys in the dark'. However, he advised against spending *too* much time on astronomy, with its limited returns.[46] This advice came as a relief to Philip. 'I am delighted that you approve of my intention to stop studying astronomy. As for geometry, I really do not know what to decide. I have a burning desire to learn it, the more so because I have always had the impression that it is closely related to military science. I shall, however, pursue this study with restraint.'[47]

There is no doubt that Philip took Languet's educational philosophy to heart. Several years later, Philip received a request from his friend Edward Denny – who was about to accompany Arthur, Lord Grey of Wilton, into Ireland – to suggest what he should read. Philip provided a programme of study that was almost precisely modelled on Languet's philosophy, and fleshed it out with more specific tips for reading – some of them, like the maps of Abraham Ortelius and the English chronicles of Raphael Holinshed, demonstrating that Philip kept abreast of recent publications. He even provided Denny with advice on intellectual time management, with a timetable of forbidding intensity:

> But now may you ask me: What shall I do first? Truly in my opinion, an hour to your Testament, & a piece of one to Tully's [Cicero's] *Offices*, & that will be study. Plutarch's discourses, you may read with more ease. For the other matters allot yourself another hour for Sacrobocus, & Valerius or any other of geography, and when you have satisfied yourself in that, take your history of England, & your Ortelius to know the places you read of; and so in my conceit, you shall pass both pleasantly and profitably. Your books of the art of soldiery must have another hour, but before you go to them you shall do well to use your hands in drawing of a plot, & practice of arithmetic. Whether now you will do these by piecemeal, all in a day, or first go through with one, you must be your own judge, as you find your memory best serve. To me, the variety rather delights me, then confounds me.[48]

Perhaps in this programme we see the kind of earnest commitment to study that worried Philip's mentor. 'You are none too cheerful by nature,' Languet pointed out bluntly, 'and study will therefore make you more melancholy still: it demands vigorous application of the mind, consumes the vital and intellectual spirits, and very much weakens the body. The finer one's talents are, the more intense are one's interests, and therefore the more harmful – and, as you know, you do not have a strong constitution.'[49] Philip replied, 'I am ready to admit that I am often more serious than my age or my pursuits require; yet I have certainly proved by experience that I am never less subject to melancholy than when I am earnestly applying the feeble powers of my mind to some high and difficult task.'[50]

Languet needed Philip to stay physically strong if he was to fulfil Languet's hopes. Years as a player in international politics had taught the older man that scattered pockets of resistance were never going to amount to a strength adequate for positive action. He was committed to bringing together powerful figures in a league – but not merely a defensive league, like the Treaty of Blois. Languet realised that what Europe's Protestant cause had always lacked was what each of its opponents possessed: a concentrated military force. A mainland Protestant army was his goal, and in Philip Sidney Languet saw his best chance of achieving it.

CHAPTER FIVE

The Company of Wise Men

IT WOULD BE easy enough to reconstruct a narrative of Philip's travels across Europe from the evidence provided in his correspondence with Languet – but we would have only half the story. The letters show how Languet attempted to control and circumscribe the younger man's movements: but they are a record of an optimistic campaign, rather than its less than certain outcome. Supplementing that correspondence with a variety of other sources gives us a version of events for the next year that strays far from Languet's plans. Indeed, a pattern emerges in which the dominant dynamic is one of Philip attempting time and again to break free of Languet's control, and to put himself in situations that alarmed, angered and saddened his self-appointed mentor.

The first signs that Philip had ideas of his own emerged within a matter of weeks. No matter how strong his affection for Hubert Languet, Philip was bound to be intrigued by what lay beyond the imperial court. Vienna was tantalisingly close to what for most sixteenth-century Englishmen was *terra incognita*: Hungary, a country that lay between the known world of Christendom and the exotic dangers of the Ottoman Empire. Under Emperor Maximilian, however, the Hungarian city of Bratislava (then called Pozsony) had been elevated to become capital of the west, and occasionally the emperor would travel there to hold court. Indeed, despite its geographical isolation, John Dee had travelled to Bratislava in April 1564 to present a copy of his *Monas hieroglyphica* – later the butt of scholarly jokes between Languet and Philip – to Maximilian. So, predictably, the inquisitive Philip announced his intention of travelling into Hungary in September 1573. Languet was passionately opposed to the idea, which he thought dangerous: although the Truce of Adrianople of 1568 had effectively suspended hostilities in Hungary, frontier skirmishes were incessant.[1]

But Philip was not to be put off, so Languet embarked instead on a plan of damage limitation. If he could not keep Philip by his side, then he could at least keep him on a tight rein. Philip was to travel directly to Bratislava. There, armed with Languet's letters of recommendation, he would stay with Languet's friend, Dr Georg Purkircher. The entire affair would last only three days. The trip started as planned, with host Purkircher receiving his young guest, with 'the courtesies which your virtue and manners deserve', as Languet observed approvingly. But soon Philip slipped his leash, heading out of the city into the Hungarian countryside. Purkircher rushed to Vienna to break the news and a furious Languet took up his pen. He had no hold over Philip, and could not pass comment on his decision to travel: he could only play the aggrieved friend:

> I have reason to complain about you; for I did not think you had so ill
> an opinion of me as not to confide your plans to me. Perhaps you
> feared that I would prepare an ambush for you along your way. When
> you left here you said that you would not be gone for more than three
> days. But now, like a little bird that has forced its way through the bars
> of its cage, your delight makes you restless, flitting hither and yon,
> perhaps without a thought for your friends; and you scarcely guard
> against the dangers that so often occur on such journeys.

Languet could hardly complain about Philip's 'noble eagerness to "observe the manners and cities of many men" as the poet says, for this is the best way to develop judgment and master our feelings'. On the other hand, he felt that his young friend should have been accompanied by more suitable men than his English retinue. As it was, Philip had 'no one to converse with along the way about various subjects, no one to tell you about the manners and customs of the peoples you visit, to introduce you to learned men, and when necessary to serve as an interpreter. I might perhaps have found you such a travelling companion, had you wished to tell me about your plan.' Tempering his tone somewhat, Languet assured Philip that his scruples arose only 'because I am anxious about you, and about the glorious flowering of your noble character, which, I hope, will eventually bring forth the delightful fruits of your many virtues'.[2] Purkircher was despatched to intercept the wayward young man at Weiner Neustadt, but it was an early sign for Languet that his protégé had no intention of being anyone's puppet.

It was also Philip's first glimpse of a side of Languet's character that was to become familiar to him over the next few years. While the two men were together, their relationship was congenial, open and genuinely warm. Once separated, however, tensions became evident. As a career diplomat whose livelihood depended on a regimented routine of letter-writing, Languet would panic when Philip – far less adept at keeping in touch – disappeared off the map. His carefully modulated letters degenerated into emotional outbursts about his love for Philip, or angry tirades about his friend's lack of affection for him. To the reader today they appear to be the writings of an infatuated older man: this may have been the case, but they also reveal the anxieties of a politician with a cause, who saw a potential instrument of his plans wandering off into dangerous territory.

Brief though it was, his Hungarian odyssey certainly made an impression on Philip. He remained interested in the Turco-Hungarian wars, asking Languet for books on the subject, commenting on Békés Gáspár (Bekessius) recruiting troops in Poland against the Turks in Hungary,[3] and enquiring into Hungary's defences.[4] More importantly for his later pursuits, it gave him ideas about the uses to which poetry could be put. 'In Hungary,' he later recalled, 'I have seen it the manner at all feasts, and other such meetings, to have songs of their ancestors' valour, which that right soldierlike nation think one of the chiefest kindlers of brave courage.' The defeat of Hungary at Mohacs in 1526 had led to a deliberate revival of nationalist fervour, which the poetic outpourings of 'that right soldierlike nation' had bolstered. In Hungary, Philip saw how poetry could be an integral part of the instilling of patriotic nationalism.

Perhaps it was encounters like this that prompted Philip to think about the role of vernacular poetry, and to remind him of other popular versifiers he had encountered. The Penshurst account books record how, on the way back from Oxford to Shrewsbury in 1566, there had been 'given by Mr Philip's commandment to a blind harper who is Sir William Holles' man of Nottinghamshire . . . 12d.'[5] Philip later commented: 'I must confess my own barbarousness, I never heard the old song of Percy and Douglas that I found not my heart moved more than with a trumpet; and yet is it sung by some blind crowder [Welsh fiddler], with no rougher voice than rude style.'[6] As George Puttenham pointed out in his 1587 work of literary criticism, *The Arte of Poesie*, blind harpers were traditionally the purveyors of 'stories of old time, as the tale of *Sir Topas*, the reports of Bevis of Southampton, Guy of Warwick, Adam Bell, and the Clymme of the Clough, and such other old romances or historical rhymes, made purposely for recreation of the common people at Christmas dinners and bride-ales'.[7] For all his classical training, Philip was unwilling to discount the emotional impact of this rough, homespun verse. Like the Welsh 'crowders', the Hungarian poets struck him as a powerful vernacular voice, which – although 'barbarous' – deserved to be taken seriously.

His time in Hungary also gave him an appetite to go further: to travel into Italy. This prospect disturbed Languet even more than had the Hungarian jaunt, and with reason. A contemporary English writer, William Harrison, wrote in all seriousness of how the sons of noblemen and gentlemen returned home from Italy with 'nothing but mere atheism, infidelity, vicious conversation, and ambitious and proud behaviour'. Even the 'earnest Protestant' returned boldly claiming that 'faith and truth is to be kept where no loss or hindrance of a future purpose is sustained by holding of the same; and forgiveness only to be showed when full revenge is made'.[8] Beyond the detrimental effects on Philip's faith, however, there was the practical issue of his own safety, since he came from a prominent Protestant family, and that would make him vulnerable in Catholic territories. There was also a more political concern. After lengthy negotiations, Henri, Duc d'Anjou had accepted the Polish crown and Languet wanted Philip on hand to meet him when he was crowned King of Poland. Notwithstanding Anjou's implication in the Paris Massacre, Languet realised that he was now a key figure in the wider field of European politics and one on whom Philip, as a French baron, might work to further Languet's ends.

On the other hand, Philip specifically wanted to visit the university city of Padua, and Languet could scarcely object to him visiting his own *alma mater*. He merely resorted to belittling what Italy had to offer, claiming that there was no point in even learning the language: the energetic attempts of the English to master Italian were 'absurd' to Languet, since 'as far as I know, there's no advantage to be gained from them. The Italians, however, get the greatest benefit from you, so they really ought to be learning your language. But perhaps,' he concluded, tongue firmly in cheek, 'you worry that you won't be able to persuade them to take your money unless your Italian is very fluent.'[9]

Determined to protect his friend, Languet once again turned to his immense network of contacts, imposing obligations on Philip with a generous selection of letters bearing his personal commendation to friends in Italy. In Venice, Philip should seek out France's ambassador there, Arnaud du Ferrier; the Huguenot writer François Perrot de Mezières; and Wolfgang Zündelin, who had been tutor to the Prince Palatine Christopher and now made his living from collecting political news and intelligence from carefully placed correspondents, digesting it and then transmitting it to another set of correspondents. In Padua, Languet recommended the Bohemian Michael de Slavata, whose family had strong connections with the Viennese imperial court; Jacob Monau, who had studied at Heidelberg and Wittenberg, and at Leipzig under Languet's friend Joachim Camerarius; Johannes Laurentius Danus, a German medical student; and Albert Laski, Palatine of Sieradz, with whom Languet hoped Philip would travel to Poland for Henri's investiture.[10]

Leaving Vienna in late October 1573, Philip took with him the entourage that had remained with him since leaving England: Lodowick Bryskett, Harry White, John Fisher and Griffin Madox.[11] We know that the five had reached Venice by Friday 6 November, when Philip raised considerable funds from the Venetian correspondent of the London-based banker Acerbo Vellutelli,[12] required in order to keep himself and his retinue suitably lodged.

Venice, then as now, was one of Europe's most cosmopolitan cities, its exoticism enhanced by the trade in luxury goods coming from the east. Once installed, however, Philip was distinctly underwhelmed by Venice's fabled beauty. To his brother Robert, he was later to despair that 'As for Italy I know not what we have, or can have to do with them, but to buy their silks and wines.' Following his own advice, he was more interested in assessing Venice's political structures. Most of Italy, Philip wrote to Robert, was in the grip of tyranny; Venice was admittedly an exception with 'good laws, and customs', but its lesson was not particularly useful to the English, since 'we can hardly proportion to ourselves, because they are quite of a contrary government' – Venice was a republic, ruled by the twenty-six members of the *Collegio* and the Council of Ten, all of whom were noblemen. Even its intellectual life was to be questioned. Some men there were 'indeed excellently learned, yet are they all given to so counterfeit learning, as a man shall learn of them more false grounds of things, than in any place else that I do know, for from a tapster upwards they are all discoursers'. The Venetians excelled other countries only in 'fine certain qualities, as horsemanship, weapons, vaulting, and such like'; for other 'more sound' qualities, 'they do little excel nearer places'.[13] 'I gather from your letters', wrote Languet, eager to capitalise on Philip's disappointment, 'that Venice's splendours have not come up to your expectations. Nevertheless, nothing else in Italy even remotely compares with them; so if you dismiss these, the rest won't appeal to you at all.'[14]

As instructed by Languet, Philip paid a visit to the Count of Hanau, another young Protestant by the name of Philip. Although only a year older than his English namesake, Philip-Ludwig had ruled the small German state of Hanau (on the Rhine in the Wetterau) since his father's death in 1561, when he was just eight. Through his parents Hanau was connected to several of northern Europe's most influential politicians. His mother came from the family of the Palatine princes and his father's mother Juliana de Stolberg had, after an early widowhood, married Count William of Nassau, and had gone on to bear him several sons, including William of Orange. This mixed family heritage, and the Hanau tradition, meant that the young count had steered clear of absolute identification with either Lutheran or Calvinist camp, which rendered him highly attractive to the pragmatic politician in Languet. Hanau embodied all the prized features of a young, malleable Protestant prince with a decent humanist education, first alongside his Nassau cousins at Dillenbourg, and later at Strasburg and Tübingen. Moreover, like Philip and Languet, he had witnessed at first hand the horrors of the St Bartholomew's Day Massacre, which had turned him into something of a Protestant activist. Forced by his high-profile Protestant affiliations to travel incognito and by routes that strategically avoided territories under the pope and the King of Spain, Venice's relatively liberal religious climate provided a welcome respite.[15]

The meeting of the Philips was a success, to Languet's delight: 'I am glad that what I wrote about the kindness of the Count of Hanau and his people you've found to be true. By my letters I only wanted to give you the chance to meet men who, I believed, love and admire excellence in any man, since I didn't doubt that your behaviour would easily be able to win them over. And wherever you go there will always be good men who will welcome you, so long as you remain true to yourself.'[16] But Languet did not leave the Hanau–Sidney friendship to chance. He ensured that Philip also made the acquaintance of Hanau's *Hofmeister* Paul von Welsperg, his friend the Hamburg-born Wittenberg graduate Matthaeus Delius, and his servant Jacques Le Goulx – all of whom were already in correspondence with Languet. Both Hanau and von Welsperg wrote to Languet, he relayed to Philip, to 'praise you to the skies and congratulate themselves on their friendship with you. They thank me for having been, so to speak, its cause. See to it, therefore, that you return their affection, that you maintain your reputation and mine, and that you vindicate the opinion good men have of you.'[17]

Building on this promising beginning, Languet cannily interwove the lives of Philip and the Hanau party. He recommended the services of Matthaeus Delius for practice in improving the pronunciation of Philip's spoken Latin.[18] But Languet was motivated by more than a desire to file Philip's classical tongues. Before long his instructions became more detailed.

> Master von Welsperg is no less fond of you than I am. Make sure you
> get especially close to him, so that you can consult him more freely
> about your business. He is an honourable man, widely experienced, who
> detects dangers far-off, as well as being by nature very kind and
> moderate. He has decided to accompany my lord the Count to those
> parts of Italy which can be visited without danger, and then to come
> here [Vienna]. Feel free to join them on this journey: you'll find no
> better or more suitable companions.[19]

Philip fell into Languet's carefully laid trap. He was determined, he announced, to travel on with the count: 'When spring comes, I shall tour all those lands alongside the noble Count of Hanau, who has announced that he plans to leave the Italians behind and visit Poland, Bohemia, and your own Saxony. So then I shall see you, my dear Languet, and I shall find more pleasure in a single conversation with you than in the magnificent magnificences of all those magnificoes.' It seemed that Languet had got his way, and that Philip would soon be restored to the safety of Vienna, but he reckoned without Philip's complicated financial and medical dilemmas. Philip's despatches from Venice in late 1573 refer to 'my entanglement in many affairs', which 'detains me from being where so many important things are to be observed and learned'.[20] So when Hanau travelled on to Padua, Philip remained in Venice, ill and 'melancholy', much to the concern of his mentor, who urged him to:

> take care of your health and not to spend so much time studying. Avoid the lagoons where you are – nothing is more unpleasant than they after one has seen the things in the city which are worth seeing. I was surprised that you stayed on for so long in that ceaseless noise and stench, especially since you write that you have not made friends with anyone you especially like. Hurry, then, to your friend the Count of Hanau in Padua, and to those other good men who are incredibly fond of you and eagerly await your company.[21]

It was not until the second week of 1574 that Philip and his retinue finally arrived in Padua, taking lodgings in a house owned by Hercole Bolognese at the Pozzo della Vacca, which seem not to have been to his taste: 'If you do not have decent lodgings in Padua,' wrote Languet, 'you can find some in the citadel of Milan, if you care to travel over there.'[22] The fact that Philip had disentangled himself from 'that troublesome business which kept you in Venice so long' was welcome news to Languet: 'you're better off living in Padua, both for your studying or your health'. In Padua, Philip would be sure to find suitable company to help him 'shake off that sometimes excessive melancholy of yours. Make sure you don't devote so much time to studying that your health gets neglected, or starts to suffer – or you'll be like the traveller who prepares for a long journey by taking great pains about his own well-being but spares no thought for the horse that will carry him.'[23] As it turned out, Philip never cut himself off from unhealthy Venice, but shuttled back and forth between that city and Padua. The journey was easily done: according to another English traveller, Richard Smith, 'Padua is from Venice twenty miles Italian; there are ordinary boats pass between both evening and morning.'[24]

Padua, Languet believed, would provide better support for Philip's academic programme. During the sixteenth century, the university of law at Padua was a bigger draw for English students than anywhere else in Europe. It could boast among its alumni scholars and politicians such as Thomas Linacre, Reginald Pole, Cuthbert Tunstall, Thomas Starkey, Richard Pace, Thomas Lupset, Richard Morison and John Caius. Both the men who held the post of Principal Secretary after 1572, Francis Walsingham and Thomas Wilson, had passed through. The university of law was made up of about twenty regional groupings called 'nations', which annually elected *consiliarii* to represent the 'nations' to the university. The English 'nation' was in continuous existence from the fourteenth to the eighteenth century, but after Elizabeth's accession the city became a refuge for a significant number of English Catholics.[25]

To an extent, Languet was successful in ensuring that Philip's social circle should be comprised mainly of German and central European noblemen, keeping him safely out of the clutches of Italians and English Catholic exiles. Philip forged friendships with Michael de Slavata;[26] Count Otto von Solms;[27] Fabian, baron and burgrave of Dohna; and Melchior, Baron von Rödern, son of the president of the Silesian parliament. However, Languet was foiled by Philip's curiosity, as Jonathan Woolfson's recent research in the Paduan archives has revealed. Although never registered at the university, Philip did play a minor role in the academic life of one of the English students there, John Hart, acting as a witness of Hart's doctoral examination in law on 7 June 1574, alongside his Welsh servant Griffin Madox and five other men.[28] This discovery usefully tempers the impression we might gain from Languet's letters. Clearly Philip *did* fraternise with the English expatriate community, many of whom were undoubtedly Catholic. Both John Hart and one of Philip's fellow witnesses, a civil lawyer named Nicholas Wendon, were listed in an official English document in 1575 as fugitives living abroad.[29] Later, during a long imprisonment in England, Hart supplied evidence on recusants to Walsingham and eventually became a Jesuit, dying in Poland in 1586; Wendon was ordained as a priest in Rome in 1578.[30]

Philip's even-handed attitude can be seen in his response to two men whom he encountered among the English community in Venice: a friend from his Shrewsbury days, and a cousin. Robert Corbett was the elder brother of Philip's schoolfellow Vincent Corbett (whom he had visited during the 1566 Christmas vacation), whom Philip described to Languet as 'my very greatest friend, a man born to high estate, yet, as Buchanan says, "whose noble manners far exceed his birth." He is a supporter of the true faith, and quite a military expert, but speaks only Italian.' Richard Shelley, on the other hand, although more closely related ('as much closer in blood as the former is in friendship'), was – like so many Englishmen in Padua (where he was *consiliarius* of the English nation in 1567) – a Catholic. 'He is well educated, for he is very well versed in Greek, Latin and Italian, and he also has some acquaintance with things French; but,' Philip admitted to Languet, 'he is very much given to papist superstition.'[31] The 'papist superstition' later took institutional form when Shelley became Grand Prior of the Knights of St John and moved to Rome, where he occupied himself with the English hospice. Yet despite their doctrinal differences, Corbett and Shelley journeyed together to Vienna, where Philip had arranged their introduction to Hubert Languet. Languet was none too impressed with this charge and his letters contain a constant comic assault on Shelley's religious convictions, which intensified when Shelley was stricken with diarrhoea while crossing the Alps. Only when Shelley came close to death did Languet drop the levity.

Despite the apparent tolerance, however, intimacy with Roman Catholics was still dangerous for a Protestant abroad. This was made vividly apparent when Philip became close to the man known as 'the English Baron': Edward, third Baron Windsor of Stanwell, a long-term resident in Venice.[32] The baron was an intelligence-gatherer for Philip's uncle, the Earl of Sussex, and regularly engaged in summarising news reports from Rome, Siena, Vinegia, Antwerp and Vienna, supplementing them with the latest from Venice, and forwarding them all to Sussex in England.[33] Now, Windsor was trying to become an agent for the English government: in June 1573, he had sent Elizabeth a 'discourse of the government of England', with the request that he become her agent. He assured her that he 'shall never be found a blab, or an utterer of matter of state, but as sure as a column of marble, for in that consisteth true nobility'.[34] In this bid, Windsor managed (at least to his own satisfaction) to reconcile religious loyalty to the pope, with patriotic loyalty to Elizabeth – a balancing act that the queen refused to recognise.

There was some alarm, therefore, when Philip forsook his customary lodgings and moved into the Windsor house, a no-go area for many of his other acquaintances. His Venice friend Wolfgang Zündelin (who had now added Philip to his list of persons to be supplied with the latest political information from across the Continent) wrote on 20 June 1574 that 'I heard that you were enjoying the hospitality of your friend the

Baron, and to seek you out in such an unfamiliar place was more than I dared.'[35] It was not long before Philip's intimacy with Windsor and others caused English tongues to wag. Languet warned him a few months later that 'your countrymen have begun to suspect your piety because you lived in Venice too intimately with those who profess a faith inimicable to yours.'[36] Languet did not approve of such public connections for his protégé; the fact that Windsor never mentioned Philip in his frequent missives to Sussex might suggest that he also realised the need for discretion on the subject.

Of course, in associating with Windsor, Philip was defying the terms of his licence to travel, which stated quite firmly that he should not 'wittingly haunt and keep with any person our subject born, that is departed out of our realm without our licence or that contrary to our licence doth remain in the parts of beyond the seas, and doth not return into our realm as he ought to'.[37] But it would be easy to read too much into these contacts, no matter how reckless they appeared from home. As an Englishman, Philip was naturally drawn to the English expatriate community in Italy, and English expatriates in late sixteenth-century Italy were quite likely to be Roman Catholics: he would hardly have had to seek them out. In England, consorting with Catholic recusants was *per se* a political statement. In Italy, consorting with Catholics was inevitable; consorting with English Catholics was more than likely, given the disproportion of Catholics within the English expatriate communities there. Philip's varying experiences with religious factions did not compromise his own Protestant beliefs, but they did give him a sense of perspective that made him more amenable to interaction with Catholics than was perhaps politically wise.

It is also possible that Philip was particularly open to suspicion because of the continued rumours of Sir Henry's links with the Spanish, which had never gone away. In 1574 the Spanish agent Antonio de Guaras wrote to Philip of Spain to report an encounter with Sir Henry. The king noted that Sir Henry 'had asked to see Guaras and spoken in great secrecy to him, and offered that he had a way to serve his majesty with six thousand chosen soldiers; and since Guaras expressed two or three times his belief as to the difficulty of doing so with the queen's will, and even more without it, he replied . . . that as security for the fulfilment of it he pledged his only heir, whose name is Philip whom his majesty lifted from the font'.[38] Once again, there is no supporting evidence for this bizarre story, but Guaras' claim underlines the complicated (sometimes contradictory) allegiances that Philip might be seen to have inherited. As a result of his time in Italy, Philip can have had no illusions about the difficulties that beset a multi-denominational or multi-factional life. On the surface, Padua was the model of an international student community where bitter political and doctrinal struggles could be left behind – or at least effectively sidelined – in favour of a liberal academic consensus, the famed *libertas Patavinas*. But it was a thin veneer, as was vividly demonstrated during the evening of 31 May 1574, the birthday of Philip's friend, the Baron of Dohna. The German nation held a banquet to celebrate the departure of two of its number, with guests that included Baron von Rödern and Michael and Albert de Slavata.[39] As the carousing guests walked back to the Slavatas' lodging-house, their high spirits irritated a group from Vicenza. Thinking that the Germans were Burgundians (their enemies), the Vicenzans drew their swords and threatened Dohna and his friends, who retaliated in kind. When it became clear that the supposed Burgundians were in fact Germans – even worse – the Vicenzans started to wield their weapons. The Germans held their ground; French, and then German reinforcements became involved; and at length the Vicenzans fled, only to be followed to their lodgings and harassed from the street by the Germans, despite some serious wounds.

Philip was probably in Venice and missed this ugly incident; he was also well out of harm's way when, in September 1575, some English and Polish gentlemen were reported to have been killed in Padua in a fight between town and gown.[40] But the involvement of his friends the Slavatas brought home to him the flimsiness of Padua's international concord: all it took was enough alcohol and a few words saw the nations regress to territorial tribes. It might also suggest a real fear behind Philip's (standard) petition to Venice's Council of Ten for a warrant for him and his retinue to bear arms – which he did as '*L'Illustre Signor Filippo Sidnei figliolo dell'Illustrissimo Signor Henrico Governatore della Provincia di Gales*' (The Illustrious Master Philip Sidney, son of the Most Illustrious Master Henry Sidney, Governor of the Province of Wales).[41]

Philip did not restrict himself to Venice and Padua. Between 5 March and 6 April 1574, he fitted in a whistlestop journey to Genoa and back, travelling via Florence on one leg of the journey, a considerable round trip that has been estimated at over 550 miles. Significantly, he seems never to have tried to go to Rome, or further south in Italy. Languet once again wrote to complain that Philip had failed to consult him about the trip to Genoa.[42] When Philip protested in writing about Languet's unnecessary concern, the latter made his motives quite clear: 'My dear Sidney, I am anxious about your welfare because I am conscious of what your origins are, what your character is, with what eagerness you strive for virtue, and what progress you have already made; and I realize how much your country can expect from you if God grants you long life.'[43]

But Languet betrayed a more personal fondness for Philip. On New Year's Day 1574, he had written to inform the young man that 'I've started cheering myself up from time to time by gazing at your portrait at the house of our most understanding friend, Abondio [the medallist who had produced a medal of Philip]. Yet I immediately pay the price for this pleasure because it brings back the pain which I felt when you left.'[44] Languet's notion of portraiture followed the belief of Leon Battista Alberti, who had written as long ago as 1435 that the 'truly divine power' of painting lay in its ability to 'make the absent present, as they say of friendship', consciously echoing Cicero's classic treatise *De amicitia* (On friendship).[45] Friends who had to be apart could therefore be made present by their image in paint.

Later in the month, Languet slipped the subject into another letter, saying he could think of no cure for the sadness that Philip's eventual departure to England would cause, 'unless a portrait of you might afford me some relief. I have one engraved on my heart which I always see before my eyes, but I implore you not to think it a burden to indulge my desire: send me your portrait, or bring it with you when you return'. He also wanted to share it with friends, who believed that Philip's alleged mental qualities would show in his face. The thought of his absent friend had even provoked Languet to an unwonted frivolity. 'Recently, the sight of your portrait at our friend Abondio's moved me so much that when I returned home I wrote these short verses (enclosed), a kind of writing I haven't indulged since I was a very young man. I want to give you myself a little something for your amusement; these little verses seem to me not inappropriate, so I would like them to be inscribed on the picture you've ordered, if there's room for them.'[46] Philip was more than happy to oblige about the portrait, since there were plenty of decent artists on hand:

> As soon as I return to Venice I shall have it done either by Paolo Veronese or by Tintoretto, who easily occupy first rank in this art. As for your verses: though it is 'a proud thing to have a much praised man praise you,' and I truly love them as a permanent token of your opinion of me, I could not be so completely immodest as to order such high praise about me to be inscribed, since I don't deserve them. Allow me to refuse this one thing, and demand anything else of me.[47]

Sadly, thanks to Philip's modesty, Languet's verses have been lost.

Ultimately Veronese (born Paolo Caliari of Verona) was chosen and work commenced in late February in his studio on the Calle di Ca' Mocenigo. 'Paolo Veronese started work on my portrait today,' Philip reported on 26 February 1574, 'so I must stay for another two or three days.' Whereas Tintoretto was a favourite for rich Venetians eager to display their wealth in thick brushstrokes, Veronese specialised in 'courtly elegance' and 'knowing nonchalance', which appealed to Philip, but the choice of Veronese was also significant for less artistic reasons. In July 1573, Veronese had been summoned before the Holy Office in Venice (the Inquisition) to explain the presence of 'buffoons, drunkards, Germans, dwarfs and other such scurrilities' in his just-completed canvas of the Last Supper for the Dominican refectory of Santi Giovanni e Paolo. Surely he was aware that 'in Germany and in other places infected with heresy, it is customary with various pictures full of scurrilousness and similar inventions to mock, vituperate, and scorn the things of the Holy Catholic Church in order to teach bad doctrines to foolish and ignorant people?' Veronese was ordered to correct the painting within three months, at his own expense. Instead, he simply retitled the painting *Feast in the House of Levi*, referring to the episode in Luke 5:30 that was suitably awash with 'publicans and sinners'.[48]

An impatient Languet – 'in this matter you are making haste very slowly,' he complained in late April 1574[49] – finally took receipt of the painting in June. 'Master Corbett showed me your portrait, which I kept next to me for several hours, feasting my eyes. But, instead of dampening it, this only increased my desire. Rather than representing you, it seems to be someone resembling you; at first, I thought it was your brother. The features are very well depicted, it looks far more youthful than it should be. You probably looked like this at twelve or thirteen.'[50] A year later, after another spell of living with the flesh-and-blood Philip, Languet commented again on the portrait:

> For as long as I enjoyed the sight of you I thought little of the portrait you gave me, and barely gave you thanks for such a beautiful present. When I returned from Frankfurt, I was led by longing for you, to frame it and hang it in full view. Then it struck me as so beautiful, and to resemble you so strongly, that I value nothing else I own more highly. Master Vulcobius is so struck by its elegance that he is looking for an artist to copy it. The painter has represented you sad and thoughtful. I would have preferred your face to look more cheerful when you sat for it.[51]

It may have been this portrait which the poet and diplomat Daniel Rogers later saw (he certainly stayed with Languet in 1577). He too remarked on Philip's youthful appearance:

> Well then (may Divine Youth long encircle with soft down those cheeks wherein it resides), who painted you, o Sidney, in such a unique manner, and who spread this rosy charm lightly over your face? Who enlivened your forehead with expression, your eyes with radiant beams? Whose art has given your lips that keen expression? . . . When I look at that image, so like your own nature, it looks back at me with eloquent eyes. But oh, why is it muter than a silent fish, why does it not speak? It imitates your habits, for you are a follower of Pythagoras' praised silence, you seem to hear much and to speak little. The rest corresponds completely: the difference lies only in this, that you speak little, but that your picture is always mute.[52]

Sadly, Veronese's portrait has been lost, but recent detective work by Sidney scholar Roger Kuin may be leading us towards it. An inventory of Languet's belongings, taken after his death, revealed a 'conterfeit van Languet ende van een Jonghen' (a picture of Languet and one of a young man). Kuin argues the picture may have been bought at auction by another of

Languet's protégés. Philippe Du Plessis-Mornay, who was living on the same street in Antwerp at the time. This would explain the presence of a portrait of 'M. Synei' in the gallery of Du Plessis' château at Saumur in 1619. Kuin further conjectures that Du Plessis may have left the portrait to his daughter Elisabeth, who was Philip's god-daughter: her belongings were sold at auction in Lower Normandy in 1697. There the trail runs cold. But it is still to be hoped that the portrait, its sitter long unidentified, may yet be found.[53]

What is striking about this correspondence is the amount of attention paid to Philip Sidney's looks. Philip's admirers and supporters often praised his physical appearance — the beauty of his face, the strength of his body. Ramus' editor Théophile de Banos was quite taken by the handsome young man: 'I well remember the first time I saw you, when I contemplated with wonder your unusual endowments of mind and body.' In a telling analogy, he reminded Philip of Pope Gregory's quip when he caught sight of some beautiful English boys: 'Not Angles, but angels' (it works better in Latin). [54] And yet we know from Moffet that Philip's 'beauty' was 'laid waste, as with little mines' by smallpox, and William Drummond recorded Ben Jonson's verdict that 'S. P. Sidney was no pleasant man in countenance, his face being spoiled with pimples and of high blood and long.' John Aubrey found another fault, opining (from others' testimony) that he was 'extremely beautiful: he much resembled his sister, but his hair was not red, but a little inclining, viz. a dark amber colour. If I were to find a fault in it, methinks 'tis not masculine enough.[55]

Throughout his early adult life Philip was objectified and to some extent feminised by the string of older men who attempted, with varying degrees of success, to control his life. It may be that these men were physically attracted to him, but there is no evidence (even from his enemies) that this was known, or assumed, to be the case. Another explanation is that their attraction was inseparable from their appreciation of Philip as an eminently eligible bachelor, his physical beauty part of a highly prized and marketable package. This would explain the portraits. There was an established tradition of taking portraits for use in marriage negotiations: in March 1571, when she was considering a match with the Duc d'Anjou, Elizabeth despatched a portrait of herself to him to prove her 'beauty and favour'; Cathérine de

Médicis responded with a crayon study of Anjou's face.[56] Languet may well have enjoyed gazing on the image of his absent friend, but he hung it in full view, advertising Philip as an ideal groom: a handsome, young, educated Protestant, son of the Viceroy of Ireland, and heir to the Earl of Leicester, favourite of the Queen of England.

Philip's itinerary was always in danger of being thrown off course by unexpected events and on 30 May 1574 there was a major surprise: Charles IX of France died, aged just twenty-nine. Panicking that the French throne might be seized from under him, his brother and heir Henri, Duc d'Anjou, fled his Polish crown under cover of night and was received by Maximilian in Vienna. From there, despite the ardours involved in crossing the Alps during the summer, Henri determined to travel to France via Italy rather than via Germany. Instead of Philip travelling to Poland to meet Henri, King of Poland, now Henri, King of France would be travelling towards Philip. For his part, Philip did not know how to react to the news of Charles' demise: 'I am at a loss what to think of it,' he wrote to Languet, 'whether his death is a wound to our cause, or, as I hope, a healing salve. The Almighty is ordering Christendom with a wonderful providence in these our days.'[57]

While desperate to have him leave Italy, Languet could not deny that this was a fabulous opportunity for Philip to observe Venice at its most spectacular, and to meet the new French king:

> If you hear that the king's arrival is imminent before your departure, you will presumably want to observe the pomp with which the Venetians receive him, for I have no doubt that it will be extraordinary and well worth seeing. You must make every effort to be presented to the king, and you can manage this either through du Ferrier, Montmorin, Pibrac, or Bellièvre. You are well known to du Ferrier; Montmorin also knows and likes you, and I have mentioned you to Bellièvre and Pibrac, both of whom have treated me with uncommon kindness.

But Philip must make strenuous efforts to work against his accustomed demeanour in order to make the most of the opportunity. 'In such a bustling crowd, as I imagine you will find yourself, you must adopt a bold stance. Bashfulness at the crucial moment is often why we lose opportunities to achieve our desired ends or even to maintain our own status.'[58] According to Languet, then, at this stage in his life Philip was not yet able to realise his potential: his personal manner was too diffident to allow him to capitalise on opportunities.

It has previously been assumed that Philip never did get to meet Henri during his splendid progress in Venice from 18 to 25 July 1574. In the fullest account of Philip's European travels, James Osborn concluded that, 'So far as can be discovered Sidney did not take advantage of the opportunity', speculating that illness and his recollection of the St Bartholomew's Day Massacre may have been the causes. Osborn also cites a letter from Philip's friend, the Frenchman François Perrot de Mezières, dated 27 August in Venice. Perrot writes:

> I shall just give you what news we have and, inter alia, what we have
> seen or heard, since you went away, of the voyage of our King, which I
> attended as far as Ferrara. I shall not say more of the honours he
> received, as I think they have already been extensively reported: as also
> what happened here and at Mantua. This we have had printed in two
> versions, and as I believe others have sent it to you, you will be able to
> see it for yourself: it has not shamed the Venetian Government.

Osborn argues that this letter 'indicates clearly that Sidney had not come to Venice to participate in the magnificent entertainments' laid on for Henri. In fact, the letter can be read more ambiguously: Perrot is filling Philip in on what has happened 'since you went away', which does not in itself rule out the possibility that Philip did see the Venetian entertainments, though he evidently did not follow Henri out of Venice, as Perrot did.[59]

And in fact there has survived a clear reference to a meeting in Venice between the new French king and Philip, in a piece of 1584 official correspondence which, although available in print since the mid-nineteenth century, seems previously to have been overlooked in this context. In a letter to King Henri, his then ambassador in London, Michel de Castelnau wrote of a lengthy audience he had had with Elizabeth, which had concluded with her saying that she desired a closer friendship with France and that the 'sieur de Chedenay' [Sidney] and her ambassador would speak of this with him further. After the audience, Castelnau continued, 'The aforesaid sieur de Chedenay came to find me to ask my advice in all things, and to beg me to write to your Majesty that he had been *gentilhomme de la chambre* of the late King your brother [Charles IX], and that going to find you at Venice, you had done him the honour of retaining him in that rank, which he regarded as a very honourable one.' There seems no reason to disbelieve Castlenau here. Philip had indeed been made a *gentilhomme de la chambre* by Henri's brother, Charles IX; all the correspondence in the weeks leading up to Henri's arrival in Venice assumes that Philip will attempt to meet the new French king. Such a meeting also explains why Perrot, in his letter of August 1574, expected Philip to know who various diplomats involved in the visit were – he casually drops in the names of Paul de Foix, Pomponne de Bellièvre, 'M. de Lansac's son.' Presumably Philip also met these men in Venice during Henri's visit.[60]

Why then is there no record of this meeting, so eagerly anticipated? We would expect to hear of it in a letter from Philip to Languet or another of his friends, or for it to be mentioned in a letter answering one of Philip's. But an examination of Philip's correspondence in the summer and autumn of 1574 reveals a strange gap. Philip wrote to Languet from Venice on 18 June, but after that there is no extant letter from Philip until 27 November 1574, when he wrote to Leicester from Vienna.[61] While it would be foolish to draw conclusions from the absence of evidence, this five-month gap could suggest that his letters from this period contained information which he thought might be compromising, and that he requested their destruction. It is easy to speculate why. In Castelnau's account, Philip appears to have used his encounter with Henri to consolidate his own rank in France – this would not have pleased many of his elders and betters in England.

Although Philip had announced his intention of returning to Vienna as early as June 1574, he fell ill again with 'severe headaches and drinking water to excess' and 'only just avoided pleurisy', according to Languet. Weakened by illness, Philip appears to have dropped out of circulation and some of his German friends left town without taking leave of him, much to his annoyance. On 4 August 1574, however, Philip drew the last tranche of the money that his father had made available to him in Venice, and presumably he and the Hanau group left shortly afterwards.[62] They travelled from Padua to Verona, over the Brenner Pass to Innsbruck, and down the Inn Valley to Passau and Ortenburg, where they visited Hanau's friend, Joachim, Count of Ortenburg, a convert to Protestantism. Lodowick Bryskett later bemoaned in verse the loss of the idyllic time that he spent travelling with Philip:

> Where is become thy wonted happy state,
> (Alas) wherein through many a hill and dale,
> Through pleasant woods, and many an unknown way,
> Along the banks of many silver streams,
> Thou with him rodest; and with him didst scale
> The craggy rocks of th'Alpes and Appenine?
> Still with the Muses sporting, while those beams
> Of virtue kindled in his noble breast,
> Which after did so gloriously forth shine?[63]

'With the Muses sporting' – a rare and tantalising hint, unsupported from the Languet correspondence, that Philip was indulging at this early date his taste for verse. Could it be that Bryskett and the others were the first captive audience of the poetic experiments of Philip Sidney?

From Ortenburg it was a gentler ride along the Danube to Vienna. Philip arrived in Vienna as August 1574 drew to a close, this time staying with Languet in his regular lodgings with Dr Michael Lingelsheim.[64] He moved easily back into the social circles he had enjoyed a year earlier, and added to them a fellow Kentish gentleman, Edward Wotton, who had served for several years in the Spanish colony at Naples, becoming an excellent linguist in the process. Wotton may well be the person jokingly alluded to by Wolfgang Zündelin writing to Philip from Venice in September as 'a man who claimed that he was going directly to you. Who he is I do not know – your English friends tell me he is a Spanish nobleman. He has told me something of his acquaintance with you; moreover, in his admittedly very brief conversation with me, he shows himself to be a man of breeding and education.'[65] Their friendship lasted until Philip's death: he bequeathed to Wotton 'One fee buck, to be taken yearly out of my park at Penshurst, during his life natural.'[66]

Together with Wotton, Philip began 'to learn horsemanship of Jon Pietro Pugliano', an Italian equerry at Maximilian's court whose homespun philosophy Philip later immortalised in the opening lines of his *Defence of Poesie*:

> He said soldiers were the noblest estate of mankind, and horsemen the noblest of soldiers. He said they were the masters of war and ornaments of peace, speedy goers and strong abiders, triumphers both in camps and courts. Nay to so unbelieved a point he proceeded as that no earthly thing bred such wonder to a prince as to be a good horseman – skill of government was but a *pendanteria* in comparison. Then would he add certain praises, by telling what a peerless beast the horse was, the only serviceable courtier without flattery, the beast of most beauty, faithfulness, courage, and such more, that if I had not been a piece of a logician before I came to him, I think he would have persuaded me to have wished myself a horse.[67]

Pugliano's stress on horsemen as soldiers points us in the direction that his teaching took. By horsemanship Philip had more in mind than the basics of saddling, or the finer points of dainty dressage. Knowledge of horses was an essential basis for any budding military leader, who had to be able to identify which horse was suitable for any particular type of service, on the battlefield or off. For an Englishman like Philip, this sort of knowledge was especially crucial, because he knew that English horses were simply not of the required standard to give the best support for English soldiers in battle. His Strasburg friend Jean Sturm put it quite bluntly in a letter to Elizabeth. England provided more horses than any other nation, he claimed, but the horses were weak. Working in the contemporary belief that it was the stallion that determined the quality of the foal, Sturm proposed that he introduce a few stallions from Germany and Friesland, forming a stud, 'which would make the offspring of the English mare more robust' and would significantly reduce expenditure on mercenaries. But it was not just the horses that were needed. Sturm proposed inviting to England 'a few German saddlers and makers of greaves and shoes' and German tailors for making clothes and blacksmiths for making coats of mail. All this should be set up, urged Sturm, under a single person, 'such as the Earl of Oxford, the Earl of Leicester or Philip Sidney'. Sturm's proposal was written in 1584, but the ideas behind it were preoccupations for Philip a whole decade before: here in Vienna, he pumped Pugliano for everything he knew.[68] The effort evidently paid off: in 1584, Christopher Clifford dedicated a treatise on the subject to Philip, choosing his dedicatee because, he claimed, of Philip's 'great knowledge and experience in horsemanship'.[69]

Philip was still fixed on travel. After a delay caused by another quite serious illness, Philip set out during October for Cracow. This brief Cracow trip (which started after 21 October and ended before 12 November) is one of those infuriating moments in Philip's life when the surviving evidence signally fails to tell us what was going on. What was Philip doing in Cracow? It was a momentous period in Poland's history. The country was still reeling from the midnight flit of its king on 18 June. Two months later, at a meeting of the Sejm, Henri was given a deadline of 12 May 1575 by which he had to return to claim his crown, but in truth no one expected him to. Henri suggested that his younger brother François, Duc d'Alençon, might come as his viceroy, but the Poles were not interested. Rival contenders were already campaigning for the vacant throne; an early favourite had emerged in the person of the Habsburg Archduke Ernst, the emperor's preferred candidate.

Philip was introduced to Andreas Dudith, one-time bishop and friend of Languet, who was now Maximilian's ambassador in Poland. Since Dudith was representing Maximilian, whose preferred candidate was the front runner for the crown, Dudith had been thrust suddenly into the centre of Polish politics – where Philip too now found himself.[70] Languet's letter of recommendation deserves some consideration. Usually in such letters Languet gave a brief account of Philip's family, but emphasised his personal virtues and qualities. In his letter to Dudith, however, Languet bluntly laid out Philip's importance to the English crown:

His father is the Viceroy of Ireland, with whom, I am told, scarcely anyone among the nobility of England can compare in *virtus* and military experience.

His mother is a sister of the Earl of Warwick and of Robert, Earl of Leicester, the most favoured at Court: since neither has children, this gentleman will probably be their heir.

His father's sister is married to the Earl of Sussex, whom I think you have met here. His mother's sister is the wife of the Earl of Huntingdon, who is related to the royal family.

Neither nobleman has any sons: so that on this one person they have placed their hopes, and him they have decided to advance to honour after his return.[71]

Languet was certainly selling Philip quite vigorously, setting him up as a young man with massive future potential, but also with the kind of contacts that made him useful right now.

But none of this explains a rumour about Philip in Poland, which has persisted through the centuries. In 1634, Antony Stafford wrote of Philip as 'A man deserving both the laurels, and the [Polish] crown to boot, designed him by the voice of many brave spirits, who discovered in him all the requisites of a king but the title'. Seven years later, Sir Robert Naunton alleged that 'through the fame of his desert, he was in election for the kingdom of Pole', but that Elizabeth refused to let him have it. Only in 1931 did Mona Wilson point out that the story probably derived from a piece by Robert Dowe in the collection of tributes to Sidney from Oxford University, published in 1587. In his piece, Dowe does indeed speak of the possibility of Philip succeeding to the Polish crown — but succeeding Stephen Bathori, who died two months after Philip himself. Wilson speculates that perhaps Philip's friends thought it possible that Sidney might eventually succeed Bathori, but the suggestion seems to belong to 1586 rather than 1575.[72] Perhaps in time the Polish archives will tell us more: for the moment, Philip's visit to Cracow remains a mystery.

At the time, the combination of Philip's ill health and an unstable political situation gave cause for concern, and his friends were all relieved when he returned from Poland safe and sound: his friend in Venice, Wolfgang Zündelin, admitted:

> I was much afraid that, scarcely recovered from your sickness, you would, through such a sudden change of air, adversely affect your newfound health and that your long and laborious journey would hardly increase your still-feeble powers, but rather weaken and destroy them. I even feared . . . that, as is common, the lawlessness of this interregnum might threaten the safety of your travel, or that you might

by some mischance have got entangled in this Polish business which rumour here [Venice] has magnified here beyond the facts.[73]

Philip himself seems not to have been impressed with Poland. A surviving letter to Leicester merely reports some stale news: 'The Pollacks heartily repent their so far-fetched election, being now in such case [that] neither they have the king, nor anything the king with so many oaths had promised, besides that there is lately stirred up a very dangerous sedition, for the same cause that hath bred such lamentable ruins in France and Flanders. Now the trouble is reasonably well appeased, but it is thought it will remain so but a while.'[74] To Burghley he wrote: 'Being returned out of Italy and detained for some time with sickness in this city [Vienna], yet could I not command my desire of seeing Poland which time notwithstanding, I might perchance have employed in more profitable, at least more pleasant voyages, from thence being of late come hither, not in very good estate of body.'[75] Philip also wrote negatively of his Polish experiences to Lobbet, who commiserated: 'I gather you are not too happy with your journey to Poland. Repentance will prevent you from going there again. But it is good that you have seen it. Beautiful countries and people will henceforth seem more pleasant to you. Be that as it may, Monsieur Bochetel has refused to believe your words and wants to follow the Samaritan's example and see for himself. Let him go ahead, I do not envy him in the least.'[76]

After his Polish spree, Philip's thoughts turned towards England. By now he had already overrun his two-year licence, and cash was running low — indeed, as the winter progressed, he was reluctantly forced to borrow money from Languet. Since Languet planned to go to the Frankfurt Fair in March, it made financial sense for Philip to accompany him that far, after following the emperor's court to Prague for the meeting of the States of Bohemia.[77] So, on 7 February 1575, the two men set out for Prague, travelling via Brno, where they visited the headquarters of the Moravian Church at Evanaice.[78] Arriving on Tuesday 22 February, Philip spent nine days in Prague. The glory days of Rudolf II's court were still two years off, and Prague was not then the glamorous city it now is. But he witnessed the arrival of the Turkish ambassador, Mohammed, whom he was surprised to see 'received with much ceremony — almost royally so, in fact'. Mohammed's retinue was closer to Philip's expectations: 'he was accompanied by the foulest gang of his villainous compatriots that ever I saw: you would say they had been hung up for a few days, they looked so like withered, wooden snakes'.[79] Philip was also received by Maximilian himself: Languet recorded on 1 March that 'The Emperor received him [Philip] a few days ago, and showed him the greatest kindness.'[80] This was a great honour for the Englishman, still just twenty years old.

Languet was required to stay on, in the household of Maximilian's physician Thaddeus ab Hajek, so Philip set out from Prague on 3 March 1575 with a French companion named Thomas Lenormand, travelling first to Dresden, then on to Leipzig, Weimar and Eisenach. Languet paved the way with a final flurry of letters of recommendation, introducing Philip to (among others) Andreas Paull, who thanked Languet effusively for arranging this new friendship with 'your noble Sidney'.[81] In Frankfurt, Philip now had access to another Melanchthon disciple, Jean de Glaubourg;[82] Languet advised him to get to know the French church pastors there, Jean-François Salvard and Théophile de Banos (whom he already knew from Frankfurt). At Heidelberg, he was introduced to Count Ludwig von Wittengenstein[83] and to Ursinus; at Strasburg, Jean Lobbet was waiting;[84] at Basle, Eduoard Biset, a native of Troyes who had been 'controleur des guerres' under Henri II and was now in exile, and Charles de Harlay.[85] Ironically, only with his own employer, Augustus, was Languet unable to prevail in obtaining an audience for Philip.

There was a reason for Languet's overkill, as he revealed to Philip in his letter of 10 March. Two days after Philip's departure, Edward Wotton had arrived in Prague with a letter from Walsingham, by now Principal Secretary of State in England. It contained the news that Philip's intimacy with non-Protestants in Venice had led some in England to doubt his allegiances. Languet vowed to defuse the situation:

> I shall write to Master Walsingham about this, and if he has formed any such opinion I shall take pains to disabuse him of it. And I hope that my letter will carry enough weight with him that he not only will believe that what I say about you is true, but will also attempt to convince others of this. Meanwhile I advise you to get to know the learned and wise French preachers where you are, to offer them

invitations, and to attend their sermons, and to do the same at Heidelberg and Strasburg. Yet don't worry about it; for I am certain that you do not doubt my affection and are aware that persons of high position take care to avoid not only guilt but the suspicion of guilt.[86]

This highly pragmatic line, stressing the importance of public image, is echoed elsewhere in Languet's correspondence of this period. It was advice he could never quite bring himself to swallow. Three days later, he remarked bitterly that 'Not only those who aspire to command must learn to dissemble, but similarly those who wish to serve princes so that they may benefit adequately from their efforts. This,' he concluded morosely, 'I have not as yet learned to do.'[87]

On 20 March 1575, Languet finally received permission from Augustus to go to Frankfurt and set out immediately, arriving at the Fair on 3 April.[88] As it turned out, by the time Languet met up with Philip at André Wechel's house, plans had changed. An 'English secretary' had arrived in Frankfurt with strict instructions to bring Philip back to England 'with the greatest possible speed, indeed without even going through France'.[89] The 'English secretary' was Thomas Wilkes, clerk to the Privy Council; his instructions used Philip as a conveniently placed cover for another mission:

As the Queen would have this matter as secretly used as may be, she would have the occasion of his journey known to be as for the meeting with Philip Sidney; yet when he shall come to the Count Palatine he shall require him to let it be understood that his coming is about a certain horrid damnable book lately made in Germany, entitled against Moses, Christ, and Mahomet, and to require that the same may be condemned and punished as so unspeakable and devilish attempt may be vanquished and suppressed.[90]

Plans were hurriedly revised. Philip rode to Heidelberg to meet up with Wilkes, and Lobbet sent Johannes Hájek, a young man (son of Languet's Prague host) whom Philip had promised to educate in England, 'gently on foot' to join him there.[91] From Antwerp, Philip wrote to the Count of Hanau, apologising that he had not visited him as he had promised: 'I was compelled to travel with such haste, by the command of the Queen and my family, that not only could I by no means perform this particular duty that I owe you, but I could not even allow for the illness with which I was severely afflicted.'[92] The mention of his family's wishes is interesting, since Languet was informed that this was all the queen's doing – could it be that Leicester or Sir Henry Sidney suggested Philip's recall?

Languet's counsel did not end at the English Channel. 'When you get to England,' he wrote, 'make sure you cultivate Cecil [Lord Treasurer Burghley] who is fond of you, and will make everything easier for you.' His advice was almost shockingly cold-blooded. 'Nothing will enable you to win his favour more than befriending his children, or at least pretending to do so. But remember that a cunning old man, long experienced in affairs, quickly detects the pretences of a young man. It will also do you honour to work on the friendship of Master Walsingham . . . Men usually have an excellent opinion of youths whom they notice seeking the company of wise men.'

Philip would need this sort of advice, wrote Languet, because he re-entered English court life at a distinct disadvantage compared to his contemporaries. 'I tell you these things as you are about to begin life at court, a kind of life in which you will come up against greater problems than your contemporaries who have already entered into their patrimonies. In other words, it is not seemly for you to indulge in a life of ease while you are still a son and heir. To put it bluntly,' he concluded, 'one who wishes to live free of scorn in the courts of powerful kings must discipline his emotions, swallow many vexations, scrupulously avoid all motives of controversy, and cultivate those men in whose hands supreme power lies. But I shall not go on, since you grasp all those things better than I.'[93]

On 4 May 1575, after almost three years on the Continent, Philip Sidney set sail from Antwerp.[94] The fruits of Languet's education could now be tested on home soil.

CHAPTER SIX

Born for Command

THE BARON DE Sidenay sailed from Antwerp, but it was Master Philip Sidney, still only twenty years old, who landed in England in May 1575. Over the following months, Philip was constantly reminded of the gulf between his European persona and the realities of his life in England. For a start, there was that embarrassing French title. Elizabeth was understandably sensitive about foreign powers doling out titles to her subjects, and it was a lot simpler to keep quiet about it. Philip pleaded with his European friends not to use the title on their correspondence: Jean Lobbet, confused, had to ask Philip in May 1575 to 'put on a piece of paper for me the title by which I should address you'.[1] He was still asking in November of that year: 'There is something I should like to ask you: whether you approve of the way I address my letters to you, or whether it should be different. I usually send them "to the house of the noble lord the Earl of Leicester". I shall await your verdict as to whether this is all right.'[2]

Other friends, with their own agendas, were less easily persuaded. When Théophile de Banos completed his life of Philip's murdered Parisian friend Petrus Ramus, he attached it to his edition of Ramus' *Commentaries*, printed by André Wechel, and announced his intention of dedicating the whole book to Philip. This was glory on a grand scale, academically prestigious and widely disseminated, but Philip's anxieties about the use of his French title were exacerbated by the thought of seeing it in print. In July 1575, he wrote to de Banos and Wechel asking them to 'leave out many praises of [my] nobility'. De Banos tried to dispel Philip's fears. 'I have seen a letter which Master Wechel received from you in which you ask him to tell me not to give you any title of honour in my dedicatory epistle to you. As that is how you wish it I shall do it: I hope, however, that you will not take it amiss if I mention in passing such things as I could not honestly pass over in silence.'[3]

Despite this assurance, when his complimentary copy of the book finally reached London in late February 1576, Philip panicked at the sight of the dedication and wrote to de Banos, urgently asking him to change it. De Banos was not impressed: 'It is impossible to do a complete job,' he pointed out, 'as two thousand copies of the *Commentaries* have already been printed.' Ultimately, however, the financial implications of reprinting were clearly outweighed by his desire to have Philip's name endorsing the book: 'Wechel and I will see to it that, at my expense, your wish may, if possible, be fulfilled at least in the other copies.' De Banos consulted Languet, who told him that 'nothing more modest could be said than to mention that noble gentleman, Philip Sidney, as belonging to the illustrious family of the earls of Warwick'. 'Had I known earlier,' wrote de Banos to Philip, 'that you would have preferred the English style about which you wrote, I would have used that title – than which nothing could be more fitted to your fame, and clear and splendid to the praise of your family's virtue.'[4]

De Banos sent Philip a copy of the corrected dedication from the Frankfurt Fair in April, from which 'you will gather that your wish has been completely fulfilled'. The volume was a great success, he reported. 'The *Commentaries* of Petrus Ramus, now in print and dedicated to you, is being bought by everyone at the present Fair, and especially by Germans – a better omen than I had hoped. We are sending a few copies to England which, because of your patronage, I have no doubt will be gladly received by the English who hold your virtue and piety in such esteem.' Even so, de Banos remained out of tune with the intricate niceties of English titles, continuing to address his letters to 'Monseigneur Philippe Comte de Sidné en Angleterre, à Londres.'[5]

All the surviving copies of the 1576 printing (there were to be two more, in 1577 and 1583) are dedicated 'To the illustrious and noble master, Master Philip Sidney, son of the pro-rex of Ireland, nephew of the earls of Warwick and Leicester'.[6] What then was the original, suppressed dedication? I would suggest that since de Banos refers to Philip preferring 'the English style', it follows that he had originally provided something non-English, presumably a reference to Philip's French barony. It seems a small matter, the form of address used in a dedication from an editor to a friend, in an edition of a late minor work by a dead scholar. But Philip must have realised the power of print not only to praise, but to damn. His French title, immortalised in printed books with their capacity for long-distance travel, could now come to haunt him in England. This explains his insistence on the long and costly process of reprinting. The affair also highlights just how important Philip was considered to be by the likes of de Banos and Wechel: they evidently believed that the simple fact of Philip's public endorsement would open up the English market to them.

Returning to England, as Languet had warned, meant returning to the realities of life as an heir. While being son of the Lord President of Wales and nephew to the Earls of Leicester and Warwick opened doors on the Continent, on home soil Philip remained just that: a son and a nephew, required to wait on his family members, while they took centre-stage. When he arrived back, he found his family in a flurry of preparations for new duties, which required them to uproot yet again. Against his better instincts, Sir Henry was busy preparing himself to return to Ireland. Although nominally back in control at Ludlow during the early 1570s, he had often been at court, advising on all matters Irish. The policies of his successor, Walter Devereux, Earl of Essex, had been disastrous and had only strengthened the resistance to English rule in Ireland. Essex was not helped by his deputy, Sir Henry's brother-in-law Fitzwilliam, who disputed his orders constantly; but the two men were allied in their condemnation of the queen and Privy Council, who refused to take positive measures to support them. Essex fell back on extreme means to maintain his position, putting to the sword the O'Neills in 1574 and ordering the Rathlin massacres in 1575. With Fitzwilliam demanding to be recalled, Elizabeth eventually turned to her tried-and-tested (if not utterly trusted) Sir Henry Sidney and asked him to serve another turn as Lord Deputy. Sir Henry, knowing the problems of Ireland to be insoluble, put up a series of demands, including a seat at the Privy Council, which he assumed would scupper his chances of being reappointed: Elizabeth, realising that she needed his expertise, for once met them.

All this was being worked out as Philip arrived home (when Walsingham wrote to Sir Henry on 15 May, he assumed that the matter was settled). As it turned out, Sir Henry would not be sworn on to the Privy Council until 31 July, and only received his letters patent appointing him Lord Deputy of Ireland on 2 August.[7] In the meantime, he remained at court, which, at this time of year, meant attending the queen on her summer progress. Elizabeth's court usually moved between a number of royal palaces, all within reasonable reach of London – Whitehall, Greenwich, Richmond, Windsor, Hampton Court and Oatlands.

During the summer, however, until the late 1570s, the queen showed herself to her people – or to a select fraction of her people, since she never travelled to the south-west or further north than Stafford – reinforcing her popular image. As the Spanish ambassador marvelled in 1568, 'She was received everywhere with great acclamations and signs of joy as is customary in this country whereat she was exceedingly pleased.'[8]

It was a massive undertaking. With the queen rode her Privy Council, which could number twenty officers, plus a huge retinue; behind them some 200–300 carts carried everything they could possibly require. Her chosen hosts were expected not simply to put out the best pewter, but to clear their house so that she could move in, even if it were only overnight. The honour of greeting the queen was expensive not only for the hosts, but for the local towns and villages who were required to provide proper gifts, sell supplies at rates determined by the court, lodge the overflow from the main house and clear up the mess afterwards.

Philip spent June in London, replenishing his worn wardrobe with something more suitable for a courtly progress, and in the process running up a bill of 'the sum of forty-two pounds six shillings of lawful money of England' to a London merchant tailor named Richard Rodway.[9] It was money he could ill afford. The Sidney family fortunes were not good. Sir Henry's finances were dangerously stretched from his periods of service in Ireland, and from fifteen years of ruling Wales. Maintaining a second Sidney residence in England and rooms in court during her husband's long absences often found Lady Sidney in dire financial straits. Her money problems were not eased by the fact that the Lord Chamberlain, who controlled the limited, highly prized and hotly contested accommodation at court, was the Earl of Sussex – her own brother-in-law, admittedly, but also the violent opponent of her brother Leicester. Sussex seems (if we believe her complaints) to have delighted in humiliating Lady Sidney.

Lady Sidney's correspondence makes truly pathetic reading. Dogged by poor health like her eldest son – she berates 'my unrecovered, unhealthful carcass'[10] – she sometimes claimed to be too weak to handwrite the personalised pleas for assistance that her situation demanded. In an important letter to Burghley requesting a lease of lands belonging to a ward he controlled, she could manage only the signature and postscript: 'I beseech your lordship pardon me I write no larger [at greater length] nor with my own hand for I am so very sick as I cannot endure to write.'[11] On one occasion, she petitioned Sussex for 'three or four linen pieces of hanging' because she had been summoned to court by the queen, 'and my chamber is very cold, and my own hangings very scant and nothing warm: myself rather a little recovered of great extremity of sickness than that I can either boast of hope of perfect health or dare adventure to lie in so cold a lodging without some further health'. It did not help her cause, however, that she had neglected to return loans of such 'wardrobe stuff' before (she blamed a wayward servant for not returning the material).[12]

Blocked by Sussex, Lady Sidney increasingly found herself lodged at court in unfamiliar, and insultingly downmarket, rooms. She complained to Sussex that the chamber she had been allotted had previously been 'but the place for my servants'. It was not fit, due to 'the coldness and wideness of it for one of my weakness and sickliness', and its design meant that she was forced to go 'through the open cloister' to reach the queen, as she was often required to do. Indeed, she continued, warming to her theme, it was precisely for those reasons that her brother, the Earl of Leicester, had allowed her five years previously to have two chambers, but now one – the better one – had been taken from her.[13]

By 1572, the Sidneys' financial difficulties had reached the point where Lady Sidney had very nimbly to turn down the honour of a barony for her husband, on the grounds they could not afford the expenses 'to maintain it withal'. To Lord Treasurer Burghley she lamented that Sir Henry was 'dismayed' with the 'hard choice' he had to make – either to shoulder the financial burden or 'else in refusing it to incur her Highness' displeasure. Titles of greater calling,' she pointed out, 'cannot be well wielded but with some amendment at the prince's hand of a ruinated start or else to his discredit greatly that must take them upon him.' Lady Sidney begged the Lord Treasurer 'as a poor perplexed woman' that 'the motion be no further offered unto him, for certes [indeed] right noble and justly renowned, most virtuous lord, if it were known unto you the strife and war between his loyal & dutiful mind to obey her Majesty's pleasure in each matter her Highness can fancy to lay upon him, and his own judgement and wants otherwise to hold the credit and countenance the same [i.e. the title] shall require.'[14] In August 1573, she was forced to beg her own servant John Cockeram to provide her ten pounds to cover expenses incurred since Sir Henry had last departed – mainly hats, gloves, medical bills and the furthering of clients' suits at court: 'under ten pounds at this present will not serve my turn . . . send it this night though you strain your uttermost credit'.[15]

This financial crisis rather tempered the glory of being required to attend on the queen. But to Philip's continental admirers, it was all grist to the mill. Joachim Möller in Prague wrote that he was delighted 'to hear that you, born to a great place, have acquired a place worthy of your great virtues with the most serene Queen of England. I pray with all my heart that you may adorn this station to the glory of God and the benefit of the Christian Commonwealth.'[16] Philip probably had less lofty ambitions for his presence on the progress, but nevertheless it was a crucial summer for the Sidneys, since the queen had chosen as the high point of her tour Leicester's estate of Kenilworth (which she had visited only briefly twice before), and Leicester was able to some extent to manipulate events to present himself and his close kin in the best light – Philip, therefore, was presumably lodged at Kenilworth, as his mother was.

The Sidney contingent at court had recently been joined by Philip's fifteen-year-old sister Mary, who was only three years old when her eldest brother left for Shrewsbury.[17] By one of those bitter twists of fate on which the Sidneys' fortunes were founded, Mary owed her place at court to the death of her sister Ambrosia, who had died on 22 February 1575 at Ludlow Castle, aged just nine. Despite his financial problems, Sir Henry ensured that an expensive and impressive monument in Ludlow's Collegiate Parish Church commemorated her life. On hearing of Ambrosia's death, the queen wrote to her Lord President, commiserating on his loss and assuring him that:

God doth nothing evil . . . He hath yet left unto you the comfort of one daughter of very good hope, whom, if you shall think good to remove from those parts of unpleasant air (if it be so) into better in these parts, and will send her unto us before Easter, or when you shall think good, assure yourself that we will have a special care of her, not doubting but as you are well persuaded of our favour toward yourself, so will we make further demonstration thereof in her, if you will send her unto us. And so comforting you for the one, and leaving this our offer of our good will to your own consideration for the other, we commit you to Almighty God.[18]

And so, as Philip joined the queen, his sister commenced her own royal attendance.

Leicester was on tenterhooks as his moment of glory approached. There had been a major crisis at Grafton, the stopping point before Kenilworth, in late June. The queen had arrived on a scorchingly hot day, only to discover that there was 'not one drop of good drink for her', Leicester reported to Burghley. The ale on site was so 'strong, as there was no man able to drink it – you had been as good to have drank malmsey [a strong sweet wine]', he continued. Evidently, however, Elizabeth did manage to down some of this undrinkable potion, because 'it did put her very far out of temper, and almost all the company beside too; for none of us all was able to drink beer or ale here. Since, by chance, we have found drink for her, to her liking; and she is well again, but I feared greatly two or three days some sickness to have fallen, by reason of this drink.' Leicester just hoped that at his house 'I pray God she may like all things no worse than she hath done here.'[19]

Leicester left nothing to chance. The entire stay would be punctuated by entertainments, penned and performed by the multitudes of scholars, poets, musicians and players under his patronage. Later, these were recorded and disseminated. Poet and author George Gascoigne published an account of the festivities, aimed at forwarding his own literary career; another report, credited on the titlepage to Leicester's protégé Robert Laneham, is now believed by some scholars to be an attack on Laneham and Leicester: although it records the events faithfully enough, the tone has been read as dripping with satire. From the two we can glean a good idea of what went on.[20]

The queen's entrance into Kenilworth on Saturday 9 July set the tone for what was to follow. When Elizabeth rode into the tiltyard in front of Mortimer's Tower, at around eight in the evening, she was greeted by the first of the allegorical performances that were to punctuate her visit. A white silk-draped sibyl emerged from an arbour to deliver a speech. In the tiltyard itself, six trumpeters, eight feet high and dressed in Arthurian costume, provided a fanfare on 'huge and monstrous trumpets'. She was stopped by a giant porter representing Hercules, who delivered his club and key to the queen only after she had heard his speech. Then, on the lower lake, three nymphs came into view on a torchlit island (in reality a raft). One, a 'Lady of the Lake', again in Arthurian garb, delivered a speech that ended with the lines 'Pass on, Madam, you need no longer stand;/The Lake, the Lodge, the Lord, are yours for to command.' Elizabeth affected hauteur that this needed to be said at all. 'We had thought indeed the Lake had been ours, and do you call it yours now? Well, we will herein common [commune] more with you hereafter.' Then, to the sound of 'loud music', the queen and her attendants rode across a seventy-foot bridge, each ten-foot section lined with gifts symbolising seven classical deities. Scholar and pedagogue Richard Mulcaster, dressed in a crimson silk doublet covered by a long blue garment, read nine lines of Latin verse. Finally, the queen was allowed to proceed into Kenilworth's inner court, where she dismounted to the sound of 'drums, fifes, and trumpets' and entered her lodgings. Even then, cannon and fireworks proclaimed the royal presence – 'the noise and flame were heard and seen a twenty mile off'.

And so it went on. At Kenilworth, it was calculated, 'in little more than a three days' space, 72 ton of ale and beer was piped up quite . . . in devout drinking alway'. Losing themselves in this 'devotion', the guests soon drank the estate dry. With good country hospitality, Leicester's neighbours managed to raise more supplies from friends – 'a relief of a forty ton' – and the guests fell 'to our drinking afresh as fast as ever we did'. Leicester had learned the lessons of the Grafton alcohol crisis well. The revellers were treated to music and dancing, fireworks and cannon, bearbaiting, audiences with local dignitaries and nobility, the conferring of the occasional knighthood. Highlights included an Italian gymnastic dancer whose spine, according to one observer, must have been like that of 'a lamprey, that has no bone, but a line like a lute string'; an historical pageant performed 'by certain good-hearted men of Coventry', depicting the English defeat of the Danes; and a speech by George Gascoigne, eager to promote himself, disguised as an 'hombre salvagio, with an oaken plant plucked up by the roots in his hand', dressed 'all in moss and ivy'. Most popular of all was 'rustic' day, the Sunday after the queen's arrival: a country-style wedding in the tiltyard followed by a morris dance, and then a quintain, the rural version of courtly tilting, in which country lads on horseback hit a target on a pivoted crossbar then had to gallop past to avoid the bag of sand swinging at the other end. 'Twas a lively pastime; I believe it would have moved some man to a right merry mood, though had it be told him his wife lay a-dying,' wrote one witness.

Philip does not appear in these published accounts, which suggests that he had a relatively low profile on the progress, but presumably he observed carefully from the sidelines. This sometimes clumsy display of provincial loyalty to the Crown was hardly the elaborate allegorical display he remembered from the Valois-Navarre wedding celebrations: the impact of many of these carefully wrought entertainments was frequently diminished – by poor acoustics, the vagaries of the English weather, and queenly whim, which was capable of cancelling a meticulously planned performance at a moment's notice. None the less, he may have seen in it some intriguing possibilities. It gave Leicester as patron a chance to commission writers to convey messages simul-taneously to his primary audience, namely the queen, an immediate audience of spectators at Kenilworth and finally, via print, to a wider reading audience. Through the use of allegory, an idea could be made clear enough to ensure that the message got through to those who wanted to read the signs, while remaining ambiguous enough to ensure that Leicester could not be personally blamed if that message turned out to be not to the queen's liking.

Philip may well have shared his impressions of the revels with a new friend, Edward Dyer.[21] The son and heir of a Somerset gentleman, Dyer was eleven years Philip's senior, and already a familiar face at Sidney family gatherings. He had been a follower of Leicester since the mid-1560s, and during Philip's absence had impressed Lady Sidney to the extent that she advised her husband's secretary Edmund Molyneux (no doubt to his great annoyance): 'In all your proceedings in my lord's causes, take the wise, noble Mr Dyer's friendly counsel, who I know doth dearly tender my lord's honour, and well doing, as much as a faithful friend may do.'[22]

The friendship between Philip and Edward Dyer became widely known and celebrated even beyond court circles. The lawyer and writer Abraham Fraunce dedicated his manuscript volume *Shepheardes logike* to Dyer, and an accompanying appendix comparing Aristotle and Ramus to Philip. Even Philip's Viennese friend, Charles de l'Écluse, knew of their friendship and dedicated his Latin translation of a Spanish herbal by

Nicolas Monardes to them jointly in 1581: 'for I unite you readily, knowing that you are joined by a note of true, indissoluble friendship'.[23] Dyer has been identified as 'Coredens' in Philip's 'Ister bank' poem that immortalised Hubert Languet: it was 'To worthy Coredens', according to Philisides, that Languet 'gave me o'er'. That line might suggest that Philip self-consciously moved from the concerns dictated by Languet's circle to a new set of issues with Dyer. At the very least, Dyer certainly seems to have become Philip's closest English friend from this point, along with schoolfellow Fulke Greville.

It is in his friendship with Dyer that we find our first concrete evidence of Philip's poetic endeavours. Many young gentlemen at court, the universities or the Inns of Court wrote poetry. This verse was circulated within élite coteries, and restricted to manuscript; print, it was felt, was not an appropriate forum for gentlemen's work – at least not until they were dead, like Sir Thomas Wyatt or Henry Howard, Earl of Surrey. It was only men of the middling classes, such as George Gascoigne, who were beginning to see the commercial possibilities of publishing their verse in print – although their objective was more likely to be patronage than cash revenue from sales of their work.

Philip and Dyer became popularly celebrated as the foremost arbiters of taste in courtly poetic wit and artistry. In 1581, Thomas Watson hoped that his *Ekatompathia* might be worthy of a place in the book chests of Philip Sidney and Edward Dyer, since it was they who determined what constituted literary excellence at court.[24] It was also known they were involved in poetic experimentation. Gabriel Harvey noted in 1580 that 'those two excellent gentlemen Master Sidney and Master Dyer, the two very diamonds of Her Majesty's Court for many special and rare qualities' were involved in 'help[ing] forward our new famous enterprise for the exchanging of barbarous and balductum rhymes with artificial verses [verses made with art], the one being in manner of pure and fine gold, the other but counterfeit and base ill-favoured copper'.[25] Harvey is here referring to the attempt, which he supported, to find new forms of English poetry that might correspond to classical metre. Sadly, however, the surviving poems attributed to Dyer display no such inventiveness – indeed, even for the 1570s they are somewhat old-fashioned, employing tried-and-tested English metrical forms. Nevertheless, Philip always talked up his friend's skill: when Geoffrey Whitney wrote a poem hailing

Sidney as the successor of the Earl of Surrey in pushing forward English poetry, Philip insisted that his praises should be directed at Dyer instead.[26]

Whatever their poetic interests, however, recreational activities always had to fit around the primary duty of courtiers like Philip Sidney and Edward Dyer: to attend their sovereign in whatever she decided to do. Elaborate though the spectacles were, the real business of the day on a royal progress was hunting, for which the queen possessed a passion. The accounts of Leicester's gamekeeper record that Elizabeth herself killed six deer during her stay. Wednesday's hart tried to escape into the lake, for which initiative the queen commanded that his life be spared, although 'he lost his ears for a ransom' (despite such regal generosity, the hart bled to death from the wounds anyway). In total, ninety-nine deer were dead by the end of the summer; both 'My Lady Sidney' and 'Mr Philip Sidney' bagged one each at Redfern Park, a mile north of Kenilworth.[27] It was probably not through poetry, but while hunting (if at all), that Philip Sidney, as a young, personable horseman, would have a chance to impress the queen favourably.

After several days' delay due to adverse weather, Elizabeth finally left Kenilworth on Wednesday 27 July, heading north for Lichfield. The progress made its slow way to Chartley Park, in the Trent Valley, on to Stafford Castle, then south to Chillington Hall, and finally to Dudley Castle, just north of the town of Dudley. It was here that Sir Henry took his leave of the queen, to return to Ireland.[28] Philip also left court temporarily, to accompany his father on his journey west via his old school town of Shrewsbury, where they were warmly received: the town corporation accounts record that there was 'Spent and given to Mr Philip Sidney at his coming to this town with my Lord President his father, in wine and cakes and other things, 7s. 2d.'[29] Knowing what he was taking on, Sir Henry seems to have regarded his third tour of duty as Lord Deputy of Ireland with apprehension. On 20 August he made a new will, with Philip acting as a witness alongside the Northamptonshire gentleman Sir Edward Montagu (one of Sir Henry's close friends, who named his seventh son Sidney in honour of the family),[30] and William Blunt, who handled his finances.[31]

Either at Shrewsbury, or possibly on the Welsh coast, Philip left his father and hurried back to the progress, which had now reached

6. Sir Henry Sidney is welcomed into Dublin.

Woodstock. There he was joined by his brother Robert, now eleven years old and beginning to tread much the same path as Philip before him, although Sir Henry had decided against sending him to Shrewsbury (their younger brother Thomas would be taught there). Robert had however followed his elder brother to Oxford, matriculating at Christ Church in May 1574 (there is an entry in the Penshurst account books for 'a great paper book and Tully's Offices [Cicero's *De officiis*]' purchased for Robert in 1575).[32] At college, he was attended by Edward Montagu (another son of Sir Henry's executor) and two servants, Rowland Whyte and Philip's European companion Griffin Madox, who travelled with him now to Woodstock. From this point on, Philip took a quasi-paternal interest in Robert's education, providing him with encouraging letters and suggestions for reading, and corresponding regularly with Robert's tutor Robert Dorsett about the education of Robert, Montagu and a further charge, the Czech Johannes Hajek, whom Philip had brought home with him from Europe.[33]

Woodstock provided its own share of entertainments, co-ordinated by the estate's owner, Sir Henry Lee, but there was one in particular that caught Philip's attention – an extended elaborate entertainment, which combined the usual spectacle with a more considered story. A fight between two knights, Contarenus and Loricus, was interrupted by a Hermit named Hermetes, who turned to the queen and told her a tale.

He described the country of Cambaya, at the mouth of the River Indus, in which a mighty duke named Occanon held sway. His sole heir was a daughter named Gaudina, 'more fair than fortunate', popular and beloved. Although Gaudina's hand was sought by many worthy admirers, Love caught her affection with a knight named Contarenus, 'of estate but mean but of value very great', who loved her in return. Soon, 'the smoke of their desires' betrayed them to her father. As Duke Occanon tried various stratagems to prevent Gaudina from marrying the 'mean' Contarenus, the story progressed through various standard romance devices – a grotto, a sibyl, a confusing prophecy. The following day, Gaudina (egged on by a Faery Queen) gave up Contarenus for reasons of state. This moment moved its royal audience, 'in such sort that her Grace's passion . . . could not but show itself in open place more than ever hath been seen'.[34]

The Tale of Hemetes was the hit of the season, and for several reasons. It combined the chivalry of pageantry and tilting with a romance story in the Greek manner – like those of Heliodorus which had just become available in an English translation.[35] This in itself was novel enough, but many in the audience felt that the story must be hinting at something closer to home. Sir Henry Lee had been associated with Leicester since at least 1566; the entertainment he commissioned, for those who wanted to see it, appeared to show a royal woman loving a noble-spirited but 'mean' knight, who loved her in return; and showed that she must give him up, for 'reasons of state'. It clearly demanded serious interpretation and even Elizabeth clamoured to possess a copy of the text so that she might consider it more closely at her leisure. George Gascoigne, who had seen some of his best work cancelled at Kenilworth, saw his big chance here and presented the queen with a manuscript copy of the Tale the following Christmas, complete with his own translations into Latin, Italian and French.[36]

The entertainment featured Philip's sister and new friend in minor roles. At the end of the first day, the Hermit escorted the queen and her retinue to a 'banqueting house', an edifice of turf and greenery, specially constructed under a great oak, liberally laced with ivy, flowers and 'spangles of gold plate'. The oak's branches were hung with emblems and poesies. The young Mary Sidney was among those ladies who were given one of 'many excellent and fine smelling nosegays made of all colours to every one whereof was annexed a post of two verses, given by a handmaid of the Faery Queen.' Mary's read:

> Though young in years yet old in wit, a gest due to your race,
> If you hold on as you begin who is't you'll not deface?

Even the couplets' simplicity seemed to imply there must be something deeper here: the French ambassador (among others) went to considerable lengths to try to decode them, in case he were missing out on crucial political truths. After Mary had been presented with her verse nosegay, Edward Dyer's voice called out to the queen from the inside of a tree with a piteous plaint of 'Despair'. His was meant to be the moan of a neglected courtier, and by January 1576 the queen had heard his call, bestowing on him a 'licence to pardon and dispense with tanning of leather', a profitable monopoly.

Although he played no part in these theatrical endeavours, Philip's summer with the queen did produce one tangible benefit: by the end of the progress, Philip had been made royal cupbearer. A signed receipt dated 10 May 1576, now in the Folger Shakespeare Library in Washington, DC, records a payment for £16 13s. 4d. for Philip's service in the post, covering one half-year ending at the Feast of the Annuciation – that is to say, 25 March 1576, suggesting that Philip was in post by September 1575. But this appointment was not as grand as it appears. First, it was something of a family affair: Henry Sidney had been appointed cupbearer to his beloved Edward VI in 1550, and soon afterwards was promoted to royal cupbearer. Second, it was poorly paid: Henry had received a stipend of fifty marks per annum (one mark equalled thirteen shillings and fourpence), and Philip's fee was scarcely more, over twenty years later. Rather than being an honour bestowed for anything outstanding Philip might be seen to have done, it seems more likely that this was a favour granted to Sir Henry at a time when the queen needed his help, perhaps as part of the deal to persuade him back to Ireland.[37]

In addition to establishing himself within the English court, Philip was also looking north. Across the Scottish border, the young king James VI was under anxious scrutiny from Protestants across Europe. Although his mother Mary, Queen of Scots was an ardent Catholic, James' education had since 1570 been in the hands of George Buchanan, an esteemed Protestant scholar. Buchanan was a friend of several of Languet's circle, including Daniel Rogers and Thomas Randolph, although Philip did not initiate a correspondence with him until 1579.[38] In the course of the 1575 progress, however, Philip did make the useful acquaintance of a young Scot named Sir John Seton, who was later to become Lord Barns, a Master of the Stable to James VI, a member of his Privy Council and an Extraordinary Lord of Session. Seton wrote from Scotland in early September to inform Philip that:

> I have presented your respects to our king, and I have conveyed to his Majesty the great desire you have to be of service to him and to kiss his hand. This, I assure you, was very well received, and his Majesty thanked you several times. I can assure you, sir, that if you intend to travel here to see his Majesty, and let me know, I shall come and meet you halfway: for this, I think, would be the very least I should do, considering the great favour you and yours have shown me.[39]

The contact with Seton shows Philip striking out on his own, beyond the carefully filtered networks supplied by his father, uncle, Walsingham and Languet. It reveals a newly acquired confidence, which he would soon display more publicly.

After he returned to London in September 1575 at the end of the progress, the only record of Philip's activities comes on 27 October, when he stood as godparent alongside Leicester, the Countess of Sussex (Sir Henry's sister Frances) and the Countess of Warwick (Leicester's sister-in-law), who was deputising for the queen, when Lady Russell's daughter Elizabeth was baptised at Westminster Abbey – very much a family affair.[40]

His return to London also led to the writing of a few long-overdue letters to continental correspondents. From London in June, before he set out on the progress, Philip had written to tell Languet that he had 'got over the usual dangers of a journey' and was 'very nearly restored to health'. But Languet had rightly predicted that Philip would lead 'a very different sort of life', and feared the change of priorities. 'I know that the court is no thrifty steward of time. I know that you will have to make yourself available to friends and relatives, who wish to enjoy your delightful company, and that you will be required to wait upon those whom it behoves young men to wait upon because of their age and rank.'[41] Languet had only one request:

> I know that it may seem absurd to ask that, surrounded by the court's bustle and so many temptations to waste time, you do not utterly neglect to practise your Latin. Because your letter demonstrates how much progress in this you have made and your proficiency in writing whenever you wish to apply your mind to it, should you drop your interest in Latin style I shall hardly be able to restrain myself from accusing you of laziness and moral weakness.[42]

Of course Languet had an ulterior motive: he intended Philip to practise his Latin by writing letters to him and his friends, maintaining their vital link with Philip in England and providing a source of intelligence right at the heart of English political life.

During the summer months Philip continued to be bombarded with letters from his continental contacts: Languet, of course, but also Wolfgang Zündelin in Venice, Théophile de Banos in Antwerp and Frankfurt, Jean Lobbet in Strasburg, and Joachim Möller in Prague.[43] Their loyalty was not rewarded: Lobbet complained that Philip did not reply to him until 28 October.[44] There was no practical reason for this: the progress contained within it Elizabeth's Privy Council, the central body for intelligence-gathering and policy-making, and its system of letter bearers to any number of locations would have been available to forward Philip's correspondence. Instead Philip seemed wilfully to cut himself off from Europe, concentrating instead on consolidating his position at the English court.

He could hardly have been surprised, then, when on 17 March 1576, Languet wrote to him in a tone that for once held no possibility of irony:

> I would write you more often if I did not assume from your ongoing silence that either our letters do not please you or that you pay them little attention. We appreciate that our friendship is of no profit to you. Yet it's not like your courteous manners so soon to forget those people who – or so your earlier demeanour suggested – do not displease you,

who love you dearly and think very highly of you. And don't imagine
that I am only speaking here on my own behalf: there are other men
whose friendship you earned here in Germany with your virtuous
qualities and courteous manners who feel exactly as I do. In their letters
to me, they lament that you have unexpectedly spurned their friendship,
which they had hoped and believed would be lasting.[45]

It was an uncharacteristically harsh tone for Languet to adopt, but it
conveyed the betrayal he felt when the young man in whom he had
invested so much time and effort, and on whom he had pledged his credit
(both financial and social), failed to deliver. The letter was enough to
sting Philip into action: 'What can you be thinking of,' he replied, 'to
torment the friend who loves you more than he loves himself? Has your
heart hardened so suddenly, my friend?' He passionately denied the
charges of 'deceit and ingratitude', and claimed that he had written on
1 February (and in a postscript revealed that letters written in January had
been intercepted by the Dutch, and only just returned). Pledging his love,
he begged Languet not to stop writing. 'You may do anything else so
long as you agree to write: claim that I am lazy, idle, even stupid, if you
wish; but don't say a word to doubt my love for you! – unless you want
to stir up this hornet's nest again. You know that I am easily provoked;
in fact, I would have answered you in the high tragic style, if I could find
the words. For this I have my court life to thank – it has sent all my Latin
into exile.'[46]

By now, April 1576, Philip seems to have found himself bored with
parochial English life and eager to renew contact with his European
friends. 'We are doing nothing here,' he lamented to Languet. 'I long to
live in your part of the world again.' A physical reminder of political life
across the Channel had come in March, when his Venice friend Michael,
Baron Slavata arrived, wanting to visit England and Scotland.[47] Philip,
who had last met the baron in Padua, reported to Languet that 'We have
Baron Slavata here; I have done what I can to make him welcome, and I
could have shown him even greater kindness had he not been, as it
seemed, keen to keep away from the more crowded places.'[48] Part of
Philip's kindness was to lend the baron money, which he later spent
considerable effort attempting to recover.

Philip's longing to get back across the Channel was fuelled by the possibility of finally seeing some military action. France was on the brink of a civil war, between the king, Henri III, and his younger brother, François – the François who had previously been Duc d'Alençon, but had now succeeded to the title of Duc d'Anjou. Anjou's career since the St Bartholomew's Day Massacre had been a classic study in self-serving ruthlessness. In 1573, he had besieged the Huguenot stronghold of La Rochelle, but two years later he had joined the Huguenots, hoping to pressurise his brother Henri into augmenting his power. Now Anjou had pitched his army of Huguenots and mercenaries near the Loire, but rather than engage him in battle, Henri forced a truce. In the same letter as he told Languet of Slavata's visit, Philip announced to Languet that the new Anjou 'has very kindly invited me through Lenormand [the Frenchman with whom he had travelled back from Prague]. I very much hope I will be able to find the means to return to you, especially if war should be declared between your side and the Turks. I want to fight my first campaign in that kind of conflict, rather than in some civil war [i.e. the French war].'[49] But Philip's excitement slowly evaporated. For him to go to France would have required a licence from the queen. The plans came to nothing.

By now Philip had learned to hedge his bets, realising that he was best advised to pursue several plans simultaneously, on the assumption that most would never come to fruition. His next endeavour was inspired by his friend Edward Dyer. The pair had a mutual acquaintance in John Dee – whose *General and Rare Memorial* of August 1576 mentions Dyer as 'my worshipful friend' – and shared Dee's enthusiasm for finding the Northwest Passage.[50] In the spring of 1576, all the talk was of the glamorous rewards that would be reaped by the discoverers of such a route: Humphrey Gilbert's *A Discourse of a Discovery for a new Passage to Cataia* promised 'great abundance of gold, silver, precious stones, cloth of gold, silks, all manner of spices, grocery wares, and other kinds of merchandise of an inestimable price'.[51] Dee and Dyer fuelled Philip's interest to the extent that when Martin Frobisher set off on his voyage of discovery (from June to October 1576), Philip, Lady Sidney and his uncle and aunt the Warwicks all contributed twenty-five pounds alongside Dyer, whose brother Andrew served as mariner on the *Gabriel*.[52]

Philip's role in this New World adventure was, for the moment at least, one of excited onlooker and interested investor. But he would travel

— not to France with Anjou, nor with Frobisher to Greenland, but to his father's domain, Ireland. Once again, to his continental admirers, this seemed only proper, the natural working out of his dynastic rights. The Wittenberg-educated poet and diplomat Daniel Rogers captured the mood of that circle in a twenty-line Latin poem, 'On Philip Sidney, a most promising and talented young man':

> Now that you have roamed through the country of Italy, now that you have met the people of France and have with wandering steps explored the states of Bohemia after seeing the towns of Germany, was it Ireland that was left for you to inspect, that land beyond the western bays? I am inclined to think that Fate has moved you to travel towards such coasts, to the distant plains of Ireland.
>
> You will not come to find yourself a visitor in these regions, like most people who live as strangers in these parts, but rather to teach them whatever you may have learned in all the other places, and so to cultivate those barbarians. Thus, Philip, you will show yourself worthy of your father whom Ireland claims for its own father. Who knows whether fate will not leave you to rule this country, a viceroy to keep the viceroy (his father) company [*Proregem prorex ut comitere patrem*]? For the house of Sidney was destined for the land of Ireland, a house that is worthy indeed to prescribe the law to a state.
>
> Therefore, young man, prepare yourself for the rule of Ireland, for you are the son of a viceroy, and born for command.[53]

Ironically, despite Rogers' understandable interpretation of events, Philip's move was facilitated not by his father, but by Walter Devereux, Earl of Essex. In December 1575, Essex had arrived back in London to petition the Privy Council to better his lot, asking for compensation for the loss of his personal fortune in the Irish campaign — both in the form of grants of lands and the official appeasement of his creditors.[54] As negotiations dragged on, Essex formed a close attachment to Philip, with whom he was frequently seen at court. The earl's agent Edward Water-house reported to Sir Henry in March 1576 that Essex 'by adoption calleth [Philip] his [son].'[55] The friendship surprised many, who knew that relations between Essex and Sir Henry had been strained for some years — and with good reason. Essex, it was popularly rumoured, had been cuckolded by his wife Lettice with Leicester. In December 1575, the Spanish ambassador De Guaras reported home: 'As the thing is publicly talked about in the streets there is no objection to my writing openly about the great enmity which exists between the earl of Leicester and the earl of Essex, in consequence, it is said, of the fact that whilst Essex was in Ireland his wife had two children by Leicester. She is the daughter of Sir Francis Knollys, a near relative of the Queen, and a member of the Council, and great discord is expected in consequence.'[56]

Finally, after five months of haggling, Elizabeth signed a warrant on 9 May 1576, reappointing Essex as 'earl marshal of Ireland' and confirming a sizeable grant of Irish territories. Essex then sold off some £35,000 worth of his lands in England in preparation for the cost of his next expedition. Although there is no positive evidence that they travelled together, it would make sense, certainly financially, that Philip accompanied Essex on his return to Ireland. If he did, then he left Holyhead on 22 July, landing at Dublin harbour on the 23rd to a warm welcome from the 'citizens of Dublin, and the gentlemen of the country', according to one report. Essex and his retinue stayed in Dublin until 8 August, enjoying a feast laid on by the Chancellor William Gerrard on 24 July and being wined and dined by several friends, including the Archbishop of Dublin and the Countess of Kildare. Setting out to meet Sir Henry, who had ridden back from the west of Ireland, Essex (and presumably Philip) were 'greatly entertained' by the Earl of Ormond on 9 August, and on the 10th Essex and Ormond met Sir Henry 'about twenty-eight miles from Dublin, where there was great show of friendly salutations of permanent friendships'. Later, Essex was publicly invested as Earl Marshal by the Lord Deputy.[57] Relations between the two men were seen to be warm, perhaps because Essex had been warned, by Walsingham, of 'the inconvenience that would ensue, as well for the public service, as his own private, in case there should not be good agreement between you'. Essex had protested to Walsingham that he 'would swallow up any injury' Sir Henry cared to do him, 'rather than break out into any disagreement'.[58]

Philip was now within the orbit of his father and his movements are readily tracked from Sir Henry's official reports to the English court. Over the previous months, Sir Henry had won plaudits for his 'success in suppressing the rebels' (Chancellor Gerrard); 'his diligence and execution of justice in all places' (the Privy Council); indeed, wrote Walsingham, 'it is no small comfort unto your private friends, to see you have so good success in your proceedings there, as your very enemies cannot but commend you'.[59] Sir Henry wrote proudly that with the single exception of Connaught, 'all the other parts of the realm, thanked be God, are in good peaceable state'.[60]

In late August, Sir Henry learned that 'two beggarly bastard boys', sons of the Earl of Clanrickarde, had raised a rebel force, attacked the town of Athenry and then fled.[61] With Philip, he set out west from Dublin Castle on their trail. They met with some success: Sir Henry was able to report to the Privy Council that he had slain some of the rebels' men and seized several of their strongholds. On 4 September, the Sidneys were in Athlone; on 16 September in Galway. Three days later, Sir Henry sent a despatch to London, declaring that he meant to return to Dublin in a circular route via Sligo and Carrickfergus. Here, however, they ran into trouble, as their enemy proved increasingly elusive in the uncharted territories. Sir Henry reported to the Privy Council from Galway on 20 September:

Since my return to this province . . . I have been still occupied, and presently I am, in a kind of an actual war, and continual search for the rebels, sometimes dispersing one part of my forces into one part of the country, and sometimes into another, as I was directed by the best intelligence, where their haunt was. But the hollow hearts of the inhabitants, and the secret lurking of the rebels, is such, and hath been yet hitherto, as I have had no great hand upon them, though I have at sundry times slain of their men, taken their prey, and some of their best and strongest holds from them . . . I hope to make an end of the matter, but if I cannot, whiles I shall remain here, by reason of their often flitting from place to place, in such secret sort, as I cannot have true intelligence of them, and where they lurk.

For Philip, eager to increase his military knowledge, the experience must have been illuminating, but intensely disappointing. This was no military campaign, but an enervating and exasperating pursuit of small pockets of resistance, often through rough terrain, much of it unknown to the English forces. By the time he wrote, Sir Henry was already tracing a route back to Dublin, 'being not a little wearied with the toilsome travail of this wearisome journey, in tracing and searching the rebels from place to place, and the ill success I have to light upon them'.[62]

In Galway, Philip caught a glimpse of what his father described as 'a most famous feminine sea captain', the legendary privateer and smuggler Grace O'Malley. O'Malley was the wife of Sir Richard Burke ('called by the nickname Richard the Iron'), a sea rover who held the County Mayo baronies of Carrowe, Owle and Irryes. O'Malley came to Sir Henry, 'and offered her services unto me, wheresoever I would command her, with three galleys and two hundred fighting men, either in Ireland or Scotland. She brought with her her husband, for she was as well by sea as by land more than master's mate with him'. Sir Henry came to an agreement with Burke, and granted him a knighthood while in Galway, but since they refused to pay taxes, or restrain themselves from piracy, the pair were hounded by the English and were finally forced to submit. 'This was a notorious woman in all the coast of Ireland,' Sir Henry later informed Walsingham. 'This woman did Sir Philip Sidney see and speak with. He can more at large inform you of her.'[63] It may well be that Grace O'Malley stuck in Philip's mind and influenced his later depiction of an Amazon in *The Arcadia* – but he had seen political Amazons enough in his encounters with Cathérine de Médicis and Elizabeth of England.

Philip came to believe that there was no place for lenity in dealing with the Irish. 'Truly,' he wrote in 1577, 'the general nature of all countries not fully conquered is plainly against it. For until by time they find the sweetness of due subjection, it is impossible that any gentle means should put out the fresh remembrance of their lost liberty.' The Irish, he continued, were 'that way as obstinate as any nation, with whom no other passion can prevail but fear'. This was proved by 'their story which plainly paints it out, their manner of life wherein they choose rather all filthiness, than any law, and their own consciences who best know their own natures'. In short, he asserted, 'under the sun there is not a nation which live more tyrannously than they do one over the other'. Therefore, lenity would not have any impact 'in minds so possessed with a natural inconstancy ever to go to a new fortune, with a revengeful hate to all English as to their only conquerors, and that which is most of all, with so ignorant obstinacy in papistry, they do in their souls detest the present government'.[64]

But Philip was also struck by another feature of Irish life. As he later wrote, 'In our neighbour country Ireland where truly learning goeth very bare, yet are their poets held in a devout reverence'[65] – an attitude he had come to believe was justified. Hubert Languet, by now feeling deserted by his protégé, wrote teasingly, 'No doubt you will write to us describing in minute detail Irish miracles and will send specimens of the birds which report has it grow on trees there.'[66] (In fact, Philip, ever the horseman, was more interested in procuring ten Irish horses, which he stabled at the Sidneys' estate at Otford.[67])

Languet's jocular tone failed to disguise his concern that Philip was growing away from him:

> I praise your filial piety for not allowing his Excellency your father to miss the sight of you any longer, as well as for showing no fear of the dangers and difficulties of such a long journey. But you must also allow him the pleasure of seeing you adorned with those virtues which wise men hope for in their children, though they dare not expect them. Of course I praise you for your high determination; but when I think of the rugged mountains of Wales, or the stormy Irish Sea, and to the consistently unhealthy autumn season I feel unusual concern about you.

The unusual concern was exacerbated by Philip's typical failure even to inform Languet of the journey, even though he had told several other correspondents:

> From your letter of June 21 from London I infer that you had no intention of informing me of your Irish trip unless you received a letter from me just as you were about to leave. Yet earlier you wrote detailed plans of the journey to other friends who informed me of them: though when you wrote me you were already well underway with preparations for the journey. Perhaps you feared I would not wish you success and considered others' goodwill toward you to be stronger than my own. Since my complaints on other occasions caused you to feel this way about me, from now on I shall not offer them, and instead reproach my ill fortune.[68]

While in Galway, bad news from Dublin reached the Sidneys. Essex was dangerously ill with dysentery. The condition was a common hazard in

Ireland: Sir Henry later wrote how many people in his train languished from the 'flux' which was 'a disease appropriated to this country, and whereof there died many in the later part of the last year, and some out of mine own household'.[69] Even as Essex was suffering, the Earl of Ormond was writing that 'I have had a touch of the loose disease, that troubleth many in this land.'[70] On 9 September, Waterhouse reported to Sir Henry that Essex had become 'sorely vexed with the flux' on 30 August, and his plan to return to England was 'very uncertain'.[71] By the 14th Essex was deteriorating: according to Waterhouse, after 'having every day and night no less than twenty, thirty, or sometimes forty stools, through which being sore weakened and nature strength diminished', the earl now saw the hand of Death beckoning to him.[72] On 20 September, he wrote to tell the queen that he was dying, asking her to favour his eldest son, Robert, 'who may be fit for more in his life than his unfortunate father hath in his possession at his death'.[73] A day later, he wrote to Burghley, asking that Robert might be raised in his household.[74]

As he faded, Essex desired Philip, then in Galway, to come to him, as he had something he wanted to discuss. 'Here heard we first of the extreme and hopeless sickness of the Earl of Essex,' recalled Sir Henry, 'by whom Sir Philip being often most lovingly and earnestly wished and written for, he with all the speed he could make went to him, but found him dead before his coming, in the castle at Dublin.'[75] Essex, they were told, 'fell asleep as meekly as a lamb', between 11 a.m. and noon on Saturday 22 September, aged just thirty-five.[76]

Philip must have guessed why Essex wanted to see him. When Waterhouse had reported that Essex was calling Philip 'his son', it was not an empty endearment. Essex's elder daughter, Lady Penelope Devereux, was now nearing marriageable age, and he thought that the son of his colleague-cum-competitor in Ireland would be a canny match.[77] Philip was certainly available. Since the aborted Anne Cecil campaign, Leicester had briefly pursued in 1573 the idea of a match for Philip with the daughter of Lord Berkeley, with whom Sir Henry was on good terms – but nothing had come of it.[78] According to a contemporary account of the earl's final anguished days, it was on the Wednesday before he died that Essex's thoughts turned to this idea:

The same day talking of many of his friends he spake of Mr Philip

Sidney. 'O that good gentleman have me commended unto him, and tell him I send him nothing, but I wish him well, and so well that if God so move both their hearts I wish that he might match with my daughter. I call him son, he is so wise, virtuous and godly, and if he go in the course he hath begun he will be as famous and worthy a gentleman as ever England bred.'[79]

This account of Essex's dying wish was supported by Edward Waterhouse, who wrote to Sir Henry:

All these lords that wish well to the children, and, I suppose, all the best sort of the English lords besides, do expect what will become of the treaty between Mr Philip, and my Lady Penelope. Truly, my lord, I must say to your lordship, as I have said to my lord of Leicester, and Mr Philip, the breaking off from this match, if the default be on your parts, will turn to more dishonour, then can be repaired with any other marriage in England. And, I protest unto your lordship, I do not think that there is at this day so strong a man in England of friends, as the little Earl of Essex, nor any man more lamented than his father, since the death of King Edward.[80]

The invocation of Sir Henry's beloved King Edward was a nice touch. What Waterhouse was saying, in the bluntest terms, was that Sir Henry and Leicester could not afford to pass up an alliance with the Essexes. But Waterhouse's role in this affair needs to be considered. It is now thought that he was the author of the anonymous, highly conventional account of Essex's final repentance and death (in which he appears as Essex's beloved 'sweet Ned'). In other words, the two pieces of contemporary evidence that we have for the Devereux–Sidney match are both by Edward Waterhouse, who had just lost his patron and may well have seen the benefits of a match that could move him smoothly into the employ of the new Lord Deputy or his son.

Even if the match had been discussed previously, an Essex connection would now have lost its allure to the Sidneys. According to Essex's will, Penelope was bequeathed a respectable dowry of £2,000, with £100 per annum income, but it was popular knowledge that Essex was in dire financial straits at the time of his death. More importantly, Sir Henry no longer needed to make his peace with Sir Walter – there was no need for Philip to marry Penelope, and (despite Waterhouse's energetic lobbying) the idea gradually faded away.

On 20 September, Sir Henry sent Philip from Galway back to the English court – his letter to Burghley asks him to 'give credit to Ph. Sidney' for all the Irish news he had not wanted to commit to paper. Sir Henry had other matters to take care of: there was talk of foul play and poison in Essex's death, that Leicester had poisoned Sir Walter so that he might marry his lover, Essex's widow Lettice. Sir Henry wrote a detailed, vigorous rebuttal of this idle talk. Only after a lengthy post-mortem, in which the physicians supported a verdict of natural causes, was Essex's body sent back to England in mid-October.[81]

Philip must have had conflicting feelings about his experiences in Ireland. He had had his first taste of military life, and it was not what he had expected. The long, tedious rides to remote sites, often without any real objective, were light years away from his Penshurst dreams of medieval chivalric knights – or, indeed, from the learned treatises on military strategy that he had eagerly devoured with Languet. At best, his father's campaign in Ireland had occasional successes; at worst, it was futile. And an ignominious early death from dysentery was not the fate he had in mind for himself. However, by the time he reached the court in mid-October, his greatest opportunity was about to reveal itself.[82]

CHAPTER SEVEN

Secret Combinations

THE POSSIBILITY THAT Penelope Devereux could be his bride had highlighted for Philip what Hubert Languet had long known – that Philip was a very eligible bachelor. Young, urbane, educated, well connected and – as everyone agreed – remarkably handsome, he would have been a catch for any lady with sufficient funds to disguise his lack of land and ready cash. In the early months of 1577, both Languet and Leicester were to set up highly desirable brides for Philip, but these matches were part and parcel of more complex political arrangements. Marriage was a powerful political tool for the rulers of Europe. Often it reinforced friendships between families. At other times, it provided a cheap, clean alternative to war. Philip's proposed brides sealed politico-religious pacts.

The story of Philip's marriage manoeuvring in 1577 is complicated, and entangled with at least two other sets of negotiations – one, an official mission on behalf of the English Crown; another, an unofficial shadow mission, on behalf of a pan-European Protestant cause. All three, however, had at their root some bad news from the Continent. On 12 October 1576, the Holy Roman Emperor Maximilian II died in Regensburg, while attending the Reichstag. Fifteen days later the Elector Palatine Frederick followed him, 'of a disease in his breast, which choked him'.[1] These two deaths shocked Protestant Europe.

What limited stability the Reformed Church had achieved in recent years on the Continent was largely due to the influence of Maximilian and Frederick. Although nominally a Catholic, Maximilian had never sought to persecute religious minorities, declaring that 'There is no graver sin than the will to tyrannise in matters of conscience.'[2] It came as no surprise that he refused to take the Roman Catholic last sacrament on his deathbed. His heir, Rudolf, by contrast, had been brought up in the arch-Catholic court of his uncle, Philip II of Spain, in Madrid. In the eyes of Languet and his friends, the Holy Roman Empire was now in the hands of Spaniards: Catholic cardinals and counsellors had the ear of the new emperor and were pouring into it the 'poison of the Roman court'.[3] At the same time the Calvinism of the Palatinate was shaken. With the passing of 'pious Fritz' – the Elector Palatine Frederick – his eldest son came to power as Ludwig VI: 'a scant Lutheran', as Burghley's Cologne correspondent Robert Colshill put it.

Hubert Languet read these signals clearly. Now, he predicted, there would be seismic changes across the empire: there were rumours that Rudolf would outlaw all Protestant sects, and several high-placed colleagues of Languet's feared for their future. They had good reason: as Elizabeth's ambassador to the French king reported in January 1577, Rudolf at Lintz had 'discharged a great number of his servants and pensionaries, and some that have served his father and grandfather ten, twenty and twenty-five years, because they did not make open profession of the Romish religion'. Among the casualties was Languet's close friend Johannes Crato von Crafftheim, who had fallen victim to a scurrilous pamphlet alleging that his medical treatment had caused Maximilian's death – a particularly unfair assertion, given that Crato had not been called to administer to Maximilian until after a rival, Catholic physician had been given his chance, and had failed. At the same time, the new elector Ludwig changed the face of Heidelberg, the city to which Philip had been sent from Paris because of its acknowledged Calvinism. There were rumours of Calvinist teachers and activists being exiled from the Palatinate, and of a new Lutheran regime being imposed.

In England, Leicester, Walsingham and Philip looked on aghast. But there was one glimmer of hope: the new elector's younger brother Johann Casimir. His father, realising what lay ahead, had bequeathed to Casimir some small lands with which he could form a principality and, in effect, a Calvinist safehouse.[4] Robert Colshill in Cologne reported that 'all the Calvinists desire Casimir for their Lord'.[5] Casimir was by no means Languet's first choice as a rallying point for German Protestantism. Better known for his military escapades in France and for his drinking than for his learning, he was none the less the only possibility. He had at least been partially raised at the French court, spoke the language and had married the eldest daughter of the Elector of Saxony.

Leicester and Walsingham wanted to test the water with Casimir and the other princes to see what arrangements they could come to, in order to minimise the damage of these shifts in power. Much to their annoyance, however, Elizabeth adopted her habitual 'wait and see' approach to affairs in Germany, as more immediate dangers in France and the Low Countries won her attention. It was almost two months after Maximilian's death when Elizabeth drafted a letter to Rudolf in Italian announcing his election to the Order of the Garter, which would be taken to him by the Earl of Sussex.[6] But it was not until February 1577 that she issued instructions for a special envoy to travel to offer condolences to the grieving widows and children of Maximilian and Frederick. Elizabeth's special envoy was named as Philip Sidney.

To many, Philip was a surprising choice. Although not a mission undertaken to divert crisis or to bring a treaty to fruition, this was a delicate embassy all the same, designed to evaluate two new regimes that threatened to be quite tricky for the English. The assignment would involve the envoy gaining audience to the Holy Roman Emperor, the Elector Palatine and other dignitaries, including Don John of Austria, Philip of Spain's Governor General in the Low Countries. Yet Philip Sidney was only twenty-two years old. His previous embassy experience was confined to a non-speaking, walk-on role in the Earl of Lincoln's Paris embassy of 1572. Even Languet, when he recommended Philip to the Elector Augustus, described him as 'adolescens'. Why then was he chosen to go?

Alberico Gentili, in his 1585 treatise on the ideal ambassador, drew attention to this anomaly when discussing how old an ambassador needed to be. He felt, however, that in this case Philip was a wise choice. 'The Romans sent young men on an embassy to Jugurtha, and I know two, hardly more than boys, who have transacted ambassadorial business with the greatest distinction: Georg Khisl, Baron of Kaltenprun, a German, and Master Philip Sidney, an Englishman – who rival one another in the outstanding qualities of their mental and moral endowment.' According to Gentili, 'there should be a careful scrutiny of what is involved in the embassy, and that the decision in the whole affair should depend on this'. The embassies of Khisl and Sidney 'were embassies of courtesy [*legationes in officium*], and there is no reason why young men should not execute embassies of this class'.[7]

Philip was chosen by the queen to signal to the world that this was no more than a courtesy embassy. But he and his friends saw it as an opportunity for something much more important. We know surprisingly little about Philip's movements in the autumn of 1576: not only because (as was his wont) Philip wrote few letters, but because, oddly, none of the letters to him has survived. After Languet wrote from Ratisbon on 8 September 1576 (informing him of Maximilian's illness), there is no extant letter from Languet to Philip until June 1577. This can partly be explained by the fact that Languet and Philip spent time together in the spring of 1577. But in autumn 1576 they were always apart. It is inconceivable that Languet would not have written to Philip about the massive upheavals in European politics of which he was such an intimate observer. The letters that passed between Languet and Philip were treasured both during Languet's lifetime and after his death. It follows then that if Languet continued to correspond with Philip between September 1576 and May 1577 (when they met again), these letters were not kept for a particular reason. My contention is that they contained references to negotiations that later proved to be too politically sensitive to risk preserving – namely, that Philip at least hoped to be part of the English envoy to Rudolf and Ludwig from the time he heard of the deaths of Maximilian and Frederick, and that both he and Languet took steps to prepare themselves.

We need to see the actions of Languet and Philip in the winter and spring of 1577 as dovetailing each other. In January 1577, Languet arrived in Prague and immediately asked to be freed from his duties to the elector, ostensibly so that he could return to France.[8] He was not asking for a complete break. He would still pass information to Augustus (partly because he still needed the financial rewards that this brought). On 23 February, he received from Augustus the required brevet and the money he was owed, and set off, first for the Frankfurt Fair, and then on to Heidelberg.[9] Freed of official duties to Augustus, Languet could now become an adviser to Casimir, employing his international networks to clear a path for Philip to negotiate a Protestant alliance.[10] By the time Languet reached Casimir, in early May 1577, Philip was already with him. It seems from the elegant way in which events worked out that both had co-ordinated their separate plans long before Philip set out from England.

While Languet's life is well documented through his massive correspondence, there are only tantalising glimpses of Philip's in the months before February 1577. Although the mission was not made public until 8 February, he seems to have prepared for it before that date, and in detail. Probably at his uncle's London residence, Leicester House,[11] he called upon the expertise of Leicester's scholarly adviser Gabriel Harvey. In the margins of his copy of Livy's *Romanae historiae principis, decades tres, cum dimidia,* now preserved in Princeton University's Firestone Memorial Library, Harvey's notes are still legible in his inimitable large, looping letters:

> The courtier Philip Sidney and I had privately discussed these three books of Livy, scrutinising them so far as we could from all points of view, applying a political analysis, just before his embassy to the emperor Rudolf II. He went to offer him congratulations in the queen's name just after he had been made emperor. Our consideration was chiefly directed at the forms of states, the conditions of persons, and the qualities of actions. We paid little attention to the [printed] annotations of [Henricus] Glareanus and others [Ioannes Velcurio].[12]

Reading together, Harvey and Philip plundered Livy books 1–3 for his exemplary examples, in a manner that Philip would be able to employ during his forthcoming encounters. What Harvey was providing here were the skills of political analysis. Elsewhere in his marginal notes on Livy Harvey wrote: 'It is fitting for prudent men to make strenuous efforts to use whatever sheds light on politics: and to increase it as much as they can. Two outstanding courtiers thanked me for this political and historical inquiry: Sir Edward Dyer and Sir Edward Denny.'[13]

We also know from John Dee's diary that Philip paid him a visit at Mortlake: on 16 January 1577, Dee recorded, 'the earl of Leicester, Mr Philip Sidney, Mr Dyer, &c., came to my house'.[14] The inclusion of Edward Dyer in this visit is intriguing. Thomas Moffet wrote that Philip, 'not satisfied with the judgement and reach of common sense, with his eye passing to and fro through all nature, pressed into the innermost penetralia of causes; and by that token, led by God, with Dee as teacher, and with Dyer as companion, he learned chemistry, that starry science, rival to nature'.[15] It may indeed be the case that Philip and Dyer consulted Dee on chemistry, but it seems more likely that on this occasion, accompanying Leicester, their purpose was closely tied to their mission.[16]

The official instructions for Philip's embassy, dated 7 February 1577, tell us only that Philip was 'being sent ambassador to Rudolf the second, emperor & his mother the empress, to condole the death of the emperor Maximilian his father: and withal he was directed to take in his way the two count Palatines, & to condole also the death of their father, then lately dead'. Philip was also to take advantage of the embassy to gather information:

> And during the time of your being there, you shall inform yourself of the young emperor's disposition and his brethren, whether he be martially inclined or otherwise, by whose advice he is directed: when it is likely he shall marry: what princes in Germany are most affected towards him: in what state he is left for revenues: what good agreement there is between him and his brethren: what partage [division of territory] they have, and how they are inclined.[17]

According to Fulke Greville, Philip took the initiative by enlarging the scope of the instructions to include the canvassing of the Protestant princes in Germany: 'under the shadow of this compliment between princes, which sorted better with his youth than his spirit [Philip], to improve that journey, and make it a real service to his sovereign, procured an article to be added to his instructions, which gave him scope (as he passed) to salute such German princes, as were interested in the cause of our religion, or their own native liberty'.[18] Greville's word in this matter carries some weight for once because he, along with their mutual friend Dyer, accompanied Philip abroad. With them also went two experienced diplomats: Sir Henry Lee, who had served in the 1568 mission to The Netherlands and the Rhineland (and who had provided the 'Hermit' entertainment at Woodstock); and Sir Jerome Bowes who, like Philip, had accompanied Lincoln to Paris in 1572. A contemporary letter reports that the party was planned to contain Richard Allen (later an envoy to the King of Denmark), Gervase Cressy, Mr Basset, Mr Stanhope and Mr Brouncker – presumably Henry Brouncker who, according to Moffet, became one of Philip's most trusted friends.[19]

As he embarked, Philip had two missions in mind: one for his queen, the other for his religion. Among his papers was a letter from Leicester for Johann Casimir; in his mind the reading he had carried out with Gabriel Harvey and John Dee. This was a once-in-a-lifetime opportunity, and he was not going to let it pass.

As he set foot on Ostend soil, Philip realised, to his great satisfaction, that he was no longer an obscure English boy travelling with a few servants. True, he was still someone's son, someone's nephew, but he himself bore the stamp of English royal approval, the imprimatur of the queen herself. Outside his lodgings he displayed a placard, which proclaimed him to the world:

Illustrissimi & Generissimi Viri
Philippi Sidnaei Angli,
Pro-regis Hiberniae filii, Comitum Warwici
Et Leicestriae Nepotis, Serenissimi
Reginae Angliae ad Caesarem Legati

The most illustrious and noble man
Philip Sidney, Englishman,
son of the Pro-rex of Ireland,
nephew to the Earls of Warwick and Leicester,
ambassador of the most serene Queen of England to the Emperor.[20]

Philip reported back in long, beautifully detailed, well-structured letters, addressed to Francis Walsingham. He wrote them in the full knowledge that they would be seen by eyes other than Walsingham's, and in the main they present as news information that was already well known to himself, and to Walsingham and Leicester. Anything more controversial or delicate was either entrusted to the verbal report of the letter's bearer or put off until Philip's return.

The first set-piece meeting was to be with Don John of Austria. Philip and his retinue made their way to Brussels, where they were welcomed by the resident ambassador Dr Thomas Wilson, while Don John came conveniently to Louvain, just seventeen miles east of Brussels.[21] It was a tricky meeting because Don John was a magnet for many disaffected English Catholic exiles, who saw in him a possible husband for Mary, Queen of Scots. But when they met on 6 March, Philip was determined not to be fazed by his glorious opposite. According to Dr Wilson, Philip – forsaking the niceties of etiquette – brought up the questions of the rebels directly, but 'notwithstanding his plain speech [Philip] had fair and sweet answers'.[22] Fulke Greville, another eyewitness, later wrote that when Philip:

came to kiss [Don John's] hand, though at the first, in his Spanish hauteur, he gave him access as by descent to a youth, of grace as to a stranger, and in particular competition (as he conceived) to an enemy; yet after a while that he had taken his just altitude, he found himself so stricken with this extraordinary planet, that the beholders wondered to see what ingenious tribute that brave, and high minded prince paid to his worth, giving more honour and respect to this hopeful young gentleman than to the ambassadors of mighty princes.[23]

Don John wrote to Elizabeth assuring her of his intention to govern the Low Countries 'peaceably and well and in friendship with England', and denying that he had ever encouraged the rebels – indeed, when some had come to him, he ordered them to go away. No man was more desirous of preserving the friendship between England and the house of Burgundy than he.[24] Sweet words, but no one was convinced.

Sailing up the Rhine, the next stop was the much-altered Heidelberg, where Philip was to greet the new Elector Palatine Ludwig, and his brother Johann Casimir. The elector turned out to be in Amberg, in the Upper Palatinate, so Philip could only speak to Casimir, who declared himself bound to Elizabeth. Philip was impressed by Casimir's sincerity: he provided a 'very good' answer, 'with a countenance well witnessing it came from his heart'.[25] Although Philip was instructed to aim for concord between the two brothers, he was to make clear to Casimir that he was Elizabeth's preferred brother:

After these general speeches delivered unto both the brethren you shall particularly let Casimir understand that as we do assure ourself greatly of his good affection and devotion towards us so may he on the other make full assurance of our friendly inclination towards him, as well in respect of the princely parts that are in him, and that he was one who the prince his father did so dearly love which cannot but yield augmentation of our affection towards him.[26]

As feared, Philip discovered 'great miscontentment' in the prince, because his brother 'begins to make alteration in religion'. The new elector had already established Lutheranism in the Upper Palatinate (Bavaria), and Casimir feared that he planned to do the same in the Nether Palatinate, by the Rhine. 'He is resolved if his brother do drive away from him the learned men of the true profession, that he will receive [them] to him, and hereof something may breed gall betwixt them if any do, but the best is to be hoped, considering Prince Lodowick [Ludwig] is of a soft nature, led to these things only through conscience, and Prince Casimir wise, that can temper well with the other's weakness.' The other German princes were a lost cause, according to Casimir, concerned only with 'how to get rich and to please their senses . . . thinking they should be safe, though all the world were on fire about them'. The sole exception, opined Casimir, was his cousin William, Landgrave of Hesse, whom Elizabeth, he suggested, should approach.[27]

No doubt Philip took advantage of his time in Heidelberg to rekindle old friendships. Thomas Moffet tells of how 'Everywhere the rich Germans manifested their beneficence [to Philip], the poor their benevolence – and all, their reverence and duty. Indeed, the emperor's noblemen – especially Casimir, and the Counts of Palatine and Hanau – began among themselves a competition in making gifts, even so as he who had sent the least thought himself most unfortunate; and graciously they offered all their services to him.'[28]

Leaving Heidelberg on 22 March, the English embassy travelled via Nuremberg to Prague, arriving on Maundy Thursday (4 April).[29] Prague was still reeling from Maximilian's funeral, which had not taken place until 22 March, nearly five months after the emperor died. What should have been a solemn memorial to a beloved ruler was disrupted by panic in the streets that Catholics and Protestants were about to attack each other: the cortège barely made it to St Vitus Cathedral.[30] Philip's audience with the emperor was scheduled for Monday 8 April. In the meantime, he sent Greville to the botanist Charles de l'Écluse in Vienna, with a letter of introduction, in which Philip described him as a 'very near relation of mine', which he hoped would 'refresh your memory of me as to make this demand on our friendship: would you be so kind as to show him the memorable parts of the city, and, much more important, to let him make your acquaintance, a thing he greatly desires?' Greville also particularly wanted 'to kiss the hands of the Archduke Ernest', so Philip wrote to arrange that with Ernest's chamberlain, Baron Prainer.[31] De l'Écluse was only too delighted to take on the charge, as he reported to Joachim Camerarius.[32] There was of course an ulterior motive: while in

Vienna, Greville negotiated with Prainer ('the emperor's cupbearer') for the ceremonial return of Maximilian's Order of the Garter.[33]

Philip was anxious about this meeting with the new emperor and had pumped Johann Casimir for information about him. Casimir could only echo the popular opinion of Rudolf, alleging 'his papistry or Spanish gravity'. But Philip learned from 'men of good judgement' that the emperor had been 'left poor, the division with his brethren not yet made, wars with the Turk feared, and yet his peace little better, considering the great tributes he pays, and the continual spoils his subjects suffer upon the frontiers'.[34] Philip, convinced of the fundamental importance of education, was suspicious of Rudolf's upbringing in Philip II's Madrid court, from the age of eleven to nineteen, at the insistence of his Spanish mother Maria (Philip II's sister), and to the dismay of his father. Rudolf's education *per se* was claimed to be excellent, particularly in rhetoric and languages: he could speak and write Spanish, German, French, Latin, Italian and even some Czech, thanks to his Czech tutor Sebastian Pechovsky. The initial verdict in Vienna and Prague was mixed: Rudolf had thrown himself into court life with a good will, but his manner was (and would remain) that of the Spanish court – cold and stiff.[35]

The meeting went as well as could be expected. A newsletter from Prague to Rome reported that Rudolf received Philip 'very graciously', and the next day made arrangements to ensure that he 'should be at no expense'.[36] When he addressed Rudolf according to Elizabeth's instructions, reported Philip – perhaps sniping at Rudolf's much-vaunted linguistic prowess – the new emperor 'answered me in Latin with very few words'. Rudolf reiterated his thanks towards 'her Serenity (for that was the term he used)', and vowed to follow his father's example.[37] In his account, Moffet described how, 'accompanied on either side by two men from the highest rank of nobles, Philip gave his right hand and his greeting to the emperor, with what looks, with what confidence, with how much grace of discourse he spoke! What a sharp impression did he make upon the hearing and minds of all – one which still remains to this day! What men from every rank did he not win over to admiration!' Sadly, Moffet's rhapsody is perhaps slightly compromised: he described this encounter as taking place in Augsburg rather than Prague.[38]

Philip discovered that Rudolf was 'wholly by his inclination given to the wars, few of words, sullen of disposition, very secret and resolute, nothing the manner his father had in winning men in his behaviour, but yet constant in keeping them. And such a one as though he promise not much outwardly, hath as the Latins say *aliquid in recessu* [something in reserve]'. Rudolf was 'most governed by one Dietrichstein the great master of his house', who 'bears the red cross of Spain and is a professed servant to that crown and inquisitors' government. The nuntio of the Pope that is now there is likewise great influence and followed by him, so that what the counsels such authors give may be easily imagined, though the effects be long in bringing forth the consequences'. The new emperor would remain a bachelor until Philip II's daughter, his first cousin (now eleven) came of age. A rival claim to her from the King of Portugal had been removed (he was now interested in 'the daughter of France') and so, by the wonders of in-breeding, Rudolf, 'to strengthen the holiness of his kinship much the more, will become both son, brother, nephew, and cousin of the king of Spain'. Philip deferred his analysis of Rudolf's appeal to the German princes until his return.

The following day, Philip delivered letters from Elizabeth to the dowager Empress Maria, but cut short his comments on her late husband, 'because in truth I saw it bred some trouble unto her, to hear him mentioned in that kind'. While expressing her support of Philip's aims in theory, the dowager empress stressed that she was withdrawing from public life. Philip also delivered letters to her daughter Elizabeth, the widow of Charles IX of France, who accompanied the empress: 'Her answer was full of humbleness but she spake so low that I could not understand any of her words.' His final port of call was to 'the young princes'.[39]

Although Languet and de l'Écluse were absent, there was one familiar face in Prague – that of the English recusant Edmund Campion.[40] Philip would first have encountered Campion at Oxford in late August 1566, when Campion gave the welcoming speech and disputed in front of the queen. By the time Philip went up to Christ Church in early 1568, Campion was established as a charismatic figure with a personal following, as well as considerable institutional prestige as a fellow of St John's, a junior proctor and a deacon. Campion not only had long-standing links with the Sidney and Dudley families, but had debts to repay, in particular to Sir Henry. After losing sponsorship from the Grocers' Company for refusing to preach publicly in London, Campion had left in August 1570 for Ireland, where his patrons included Sir Henry, who saved his life in the spring of 1571 by warning Sir James Stanihurst that Campion was in danger, following Elizabeth's excommunication by Pope Pius V – another example of Sir Henry's pragmatic even-handedness to Catholics. Campion fled to Bohemia, where he trained as a Jesuit, and in return made Sir Henry the hero of his *Two Bokes* of Irish history. In time, Campion was appointed a professor of rhetoric at the Jesuit College in Prague, and soon became a valued orator at Maximilian's court.

In Prague, Philip apparently spent some time with Campion, as he had with other Catholics in Italy – time that Campion quickly used to his own advantage. In a letter to John Bavand, Campion explained excitedly how, a few months previously, Philip Sidney had come to Prague as an ambassador 'magnificently provided'. He had 'much conversation' with Campion, 'I hope not in vain', the Jesuit continued, 'for to all appearance he was most eager.' Philip, he alleged, 'asked the prayers of all good men, and at the same time put into my hands some alms to be distributed to the poor by him, which I have done.' This was hot news: 'Tell this to Dr Nicholas Sanders,' Campion urged, 'because if any one of the labourers sent into the vineyard from the Douai seminary has an opportunity of watering this plant, he may watch the occasion for helping a poor wavering soul.' Philip Sidney would be an incredible catch for English Catholicism. 'If this young man, so wonderfully beloved and admired by his countrymen, chances to be converted, he will astonish his noble father, the Deputy of Ireland, his uncles the Dudleys, and all the young courtiers, and Cecil himself.' The matter had to be handled with exquisite care. 'Let it be kept secret.'[41]

Campion's claims to have met Philip are not uncorroborated. In a speech drafted in 1581 when on trial for harbouring Campion, Sir Thomas Tresham intriguingly referred to Campion being 'well reputed of . . . by Protestants of good account that returned from the emperor's court', although these Protestants remain tantalisingly anonymous.[42] Two later accounts, by Father Robert Persons and Father Thomas Fitzherbert, also testify to the meeting. In Fitzherbert's account, written in 1628, he claimed that 'Sidney had the courage to confess in England that one of the most memorable things he had witnessed abroad was a sermon by Campion which he had attended with the Emperor in Prague.'[43] The account by Persons, however, suggests a much more hole-in-the-wall affair: it was difficult, he wrote, for Philip to arrange a meeting with Campion, because 'he was afraid of so many spies set and sent about him by the English Council'. Despite this, Philip 'managed to have divers large and secret conferences with his old friend', and 'after much argument' professed himself to be 'convinced'. However, Philip explained, he had to 'hold on the course which he had hitherto followed', although he did promise never to hurt or injure any Catholic ('which for the most part he performed,' admitted Persons). He also promised that Campion 'should find him a trusty friend' – a promise that he failed to keep, Persons argued, since when Campion was condemned to death four years later, Philip failed to use his influence (being then 'in most high favour'), 'for fear not to offend'.[44]

What was Philip Sidney doing talking to Edmund Campion in Prague? His involvement may have been limited to accompanying Rudolf to one of Campion's sermons. But Philip may also have considered that Campion would provide a different angle on the local situation from his own sources, most of whom were politically and doctrinally motivated Protestant partisans. Persons' account of Philip operating within a spy-infested retinue appears paranoid, but Philip could indeed have thought it well-advised to keep such meetings secret. On the other hand, Persons is right to claim that Philip made no attempt to save Campion when he was arrested, interrogated and eventually executed in England in 1581. Talking to an English expatriate Catholic preacher in Prague, a city under the control of a Catholic emperor, was essentially different to intervening on behalf of a Catholic recusant accused of treason in England, where the head of state was also the head of the Anglican Church. Philip certainly omitted to mention the encounter in his written missives to Walsingham and Burghley. Like his father, Philip refused to allow his sincere doctrinal loyalties to get in the way of the most productive pursuit of his political life.

There was to be one final banquet thrown by the emperor before the English party left Prague on Sunday 20 April, with Philip bearing a letter of thanks to the queen and 'most honorific gifts', including a chain of gold; Moffet mentions 'from the Emperor a generous fee for the embassy, along with still more ample good will'.[45] Moffet also describes how, after the mission was accomplished, 'being entertained afterward with public and private ceremonies and banquets of various nationality –

Greeks, Romans, Italians, Frenchmen, Germans – he [Philip] responded to each man in his own tongue. When called upon, he uttered his opinion concerning each topic raised, in such chaste and polished phrasing that his every speech seemed framed and adorned by art.'[46]

Travelling via Nuremberg, where he met up with the Camerarius brothers,[47] Philip arrived back at Heidelberg on 30 April, meeting Elector Ludwig, now returned from Amberg, the following day. Philip delivered his usual messages of condolences from the queen and her hopes that he would unite with his brother, but had to rely on the translating services of Ludwig's vice-chancellor, who answered rather vaguely with commonplaces about 'the necessity of brothers' love', while avoiding any specific comment on Casimir. Philip was 'bold to add in my speech' to urge Ludwig, in the queen's name, 'to have merciful consideration of the church of the religion, so notably established by his father as in all Germany there is not such a number of excellent learned men, and truly would rue any man to see the desolation of them'. He also argued that 'violent changes' were dangerous for even the mightiest princes; that if Ludwig abolished all his father had instituted, he would wrong, and even condemn, his father – and, Philip added slyly, give a precedent to his own descendants 'to handle him the like'.

This was all well beyond his remit, but, as Philip reasoned to Walsingham, even if Ludwig did not pay any attention, it was important that the church in Germany should know that Elizabeth was thinking of them. 'This I hope will be taken for sufficient cause therein, of my boldness.' Philip received no reply from the vice-chancellor but later, through another interpreter, Ludwig answered that 'for her Majesty's sake he would do much, he misliked not of the men, but must be constrained to do as the other princes of the empire'. And with that Ludwig departed to the baths 'for the last remedy of his infirmity',[48] sending Elizabeth a formal thank-you for her letter.[49]

It was now, at Heidelberg, that the strands of Languet's and Sidney's plans were pulled together. From the surviving correspondences of Languet, Augustus and Casimir, we can establish that various meetings here were long planned, and quickly reported. On his arrival, Philip was met by Dr Dietrich Weyer, Steuerburg von Lewenstein and Peter Beutterich, three members of Casimir's retinue. They promptly relayed the news of the English envoy's arrival to Casimir, who was in nearby

Kaiserslautern, while Philip wrote to inform the Landgrave of Hesse that he would soon be visiting him. The following day, Philip finally met up with Languet in Heidelberg. After quitting Augustus, Languet had had to fulfil a commitment to visit the Frankfurt Book Fair, where he was so besieged by visitors at Wechel's lodgings that he was unable to visit any library or even to leave the house.[50] But he managed to get to Heidelberg by 2 May to meet Philip – evidently an important meeting, as he bothered to announce it to Augustus.[51] The news of Languet's arrival was also despatched to Casimir. On the 3rd, Philip reported to Walsingham that Casimir was the lynchpin to any operation: 'How his brother and he stand I will likewise refer till my return and that I have spoken [again] with Prince Casimir . . . What I shall find among these princes truly I know not till I have spoken with Prince Casimir. I go tomorrow to Kaiserlautern, but I see their proceedings such that my hope doth every day grow less and less.'[52]

On 4 May, therefore, Philip, Languet and the others all set off to visit Casimir, and got down to business.[53] Casimir broached his plan to hold a summit meeting in Frankfurt in September of representatives from all the churches who felt threatened by the Lutherans.[54] In an official letter to Elizabeth's Privy Council, Casimir promised to join a Protestant League if it were formed, and to use his influence to persuade his relatives, including William, Landgrave of Hesse (the Landgrave was, in Philip's words, 'the only prince Casimir makes account of'[55]) to subscribe. He pledged 100,000 dollars in currency to promote the cause, asking in return what Elizabeth would offer. He discussed in detail and at length with Philip the form of a general agreement to be signed by all reformed churches: he himself would contact the churches in France, Poland, the Low Countries and Switzerland.[56] Later in the month, the landgrave wrote to pledge his support.[57]

As late as 3 May, it was Philip's intention to visit the Landgrave of Hesse to deliver Elizabeth's letter in person. But at the last minute his plans were changed. Philip was forced to send Richard Allen instead, when instructions arrived for him from England: he was to return home at once to report on the situation.[58]

Following orders, Philip headed for England, accompanied as far as Cologne, throughout most of May, by Languet. It was a happy month for the two men, almost too happy: 'I felt an incredible satisfaction,' Languet later wrote, 'from being together for so many days, but now I feel like a man who drinks thirstily and deeply of cold water when he is too hot, and by doing so, brings on a fever.'[59] They met up with Pietro Bizari, Philip's friend from his Paris days, in Cologne. Before they were all forced to part, Philip finally succeeded in extracting from Languet his word that he would come to England to visit him.[60]

We know from the letters written in the months after they separated that Languet and Philip had had some serious discussions during their journey about Philip's future. At Mainz, Languet had taken Philip aside to put a proposal to him. He had found a bride he thought worthy of his protégé, but Philip was to keep this secret. The lady in question was a princess. Philip asked for time to consider the proposal. He was not the only one involved: others had to be asked.

Who was this 'princess'? Languet's letters following this revelation are all written in an allusive style, with references to 'she whom you know of ', rather than any open identification, which suggests that the matter was quite delicate. It seems from a comment in one letter that the princess had given her word to her brother that she would not commit herself elsewhere until she had a definitive response from Philip.[61] If the patriarch of her household, to whom she had to answer, was her brother, this suggests that her father was dead. In 1776 David Dalrymple, who edited Languet's letters to Sidney, suggested that the princess must be Ursula, sister to Prince Johann Casimir. This remains the most obvious choice, and would explain the lack of a father. Languet wrote during the summer that he had been stalling the party of the prospective bride; since all his letters during June and July were written from Frankfurt, it would follow that that party must have been in Frankfurt or somewhere close[62] (in September, Languet mentions to Camerarius that he had often been called to neighbouring courts).[63] On one occasion, he also relayed to Philip what their 'mutual friend' had written – and quoted that friend in French. Unlike most of the German princes, Casimir's preferred language was French.[64]

Languet's letters during the following months are littered with almost impatient attempts to force an answer. On 14 June, he writes: 'See that you remember what I said to you at the mouth of the Maine, and write about it as soon as you can, as you've promised several times.'[65] A month later, he reiterates: 'You remember how often I have begged you to let me know as soon as possible the opinion of your [friends] of the matter I spoke to you about at the mouth of the Maine, and you promised that you would do so.'[66]

The situation became more complicated when Philip reached the Low Countries. Philip wrote to Languet from Bruges on 6 June that there were reasons that almost made him 'despair of the possibility that this would turn out successfully'; he asked Languet, as far as he could, 'to dampen the hopes of the other parties'. Languet was not sympathetic. 'You should have found out what your people wanted, and let us know immediately as you promised to do,' he complained. He assumed it was family pressures that were causing Philip to procrastinate:

I know what has occurred to you to make you consider the matter a difficult one to pull off, for when the other parties discussed the project with me it occurred to me immediately that you were the son of a family . . . I could have had your justification ready if you responded, and I would still have it ready now had I your letter. And I beg you by our friendship to send it, lest our friends believe they are being slighted by you, or that I have not acted in good faith.[67]

When Languet returned from Cologne he wrote to the 'mutual friend', reporting how Philip had liked the proposal and was grateful for their thought, but (as he put it to Philip) that 'you could not come to any determination on the subject until you had talked with those who had a hold over you; that you promised to discover what they wanted as soon as you returned home, and to let us know the verdict'.[68] In July Languet received a letter from that 'mutual friend', the content of which he relayed to Philip: 'We are waiting for the decision on your part, that is of whom you know. On our side we're assured, having the consent of the principal person. Monsieur Ley has spoken of it.' 'Monsieur Ley' remains unidentified – could this be a reference to Philip's embassy companion Sir Henry Lee?

Languet was boxed into a corner:

You see in what a situation I am placed. I really have been afraid because of this to go to them, although they have invited me on more than one occasion, and I have had to invent various excuses for not going, for I did not wish to let them lose all hope of wrapping up the business, until I heard from you that no hope remained. For although I think that the thing is very difficult I don't think it's utterly impossible. What if your fortune or some good genius should infuse into your friends or even your Zenobia [presumably Elizabeth] a spirit of liberality towards you?

Now he had no choice. 'I am now summoned by our friends on affairs of such importance that I have to heed the call. When they ask me for the latest on this matter of ours I can say nothing except that I haven't heard from you.'[69]

By the end of September, by which time Philip was back in England, Languet warned him that 'both your reputation and my own have begun to suffer with our friends here', because 'they believe that you changed your mind in Holland, and that you preferred another proposal over the one we agreed.' Even worse for Languet:

they believe that I know all this, but that I'm pretending to them. I called God as witness that I knew nothing of those things which they were saying about you, that I did not believe they were true, and that I had not to that point received any letter from you – and indeed, I haven't received yours which you say you wrote on July 23. After I have learned what you want in this matter I shall bring it about, as I hope, that they will accept in good part whatever you decide on, without lessening their affection for you.[70]

In October, the stakes were raised, when Languet reported on the 9th that Jean-George, Elector of Brandenburg since 1571, a Protestant widower in his fifties, was 'said to be looking eagerly in the direction' of the princess, but 'constancy has not yet yielded to his rank and greatness, so strong are the hopes which she has conceived. So now she will sigh when she discovers the uselessness of her constancy and the frustration of her hopes. I beg you to pardon me if perhaps I've been too insistent in demanding an answer to the matters we agreed upon.'[71] By the end of November, frustrated with the princess's non-committal, Brandenburg had married a daughter of the Prince of Anhalt.[72]

Although Languet did not know it, he hit home when he wrote to Philip that 'you changed your mind in Holland'. There, Philip had finally met one of his heroes: William the Taciturn, Prince of Orange. He had always wanted to visit him: Languet noted, 'I saw you burning with the desire to speak to Orange, and form a friendship with him.'[73] When Philip set off back to England, however, Languet advised against the idea, arguing that Philip should obey Elizabeth's command to return directly. However, on his way home through Brussels, the situation changed. In Languet's account, Philip received a letter from the queen in which he was commanded 'to visit the Prince of Orange and attend the baptism of his daughter in her name' at Middelburg, on the island of Walcheren.[74] Either Languet misremembered the details (which seems highly unlikely) or Philip had not been totally honest about the circumstances behind his change of itinerary. For it was not his sovereign whom Philip was representing at the baptism, but his uncle Leicester. On 8 May, Leicester had sent Edward Dyer to Orange to express his delight at the invitation he had received and to suggest a stand-in: his nephew Philip Sidney who, as it happened (or so Leicester said), was at that moment sailing down the Rhine so that he might kiss the hands of his Excellency the Prince of Orange. (Failing that, Leicester could substitute Dyer, but he apologised in advance for Dyer speaking only Latin and Italian.) Dyer then took Leicester's message to Philip in Brussels.[75]

Quickly retracing their footsteps, Philip's retinue travelled through Bruges, Ghent, Antwerp and Breda to Middelburg, where William and his wife, Charlotte de Bourbon, were staying, arriving on 27 May.[76] There, for the first time, Philip met William of Orange. The prince was a striking figure, not least because he signally failed to conform to popular expectations of princeliness. Thomas Fuller later wrote that 'In people's eyes his light shined bright, yet dazzled none, all having free access unto him: everyone was as well pleased as if he had been Prince himself, because he might be so familiar with the Prince.'[77] Fulke Greville vividly described his unorthodox appearance: 'His uppermost garment was a gown, yet such (as I dare confidently affirm) a mean-born student, in our Inns of Court, would not have been well pleased to walk the streets in. Unbuttoned his doublet was, and of like precious matter, and form to the other. His waistcoat (which showed itself under it) not unlike the best sort of those woollen knit ones, which our ordinary watermen row

7. William of Orange.

us in.' When Greville met him in Delft, the prince's chosen company was 'the burgesses of that beer-brewing Town: and he so fellow-like encompassed with them, as (had I not known his face) no exterior sign of degree, or deservedness could have discovered the inequality of his worth or estate from that multitude'.[78]

The Middelburg meeting came at a crucial moment in Low Countries politics. On 12 February, Don John of Austria had signed the Perpetual Edict with the States General, the body of representatives from the various states comprising the Low Countries. This edict enforced the terms of the Pacification of Ghent in return for obedience to Spain and the imposition of Roman Catholicism as the official religion. Orange had refused to sign the edict, and the states of Holland and Zeeland (his powerbase) withdrew their delegates in protest at the States General's acceptance of these terms. Seeking to settle the matter quickly, Don John proposed a meeting between his representatives and Orange's: William agreed, and attended in person. Two weeks of talking did not cause him to bend, however, and the conference broke up on 27 May.

In comparison with the stilted encounters with Don John and Rudolf, the first meeting of William and Philip was a huge success. In addition to his official position at the baptism of Elisabeth, Philip talked at length with the prince. From their three days (28–30 May) of meetings emerged a tract penned by Philip entitled 'Certain notes concerning the present state of the Prince of Orange, and the provinces of Holland and Zeeland, as they were in the month of May 1577'.[79] This was an incisive analysis of the strengths of the Low Countries, which stressed the strategic importance of Orange in any conflict against Spain and highlighted his current, healthy position. On 2 June, William wrote to Elizabeth relating what Philip would write, and assured her that he, along with other officials in Holland and Zeeland, desired to serve her. He had 'asked Mr Sidney, ambassador of your Majesty to the emperor, to do us the honour of declaring more particularly' the details of the agreement he proposed.[80] These suggested an alliance whereby Orange would give Elizabeth ports in Holland and Zeeland, with ships, sailors, materials, spare parts and stores for the English navy; in return she was required to close English ports to Spanish forces, and protect commerce along the lines of the old Burgundy treaties. She would then, at length, grant the States General an annual loan of £50,000 should war be prolonged.

William was impressed with the young Englishman, and made his liking known. Later in the year another English representative, Daniel Rogers, was able to tell Elizabeth that William 'had conceived a great opinion' of Mr Sidney.[81] But Philip had a more immediate impact, news of which soon reached intelligencers. On 1 June 1577, a Spanish merchant in London named Antonio de Guaras wrote to Don John to inform him that Philip was 'busy arranging a secret marriage with the Prince of Orange's daughter by his first wife . . . [The Prince] will give him as dowry the government of the provinces of Holland and Zeeland.'[82] The proposed bride was William's eldest daughter Marie of Nassau, now about twenty years old.

This proposal had very different ramifications from the match proposed by Languet. A marriage with Casimir's sister would indicate English support for a Protestant alliance, without much power, and would consolidate Languet's position as an international power-broker. A marriage with Orange's daughter, on the other hand, would cement an alliance between Orange and Leicester, draw both of them away from the need to treat with France and provide Philip with a considerable personal presence in the Low Countries. For the first time, Philip's loyalty to Languet's vision of pan-European Protestantism came into direct conflict with Leicester's more localised ambitions.

Unsurprisingly there is no record of these negotiations in the extant correspondence of either Philip or Orange. However, Roger Kuin's assiduous researches into the Archives of the Royal House in The Hague have supported this hypothesis.[83] Marie usually resided with her uncle, Count Louis of Nassau, at Castle Dillenburg; in March 1577 she was staying at a country house at Siegen in the Rhineland. A letter to her father, written on 19 March, indicates that he has asked her to come and join him, a plan she thinks may be difficult because her pregnant aunt is about to enter her lying-in period. This means that William had written requesting her presence in early March – that is, before Leicester suggested that Philip should attend the baptism. Could it be that Orange originally had Leicester in mind as a groom?

Orange wrote again on 5 May, a letter that was evidently sent with some despatch, as Marie replied the following day. She writes of how he asked her 'to tell you what I think of joining you there; since you desire it so much, it will be a great pleasure for me'. She would leave it to her father to send Bruninck or someone else to fetch her, and she would 'take care to be ready, for I will hardly take anything with me, and will leave everything at Dillenburg, as M. [her father] tells me I will have to return there'. Missing the point of his urgency, however, she asks if she might stay another four or five weeks to help her aunt with the delivery. Orange had asked her to speak of her leaving to her uncle and grandmother. This was clearly a serious order.

As it turned out, the pregnancy ended sadly, with Marie's aunt being delivered prematurely of a stillborn girl. On 25 May, Marie wrote to her father from Dillenburg with this news, leaving everything in her father's hands; Kuin argues that it is not impossible that she could have reached Middelburg in time for the christening, or shortly thereafter. For those with a poetic streak, the conclusive proof might be held in some sentimental lines Philip penned 'To the tune of Wilhelmus van Nassau', a French melody that was usually sung to patriotic Dutch lyrics by Marnix van St Aldegonde. Philip's version, dealing with a 'she' who is 'nature's sweetest light', sadly lacks specific details of the 'she' in question.[84] Without the central correspondence (between Philip, Languet and Orange, for example), it is impossible to prove this case conclusively. But it does appear that Philip Sidney had just been offered his second princess in a single month.

Philip reached English soil sometime around 8 June 1577, and quickly made his way to the court at Greenwich. There he spent two days being debriefed, primarily by Walsingham and the queen, but also by Burghley, Leicester and other privy councillors, all with their own agendas. Sir Henry's secretary Edward Waterhouse wrote to assure his master that 'Mr Sidney is returned safe into England, with great good acceptation of his service at her Majesty's hands; allowed of by all the lords to have been handled with great judgement and discretion, and hath been honoured abroad in all the princes' courts with much extraordinary favour . . . God blessed him so, that neither man, boy, or horse failed him, or was sick in this journey; only Fulke Greville had an ague in his return at Rochester.'[85]

Walsingham was even more enthusiastic. Philip's embassy had been 'very sufficiently performed', he reported to Sir Henry, and his 'relating' of his journey at Greenwich was 'gratefully received, and well liked of her Majesty'. Indeed, he rhapsodised:

The gentleman hath given no small arguments of great hope, the fruits whereof I doubt not but your lordship shall reap, as the benefits of the good parts which are in him, and whereof he hath given some taste in this voyage, is to redound to more than your lordship and himself. There hath not been any gentleman, I am sure these many years, that hath gone through so honourable a charge with as great commendations as he: in consideration whereof, I could not but communicate this part of my joy with your lordship, being no less a refreshing unto me, in these my troublesome business, than the soil is to the chased stag.[86]

While Philip had finally made his mark on the English court, his embassy had sealed his lasting reputation on the Continent, providing a concrete validation of his much-vaunted potential. Walsingham noted 'the honourable opinion he hath left behind him, with all the princes with whom he had to negotiate, hath left a most sweet savour and grateful remembrance of his name in those parts'. His words were borne out by later traces of the embassy's impact. When Lambert Daneau came to dedicate his *Geographiæ Poeticæ* to Philip in 1580, he added to his standard list — 'son of Henry prorex of Ireland, nephew of the earls of Warwick and Leicester' — the billing of 'legate of Elizabeth, most serene Queen of England to the Emperor Rudolf, and other princes'.[87] As Fulke Greville later put it, this mission was 'the first prize which did enfranchise this master-spirit into the mysteries, and affairs of state'.[88] The German poet Paulus Melissus, laureate to Maximilian, penned a remarkably ornate verse tribute to Philip, whose voice 'by its serenity, could hold the emperor's eye and speech spell-bound', as he sailed away down the Rhine:

> O, Sidney, renowned for your study of the Muses, son of the Viceroy of Ireland, again you will sail down the Rhine to return to your native country along the wide waves of the vast Ocean. The illustrious Queen of your *Britannia* is eager to learn what you will have to report from the Imperial Court on your return as your Ambassador.[89]

Melissus, a neo-Latin poet with interest in vernacular poetry, appears to have corresponded with Philip, but sadly their letters are now lost.[90] Pietro Bizari wrote in 1579 of how in his embassy Sidney 'was so clearly the exemplar of the heroic spirit and the prudent, well-educated young man, that anyone could anticipate where his precocious and unique talent might direct him'. These were 'the rude beginnings of greater events, results of the highest significance may be expected'.[91] Alberico Gentili's treatise *De legationibus* (1585) concludes resoundingly by claiming that 'a living image and example of the perfect ambassador . . . can be found and demonstrated in one man only — a man who has all the qualities which are needed to make this consummate ambassador of ours, and has them indeed in greater abundance and on a more generous scale than is required. That man is PHILIP SIDNEY.'[92]

William of Orange was eager for negotiations for a Protestant League to get under way, as Thomas Wilson relayed to Walsingham.[93] For once, Elizabeth seized the initiative, and started to build on the foundations that Philip had laid. In June emerged the outline of the proposed treaty 'between the Queen of England and the Protestant Princes of Germany'. All princes willing to enter into a defensive league against the pope — no matter what their particular affiliation – would suppress their points of difference until those matters could be peaceably resolved. The princes would all contribute monies to sustain forces to be employed 'in the general defence of the common cause of religion'. These monies would be invested with merchants, and the interest arising would pay the pensions of some of the principal German reitmasters (commanders of mercenaries). The princes associated in this treaty would support one another if they were attacked on religious grounds; and they would aim, in the longer term, to draw in other princes, the free towns and Swiss cantons.[94] This was very much a Languetian plan of pooled resources supporting a Protestant army, relying not on any individual prince's force, but on a standing army of mercenaries.

But it was not Philip who pushed these plans forward. Elizabeth had become increasingly conscious and then suspicious of Philip's role in the process. Perhaps it occurred to her that, cleverly substituted for Leicester at the baptism of Orange's daughter, Philip had contrived to become something of an intimate of Orange, and even to inveigle his way into the Orange royal family.

Elizabeth's concern may have been fuelled by envious tongues. Thomas Moffet recalled how, on Philip's return from Prague, 'A few, to be sure, were observed to murmur, and to envy him so great preferment; but they were men without worth or virtue, who considered the public welfare a matter of indifference – fitter, in truth, to hold a distaff and card wool among servant girls than at any time to be considered as rivals by Sidney.' Whether provoked by others' envy or her own suspicions, however, Elizabeth's instructions for Daniel Rogers, completed on 22 June 1577, make plain with startling clarity her objections to Philip:

> We have in all our former actions, in these their late troubles, sought by all means to bring the provinces of the Low Countries that were at discord and divided, to an unity. If now, after such a course taken, we should, without further offence given, seek to dismember the body and pluck th'one part thereof from th'other, by withdrawing the subject from the Sovereign, we should enter a matter which should much touch us in honour and might be an evil precedent for us even in our own case. For we could not like that any foreign prince should enter into any such secret combination with our President of Wales or Deputy of

Ireland or any other governor under us, which might any way estrange him from th'obedience he oweth us.[95]

Elizabeth's examples of 'governor[s] under us' were not randomly chosen. The President of Wales and Deputy of Ireland were united in the body of one man, Sir Henry Sidney. The fact that she saw a possibility of Sir Henry entering into 'secret combination' suggests that Elizabeth's immediate concern was that the Sidney *family* might become estranged from their due obedience to her, rather than just the son Philip. With Philip Sidney as a leader in the Low Countries and Sir Henry ruling Ireland and Wales, there would be a distinct overload of power in the Dudley clique. Elizabeth could not safely tolerate this, and Philip was suddenly left out of future negotiations.

And so it was that Daniel Rogers (who had been with William of Orange while Philip travelled to Prague) was sent back at the end of June to consolidate Philip's work. Rogers was chosen precisely because of his low profile: 'This negotiation might seem to demand a person of more consequence than Rogers, but she thinks it better to send him so that the matter may be arranged the more secretly.'[96] Once again Rogers was sent to counsel Orange, bearing a letter that contained Elizabeth's gratitude for the honourable treatment afforded Philip.[97] In July, he accompanied Orange from Alkmaar to Enkhuizen with a company that included Janus Dousa and Marnix de St Aldegonde, who all enquired after Leicester, Philip and Edward Dyer.[98] By the beginning of August – still hoping for a link with Leicester via Philip – Orange claimed that the German states were too splintered to bring about an effective Protestant League, and suggested that England should instead unite with Holland and Zeeland.[99]

Orange's fears were borne out by Rogers' experiences over the next two months. In August Rogers travelled to Frankfurt and stayed with Languet, delivering a letter from Philip that softened Languet's irritation at his friend's tardiness at replying to his letters.[100] Rogers met Casimir at the end of August, who agreed that there were obstacles to the League, but thought these were confined to the quarrels between Lutherans and Calvinists. Rogers was then replaced by Robert Beale, clerk to the Privy Council, who was charged with dissuading the Lutheran princes from condemning their Calvinist-inclined peers as heretical, arguing that

Protestant unity was more indispensable than ever in the face of the strengthening Catholic threat.[101] Languet played a crucial role in preparing the ground with Casimir for both Rogers and Beale, both fellow Melanchthon pupils; in September 1577, Casimir ordered Languet to accompany Rogers to Ems to meet him and assist him in his meeting with the Landgrave of Hesse. Languet also kept Augustus informed of the progress of the English campaign, stressing Elizabeth's desire not to force a division between Lutheran and Calvinist, but rather to strengthen anti-Catholic unity.

At Ems, the landgrave declared that the League was an impossibility as long as Saxony continued to underwrite the 'ubiquitarian zeal' of 'certain mad divines', by which he meant the Lutheran theologians. Within a few days, Ludwig's enthusiasm had also evaporated. The League, he declared, was an attempt by the English to meddle in German affairs, and he would have no part in it. Casimir still held out a vain hope that if enough other German leaders could be persuaded to join, then the absence of Ludwig was not fatal, but the damage had been done.[102] It was enough to scupper the plan: on 31 October, a year and four days after Elector Frederick's death, Walsingham told Rogers that the plan was finished as far as Elizabeth was concerned.[103]

Philip had to bide his time in England while first Rogers, then Beale, pursued the plans he himself had made possible. It was not a happy time for him. Elizabeth's suspicion put him in an awkwardly powerless position on home soil. For example, when Henry, Duke of Lichtenstein visited the English court, Philip was expected to receive him. But his uncle and father were at Bath, and Philip lacked the means to entertain himself, let alone a visiting European duke. To Languet, he admitted freely that he was jealous of Robert Beale, negotiating in Germany: 'I love him, and yet I envy him.'[104] Philip was not completely sidelined, however, during the long summer. He 'formed an acquaintance' with a visiting nobleman named de Tamars. On the Continent he remained a presence by adding his own personal letters to the official letters from Elizabeth; despatches from Rogers testify to interest in Philip's whereabouts from Casimir.

He also tried to raise Languet's profile with the queen. When Martin Frobisher returned from his second voyage (in which Philip had invested fifty pounds) with 200 tons of ore, Philip asked Languet to provide a learned discourse on mining to help the English effort: 'we know that we're no more skilled in that art than we are in wine-making'. Languet could in this way help a major new English initiative. 'Please remember to write in a style which will live up to your reputation here, which is considerable. For if you allow me, I want to show your letter to the Queen. This business is indeed of great importance.'[105] Languet missed the point of this and wrote a few pages about his fears that England would be 'seduced by a desire for gold', leading to the shedding of much English blood.[106] Not surprisingly, when Philip tried, via Leicester, to procure from Elizabeth some reward to mark Languet's vital contribution – Languet declared to Beale that he had not suggested this – it was in vain.[107]

Despite the queen's actions, Philip's marriage negotiations refused to go away, thanks to the persistence of his friend. At the end of February 1578, Robert Beale, Daniel Rogers and Peter Beutterich arrived back in London, bearing letters from Languet. Marriage, apparently, was still on the cards, although it seems that Languet may have found yet another potential bride. Philip's reply was comically exasperated:

> I wonder, dearest Hubert, what you're thinking of: when I've not yet done anything worthy of myself, you want me tied in the chains of matrimony; and without specifying which lady, but just praising the state itself, although you've not set the example yourself. As for the lady (of whom I acknowledge how unworthy I am), I've let you know my reasons long ago – in brief, it's true, but as well as I could. Now, however, you seem to have another idea in mind, and I beg you to let me know what it is . . .[108]

It may be that Philip tried to laugh off this new proposal because he was still interested in the Orange match. As late as April 1578, Mendoza reported to Philip of Spain:

> There is much talk here of a marriage between Philip Sidney, Leicester's nephew, the heir of Henry Sidney, of the earl of Warwick, and of Leicester's property, and a sister of Orange [Mendoza is perhaps mistaken about the relationship], who enters very willingly into the suggestion, and promises as a dowry to make him lord of Holland and

Zeeland, by this means and other gifts gaining over Leicester, who has now turned his back upon France, to which he was formerly so much attached.[109]

It is striking that these terms, offered by Orange to Philip and Leicester, echo those he offered to Elizabeth scarcely a year earlier – since he has been unable to convince the queen, the Dudley dynasty is clearly the next choice. But by now Philip Sidney was stuck back in England, unable to travel without a licence from his queen – and she was not about to provide his passport to a princess.

CHAPTER EIGHT

The Perfect Courtier

RESTRAINED BY ELIZABETH from taking his part in Europe's Protestant politics, Philip bestowed his energies where they might be of use: at Elizabeth's own court, in favour of his father. He had returned to find that Sir Henry's position in Ireland, always very difficult, had deteriorated sharply during his absence. When the Lord Deputy requested further funds during the summer of 1577, Elizabeth responded to him abruptly: 'You gave us hope to diminish our charges and increase our revenue, but we find the former still to be great and the latter . . . is much decayed.'[1] The signals were clear. By August, Sir Henry was writing to Leicester: 'It is bruited [rumoured] here that I am to be revoked, and that speedily. The bruit doth no good, but if it be intended the sooner the better, for the queen and for myself. I attest God I had rather have the Harry Beswyche office in Kenilworth, than Sir Harry Sidney's in Kilmaynham.'[2]

Even before Philip went to Prague, he was being relied on by Sir Henry to present his case at court. From a letter that Sir Henry wrote from Dublin to Philip in March 1577, we can glimpse the kind of service Philip was supposed to provide. The letter was carried by Sir Cormock McTeigh McCarty, whose service Sir Henry wanted to recommend. 'I would have you make him known to my lords your uncles, and to other your friends in the court,' he wrote to his son, 'as a special man of this country's birth and his training, and breeding up.' Sir Henry's word was clearly not enough – he needed Philip's courtly finesse, and his close association with Leicester and Warwick, to carry his plans through.[3]

In the autumn of 1577, Philip's skills were called on more than ever before, as Elizabeth engaged Sir Henry in a tedious pitched battle-by-letter over his imposition of the 'cess' (land-tax) on lords living within the borders of the Pale. These lords claimed exemption by customary practice; Sir Henry's investigation into the archives he had 'laid up' at Dublin Castle suggested that this claim was bogus. A delegation of three Palesmen sent to the English court to protest had been imprisoned, but Elizabeth's favourite, Ormond, was intervening with the queen for the Palesmen.[4]

Philip was angry on his father's behalf. In Waterhouse's words, he imputed to Ormond 'such practices as have been made to alienate her majesty's mind' from his father, and matters soon came to a head. In September 1577, there were, as Waterhouse delicately put it, 'some little occasions of discourtesies . . . passed between the earl of Ormond and Mr Philip Sidney'. The discourtesies were founded on the niceties of court etiquette: passing each other one day, Ormond spoke to Philip, but Philip said nothing in response, remaining instead 'in dead silence of purpose'. Although this was a huge snub to a social superior, nothing much came of Philip's rudeness: Ormond announced magnanimously that 'he will accept no quarrels from a gentleman that is bound by nature to defend his father's causes; and who is otherwise furnished with so many virtues, as he knows Mr Philip to be'.[5]

His punctilious impudence effectively foiled, Philip determined instead to fight his father's corner in another way. An occasion was presented by the arrival at court of Sir Henry's Lord Chancellor, William Gerrard, who had journeyed from Ireland to present the Lord Deputy's case. Waterhouse informed Sir Henry that 'I have obtained that at my Lord Chancellor's coming, your lordship's matters shall have present hearing: and I think that to the cess rates, Mr Philip, Mr Whitten and I shall be called to assist him.' Master Philip was to be present because

> Mr Philip had gathered a collection of all the articles, which have been
> enviously objected to your government, whereunto he hath framed an
> answer in way of discourse, the most excellently (if I have any
> judgement) that ever I read in my life; the substance whereof is now
> approved in your letters and notes by Mr Whitten. But let no man
> compare with Mr Philip's pen. I know he will send it to your lordship,
> and when you read it you shall have more cause to pray God for him
> than to impute affection to me in this my opinion of him.[6]

Only one manuscript copy of the document survives, with only the last four answers intact, which suggests that it was not written for circulation. Indeed, it may merely have formed the basis for Philip's *viva voce* performance with Gerrard, Whitten and Waterhouse before the Council.[7] The 'Discourse' answered seven of the Palesmen's complaints (as Sir Henry had done in a letter of the previous month to the queen).

In Philip's appraisal, no doubt informed by his experiences there a year earlier, Ireland was an extreme country, which required extreme action. In his opinion, there were three possible solutions to the problem: 'Either by direct conquest to make the country hers, and so by one great heap of charges to purchase that which indeed afterwards would well countervail the principal; or else by diminishing that she doth send thither; or, lastly, with force and gentleness, to raise at least so much rents, as may serve to quit the same charges.' The third, in Philip's view, was necessary, but only as a softener before undertaking the first option. Whether or not the merits of Philip's representations were the cause, the queen finally conceded to Sir Henry that 'sufficient matter was produced by the Chancellor for justification of you and that Council, and all your doings in the continuance of the cess'.[8]

Philip was not merely ventriloquising Sir Henry Sidney. In the 'Discourse' we get a glimpse of a young man whom many believed could one day become Lord Deputy of Ireland himself. In his letter of advice to his eventual successor, Lord Grey, Sir Henry rather pointedly stated that his son Philip 'most earnestly and often hath spoken and written to do this loving office'.[9] Sir Geoffrey Fenton – who a decade earlier had dedicated his book of prose fictions to Lady Sidney, and was now an official in Dublin – suggested in 1580 that Leicester might obtain a grant of Lord Barry's lands, either for himself or to reward court friends. Kerry would be an ideal choice for the latter. 'If your lordship so like, it might be transferred to my lord of Warwick or else to Mr Philip Sidney by the title of Baron of Kenny.'[10] Philip may have seen the protection of his father's regime in Ireland as having long-term benefits for his own promotion.

But Philip had won the battle, only for Sir Henry to lose the war. Even as Elizabeth's anger appeared to cool in January 1578, Walsingham detected that she would probably recall the Lord Deputy from Ireland on the pretext of a conference to discuss the trimming of expenses there. His friends on the Privy Council urged the queen to give Sir Henry some reward, to counter the humiliation that public recall would inflict. But only a month later, in February 1578, Sir Henry received the call to come home.

Philip took it on himself to manage Sir Henry's recall, anxious to make it look as good as possible. At first he advised him to return 'as soon as conveniently you might', since he had assurances from 'the best sort' that Sir Henry's return should be met with 'honourable considerations . . . particularly to your lot'. However, by late April events had led Philip to change his mind: 'So strangely and diversely goes the course of the world by the interchanging humours of those that govern it, that though it be most noble to have always one mind and one constancy, yet can it not be always directed to one point; but must needs sometimes alter his course, according to the force of others' changes drives it.' Now, in Philip's case, 'it makes me change my style, and write to your lordship, that keeping still your mind in one state of virtuous quietness, you will yet frame your course according to them. And as they delay your honourable rewarding, so you by good means delay your return, till either that ensue, or fitter time be for this.'

Philip had a suggestion. The queen's letters had prescribed the date when the Lord Deputy should leave Ireland: however, the deadline had already passed by the time her messenger reached Dublin with instructions. Sir Henry should use this to buy time. He was 'to write back, not as though you desired to tarry, but only showing that unwillingly you must employ some days thereabouts'. He could also add that he needed Chancellor Gerrard to return to Ireland: 'for by him your Lordship shall either have honourabler revocation, or commandment of furder [further] stay at least till Michaelmas, which in itself shall be a fitter time; considering, that then your term comes fully out, so that then your enemies can not glory it is their procuring'. In the meantime, Philip assured his father, his friends could 'labour here to bring to a better pass, such your reasonable and honourable desires, which time can better bring forth than speed. Amongst which friends,' he pointed out, 'before God there is none proceeds either so thoroughly or so wisely, as my lady my mother. For mine own part, I have had only light from her.' Evidently Lady Sidney was still working busily on her husband's behalf at court.

Leaving the final choice to his father (but making it clear that 'for mine own part (of which mind your best friends are here) this is your best way'), Philip pleaded to be kept informed by Sir Henry himself:

> I beseech you with all speed I may understand, and that if it please you
> with your own hand; for truly Sir, I must needs impute it some great
> dishonesty of some about you, that there is little written from you, or to
> you, that is not perfectly known to your professed enemies. And thus

much I am very willing they should know, that I do write it unto you: And in that quarter, you may, as I think, look precisely to the saving of some of those overplusages, or at least not to go any furder; and then the more time passes, the better it will be blown over.[11]

What is striking about Philip's reaction to the perceived slur on his father's reputation (which naturally threatened to visit itself on the son) is his pragmatic flexibility, allowing him to change course according to 'the interchanging humours' of the world's governors. It was a pragmatism instilled by Hubert Languet, demonstrating an admirable ability to read the nuances of a complex situation, and to respond accordingly.

The affair also revealed Philip as a man experienced in the technicalities of international correspondence: he insisted on Sir Henry writing in his own hand, without involving any third party, because he had reason to believe that the Lord Deputy's rule was being routinely sabotaged by the civil servants about him, who dealt with his paperwork. In time, he tracked down the leak – to Sir Henry's secretary, Edmund Molyneux. On 31 May 1578 Philip made the situation brutally plain in a strikingly abrupt letter:

Mr Molyneux,

Few words are best. My letters to my father have come to the eyes of some. Neither can I condemn any but you for it. If it be so, you have played the very knave with me; and so I will make you know if I have good proof of it. But that for so much as is past. For that is to come, I assure you before God, that if ever I know you do so much as read any letter I write to my father, without his commandment, or my consent, I will thrust my dagger into you. And trust to it, for I speak it in earnest. In the meantime farewell.[12]

Molyneux professed himself devastated by Philip's letter, 'the sharpest that I ever received from any'. He could not deny that he read Philip's letters, but he protested that he did so simply because he enjoyed reading them so much: 'I must confess, I have heretofore taken both great delight and profit in reading some of them.' This was his only motivation, he claimed, and Philip wrongly accused him of sabotaging his father's correspondence. 'It is (I protest to God) without cause, or yet just ground

of suspicion you use me thus'), tartly commenting on Philip's melo-
dramatic threats: 'you might have commanded me in a far greater matter,
with a far less penalty'.[13] Philip seems to have harboured resentment of
Molyneux, justified or not: he attacked the secretary again in April 1581
when he became convinced that Molyneux was blocking Fulke Greville's
bid to win the office of Clerk of the Signet to the Court of the Council
in the Marches of Wales, a lucrative post newly brought into being by
Sir Henry's administrative initiatives.[14]

Rumours about Sir Henry's future abounded – he was to be given
charge of Mary, Queen of Scots, or to lead a force of 10,000 men into
Flanders – rumours that the Spanish ambassador Mendoza promptly
broadcast to Spain. After a stalling period in which he endeavoured to
bring Ireland to a state of 'universal quiet', Sir Henry travelled back,
bringing as booty 'that arch traitor' the Earl of Clanrickard and his son.
According to Edmund Molyneux, as he boarded the ship that would take
him away from Ireland for the last time, Lord Deputy Sidney turned to
the Psalms: 'And at his very entering into the ship for his farewell unto
that whole land and nation, he recited the words of the 114th Psalm . . .
alluding thereby to the troublesome state of Moses in the land of
Egypt.'[15] Ireland had taken its toll, and by now Sir Henry was seriously
ill. He stopped in Chester for ten days (18–28 September) to try to regain
his strength, and finally returned to court some six months after his recall.
As he later remembered, it was not a happy occasion: 'When I came to
the Court to know how I was entertained, I confess well, but not so well
as I thought and in conscience felt I had deserved . . . Notwithstanding
all these my painful services I was accounted *servus inutilis* [a useless
servant] for that I had exceeded a supposed commission . . . and although
somewhat I had exceeded in spending her Majesty's treasure, I had too
far exceeded in spoiling my own patrimony.'[16]

Sir Henry's rule in Ireland had many supporters. After his death,
Auditor Jenyson proclaimed to Lord Burghley that 'Sir Henry Sidney
was of great credit and also famous in this government as by divers his
erections appeareth, and most chiefly by the bridge of Athlone, which is
one of the best acts done for the commonwealth.'[17] The Irish State
Papers are littered with flattering comments: 'If Sir Henry Sidney can but
sit in his chair he will do more good than others with all their limbs'; 'Sir
Henry Sidney is cried for by the children in the street'; 'The public desire

Sir Henry Sidney above all others to be Lord Deputy.'[18] In his heart, Sir Henry knew that it was not bad leadership, but the battle over the cess, that had lost him Ireland. 'Trust me, my lord,' he wrote to his successor, Lord Grey, 'this one particular was the thing that chiefly brake my back.'[19] Philip's father was no longer King of Ireland.

Elizabeth's behaviour towards Sir Henry reinforced the perception that the Sidneys could do little right in her eyes. But then, her concern about the Dudley–Sidney axis had not been helped by the fact that the families had engineered another high-level alliance, this time with the Herberts. Philip's sister Mary was now fifteen, and quite a catch: John Aubrey later wrote of her, 'She was a beautiful lady and had an excellent wit, and had the best breeding that that age could afford. She had a pretty sharp-oval face. Her hair was of a reddish yellow.'[20] As early as December 1576, court gossip had it that Mary would be the next 'lady of Wilton', third wife of the forty-year-old widower Henry Herbert, second Earl of Pembroke.[21] Pembroke already had extensive and long-standing links with the Dudley and Sidney families, stretching back to the days of the Duke of Northumberland, and reinforced by Pembroke's interest in Wales. Indeed, in 1553 Pembroke, then Lord Henry Herbert, had married Lady Catherine Grey, sister of Lady Jane, as part of Northumberland's campaign to place Lady Jane on the throne (the marriage was later annulled, as politically embarrassing).

For the Sidneys the prospect of Mary's marriage was a financial nightmare. After years of subsidising his official duties in Wales and Ireland, Sir Henry simply could not raise the dowry, but he desperately wanted this son-in-law. While still in Ireland, he wrote to Leicester 'protesting before the Almighty God that if He and all the powers on earth would give me my choice for a husband for her I would choose the Earl of Pembroke'. He had one request: 'Good my Lord, send Philip to me; there was never father had more need of his son than I have of him. Once again, good my Lord, let me have him.'[22] But at that moment Philip was about to go to Prague, and could not help his father. Even without Philip, Sir Henry contrived to bring the match to fruition, turning instead directly to Leicester, and on 21 April 1577, Mary Sidney became the Countess of Pembroke.[23] Sir Henry was ecstatic at the match and wrote to Leicester: 'I pray you let me know what sum of money and at what days you have ordered me to pay my lord of Pembroke. I am made very happy by the match. If God should take me away it would be more charge to your nephew [Philip] or yourself than if it be done in my time.'[24] The marriage negotiations were, as usual, complex, and Sir Henry was inevitably late in raising the staggered instalments of the £3,000 dowry. In September 1577, he was forced to beg Walsingham to rubber-stamp payments due to him: 'I beseech you, sir, favour me in getting my payment for my warrant of £3,000 and the £1,600 which I laid out for debt due before my entering into charge . . . I have no other means to satisfy my lord of Pembroke for my daughter's marriage money but this way.'[25] After an initial payment of £1,500, Sir Henry borrowed £1,000 on 15 December from his brother-in-law Sir James Harrington. The final payment of £500 was not made until 3 February 1578.[26]

Pembroke represented a good marriage for Mary. The jointure agreement details quite an array of land and properties settled on her for life.[27] Her energies were to be expended in maintaining and entertaining in her husband's multiple homes: estates at Ramsbury, Ivychurch and Wilton in Wiltshire; and a London house at Baynards Castle. Philip quickly took advantage of these new residential possibilities, perhaps to avoid the cramped, expensive accommodation at court, and damp outposts in Wales and Ireland. In Wilton, Philip found an ideal rural retreat, to which he would return time and again over the next few years: he was certainly there in August, September and again in December 1577. Wilton was a large, quadrangular house, surrounded by a high wall, which the earl's father had built at some considerable expense from stone quarried at Chilmark on land granted to him following the dissolution of the Abbey of Wilton (which had a 700-year history) in 1539.[28] Philip featured it in his poem 'The 7 Wonders of England', written sometime between 1577 and 1581, playing on the estate's proximity to Stonehenge:

> Near Wilton sweet, hugh heaps of stones are found,
>   But so confused, that neither any eye
>   Can count them just, nor reason reason try
> What force brought them to so unlikely ground.[29]

Although he had not previously been close to his sister (Mary was only three when he left for Shrewsbury, and they probably only got to know each other on the 1575 progress), they quickly became fast friends. Philip's brotherly affection even led to scurrilous rumours (according to John Aubrey) that 'there was so great love between him and his fair sister that I have heard old gentlemen say that they lay together, and it was thought the first Philip Earl of Pembroke [the fourth earl] was begot by him'.[30] As with so much of Aubrey's information, there is nothing to support this accusation, or to suggest that the rumour was ever current. However, it might betray a real anxiety – that something untoward was going on at Wilton. The Wiltshire estate did seem to attract some of England's most politically dangerous figures. In June 1577, the newly-weds welcomed to Wilton some early visitors: the Earls of Leicester and Warwick; Leicester then went privately with Pembroke to Buxton spa. Two months later, Philip and Robert Sidney (on vacation from Oxford) came to stay with their sister. At Christmas, one commentator noted that Leicester had disappeared from court and gone to Wilton 'to sport there awhile, making merry with his nephew, the earl of Pembroke', before returning just before Christmas.[31] Wilton soon established itself as a base away from town not only for the Herberts, but also for the Dudleys and Sidneys. In such a group, so closely knit by familial and marital bonds, it was difficult to spot where a family gathering ended and a political summit began.

Wilton was no doubt one setting for heated discussions about how the Protestant cause should proceed in Europe. Although negotiations for a formal Protestant League had collapsed, some of the main players were still desperate to gain English support and, given Elizabeth's recalcitrance, Leicester was their new target. William of Orange led the attack. On 3 October 1577, Elizabeth's ambassador in Brussels, William Davison, wrote to tell Leicester: 'I find the prince the most desirous man in the world of your Lordship's coming over, and it is the string he daily harps on; but as one careful, I think, above all men of your honour's welfare.' Orange appreciated the difficulties this plan might entail, especially Leicester's long absence from court, which might prejudice the very cause they had in mind – given that by Leicester's 'credit and presence there all their causes have the better speed and success'. Notwithstanding, 'to come over and remain here a while to set all things in good order, and to bring with your lordship some such qualified person as, in case you should be revoked, might be fit to take the charge, he thought it would greatly advance their cause'. Davison and Orange then:

> fell to speak particularly of persons to supply your room [to fill your office], to the which I named my good lordship of Warwick, your lordship's brother, or, if that might not be, Mr Philip Sidney, both men so agreeable to his Excellency as in a world I could not have made a choice to his better contentment, for the honourable opinion he hath both of the one and other; but he would have all referred to your lordship's own direction upon this point.[32]

More pressure came from Johann Casimir. In December 1577, Daniel Rogers and Casimir's minister Peter Beutterich left Germany for England with a new proposal. As Languet explained to Philip:

> you will discover that the illustrious Prince Casimir has high regard for you, and wants to do you service . . . Rest assured that it's not only the Spaniards and the French who desire the overthrow of those in Flanders who are taking up arms to maintain their liberty; there are also some of Germany's leading princes who want the same, and are eager to make good use of any opportunity . . . If you give some thought to the Germans, you will be doing a thing not unworthy (to my mind) of your greatness as a nation, and would add to your influence considerably.

Languet suggested that one means of accomplishing this 'would be to hold several military officers to your [i.e. England's] interests with a small yearly stipend. You couldn't use them to raise troops, but it would increase your influence significantly, and you would be more highly regarded in Germany than you have been up to now. And occasions would no doubt arise when you could put obstacles in the way of those who look to hurt you.' In order that these officers would not be 'like the individual twigs of a broom, unfit for working, and therefore useless to you', Languet proposed that a leader should be appointed – 'some man, eminent in moral character and social rank, whose authority might tie them together, and who should exert control over them through a subsidy provided by you'. Unsurprisingly he had a candidate to propose:

to no man could a command like this be trusted more advantageously than to the most noble Prince Casimir. As you well know without me telling you, he's the only man in Germany to whom it could be trusted at all – whether it's in respect to his devotion and respect for her gracious Majesty and your country, or to the splendour of his birth, or his age, now in its prime, or his martial prowess and experience, or the reputation he has with military men.[33]

Languet's proposition was neither a pipe-dream nor a shot in the dark. For a time it seemed that Philip Sidney might go to the Low Countries with Casimir. On 1 March 1578, Philip wrote to Languet, tentatively, that he believed the queen would do 'what you wrote to me about' for the sake of Prince Casimir, but warned that it 'is not our nature' – by which he meant Elizabeth's nature – to do anything in a hurry. He was by now desperate to act: his mind, he told Languet, began 'to lose its strength, and to relax without any reluctance. For to what purpose would our thoughts be directed by various kinds of knowledge, unless room be afforded by putting it into practice, so that public advantage may be the result, which in a corrupt age we cannot hope for.'[34]

Finally, in April 1578, Casimir sent a formal request directly to Philip for an English force to support his own 'moderate forces' with which he would march into Flanders, as Elizabeth proposed. 'I have begged her to appoint some gentleman to be attached to me to assist me in her name at all deliberations. I have desired that this should be yourself, for the singular opinion I have of your virtue, and the pleasure I should receive from frequent conference with you. If her Majesty thinks well to send some one, I pray you do not refuse this charge.'[35] It was Daniel Rogers who had to put the notion to Elizabeth that Casimir 'desires her Majesty to send some man of good estimation and calling, who may continually during the war remain about him and be present at all deliberations. He especially desires Mr Philip Sidney to be sent, a gentleman whom for his noble towardness and virtue he has greatly in admiration.'[36]

In April, Walsingham was informed that Philip's departure was imminent.[37] According to the Spanish ambassador Mendoza in mid-June

the Queen has appointed Lord Howard to be Admiral of the six ships which are being fitted out with Henry [sic] Sidney, a nephew of

Leicester's, to be Vice-Admiral, the other captains being selected men. It is understood that these ships will take three standards of infantry raised by the guilds or trained bands of this city, although some suspect that they will go over to Flanders. Walsingham is going there, and he is such a devilish heretic that he constantly favours those like himself, and persecutes the Catholics in order to pledge the Queen more deeply to his way of thinking.[38]

Certainly, the Privy Council called Philip to court on 5 June with this message: 'To Mr Philip Sidney that where her Majesty intendeth forthwith to set certain of her ships to the seas wherein his service to be used, he is therefore required immediately to make his repair to the Court with all expedition, to receive such charge as shall be committed unto him in that behalf.'[39]

At this moment, hoping to force the pace, Philip put his pen to work again. But the result this time was not a political tract, but an entertainment, which has come to be known as *The Lady of May*, in which Philip put to work some of the ideas he had gleaned from seeing Sir Henry Lee's entertainment at Woodstock. As with Lee's piece, *The Lady of May* required the presence of, and participation of, the queen herself. The scene was the garden of Leicester's residence at Wanstead, at the beginning of May 1578. As Elizabeth walked in the garden, she was accosted by 'one apparelled like an honest man's wife of the country', who beseeched her to intervene in her daughter's dilemma. Her 'poor daughter', the wife explained, was 'oppressed with two [suitors], both loving her, both equally liked of her, both striving to deserve her': one a forester named Therion, the other a shepherd named Espilus. Elizabeth was asked to choose between the two, who battled to prove their worth in an exchange of verses. The contest was then seconded in a debate between Dorcas, an old shepherd, and Rixus, a young forester, moderated by a pedantic schoolmaster named Rombus, given to bilingual malapropisms. The queen made her judgement, and Rombus completed the entertainment with a tongue-in-cheek portrayal of Wanstead's owner as an arch-Catholic:

In this our city we have a certain neighbour, they call him Master
Robert of Wanstead . . . he is foully commaculated with the papistical

enormity . . . The *bonus vir* is a huge *catholicam*, . . . I have found *unum par*, a pair, *papistirocum bedorus*, of Papistian beads, *cum quis*, with the which, *omnium dierum*, every day, next after his *pater noster* he *semper* suits 'and Elizabeth', as many lines as there be beads on this string.[40]

Leicester's 'papistical enormity' was happily revealed to be no more than his idol-worship of Elizabeth herself.

This may sound slight enough, but recent critics have shown how, placed in its immediate contexts, this little entertainment could yield fascinating interpretations. The Wanstead visit by the queen came as a mission to the Low Countries was being mooted. Two days before the court arrived, on 11 May 1578, Walsingham wrote to William Davison intimating that the queen was pondering whether to send him and 'some persons of quality to deal effectually with the States', while Leicester was labouring 'greatly to be employed in this journey, and is not without hope to obtain it'.[41] In *The Lady of May*, Therion and Espilus personify debates about action versus inaction, risk versus security, aggression versus passivity. It is a May Day event: the queen is asked to choose the May King, who was traditionally Robin Hood. Therion is, like Robin Hood, a forester, a venison-stealer, and 'sweet Robin' was Elizabeth's affectionate nickname for Leicester.[42] Could it be that the active, spontaneous Therion suggested active political intervention, inviting Elizabeth to endorse Leicester as her envoy to the Low Countries – and, by extension, to endorse Philip's involvement there?

If so, it did not work. Philip's highly allusive little drama had one major flaw in performance – it left the writing of the crucial line of the script to its audience. Whereas in the Kenilworth entertainments of 1575, Elizabeth was only ever called on to fulfil a function, here she was allowed to make a choice. Deliberately going against the grain of the piece, Elizabeth chose Espilus, and Leicester ended up taking the waters at Buxton again rather than sailing off to the Low Countries.[43]

By July, Elizabeth had arrived at a compromise: Philip might go, but only as a private person, not as her representative. It was a bitter blow to Leicester, but it was better than nothing. To Sir Christopher Hatton, he reasoned: 'Since my hap is not to be in so honourable a voyage nor ch[arge?], I would be most glad that my nephew might go to Casimir; and if he may not as from her Majesty, yet after the other sort, you say her

Majesty could like of. I beseech you further it, and I shall be most glad it may be obtained.'[44] When Sir Henry heard of Philip's plans to join Casimir, he was preparing to return from Ireland. The thought of making his way through the complexities of court life without his son to steer his path terrified him, as he wrote to Leicester:

> I understand by Philip that he hath put on a determination to go into the Low Countries to serve the States in company and under the conduct of Casimir, which if it be so, what lack his presence shall be unto me at my coming over, having to answer so many complaints and informations as the malice of my enemies here devised against me, I leave to your lordship to consider. But if the matter be not of that weight as his stay shall be requisite to assist me I would not then hinder his determination in a matter wherein he is to purchase himself so much honour and credit to stay him.[45]

For others, however, Philip's imminent departure was an exciting prospect. In July, when Elizabeth's summer progress came to Audley End, near Cambridge, Gabriel Harvey compiled a volume of verse commending those he saw as her principal courtiers: Leicester, Burghley, Hatton, Oxford – and Philip Sidney. He presented Philip as the image of the perfect courtier, and dedicated one elogium to Philip 'a little before his departure'.[46] Abraham Fraunce, a fellow Shrewsbury alumnus and now an undergraduate at St John's College, Cambridge, dedicated to Philip a manuscript volume that brought together a summary of Ramist logic and a collection of *imprese*, or emblems. The coloured binding depicts a scene from the *Aeneid* in which Achaemaendis, the castaway whom Odysseus has left with Polyphemus, begs to be rescued by Aeneas and his men. The significance of the scene is not deeply buried. Between Achaemaendis' feet are the initials 'A.F.' (Abraham Fraunce). If the point is not clear enough, the back cover has valedictory verses praising Philip's wisdom, strength and eloquence. Fraunce is pleading with Aeneas/Philip not to be left behind as Philip embarks on his sea voyage.[47]

Finally, in early August 1578, Philip was given formal leave to go, but events abroad dictated that Elizabeth had reconsidered his role once again. Much to her horror, Casimir had let it be known that the queen supported his march into Brabant, information that she had wanted kept quiet. Now, she made clear, Philip had to be the bearer of a poisoned chalice to Casimir, a duty that hardly redounded to his international honour. As Leicester wrote bitterly to Walsingham:

> When my nephew Ph. was to take his leave and receive his dispatch, among other small comforts he should have brought to the Prince, he was specially commanded by her Majesty to tell duke Casimir that she marvelled not a little, and was offended with him for giving out that his coming was by her means, and that she misliked any such speeches, and prayed her name might not be so abused, since she did not command him to come, but the States had entertained him and they should maintain his coming; with such other small encouragement to that prince, whose cause of coming you and I and almost all men know. Yet this earnestly has she commanded Ph. to say to him, writing such a letter besides of cold comfort that when I heard of both, I did all I could to stay him at home; and with much ado I think I shall, seeing I know not what he should do there but bring discouragement to all her best friends. For my part I had rather he perished in the sea than that he should be instrument of it.[48]

Eighteen months earlier, Philip had been the proud representative of the English queen, with a daring plan to reconfigure European Protestant politics. Now he was to be the vehicle through which Elizabeth was to dash any hopes that plan might have raised. Leicester realised the damage this could inflict on Philip's personal credibility with his continental allies, and was able to convince Philip that he could not undertake this mission. This was probably the result that the queen was aiming for. Fulke Greville recalled that, when he attempted to go to see Casimir's manoeuvres, 'my horses, with all other preparations being shipped at Dover, with leave under her bill assigned: even then was I stayed by a princely mandate, the messenger Edward Dyer'.[49] It may well be that *had* Philip decided to go, then he would have been called back, at the last moment, as Greville was – with their friend Dyer forced to bring the bad tidings.

For Philip it signalled the end of his attempts simultaneously to please the queen and follow his political conscience. He retired to Wilton, where in November, the three families met up to celebrate Mary's seventeenth birthday.[50] The festivities were a useful pretext for a reassessment of their strategy.

Elizabeth's withdrawing of support from Casimir's military efforts occurred as she resumed marriage negotiations, this time with the French king's younger brother, François, Duc d'Anjou. Philip remembered Anjou from his time in Paris when he had been the Duc d'Alençon. Only two years earlier, Philip had considered going to fight with Anjou: by the end of 1576, however, Anjou had renounced his Huguenot affiliations and returned to his brother Henri's court. In the spring of 1577, he had been implicated in a savage massacre of Huguenots in the Loire Valley. In February 1578, Henri had placed him under arrest; escaping, Anjou turned his sights to the Low Countries, making it known that he was willing to fight for whoever wanted him – Don John or William of Orange.[51]

Since Elizabeth had declined to intervene, William of Orange was finally forced to accept Anjou's offer. In August 1578, a treaty was signed by which Anjou became 'defender of the liberty of the Netherlands against the tyranny of the Spanish and their allies'. Although the situation was partly of Elizabeth's making, this raised the spectre of a French-controlled Low Countries, a possibility she found as unappealing now as it had been six years earlier. Suspicious that the whole arrest-and-escape story was a ruse concocted by Anjou and Henri, designed to facilitate France's annexation of the Low Countries, Elizabeth sent an embassy led by Walsingham and Cobham to investigate in May 1578; they soon confirmed that Anjou was acting on his own initiative, without the support of his brother.

Satisfied by her ambassadors' report, Elizabeth held out an offer of aid to Anjou to help his campaign, to prevent the Low Countries falling into Henri's hands. In return, Anjou revived the question of marriage, and in July 1578 sent over his Chamberlain in Ordinary, the Sieur de Bacqueville, to make a formal proposal. Elizabeth prevaricated, sending Bacqueville to France in September, with the clever message that she could never marry a man on whom she had not first laid eyes. Only after several months did she agree that Anjou's ambassador Jean Simier might come to commence real negotiations.[52]

However, just as Simier was setting out from Paris in December, a new problem arose. As the Spanish ambassador Mendoza reported to Philip II on New Year's Eve, the French king had 'welcomed and entertained' a brother of the Earl of Morton, whose regency in Scotland had just collapsed. It was by no means clear what the purpose of the visit was, but in the meantime the English ambassador in France advised that 'it would be desirable that the Queen should send some one to the king of France to make an excuse for M. de Simier's coming being delayed. She has therefore sent Philip Sidney.'[53] Philip may have jumped at the chance of being part of any plan to delay the marriage negotiations, but soon enough Simier, who had been stalled at Calais, was allowed to proceed to London, where he arrived on 5 January 1579.

Philip soon welcomed another, far more desirable set of guests. Casimir had arrived at the 'patriot' camp in Brabant on 26 August 1578, along with 12,000 mercenaries. However, in October he had ridden to support the ultra-Calvinist group in Ghent in their fight against some mutinous troops dubbed the 'Malcontents'. This effectively put him in opposition to the more religiously tolerant policies of William of Orange. By January, Casimir was stuck in Ghent with troops he could not afford to pay: it seemed to him that his only option was to flee back to Germany. But then he fell on the idea of travelling to England, which would also give him a chance to explain himself to Elizabeth, who had to all intents and purposes abandoned him. A retinue of some twenty-five or thirty people was hastily assembled, including Hubert Languet, who overcame his fear that the sea journey might be the last straw for his fragile health. Casimir announced disingenuously that he had decided 'to make a voyage into England to see her Majesty before he return home being so near the seas as he is'.[54]

Elizabeth commissioned Philip to meet Casimir as he disembarked. After the Simier muddle, this was a commission he relished, not least because it reunited him with Languet, whom he had last seen over eighteen months earlier. Philip escorted the party to the Tower of London, where they arrived during the evening of 22 January.[55] Casimir was welcomed by various noblemen, and then 'conveyed by cresset light and torch light to Sir Thomas Gresham's house in Bishopsgate Street, where he was received with sounding of trumpets, drums, fifes, and other instruments of music, and there both lodged and feasted till Sunday next'. From there he was fetched to the court at Westminster, where he was granted an audience with the queen, and was lodged at Somerset House. A contemporary account detailed the events:

> In the week following he hunted at Hampton Court. On Sunday, the first of February, he beheld a valiant jousting and running at the tilt at Westminster; on the next morrow he saw them fight at barriers with swords on horseback. On Tuesday he dined with the Lord Mayor of London; on Wednesday with the Duchess of Suffolk at her house called the Burgokening or Barbican, by Redcross Street; on Thursday at the Stilyard, etc. On the 8th of February the Queen made him Knight of the Garter, by delivering to him the collar and putting the Garter on his leg at Whitehall. On the 14th of February he departed from London homewards, with great rewards given by the Queen's Majesty, the nobility, men of honour, the Mayor of London, and citizens of that city.[56]

The City of London presented Casimir with 2,000 crowns' worth of chain and plate. This was full VIP treatment.

Throughout the festivities Leicester was constantly at Casimir's side, and entertained him at his estate in Wanstead. Sir Henry Sidney took Casimir, and probably Languet, to Paris Garden, which lay opposite his house at Paul's Wharf. This was also the first time that Sir Henry had met these two champions of his son and he spared no expense, as his accounts compiled by John Pakenham indicate:

> For my boat-hire from the Court to follow your lordship [i.e. Sir Henry] when you went in haste to meet Duke Casimir the 20th of January . . . 3s. For my boat-hire when your lordship went to the Parrish Garden [Paris Garden] with Casimir, going and coming . . . 3s. For money given to your lordship to give unto Dethick, the goldsmith, for colouring my chain which your lordship gave unto Mr Languet, and for his pains in going and coming to your lordship, the 14th of February . . . 15s. For the price of my chain which your L. gave to Mr Languet the same day . . . £45.[57]

Sir Henry's generosity had its limits: it seems that it was poor Pakenham who provided the chain to be presented to Languet!

Although they did not yet know it, this was the last time that Languet would see Philip. Fulke Greville tells the sad story of their farewell: 'At the sea they parted, and made many mutual tears ominous propheciers of their never meeting again.'[58] The truth was less romantic. Philip Sidney and Hubert Languet never said goodbye. Casimir decided to leave as he had arrived, on the spur of the moment, 'as if they were taking leave of enemies, not of friends', complained Languet, who wanted to say goodbye to Philip and to Edward Dyer,[59] whose friendship he counted 'a precious gem added to my store'. In retrospect, however, he admitted in a letter to Philip that he would have had nothing for him 'but tears and sighs'. Taking his leave of Sir Henry, who – unlike his son – was able to accompany Languet to Dover, Languet sailed back to Flushing, this time with Fulke Greville, 'whom during our journey I discovered to be a great admirer of your character, and strongly attached to you', he assured Philip.[60]

After the débâcle in Ghent, Languet's confidence in Casimir quickly ran out. His next choice of employer was predictable enough: within months he realigned himself with William of Orange, winning for himself a place of influence with the prince comparable to that of his chaplain Loiseleur de Villiers, as Gilpin remarked to Walsingham.[61] Languet may well have been chosen in order to help William draft his tract, entitled *An apologie or defence, of my Lorde the Prince of Orange*, in response to the '*ban de proscription*' published against him by Philip II:[62] Du Plessis recalled how William called himself and Languet to comment on the draft prepared by Villiers. Languet was certainly involved in disseminating the document, sending copies to George Buchanan and Robert Beale in February 1581, although characteristically he admitted to Beale that he would have preferred the text to have been less vehement.[63] As political life became ever more vehement, it was at Orange's side that Languet would spend his last years.

For all the splendour of the reception for Casimir, there was no disguising the fact that it was splendour underwritten by the Sidneys and Leicester, rather than by the queen, for whom Casimir had come. Elizabeth was busy lapping up the attentions of Anjou's confidant Jean de Simier, 'a most choice courtier', according to William Camden, 'exquisitely skilled in love toys, pleasant conceits, and court dalliances'.[64]

Punning on the French *simiesque* (ape-like), Elizabeth dubbed Simier her 'ape'. She talked with him several times a week, and entertained and gifted him as if he were the bridegroom. For the first time in many years, her closest counsellors realised that the queen was serious about the marriage. Leicester wrote to Davison in late February 1579: 'I should say conjecturally by that I newly hear and find in her deep consideration of her estate and that she is persuaded nothing can more assure it than marriage, I may be of mind she will marry if the party like her.'[65] From the end of March until early May 1579, the Privy Council debated the possibility of marriage, with factions emerging. At the end of April, Elizabeth asked each member of her Privy Council to give her their advice in writing. The response showed a council deeply divided, with her two most powerful ministers in discord: Lord Treasurer Burghley in favour of the marriage, Secretary Walsingham vigorously against. To the French, however, Elizabeth still played hard to get: despite all this courtly foreplay with Simier, she refused to deal directly with him on the question of marriage. Simier was passed on to the Privy Council, who reiterated the queen's dictum that she must see the groom first. He replied that he had to refer the matter to his master.

Anjou was now ready to come. During the past year his Low Countries campaign had deteriorated into a series of embarrassing fiascos: his troops had deserted and some of his supporters in the south had defected to the Prince of Parma, the new commander of the Spanish army. Anjou had been forced to withdraw back into France. To Elizabeth he wrote that this was a tactical withdrawal, undertaken precisely so that he might visit her in England. By now, the plans had become public knowledge and bets were being taken on their outcome. 'I know a man may take £1,000 in this town,' wrote Gilbert Talbot to the Earl of Shrewsbury in May, 'to be bound to pay double so much when Monsieur [Anjou] comes into England, and treble so much when he marries the Queen's Majesty.'[66] Sermons were also being preached against the marriage – including one in front of Elizabeth on the first Sunday of Lent – until the queen prohibited ministers from preaching on any scriptural text that might be interpreted as relevant to the issue.

When it was finally decided that Anjou should come, Leicester retired to his estate at Wanstead, incensed: he did not attend any Privy Council meetings between 15 June and 6 July.[67] Philip's Oxford contemporary

William Camden, writing in 1615, alleged that Leicester did his best to undermine Simier: he 'spread rumors abroad that by amorous potions and unlawful arts he [Simier] had crept into the Queen's mind and enticed her to the love of Anjou'. According to Camden, Simier – who 'left no means unassayed to remove Leicester out of place and grace with the Queen' – finally played his trump-card in late June 1579: he let Elizabeth know that Leicester had secretly married his long-term mistress, Essex's widow Lettice Knollys.

In Camden's version, on hearing the news from Simier, Elizabeth was distraught and furious, growing 'into such a chafe'. Coming on top of the secret marriage of another favourite, her '*mouton*' Sir Christopher Hatton, she viewed Leicester's marriage as nothing short of treachery. Leicester was placed under house-arrest at Greenwich and would have been sent to the Tower of London, had the Earl of Sussex – of all people – not intervened on his behalf. Sussex persuaded the queen 'that no man was to be molested for lawful marriage, which amongst all men hath ever been honest and honored. Yet glad he was that by his marriage he [Leicester] was now out of all hope of marrying with the Queen.'[68] Camden's version of events is supported by two contemporary letters. According to a gleeful Mary, Queen of Scots, writing on 4 July, Leicester's marriage might even have been the final push that made Elizabeth agree to see Anjou: 'Leicester and Hatton are married secretly, which hath so offended the queen, that it is thought she has been led upon such miscontentment to agree to the sight of the duke.'[69] Two days later, the Spanish ambassador Mendoza wrote that Leicester himself 'has retired to a house of his five miles away where the Queen has been to see him, and where she remained two days because he feigned illness. She afterwards returned secretly to London. A sister of Leicester's of whom the Queen was very fond, and to whom she had given apartments at Court, retired at the same time as her brother.'[70] Elizabeth's sense of betrayal evidently stretched to her trusted lady-in-waiting; for Philip's mother attempting to lead a court life as Leicester's sister finally became too difficult, and she retired to Penshurst.

Leicester's biographers have been deeply sceptical of Camden's claims that this was the moment when Elizabeth discovered that he was married. The liaison with Lettice Knollys was well known to those on the diplomatic circuit. In early 1578, Lettice announced to Leicester that she was pregnant; he responded by marrying her secretly in the spring, in a ceremony at Kenilworth, establishing her comfortably in Wanstead Hall, Essex (just two days before Elizabeth arrived to be entertained with *The Lady of May*) and then marrying off his former mistress Douglas Sheffield to Sir Edward Stafford. A second marriage ceremony was held at Wanstead on 21 September 1578, in the presence of Lettice's father Sir Francis Knollys, Leicester's brother Ambrose and the Earl of Pembroke, Mary Sidney's husband. Lettice's baby did not survive, but for Philip the implications of all this were severe: if Lettice were to give birth to a legitimate child who lived, then Philip would be ousted from his position as heir to the Dudley brothers (Ambrose was still childless).

Whatever the truth of the matter, on 16 June 1579 the Privy Council granted Anjou a safe-conduct, and (after persuading his brother to provide him with a licence) the duke reached Greenwich on 17 August. At Elizabeth's insistence, Anjou had travelled incognito, fearing for his safety; she had gone as far as to forbid anyone to speak of his arrival, or to carry a firearm in the vicinity of the court. As it turned out, Anjou's visit was uneventful, filled with the usual receptions and entertainments at Richmond and Greenwich. Elizabeth appeared smitten and Anjou attracted a new coterie of mainly Catholic followers, including members of the Howard family, Sir Edward Stafford, the Duke of Northumberland and Charles Arundell.

The group also included Edward de Vere, Earl of Oxford, the man who had won Anne Cecil (or rather, her father Lord Burghley) from Philip a decade earlier – and it was Oxford who was to spark a showdown between the pro-Anjou camp and the anti-marriage campaigners. Although Philip had maintained good relations with members of the French embassy, in this tense atmosphere he was more alert to slights from his English contemporaries. As Fulke Greville tells the story, Philip was 'one day at tennis', when an English peer – Oxford – 'born great, greater by alliance, and superlative in the prince's favour, abruptly came into the tennis-court'. His birth, alliance and royal favour combined to make Oxford particularly arrogant and, according to Greville, 'he forgot to entreat that which he could not legally command'. Failing in his attempts, Oxford was reduced 'at last with rage (which is ever ill-disciplined)' to command Philip and his companions to get off the tennis court.

Philip answered 'temperately', 'that if his Lordship had been pleased to express desire in milder characters, perchance he might have led out those that he should now find would not be driven out with any scourge of fury'. The answer only exacerbated the earl's anger, and 'like a bellows blowing up the sparks of excess already kindled' made Oxford call Philip a 'puppy'. The offence was made worse by the fact that the French commissioners had been granted an audience in the private galleries that overlooked the tennis court, and their attention was soon attracted by the angry exchange below. Philip realised this, 'and rising with inward strength by the prospect of a mighty faction against him, asked my Lord with a loud voice that which he heard clearly enough before'. Oxford repeated the insult. Philip, 'resolving in one answer to conclude both the attentive hearers and passionate actor, gave my Lord a lie, impossible (as he averred to be retorted) in respect all the world knows puppies are gotten by dogs and children by men'.

Both men stood silent ('like a dumb show in a tragedy,' remarked Greville) until Philip – realising the wrong that had been done to him, in the presence of 'foreign and factious' men – 'with some words of sharp accent led the way abruptly out of the tennis-court, as if so unexpected an accident were not fit to be decided any farther in that place'. Oxford proceeded to play tennis. According to Greville, Philip spent a day expecting to hear from the earl, but when no message came, sent 'a gentleman of worth to awake him [Oxford] out of his trance, wherein the French would assuredly think any pause, if not death, let a lethargy of true honour in both'. This, as intended, provoked Oxford into sending a challenge to Philip, but matters had now come to the attention of the Privy Council and they 'took notice of the differences, commanded peace, and laboured a reconciliation between them'.[71]

Greville's version of events, however, does not tally with that implied in a letter from Hubert Languet, who identifies Philip rather than Oxford as the sender of the challenge, and berates him for it. The entire incident gave him 'great pain. I know that by an ancient custom recognised throughout Christendom, a nobleman is disgraced if he does not take offence at such an insult; but I still think it unfortunate that you were lured into this quarrel, although I appreciate that no blame can be attached to you for it.' He advised Philip:

take care lest, influenced by swashbucklers, you overstep the bounds of your native modesty. In this quarrel, although your position was sound, you went further than you should, for when you had thrown back the insult, you should have said no more; but instead, carried away by your short temper, you sent a challenge to him, and by that means you have deprived yourself of the choice of weapons if this disagreement ever comes to a duel . . . If you had stood firm after you had given your adversary the lie, he would have been forced to challenge you.

Falling back easily into tutorial mode, Languet recommended a work on duelling by the English writer William of Neuberg, who 'quotes the decrees of a synod which utterly condemned duels, forbidding Christians to take part in them'. He was also worried for Philip's safety: 'Since your opponent has linked himself to Anjou's party, if your wooer [Anjou] returns to you surrounded by French noblemen, you must be on your guard, for you know how volatile my countrymen are.'[72]

Whether or not Philip threw down the gauntlet, the response of the queen, in Greville's account, was unequivocal and deeply wounding to Philip. She lectured him on 'the difference in degree between earls, and gentlemen; the respect inferiors ought [owed] to their superiors; and the necessity in princes to maintain their own creations, as degrees descending between the people's licentiousness, and the anointed sovereignty of crowns: how the gentleman's neglect of the nobility taught the peasant to insult upon both'. Philip replied ('with such reverence as became him'): 'First, that place was never intended for privilege to wrong', and gave as an example Elizabeth herself, who despite her position, 'yet was she content to cast her own affections into the same moulds her subjects did, and govern all her rights by their laws'. He implored the queen to consider that, although Oxford was 'a great lord by birth, alliance, and grace; yet he was no lord over him: and therefore the difference of degrees between free men, could not challenge any other homage than precedency'. Philip went on to cite the example of her father, Henry VIII, 'who gave the gentry free, and safe appeal to his feet, against the oppression of the grandees; and found it wisdom, by the stronger corporation in number, to keep down the greater in power', lest 'the over-grown might be tempted, by still coveting more, to fall (as the angels did) by affecting equality with their maker'.[73]

As this little history lesson to his sovereign suggests, Philip was unrepentant. On 28 August he wrote to Sir Christopher Hatton: 'As for the matter depending between the Earl of Oxford and me, certainly, sir, howsoever I might have forgiven him, I should never have forgiven myself, if I had lain under so proud an injury, as he would have laid upon me, neither can anything under the sun make me repent it, nor any misery make me go one half word back from it: let him therefore, as he will, digest it: for my part I think, tying up, makes some things seem fiercer, than they would be.'[74]

At around the same time as this nasty, high-profile clash damaged him in the eyes of the queen, Philip undertook a task that threatened even worse repercussions. Leicester returned to court in late August still 'in great grief' about Elizabeth's marriage plans; after an audience with the queen, according to Mendoza, 'his emotion was marked'. This spurred him to call a conference of his close-knit group. Mendoza continued: 'A meeting was held on the same night at the Earl of Pembroke's house, there being present Lord Sidney and other friends and relatives. They no doubt discussed the matter, and some of them afterwards remarked that Parliament would have something to say as to whether the Queen married or not. The people in general seem to threaten revolution about it.'[75] Once again, Pembroke's house (this time his London residence Baynards Castle) was the chosen location for a summit meeting of Leicester's familial and political allies. Although 'Lord Sidney' probably refers to Sir Henry, it is more than likely that Philip was also among the 'friends and relatives', and it must have been at this gathering (or one like it) that the plot was hatched for Philip to write a letter to Elizabeth, advising her against the marriage.

This letter needs to be seen in context. A printed anti-marriage tract, John Stubbs' *The Discoverie of a Gaping Gulf whereinto England is like to be swallowed by another French mariage*, published at the same moment, led to the writer and a distributor having their right hands publicly amputated: Philip's letter, however, was of another genre altogether. Indeed, it was a standard exercise for counsellors that year: Burghley drew up a long memorandum listing and countering objections to the match; the Bishop of Ely penned a letter directly to the queen; Walsingham wrote a summary of the relative dangers posed by an unmarried queen and a French-married queen entitled 'A Consideration of the diseased state of the realm and how the same may in some kind of sort be cured'.[76]

Philip's *Letter* claims to come from a man who already has access to the queen, and who is in the habit of offering his opinion on matters of state. After assuring Elizabeth that his 'shallow' words come 'from the deep wellspring of most loyal affection', Philip reminds her that they 'have already delivered to your gracious ears what is the general sum of my travelling thoughts', concerning 'the continuance of your safety', and he would now address 'the reasons that make me think the marriage of Monsieur [Anjou] to be unprofitable for you'; then he would answer 'the objections of those fears which might procure so violent a refuge'.

According to the *Letter*, the marriage was dangerous to the state: Elizabeth was presently in a strong position and change would be harmful – 'What makes you in such a calm to change course? To so healthful a body, to apply such a weary medicine? What hope can recompense so hazardous an adventure?' More particularly, it would further divide the country's existing 'two mighty factions', since the match would be abhorrent to Protestants, while it would strengthen the position of papists and malcontents, especially given Anjou's fickleness, ambition and bad companions. Anjou had the potential to become strong in England because of the power of English papists; already the Frenchman's natural inclination to military action – and the support of his brother – posed a threat.

Philip made his only reference to the horrors of the St Bartholomew's Day Massacre: 'the very common people will know this: that he is the son of the Jezebel of our age; that his brother made oblation of his own sister's marriage, the easier to make massacres of all sexes'. With this heritage, Anjou could not be trusted. 'He himself, contrary to his promise, and against all gratefulness, having had his liberty and principal estates chiefly by the Huguenots' means, did sack La Charité and utterly spoil Issoire with fire and sword.' (Philip was probably overstating the case here, since Anjou could not be entirely blamed for these events.)

The queen herself was at risk from Anjou: he vacillated constantly, his presence would give rise to considerable ill feeling, and he brought with him absolutely no advantage. Philip played on the queen's vanity, referring to the duke's 'sometimes seeking the King of Spain's daughter, sometimes your Majesty'. The apparent motives for the marriage were weak. England was afraid to stand alone, but there was no realistic prospect of a secure league with Anjou. If Elizabeth feared the contempt of her subjects, she was ill advised: her long reign signalled security; the uncertain succession was irrelevant given the widespread love for the queen (although marrying Anjou might jeopardise this); calumny should be ignored. Love, which the queen had in abundance, was the best weapon against contempt; fear was the alternative, but that could be increased only with danger. In conclusion, the queen's glory and strength lay in her standing alone. Anjou could neither help her nor endanger her – except by marrying her. 'Lastly', Philip concluded, 'doing as you do, you shall be as you be: the example of princes, the ornament of this age, the comfort of the afflicted, the delight of your people, the most excellent fruit of all your progenitors, and the perfect mirror to your posterity'.[77]

It is clear from Mendoza's report that Philip was commissioned to write this letter, which in fact had a range of sponsors, notably Leicester. As Languet later reminded Philip, he had been 'ordered to write as you did by those whom you were bound to obey'.[78] Since Leicester had been effectively silenced by Simier's intervention, it was important to find another voice that he could control, but which was sufficiently familiar to the queen. But the fact that the *Letter* bore Philip's name is intriguing. If the tennis-court débâcle happened before the letter was drafted, then perhaps it was felt that Philip had nothing to lose by having the letter carry his name. If the letter preceded the Oxford incident, then we might see Elizabeth's reaction to that event as partially a displaced response to the letter. But in fact Philip appears not to have suffered unduly from being identified as the author of the *Letter*: his later absences from court, often ascribed to the offence that it allegedly caused, can be shown to have their roots elsewhere.

Philip's letter circulated only in its original manuscript form (it was not printed until 1663). At least twenty copies are known to have survived, which suggests that its dissemination was significant, although several of these are seventeenth-century copies.[79] Certainly, Languet wrote to express how glad he was that 'your letter about the duc d'Anjou has come to the attention of so many . . . no right-thinking man can blame you for putting forward freely what you thought good for your country, nor even for overstating some details in order to make the case for what you thought expedient'.

Languet admired Philip's courage 'in freely admonishing the Queen and your fellow countrymen of that which is to the state's advantage'. But he was once again alarmed by what he saw as his friend's recklessness:

> You must beware not to go so far that your conduct becomes more unpopular than you can bear . . . Remember that you may be deserted by most of those who now take your side. For I have no doubt that many will run to the safe side of the vessel, when they discover you cannot resist the Queen's will, or that she is seriously offended at your opposition . . . You should persevere as long as you can in doing anything to benefit your country; but when you find that your opposition draws on you nothing but dislike and aversion, and that neither your country, your friends, nor yourself derive any advantage from it, you should give way to necessity, and reserve your strength for a more suitable occasion; for time itself will bring you occasions and means of serving your country.

Languet was also alarmed by the animosity Philip had somehow aroused in Anjou, which could have long-term effects beyond English shores. 'I wonder why Anjou has taken against you. If he hates you simply because you opposed him in England, he will soon be reconciled, and you need only say that you acted not out of personal ill will, but for the good of your country. You gain neither advantage nor honour by quarrelling with men of his rank.' Anjou's continuing enmity would severely limit Philip's horizons. 'Anjou's party and his influence are increasing here [in the Low Countries], and if you annoy him by opposing him in England, you will hardly be well received here, let alone in France. You're barred from Spain and Italy thanks to your religion, and so Germany would be your only refuge if you were forced to leave your country.'[80]

Philip was further reminded of how his profile abroad had been damaged from Fulke Greville, who visited William of Orange during 1579. Orange asked Greville to commend his service to Elizabeth, 'and after crave leave freely to open his knowledge and opinions of a fellow-servant of his that (as he heard) lived employed under her'. He told Greville (for Elizabeth's consumption) 'that, if he could judge, her Majesty had one of the ripest and greatest counsellors of state, in Sir [sic] Philip Sidney, that at this day lived in Europe; to the trial of which he was pleased to leave his own credit engaged till her Majesty might please to employ this gentleman, either among her friends or enemies'.

Returning to England, Greville told Philip of this exchange. At first, Philip rejected Orange's appraisal, but at length 'for my satisfaction, freely added these words', as Greville recalled: 'first, that the Queen had the life itself daily attending her, and if she either did not or would not value it so high, the commendation of that worthy prince could be no more (at the best) than a lively picture of that life, and so of far less credit and estimation with her'. Philip reasoned that 'princes love not that foreign powers should have extraordinary interest in their subjects, much less to be taught by them how they should place their own, as arguments either upbraiding ignorance or lack of large rewarding goodness in them'.[81]

Perhaps to strengthen his hand with Elizabeth, Philip spent much of the winter at court and in London. On New Year's Day 1580, he presented the queen with a covered crystal cup – as Elizabeth accepted his gift, we must assume that he had remained *persona grata* with her. Philip was still in London on 16 January when Fabianus Niphus wrote to Dannewitz, the secretary of Archduke Matthias of Austria, another party interested in the Low Countries, that 'Philip Sidney, a young man of eminent wit and virtue, is wholly with us, and displays great affection for our prince'.[82] It was not a coincidence that Philip chose to spend his time with the ambassadors of foreign princes. The possibility of the Anjou marriage had strengthened his resolve to leave England and to join William of Orange's army, a notion that appealed greatly to Languet, who felt that Orange's commander, La Noue, was the ideal figure under whom to serve. But Languet, freshly anxious for his protégé, warned that Philip must make up his mind for himself and not discuss such plans in public. As he reminded him, 'Last year, as you know well, you gave hope to some people that you were coming here [into the Low Countries], and while it was no fault of yours that you didn't come, if there was a repeat performance, many would think it a lack of constancy in you.'[83]

Languet was right to advise caution: once again, nothing came of these hopes.

CHAPTER NINE

Fancy, Toy and Fiction

HILIP'S NEGOTIATIONS WITH European princes and his
contretemps with English nobles may have filled the pages of his
letters and the despatches of the diplomatic *cognoscenti*. To those in
the wider world, however, whose knowledge of him was dependent on
what they read in printed books, his fame was growing in a different
direction – as a poet.

This new reputation sprang at least partly from the self-publicising
writings of two men who were acquainted with Philip: Gabriel Harvey,
the Cambridge scholar with whom Philip had read Livy before setting
out to Prague, and the poet Edmund Spenser, who worked briefly as
secretary to the Earl of Leicester. In 1579, Spenser dedicated his
anonymously published *The Shepheardes Calender* to Philip, invoking him on
the title page, and referring to him as 'the precedent of all chivalry'. As if
to validate this rather grand dedication, the following year a collection of
letters (dating from October 1579 to May 1580) between 'Immerito'
(Spenser) and his friend Harvey was published, laying claim to a
friendship with Philip. In the correspondence, Immerito boasts that 'the
two worthy gentlemen, Master Sidney, and Master Dyer . . . have me, I
thank them, in some use of familiarity'.[1] Later there is a casual allusion
to the 'delicate, and choice elegant poesy of good M. Sidney's, or M.
Dyer's (our very Castor, & Pollux for such and many greater matters)'.
Harvey signs off with strict instructions not to show 'these patcheries,
and fragments' to anyone except 'the two gentlemen', and possibly 'to my
good friend M. Daniel Rogers', another member of Philip's circle.[2]

The 'Master Sidney' who emerges from the Spenser–Harvey correspondence is a poetic experimenter, who has been attempting to
introduce classical metrical quantity into English vernacular verse.
Immerito claims that Philip gave him a copy of 'the rules and precepts of
art, which you observe in quantities', originally devised by one Thomas
Drant, but 'enlarged with M. Sidney's own judgement, and augmented
with my observations'. Spenser may be a reliable source here: Philip's
name crops up twice in Latin eulogies published in 1576 in *Praesvl* by
Drant, a preacher who worked in London and at court. There are extant

copies of a short treatise by Philip which suggests that he did indeed develop Drant's rules. While this indicates a strong interest in how the English vernacular might differ in its structures, word lengths and pronunciation from classical languages, it seems from what has survived of Philip's poetic works that, ultimately, he could not make classical quantities fit with pesky English pronunciation.[3]

It is tempting to take the Immerito–Harvey correspondence at face value, and to see Philip as part of a glittering courtly poetic sub-culture. At one point, Harvey refers jokingly to an 'areopagus' (after the hill court of ancient Athens), suggesting that the four men were part of a formal academy of English literature – an idea that some literary critics have found understandably appealing. But when read closely these letters do not claim intimacy for either Spenser or Harvey with the gentleman-poets. The pamphlets should probably be seen less as proof of the poets' intimacy and more as a public claim for that intimacy, designed to further the careers of Harvey and (the still anonymous) Spenser. (It may have paid off. By late 1580, Spenser found himself in the retinue of Lord Grey on the way to Ireland – quite probably a result of Sidney influence.) What is more, far from being part of a courtly areopagus, Philip was writing most of his important verse far away from the bustle of court.

In March 1580, Philip returned to Wilton, to be with his sister Mary during the final weeks of her first pregnancy. After her son William was born on 8 April, Philip stood in for Leicester as godfather at the baptism; the other godparents were the Earl of Warwick, who travelled to Wilton to stand 'in his own person', and the queen herself, showing great favour to the young couple.[4] It was the best of starts in life for the child who would go on to become Earl of Pembroke and inadvertently achieve immortality as the patron of William Shakespeare.

Philip was still at Wilton in late July 1580, when Mary's pregnancy was no longer a genuine excuse. He wrote to Leicester on 2 August to explain his continued absence from court:

> Right honorable and singular good Lord. I have now brought home my
> sister, who is well amended both of her pain and disease. For myself I
> assure your lordship upon my troth, so full of the cold as one cannot
> hear me speak: which is the cause keeps me yet from the court since my

only service is speech and that is stopped. As soon as I have gotten any voice I will wait on your lordship if so it please you.[5]

With Elizabethan England's love of figurative language, we might be tempted to read the 'cold' that prevents Philip from speaking as some form of hostility from the queen. In fact, as the letter goes on to show, his withdrawal from court life had a more practical cause: he no longer had the funds to finance it:

> Although it be contrary to that I have signified to her Majesty of my want, I doubt not her Majesty will vouchsafe to ask for me, but so long as she sees a silk doublet upon me her Highness will think me in good case. At my departure I desired Mr ViceChamberlain he would tell her Majesty necessity did even banish me from the place. And always submitting myself to your judgement and commandment, I think my best [i.e. option], either constantly to wait, or constantly to hold the course of my poverty, for coming and going neither breeds desert, nor witnesseth necessity.[6]

Despite being told that Philip cannot afford to attend on her, the queen seems incapable of understanding this – if he can afford to wear a silk doublet, then surely he can afford to be at court. So Philip decided, rather than dashing to and from court when funds permitted, simply to absent himself for a longer term. The cold, presumably, was a real ailment, which was also keeping Philip from Leicester's company: 'I hope within 3 or 4 days this cold will be past, for now truly I were a very unpleasant company keeper.'[7]

What this self-enforced exile provided, however, was an opportunity to consolidate other interests, which Philip had been able to pursue only piecemeal during the intrigue-filled days at court. In his sister Mary he found a fellow lover of literature and drama, and in Wilton he discovered a perfect place to write. Wilton was the setting for a verse drama sometimes attributed to Philip: 'A Dialogue betweene two shepherds, uttered in pastoral show, at Wilton'. It may be that some of Philip's early writings were devised for his sister's entertainment – or even in collaboration with her: in later years, Mary herself was to write 'A dialogue betweene two shepherds, Thenot, and Piers, in praise of Astrea

... at the Queen's Majesty's being at her house at Wilton, Anno 1599'.[8] She went on to become an accomplished and respected poet in her own right, and a renowned patron: 250 writers dedicated their work to the Herberts, including such luminaries as Spenser, Jonson, Thomas Nashe, playwrights Philip Massinger, John Ford and George Chapman, and Sir Thomas Browne. The family's tutors included Samuel Daniel, Michael Drayton and Henry Peacham. In John Aubrey's words, Wilton House was 'like a college, there were so many learned and ingeniose persons. She was the greatest patroness of wit and learning of any lady in her time.'[9]

Philip's single greatest literary achievement is inextricably bound up with Mary and with Wilton, and it was probably during this summer of 1580 that it was completed. *The Arcadia*, an epic romance in five books with eclogues and songs, was dedicated 'to my dear lady and sister the Countess of Pembroke' from 'your loving brother, Philip Sidney'. Philip credited Mary with commissioning the book: 'You desired me to do it, and your desire to my heart is an absolute commandment.' Mary was not only the catalyst for the work, but its eager first audience: 'Your dear self can best witness the manner, being done in loose sheets of paper, most of it done in your presence, the rest by sheets sent unto you as fast as they were done.' The birth of *The Arcadia* was implicitly likened to the birth of Mary's son, as 'this child which I am loath to father ... if it had not been in some way delivered, [it] would have grown a monster, and more sorry might I be that they came in than that they gat out'.[10]

In fact, the gestation period for *The Arcadia* was considerably longer than a summer at Wilton. Edmund Molyneux claimed that Philip started work on it 'not long after his return' from Prague in 1577, 'and before his further employment by her majesty, at his vacant and spare times of leisure (for he could endure at no time to be idle and void of action).'[11] However, the romance was the culmination not only of the previous three years' experiences, but of almost twenty years of voracious reading on Philip's part.

Romances had certainly formed part of Philip's education, for we know he read Belleforest's French translation of Bandello's short stories to improve his French while at Shrewsbury. While travelling on the Continent he must have practised his Italian with Lodowick Bryskett by reading the vernacular romance by Jacopo Sannazaro, which gave him his own title – *Arcadia*. England had its own rich canon of romance literature, often based on the chivalric adventures of the Arthurian legend, perhaps the most famous being Malory's *Morte D'Arthur*. And, in the summer of 1575, Philip had seen new possibilities in the romance genre when he witnessed Sir Henry Lee's entertainment at Woodstock, with its novel blend of Greek romance and English chivalry. He had been particularly struck by the impact all this had on its audience, who scrambled to obtain a written copy so that they could decipher the hidden meaning they assumed must lie in Hermetes' tale.

The Arcadia draws on all these influences. In addition to Sannazaro critics have discerned traces of other romances: Heliodorus' *Æthopian Historie*, translated a few years earlier by Thomas Underdown; Apuleius' *Golden Ass*, in a version by William Adlington; *Amadis de Gaul* in French; Montemayor's *Diana* (and its sequels) in Spanish. But it was a strange genre for a scholarly, politically astute writer to choose. Romance was often denigrated as the province of women, its subject matter regarded as either ridiculous or overly sexualised. Certainly it was not the domain one would expect a pupil of Hubert Languet to inhabit – but then this work, being in English, was significantly not one that Hubert Languet would be able to read. Philip was addressing a specifically English audience with his romance, and playing with traditional vernacular forms. The plot of *The Arcadia* is as convoluted as any romance reader could desire, replete with a mysterious prophecy, chivalrous knights, beautiful damsels in distress, marauding lions, bizarre disguises, cross-dressing and sudden reversals of fortune, with a fair amount of its trademark illicit sex thrown in for good measure. In his dedication to the Countess of Pembroke, Philip presented *The Arcadia* as a worthless product of his feminised leisure time at Wilton: 'Now it is done only for you, only to you; if you keep it to yourself, or to such friends who will weigh errors in the balance of goodwill . . . for severer eyes it is not, being but a trifle, and that triflingly handed . . . Read it then at your idle times, and the follies your good judgement will find in it, blame not, but laugh at . . . looking for no better stuff than, as in a haberdasher's shop, glasses or feathers.'[12]

Some took Philip at his word. As late as 1631, Thomas Powell was advising husbands on how to control their wives: 'Instead of reading Sir Philip Sidney's *Arcadia*, let them read the grounds of good huswifery.' But others knew better. Although Philip wrote of himself as one 'who (I know not by what mischance, in these my not old years and idlest times' had 'slipt into the title of the poet', in fact he took that title extremely seriously. Written alongside *The Arcadia* was *The Defence of Poesie*, a full-length analysis of the importance of poetry, in which Philip felt he had to 'say something unto you in the defence of that my unelected vocation'. He claimed that he had 'just cause to make a pitiful defence of poor poetry, which from almost the highest estimation is fallen to be the laughing-stock of children', and started his *Defence* in the loftiest vein, claiming that the earliest Greek philosophers were poets. *The Arcadia* was, to Philip, a serious endeavour.

Although the form was romance, *The Arcadia* shared features with other literary forms. It was divided into five acts, reminiscent of the classical drama that Philip had read at Shrewsbury (drama being studied for its form). It also drew on the long tradition of pastoral poetry. As George Puttenham put it, in his *The Arte of English Poesie*, the pastoral was designed 'under the veil of homely persons, and in rude speeches to insinuate and glance at greater matters, and such as perchance had not been safe to have been disclosed in any other sort; which may be perceived by the *Eclogues* of Virgil, in which are treated by figure matters of greater importance . . . These Eclogues came after to contain and inform moral discipline, for the amendment of man's behaviour.'[13] In his own *Defence of Poesie*, Philip noted that Virgil's *Eclogues* 'can show the misery of people under hard lords or ravening soldiers, and . . . what blessedness is derived to them that lie lowest from the goodness of them that sit highest; sometimes, under the pretty tales of wolves and sheep, can include the whole considerations of wrong-doing and patience'.[14] This is precisely the quality that William Webbe, writing in 1586, noted in Spenser's *Shepheardes Calender*: 'There is . . . much matter uttered somewhat covertly, especially the abuses of some which would not be too plain withal'.[15]

Indeed, *The Shepheardes Calender* was listed in Philip's *Defence of Poesie* as one of only four worthwhile vernacular verse works in the English canon, stating it 'hath much poetry in his eclogues, indeed worthy the reading, if I be not deceived'.[16] *The Shepheardes Calender* also contained a plea for an English vernacular literature, which was taken up by Philip in his *Defence*. Although he is slightly sniffy about the faux-archaic style that Spenser adopts ('That same framing of his style to an old rustic language I dare not allow, since neither Theocritus in Greek, Virgil in Latin, nor Sannazaro in Italian did affect it'), by naming this extremely recent text as one of the greats of English poetry, he was signalling shared ground with Spenser's mix of politics and religion. It was here, rather than in experimentation with verse quantities, that Sidney's and Spenser's interests truly overlapped. Indeed, one of his followers, George Whetstone, believed in 1587 that Philip was in fact the author of the *Calender*: 'the reputed work of S. Phil. Sidney a work of deep learning, judgement & wit disguised in Shep. Rules'.[17]

Seen in the pastoral tradition, *The Arcadia* immediately becomes a highly political text – which might make us reconsider Philip's deliberate situating of its composition at Wilton. Although one reading of the book was as a romance written firmly in women's space, away from the court, Philip knew that Wilton also called attention to *The Arcadia's* political potency. As a known gathering place for the Pembrokes, Dudleys and Sidneys, the Wiltshire house provoked considerable mistrust at court. Even when Sir Henry came to Wilton for his grandson William Herbert's christening, his visit raised royal suspicions. Walsingham wrote to tell him that the queen 'hath commanded me to recommend unto your lordship the more earnestly, for that she is given to understand, that your lordship doth sometime resort to Wilton; which . . . she somewhat misliketh'.[18] This might explain why Molyneux wrote in 1586 that the book had been kept a great secret, its circulation jealously guarded: 'Few works of like subject hath been either of some more earnestly sought, choicely kept, nor placed in better place, and amongst better jewels than that was; so that a special dear friend he should be that could have a sight, but much more dear that could once obtain a copy of it.'[19]

Exclusiveness bred suspicion. *The Arcadia's* original élite circulation encouraged the belief that it must be hiding a closely kept secret. From its first publication in 1590 to the present day there has been no lack of readers attempting to read *The Arcadia* as some form of allegory. In 1628 Henry Oxinder attempted to read off the characters against prominent members of the Sidney and Devereux families; sixty years later, John Aubrey commissioned another key from one Mr Tyndale – while some identifications remained constant, Tyndale suggested some very different ones from Oxinder. In recent years, *The Arcadia* has been read as an allegory of European Protestantism, of the succession question in England and of the threat of Elizabeth's marriage to Anjou.[20]

Philip would probably have been delighted by these interpretations –

not any particular interpretation, but the sheer range of them. For while *The Arcadia* deliberately allows – indeed, may even encourage – localised identifications, it is ultimately not a *romance-à-clef*. In *The Defence of Poesie*, Philip wrote against this kind of reading. Responding to the charge that poets 'give names to men they write of, which argueth a conceit of an actual truth', Philip asks: 'doth the lawyer lie then, when under the names of "John of the Stile" and "John of the Nokes" [the early modern John Doe and John Roe] he puts his case?' The only reason that poets name their characters 'is but to make their picture the more lively, and not to build any history'. Instead, readers should 'use the narration but as an imaginative groundplot of a profitable invention' – they should work through the text to something further.

In his 'imaginative groundplot', Philip raises moral, philosophical, political and ethical issues to be debated. Should a prince abdicate his government? Does a king have the right to take over the government of a neighbouring nation when that nation is in trouble? What does it mean for a woman to rule a kingdom or lead an army? *The Arcadia* is a romance, certainly, but all the commonplace romance elements are interrogated. Romance was known for its rape and adultery – but should there not be consequences for the perpetrators? Even with a guaranteed happy ending, should a promise of marriage sanction sexual relations? The cross-dressing, so important to the plot, is used to raise questions about gender and politics: one of the heroes, disguised as an Amazon, is able to subdue the mutinous crowd with 'her' rhetoric, but is this a woman's rhetoric, or the rhetoric of a man? Can a man's words have greater impact when delivered by a woman?[21]

The Arcadia was written to provoke questions, not necessarily to answer them. It provides a record not of Philip's consistent political philosophy, but of his ongoing intellectual enquiry. That enquiry did not come to an end at Wilton with the book's dedication to Mary; rather, he soon started to rewrite his romance – and to reconsider his ideas in the light of his ever-changing political position.

As Philip developed his fiction, he started deliberately to blur the edges between his literary works and his self-presentation at court and elsewhere, writing himself into his poetry in a number of guises, and writing his poetry into his own life. This happened most vividly in the highly stylised chivalric tilting that gained in popularity at court during the 1570s.[22] Edmund Molyneux claimed that 'at jousts, triumphs, and other such royal pastimes (for at all such disports he commonly made one) [Philip] would bring in such a lively gallant show, so agreeable to every point which is required for the expressing of a perfect device (so rich was he in those inventions), as, if he surpassed not all, he would equal or at least second the best'.[23]

We can get some idea of the power of a typical tilt from an eyewitness description of the 1584 Accession Day celebrations. At noon Elizabeth and her ladies sat at the windows of a long room in Whitehall Palace looking out over the barrier where the tournament was to be held. Around the barrier, stands were available for anyone willing to pay twelvepence to see the spectacle. From the queen's room, a staircase led down to the tiltyard. All those wishing to fight 'entered the lists' in pairs, to the blast of trumpets. The tilters wore easily distinguished costumes and carried *imprese*, plasterboard shields bearing images and mottoes. Their servants, who lined the barrier, were also in co-ordinated costume.

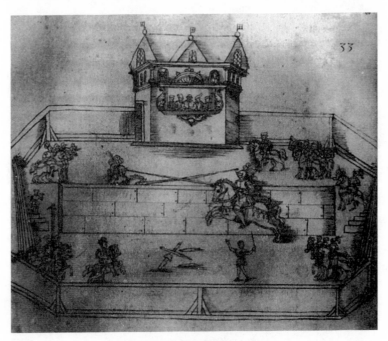

8. Tilting at Elizabeth's court.

'Some of the servants were disguised like savages, or like Irishmen, with the hair hanging down to the girdle like women, others had horse manes on their heads, some came driving in a carriage, the horses being equipped like elephants, some carriages were drawn by men, others appeared to move by themselves; altogether the carriages were of very odd appearance.' Even the drive to the tiltyard was fancifully conceived: 'Some gentlemen had their horses with them and mounted in full armour directly from the carriage.'

The event was rich in arcane ritual, highly ironised:

> When a gentleman with his servant approached the barrier, on
> horseback or in a carriage, he stopped at the foot of the staircase leading
> to the queen's room, while one of his servants in pompous attire of a
> special pattern mounted the steps and addressed the queen in well-
> composed verses or with a ludicrous speech, making her and her ladies
> laugh. When the speech was ended he in the name of his lord offered to
> the queen a costly present, which was accepted and permission given to
> take part in the tournament.[24]

Philip made particularly good use of 'devices' or mottoes, emblems often placed on the shield, designed to send signals about the wearer and his present state (whether emotional or political). His inventiveness in this area might have been inspired by the recent collections of *imprese* by Paolo Giovio and Girolamo Ruscelli (he recommended Ruscelli's book to Languet in Venice): subsequent remarks by Henry Peacham and John Aubrey record Philip's contributions as central to the development of the genre in England.[25]

Philip's *imprese* were eagerly commented on. William Camden wrote: 'Sir Philip Sidney, to note that he persisted always one [i.e. that he was constant], depainted out the Caspian sea surrounded with his shores, which neither ebbeth nor floweth, and over it "Sine refluxu" [without flowing]'. Another favourite was *vix ea nostro voco*, a tag taken from lines in Ovid's *Metamorphoses*, meaning 'I scarcely call our ancestors' deeds our own.' This implied a pride in his ancestry, but an even greater pride in his own achievements.[26]

The *imprese* allowed observers to elaborate on Philip's possible meanings. His protégé Abraham Fraunce included two of Philip's *imprese* in his collection. One was a sheep marked with the planet Saturn and the motto '*Macular modo noscar*' (I am marked so I may be known). Fraunce developed the motto in three Latin verses, the last of which read:

Is a flock or a people a greater source of praise? the sheepfold or the court? Both the flock and the people, the sheepfold and the court are pleasing. Agamemnon was the king of peoples, a shepherd of the people. He was *the shepherd of his people*; the whole of Greece was his flock. His court is in the sheepfolds: the gods also have dwelt in the forests. Even the god Apollo fed his wandering flock.[27]

In this explanation, Fraunce wittily attempts to contrast the court (*aula*) with the sheepfold (*caula*). But he concludes by drawing the two together in an allusion to Homer's depiction of Agamemnon in the *Iliad* as the shepherd of the people. As Agamemnon was the leader of the Greek forces at the siege of Troy, Fraunce can in this way link the shepherd-poet with the shepherd as leader of men.[28] It showed that at least one observer appreciated Philip's games with fact and fiction.

Just as Sir Henry Lee invented 'Loricus' and later 'Laelius' to represent himself in the tiltyard, so Philip invented the persona of the shepherd 'Philisides', playing on his own name. As if to emphasise the fictional elements of his chivalric persona – and the possible political implications of his fiction – in a later version of *The Arcadia* Philip even inserted a clash between Laelius and Philisides:

The first that ran was a brave knight [Laelius], whose device was to come in all chained, with a nymph leading him. Against him came forth an Iberian [Philisides], whose manner of entering was with bagpipes instead of trumpets; a shepherd's boy before him for a page, and by him a dozen appareled like shepherds for the fashion, though rich in stuff, who carried his lances, which though strong to give a lancely blow indeed, yet so were coloured with hooks near the morne [lancehead] that they prettily represented sheephooks. His own furniture [equipment] was dressed over with wool, so enriched with jewels artificially placed that one would have thought it a marriage between the highest and the lowest. His impresa was a sheep marked with pitch, with this word 'Spotted to be known.'[29]

9. Designs for Sir Henry Lee's armour.

Philip, as Philisides, rode into *The Arcadia* bearing his own *impresa*. It was a bizarre conflation of real life and literature, which produced its own mythology: Philip Sidney, the shepherd-knight.

After his months at Wilton, it was time to return to court and fall into line. Philip's New Year gift to Elizabeth for 1581 was a delicious piece of arch wit: 'a jewel of gold, being a whip, garnished with small diamonds in four rows and cords of small seed pearl'. This appeared to be a symbol of submission (Philip hands the whip over), but it was also a reminder that he *had* a whip in the first place.[30] The submission conceit was taken further when Philip participated in a tournament on 22 January 1581, which had been initiated on Twelfth Night by 'Callophisus', Philip Howard.[31] The joust was part of Howard's campaign to present to the queen his claim to the disputed earldom of Arundel.[32] In his challenge, Howard declared himself a prisoner to Elizabeth's beauty, 'finding the place of his imprisonment so strong as he cannot escape'. The Earl of Oxford appeared as 'The Knight of the Tree of the Sun' to confront the 'Red Knight': Howard's second, Sir William Drury. Oxford was seconded by 'The White Knight': his twenty-year-old nephew Edward, Lord Windsor. Philip must have played the Blue Knight: he was to wear blue again in his next tournament, and the Blue Knight made a great deal of being a lover of horses, a standard play on 'Phil-Ip'.[33] With the New Year's whip hopefully still fresh in the queen's mind, the Blue Knight reiterated his subjection, claiming that the queen 'by remembrance of her name only stirreth up all desires to virtue, and by the perfections of her beauty and good graces subdueth the stoutest heart of her beholders'.

This activity may have provided Philip with welcome relief from his official duty at the time: sitting in the House of Commons. Sir Henry had requested both Ludlow and Shrewsbury to return his son as MP for the session beginning in January 1581. When both agreed, Philip chose Shrewsbury, and was replaced in Ludlow by a by-election. The short sitting was packed with novice parliamentarians, none of whom made any great impact on the floor of the house, but Philip did serve on two committees: one to discuss a proposed subsidy (on 25 January) and one to discuss slanderous practices (1 February).[34] He never, however, went on to distinguish himself in traditional parliamentary politics.

He had other matters weighing on his mind. In April 1581, Leicester's wife Lettice provided the earl with a legitimate male heir. The exact date of the birth remains unknown – indeed, the date of the baptism remained hidden until Dr Simon Adams unearthed it recently after four centuries[35] – but the likelihood must be that Philip quickly knew of it, and knew too that he was no longer Leicester's heir. William Camden later wrote: 'Sir Philip Sidney, who was a long time heir apparent to the Earl of Leicester, after the said earl had a son born to him, used at the next tilt-day following SPERAVI, thus dashed through, to show his hope therein was dashed.'[36] 'Speravi' (I used to hope) referred the spectators back to Philip's old motto 'Spero' (I hope),[37] and challenged them to discover why his hope was dashed.

It may be that the 'speravi' motto was used in the lavish entertainment in which Philip participated in May, sending signals to an international audience since the tilt was attended by the French. Anjou had accepted the sovereignty of the Low Countries on 23 January 1581, further enhancing his status as a marital prospect for Elizabeth. A French embassy reached Dover on 17 April and entered into London in great splendour. Leicester and Pembroke were required to meet Anjou, a pointed command that required them to fall publicly into line.[38] From 21 April to 14 June, Elizabeth fêted her French guests, with the full panoply of courtly diversions including, on Whitsun Monday 15 May and Tuesday 16 May 'a triumph in most sumptuous order' at Whitehall. Here 375 men had been labouring since Easter Day on a massive, elaborate banqueting house, at a cost of £1,744 19s., and two broken legs.[39]

The triumph concerned the attempts of four 'Foster Children of Desire' to assault the 'Fortress of Perfect Beauty' (the gallery at the end of the tiltyard, where the queen sat).[40] Two days of tilting and rhetorical sparring followed, in which the twenty-two defenders established that the queen was Heavenly Beauty, and above earthly desires, 'the most renowned and divine sun' who gives 'indifferent succour' to all, rather than favour to one. The second day ended with the Children's realisation that their assault was misguided, and they acknowledged 'this fortress to be reserved for the eye of the whole world, far lifted up from the compass of their destiny'. They were wrong to think Violence could accompany Desire:

> They acknowledge that Desire received his beginning and nourishment of
> this fortress, and therefore to commit ungratefulness in bearing arms
> (though desirous arms) against it. They acknowledge noble Desire should
> have desired nothing so much, as the flourishing of that fortress, which
> was to be esteemed according to itself's liking . . . Therefore they do
> acknowledge themselves overcome, as to be slaves to this Fortress for ever.

At the most basic level, the rejection of Desire suggested Elizabeth's rejection of Anjou's desire; it also added helpfully to the myth of Elizabeth as Virgin Queen, who rejected all such advances. But there were other, more complex interpretations to be gleaned.[41]

The four Foster Children of Desire, who demanded of Elizabeth that 'you will no longer exclude virtuous Desire from perfect Beauty', were Philip Howard, who had won the earldom of Arundel; Frederick, Baron Windsor; Philip Sidney; and – replacing Oxford, who was again out of favour – Fulke Greville. The four challengers entered the tiltyard in magnificent display. Philip was particularly striking:

> Then proceeded M. Philip Sidney, in very sumptuous manner, with
> armour part blue, and the rest gilt and engraven, with four spare horses,
> having caparisons and furniture very rich and costly, as some of cloth of

gold embroidered with pearl, and some embroidered with gold and silver feathers, very richly and cunningly wrought. He had four pages that rode on his four spare horses, who had cassock coats and Venetian hose all of cloth of silver, laid with gold lace, and hats of the same with gold bands, and white feathers, and each one a pair of white buskins. Then had he a thirty gentlemen and yeomen, and four trumpeters, who were all in cassock coats and Venetian hose of yellow velvet, laid with silver lace, yellow velvet caps with silver bands and white feathers, and every one a pair of white buskins. And they had upon their coats, a scroll or band of silver, which came scarf-wise over the shoulder, and so down under the arm, with this poesie, or sentence written upon it, both before and behind, *Sic nos non nobis*.[42]

It has been suggested that Philip was heavily involved in writing this triumph. If so, it provided a new challenge to his chosen method of self-presentation. Here he wanted to show himself to best advantage, but the role in which he was cast placed him on the wrong team. Philip, who had publicly opposed the marriage, was made to represent Anjou's Desire – but within that role, he was able to insist that he was not acting for himself. *Sic nos non nobis* was an adaptation of the familiar motto *Sic vos non vobis*, meaning 'thus we are not for ourselves', or 'we do not for our own sake'. The tilt showed that allegorical meanings could be cleverly nuanced by more personalised readings. Not that everything was clear to the audience. Even Henry Goldwell, who collected and published the materials, left out some sections, 'for that some of them be mystical and not known to many'.

By all accounts, the entertainment was a success. One observer, Thomas Milles, reported to William Davison: 'The tilt I saw from the beginning to the ending and cannot but report great honour to be won at all hands. The men are already gone to Windsor and there it is generally expected that their departure will not be long after. The general fear of the marriage is well laid down.'[43] It seems that the message had hit home. If Philip did have a hand in the 'Foster Children' entertainment, then perhaps for once his literary efforts did achieve their hoped-for political impact. Elizabeth once again rejected Anjou.

Philip also made the 'Foster Children' tilting the subject of a sonnet:

Having this day my horse, my hand, my lance
  Guided so well, that I obtain'd the prize,
  Both by the judgement of the *English* eyes,
And of some sent from that sweet enemy *France*,
Horsemen my skill in horsemanship advance:
  Town-folks my strength; a daintier judge applies
  His praise to slight, which from good use doth rise;
Some lucky wits impute it but to chance;
  Others, because of both sides I do take
My blood from them, who did excel in this,
Think *Nature* me a man of arms did make.
How far they shoot awry! the true cause is,
  Stella look'd on, and from her heav'nly face
Sent forth the beams, which made so fair my race.[44]

If Philip really did pen the sonnet on or around 'this day' of the 'Foster Children' tilt, then in May 1581 he was already writing the sequence of 108 sonnets, irregularly interspersed with eleven 'songs', which was posthumously published as *Astrophil and Stella*. This, his most enduring poetical work, concerned the unrequited love of the poet's persona 'Astrophil' for a disdainful, unavailable lady, 'Stella'. It would follow, then, that 'Stella', according to this, was a controlling force in his life in May 1581. For Stella was Lady Penelope Devereux, the daughter of the Earl of Essex, and (at least according to Edward Waterhouse) Philip's intended bride in 1576. But by that May the chance of her ever becoming Philip's wife had disappeared.

Since 1577, the two Devereux sisters had been the responsibility of the Earl and Countess of Huntingdon. When, on 27 February 1581, Lord Rich died, leaving a twenty-year-old son named Robert, Huntingdon saw a chance to marry Lady Penelope, who had been received by the queen at court a month earlier.[45] Petitioning Burghley for his support, Huntingdon made his case clear: 'Hearing that God hath taken to his mercy my Lord Rich, who hath left to his heir a proper gentleman and one in years very fit for my Lady Penelope Devereux if with the favour and liking of Her Majesty the matter might be brought to pass.'[46]

Robert Lord Rich was young, extremely wealthy and properly Puritan-leaning: the marriage duly took place at the beginning of

November 1581. Yet, around this time, Lady Penelope seems to have been thrown into Philip's company quite often, both at court and elsewhere. Just before the wedding, the Countess of Huntingdon visited Wilton for the christening of the Countess of Pembroke's daughter Katherine, who was born on 15 October, and it may be that Philip and Lady Penelope met there for the last time before her marriage.[47] The match seems not to have been to the bride's liking: her second husband Charles Blount, later seeking to prove the legality of his marriage, argued that Penelope, 'being in the power of her friends, was by them married against her will unto one against whom she did protest at the very solemnity, and ever after: between whom from the first day there ensued continual discord, although the same fears that forced her to marry constrained her to live with him'.[48]

Philip was at Wilton over Christmas in December 1581, and no doubt made headway with his new literary project.[49] Ironically, Penelope's marriage, though possibly a personal disappointment, was a necessary inspiration. The sonnet as a genre came with its own inbuilt expectations: the poet laments his hopeless love for an unattainable woman, often a married woman. Philip named his woman 'Stella' (star) and his poetic persona 'Astrophil' (lover of Stella/star), but of course 'Phil' also pointed to Philip Sidney himself. Like his *Arcadia*, *Astrophil and Stella* signals its own autobiographical elements, and draws its readers into an interpretative game.

Beyond the obvious sign of the name, there are more easily decodable clues as to Astrophil's identity. In sonnet 30, he refers to 'How Ulster likes of that same golden bit,/Wherewith my father once made it half tame', a clear reference to Sir Henry's policy of imposing the cess on the English Pale. In sonnet 65, Astrophil tells Stella, 'Thou bear'st the arrow, I the arrow head' – a reference to the silver arrowhead in the Sidney arms. And while 'Astrophil' was clearly readable as Philip, the identity of Stella was scarcely less well obscured. Penelope's married name 'Rich' is mentioned three times, and at length in sonnet 37, in which Astrophil states he 'must a riddle tell':

> Towards Aurora's Court a Nymph doth dwell,
>   Rich in all beauties which man's eye can see:
>   Beauties so far from reach of worlds, that we

Abase her praise, saying she doth excel:
  Rich in the treasure of deserv'd renown,
  Rich in the riches of a royal heart,
  Rich in those gifts which give th'eternal crown;
  Who though most rich in these and every part,
    Which make the patents of true worldly bliss,
    Hath no misfortune, but that Rich she is.[50]

But, as with *The Arcadia*, the attempt to identify individuals in Philip's work can diminish its complexity and multiple resonances. Stella is often only a cipher, a means to explore the many sides of Astrophil – lover, poet and courtier. Perhaps above all, *Astrophil and Stella* is a dazzling play with language, metre and imagery. In the first printed edition of the sequence, a pirated 1591 version by Thomas Newman, the pamphleteer Thomas Nashe described it as a 'theatre of pleasure', where 'you shall find a paper stage strewed with pearl, an artificial heav'n to overshadow the fair frame, and crystal walls to encounter your curious eye, whiles the tragicomedy of love is performed by starlight . . . The argument cruel chastity, the Prologue hope, the Epilogue despair.'[51]

There is also a chance that Philip's skill at forcing the reader to interpret this work autobiographically as thwarted passion may in fact obscure other functions served by Lady Rich. Her courtly clique had strong connections with Huguenot France. She was an active patron of Leicester's secretary, Jean Hotman: one letter reveals her acquaintance with Buzanval, the Huguenot Henri de Navarre's ambassador in England, and with Philip's brother Robert, Horatio Palavicino and Henry Constable.[52] These were all men who worked closely with Henri de Navarre. Constable wrote verses to her – as he did to Louise de Coligny, wife of William of Orange. Could what appears on the surface to be a simple unrequited love story, given Philip's love of hidden messages, be of more political consequence? Sadly, there is too little evidence to make the case, but the possibility is intriguing.

In the early summer of 1581 Philip received a letter written on 13 May in Tunis addressed '*Al Illustre Filipe Cidnei mi amado Sobrino* [my beloved nephew]'.[53] Its author was Dom Antonio, the pretender to the Portuguese throne, who was disputing Spain's usurpation of the throne after the battle of Oporto in August 1580, when Antonio had been crushed by the Duke of Alva, Philip II's military genius. Philip Sidney spoke for many when he wrote to his brother Robert in October 1580: 'Portugal we say is lost.'[54]

Dom Antonio clearly regarded Philip as an international player, and wanted him to be involved in his bid for power. He was now preparing men and ships, and wrote to Philip that 'Though many more should go if I did not see you in the company, I shall say, *Numerum non habet illa suum* [it does not have its full complement].'[55] But the treatment of Dom Antonio's cause by Elizabeth graphically shows how Philip, still sought-after by foreign powers, was sidelined at home. When Dom Antonio appeared in England in June 1581, intending to fit out a naval force against Spain, Elizabeth agreed (at Leicester's suggestion) to allow Dom Antonio to lodge at Baynards Castle – Pembroke's London base. A plan was hatched whereby Sir Francis Drake would lead an expedition to seize the Azores in the name of the Pretender. Preparations went ahead, but ultimately (at Burghley's urging) Elizabeth decided she could not face spending the money such an arrangement would cost – indeed, had she not already spent £12,000 buying Braganza jewels from Dom Antonio so that he could fit out his fleet at Plymouth?[56] It was made clear to Antonio that he should leave England. According to Mendoza, Philip (along with brother-in-law Pembroke) was chosen by the queen to escort Dom Antonio to his ship – partly to prevent him capturing two valuable Spanish ships on the Downs, as it was rumoured he planned to do. A few days later, when Dom Antonio was finally about to set sail, Philip was commanded to chase after him to Gravesend with a message from the queen.[57] It was almost as if Elizabeth were trying to humiliate Philip in front of his foreign friends.

Beyond the personal shame, there was the usual financial embarrass-ment. Stuck in Dover for some time, Philip's patience and his money ran out.[58] To Sir Christopher Hatton he complained: 'the delay of this prince's departure is so long, as truly I grow very weary of it, having divers business of mine own and my father's, that something import me, and to deal plainly with you being grown almost to the bottom of my purse'. He begged Hatton to 'do me a singular favour, if you can find means'; namely:

to send for me away, the king himself being desirous I should be at the

Court, to remember him unto her Majesty, where I had been ere this time, but being sent hither by her Highness, I durst [dared] not depart without her especial revocation and commandment. The Queen means, I think, that I should go over with him, which at this present might hinder me greatly, and nothing avail the king for any service I should be able to do him. I find by him, he will see all his ships out of Thames before he will remove: they are all wind bound, and the other that came hither, the wind being strainable at the east, hath driven them toward the Isle of Wight, being no safe harbour here to receive them: so that he is constrained to make the longer abode, if it were but to be waffed [wafted] over. I beseech you Sir, do me this favour, for which, I can promise nothing, seeing all is yours already.

Philip was back in London on 10 October,[59] but his comment that all was Hatton's already was literal as well as metaphorical. Philip was falling heavily into debt, and Sir Christopher had lent him more. Throughout the last months of 1581, Philip dashed off begging letters to his powerful friends and patrons, but only the queen offered him anything – and that was income from recusancy fines, and property seized from Catholics. This again was a barbed comment. The Parliament of January to March 1581, in which Philip had sat, was notable for clamping down on recusancy. Despite his public associations with Walsingham and Leicester, Philip displayed a more tolerant aspect in replying to a plea from Lady Kytson, whose father, the recusant Sir Thomas Cornwallis, had been banished to his Suffolk estates at Elizabeth's accession.[60] At Lady Kytson's request, Philip petitioned Walsingham (both by letter and through Greville) to intercede on behalf of Sir Thomas, and informed Lady Kytson (incorrectly as it turned out) that 'there is a present intention of a general mitigation, to be used in respect of recusants', assuring her that 'there is meant a speedy easing of the greatness of your burden. I assure you, madam, upon my faith, I dealt carefully and earnestly, owing a particular duty unto Sir Thomas, which I will never fail to show to my uttermost, and if otherwise have been thought, I have been mistaken, and if said, the more wronged.' Elizabeth's backhanded generosity in granting Philip the recusancy fines seems to have been aimed squarely at such kindness and possibly even at his alleged friendships years before in Venice.

Philip was perturbed at the moral choice he had to make. 'Truly I like not their persons and much worse their religions,' he lamented to Leicester, 'but I think my fortune very hard that my reward must be built upon other men's punishments.'[61] Ultimately, there was no contest: he needed the money.

Ironically, it was the final chapter in the increasingly farcical Anjou marriage negotiations that finally allowed Philip to return to the Continent.[62] In the autumn of 1581, Anjou made one final attempt to win Elizabeth as his bride, staying in London for three months from 1 November. Matters were bogged down in their usual way when, on the morning of the 22nd, to everyone's surprise, the queen forced the pace. As she and Anjou, with Leicester and Walsingham, were walking in a gallery, the French ambassador entered and announced (in Mendoza's account):

> that he wished to write to his master, from whom he had received
> orders to hear from the Queen's own lips her intention with regard to
> marrying his brother. She replied: 'You may write this to the king: that
> the duke of Anjou shall be my husband,' and at the same moment she
> turned to Anjou and kissed him on the mouth, drawing a ring from her
> own hand and giving it to him as a pledge. Anjou gave her a ring of his
> in return, and shortly afterwards the Queen summoned the ladies and
> gentlemen from the presence chamber in the gallery, repeating to them
> in a loud voice in Anjou's presence what she had previously said.[63]

The French king sent a representative to finalise the terms (both political and financial) of the match, but as ever the path to true love was not smooth. Elizabeth demanded terms (most painfully the restitution to England of Calais) which served only to exasperate Henri. Having committed herself so publicly, the queen came to hate the very idea of marrying, and it soon became clear – to everyone but Anjou, who was still, embarrassingly enough, at the English court – that the marriage was impossible.

Anjou had to be made to leave, but he was deaf to entreaty. Mendoza wrote incredulously that 'the tricks which the Queen is playing to get rid of Monsieur are more than I can describe.' It was pointed out to Anjou that his honour was being violated by the string of victories being enjoyed by the Spanish commander Parma in the Low Countries; he replied that it was only to win Elizabeth that he had ever shown any interest in the Low Countries. He would not leave until the marriage had taken place. In the end, only the lure of money could move this most steadfast of suitors. On 15 December, Elizabeth agreed to lend him £60,000, on the condition that he would repay it within six months of her demanding him to do so. Anjou now agreed to leave, provided she promise to marry him a few weeks later and laid on an escort to Holland 'meet for his greatness', which would make it clear to his detractors that he was leaving the country without shame.[64] Elizabeth was forced to concede.

The magnificent envoy, totalling over 600 men, started out on 1 February 1582, including in its ranks Lord Howard, the Vice-Admiral, Leicester, Hunsdon, Willoughby, Windsor, Sheffield, Sir William Drury, Walter Ralegh, Fulke Greville, Edward Dyer and, naturally, Philip Sidney. Elizabeth herself accompanied this bizarre public-relations exercise as far as Canterbury, where she celebrated her forthcoming marriage with sumptuous feasting and lamented Anjou's imminent departure with a good deal of public weeping. Monsieur must, she commanded, address his letters to his wife, the Queen of England.[65]

On 7 February, fourteen vessels took Anjou and his retinue to Flushing, where he was welcomed by William of Orange, St Aldegonde, the States of Brabant and the Deputies of the States General with (according to one observer) 'all manner of tokens of joy'. Philip was able to introduce Leicester to William of Orange, whom he had never met. William expressed his delight at meeting his ally after so many years and his wife was enchanted by the earl's attention to her young daughter Louisa Juliana. On 19 February, Anjou entered Antwerp, processing through a series of triumphal arches and decorated streets to the palace, where he was installed as Duke of Brabant. For a week ordnance was fired and bonfires blazed, in his honour.[66] But to many, it was Leicester who was the important presence. He rode into Antwerp ahead of Anjou, with Orange and the Prince Dauphin. A magnificent folio volume describing Anjou's entry was dedicated to Leicester and a copy forwarded to him by Orange's own chaplain, De Villiers.[67] Some even believed that without Leicester in tow, Anjou would not have 'been received as a friend, much less invested as their lord'.[68]

For Philip, the visit to Antwerp and his meeting again with William of Orange, must have been tinged with sadness, for it took place without his greatest mentor. At the end of October 1580, Languet had accompanied Orange into Holland – surprisingly, the first time Languet had ever travelled there. Languet's letter to Philip of 28 October 1580, mentioning this mission, is the last known correspondence from Languet to his protégé. Together, Orange and Languet spent some time in Delft, where Languet fell ill. At the beginning of March 1581, Orange left Delft for Amsterdam and Languet returned to Antwerp, a city now in a state of near-revolution. 'It's as if we were in an interregnum here,' he wrote to Crato. 'Nobody uses the name of the King of Spain anymore in public acts, but neither do they use Anjou's.'[69] In Languet's letters to Augustus, the decline of Antwerp is graphically shown, day by day. The loss of Breda devastated Orange's revenues and terrified the Antwerpians, who responded by forbidding the practice of Catholicism, expelling all priests and sealing up the convents.

By September, half the population had been struck down by a fever, including Languet himself, who was only able to write a short letter to Augustus on 2 September. He died on 30 September, in the house known as 'den Coninck Melchior' (King Melchior) on Lange Nieuwstraat, owned by the rich Calvinist merchant Louis Malepert. In his last days, he was attended by Charlotte Arbaleste, wife of another of his protégés, Philippe Du Plessis, who was living on the same street.[70] Since he died intestate, most of Languet's belongings were sold at auction, and an inventory reveals the contents of his two rooms. It was a forlorn spectacle: a chest of clothes, another of new clothes and shirts, a chest with books bound and unbound, a collection of papers, a rapier, some hats and two pictures: one of Languet himself and one of a young man, perhaps the Veronese portrait of Philip.[71]

CHAPTER TEN

Heroical Designs

I T WOULD BE too easy to fall into the trap of believing that Languet's death spelled the end of Philip's active intervention in European politics. In purely quantitive terms, the surviving evidence might encourage this verdict. By a quirk of fate, one large volume of Philip's letters from European correspondents during the mid-1570s has survived, while other letters presumably have not. The effect of this volume, combined with the carefully preserved letters from Languet, is to make it appear at first glance as if Philip's dealings with mainland Europe were largely confined to the period before Languet's death.

However, from the handful of letters that have survived, and the references in other correspondence (above all, Walsingham's), it is clear that Philip remained a prime mover in his sphere of European politics until the end of his life. In addition to the circles set up by Languet, Philip had gained new correspondents all over Europe: Dom Antonio's agent Antonio d'Avigna;[1] in Paris, the Italian Sebastiano Pardini providing an alternative to the missives of ambassador Cobham;[2] in Bièvre, François Perrot de Mezières;[3] in Antwerp, Anjou's servant Alfaranti de Viçose, the Sieur d'Alfeyran,[4] and Frederich Schwartz von Ruissingen,[5] as well as Charles de Fremyn, Walsingham's chief intelligencer there.[6] In their letters, these correspondents invariably link Philip with Leicester, sometimes with the Earl of Warwick, and occasionally with his peers Fulke Greville, Edward Dyer and Stanhope. But Philip Sidney is seen to possess qualities that would make him a viable leader in his own right. In April 1582, Charles de Fremyn reported to Walsingham that there were calls from some Englishmen in the Low Countries for 'a certain number of cavalry, led by some honourable gentleman recommended by her Majesty and it seems to me that Mr Philip Sidney would be well suited for this'.[7]

Foreign scholars and publishers continued to dedicate their books to him. Some of these were from long-time admirers: Henri Estienne (Stephanus) dedicated his edition of Herodian to Philip in 1581,[8] and André Wechel's press produced Franciscus Junius' Hebrew grammar in 1580. In his dedicatory epistle, Junius addressed Philip as 'son of

246

England's President over all Wales, nephew of the renowned Earls of Warwick and Leicester', and thanked him for his personal kindnesses towards him (they may have met during Philip's travels in 1577). Like de Banos four years earlier, Junius believed that Philip was the key that would open up English markets for his book: 'the result of this preface in honour of your great name will be that England will approve of whatever you approve of and will be happy to accept whatever you accept willingly'.[9] In 1582, his friend from his Vienna days, Charles de l'Écluse, dedicated to Philip his translation of Nicolas Monardes' *Simplicium medicamentorum historiae liber tertius* from Antwerp.[10] But Philip's influence was beginning to be felt even further afield. In 1580 Lambert Daneau dedicated his *Geographiæ Poeticæ* to Philip from Geneva, which he had never even visited.[11] The Italian Gentili brothers, Alberico and Scipio, thought it worthwhile to associate themselves in print with Philip's name. In 1581, Scipio dedicated his paraphrases of the psalms of David to Philip; three years later, a second volume followed. Alberico, as we have seen, memorialised Philip as the ideal ambassador in his *De legationibus*, and dedicated the book to him in 1585.[12]

Despite his continuing prestige on the Continent, Philip's position at home was, if anything, even worse than it had been in 1575. The birth of the baby Lord Denbigh had unseated him as heir to Leicester, and indeed to Warwick. The obvious path for him to take was still Ireland, with which he was inevitably associated: in 1581, John Derrick published his book *The Image of Irelande*, lauding Sir Henry, and dedicated it to Philip as his 'son and heir'.[13] His father had attempted to lure him back to Ireland, but in vain. When news came in the spring of 1582 that Lord Grey de Wilton was to be recalled from his Lord Deputyship in Ireland, Sir Henry let it be known that he would serve as Lord Deputy one more time, on one condition: if Philip 'will assuredly promise him to go with him thither, and withal will put on a determinate mind to remain and continue there after him, and to succeed him in the government (if it may so like her Majesty to allow him) he will then yield his consent to go'. If these conditions were not met, then Sir Henry vowed that 'he will not leave his quiet and contented life at home, considering his years, and the defects of nature, that commonly accompany age, to enter into so toilsome a place, both of body and mind, but only to leave some memory and worthy mark to his posterity'.[14] The deal did not appeal – although whether to Elizabeth or to Philip is unknown – so Sir Henry, and his son, stayed in England.

Philip Sidney was twenty-eight years old, unmarried and with no prospect of a significant official position. Accordingly, he found himself increasingly drawn to the financial and political benefits that might be gained from a well-chosen bride. It seems that, at one point, Philip flirted with the idea of marrying Penelope Rich's younger sister, Dorothy Devereux: in Leicester's will dated 30 January 1582 (which was later superseded) he bequeathed £2,000 to further a match between Philip and Dorothy.[15] Evidently this came to nothing, and Philip was already considering a match where his future father-in-law would have domestic political muscle. Sir Francis Walsingham had lost his daughter Mary in 1580, leaving another daughter Frances as his sole heir. Philip had encountered Frances when she was still something shy of her fifth birthday, as they sheltered together in the English embassy at Paris during the Massacre of August 1572. Now fifteen-year-old Frances was of marriageable age, and Walsingham was an attractive prospect as father-in-law.

For Walsingham, the Sidneys were not a safe bet financially, but he appreciated Philip's potential in other ways. Besides, he had a vested interest in settling Frances as quickly and quietly as possible. In 1581, a man named John Wickerson had made 'a rash contract with Mistress Frances', then only thirteen or fourteen. These 'clandestine' marriages, which possessed a certain legal validity, were the bane of every father seeking to control his child's future. Walsingham was powerful enough to have Wickerson committed to the debtors' prison of Marshalsea and so remove this threat to his plans for Frances.[16]

The Sidney–Walsingham match was spoken of in family circles as early as autumn 1581 by Philip's friend Edward Denny, a fellow tilter and recipient of Philip's suggestions for reading. Denny was related to Walsingham (whose mother was born Joyce Denny) and wrote on 6 October 1581 asking 'that I may be most humbly commended to my good lady, and to my cousin Frances, and I beseech you, good sir, make a great account of my matchless master Mr Sidney. I speak it the rather for your own good to hold now to you the most worthy young man in the world.' Philip is punningly 'matchless' – without peer, and without a wife. Two months later, Philip himself dropped a hint in a letter to Walsingham, offering his 'humble salutations . . . to yourself, my good lady, and my exceeding like to be good friend' – a deliberately ambiguous reference to Frances.[17]

By February 1583, the news was out on the English political scene. Burghley wrote to Walsingham that 'I hear of the comfortable purpose toward for your daughter. God bless it; as I would any of my own so is that great hope.'[18] By May, word had spread to the Continent: Jean Lobbet sent his congratulations from Strasburg to Sir Francis:

> I have been very glad to hear of the alliance to be between you and Mr Philip Sidney, who is to marry your daughter. I think I saw her in your house at Paris. I rejoice with them both, and it seems to me that the match is well made; I pray God to give it his blessing, which I am sure he will, as is promised in the 128th Psalm. Please greet Mr Philip Sidney from me, and his brother Mr Robert at the same time and congratulate them on so honourable a connexion.[19]

For several months, however, it appeared that the nuptials would never take place. Walsingham apparently came to believe that Sir Henry was not wholly behind the plan. On 1 March 1583, Sir Henry Sidney wrote a lengthy letter to Walsingham, effectively a narrative *curriculum vitae*. While the letter now serves as a useful treasure trove for historians of Welsh and Irish history, Sir Henry's immediate purpose was to counter the Secretary's suspicions. 'I have understood of late that coldness is thought in me in proceeding in the matter of marriage of our children. In truth, sir, it is not, nor so shall it ever be found; for compremitting the consideration of the articles to the earls named by you, and to the earl of Huntingdon I most willingly agree and protest I joy in the alliance with all my heart.'

Sir Henry's reservations lay in the news (which Walsingham had relayed to him on 3 January) that the queen had refused in any way to relieve Sir Henry's 'decayed estate'. Now, he wrote, he would have to sell lands 'to ransom me out of the servitude I live in for my debts, for as I know, sir, that it is the virtue which is, or that you suppose is, in my son that you made choice of him for your daughter, refusing haply far greater and far richer matches than he'. In return, Sir Henry had been confident that by Walsingham's means he would obtain 'some small reasonable suit of her Majesty'; as he pointed out, 'I might have received a great sum of money for my goodwill of my son's marriage, greatly to the relief of my private, biting necessity.' The money was not forthcoming.[20]

A second stumbling block came from the queen, who let it be known that she was displeased with the negotiations. To Sir Christopher Hatton, Walsingham mused that 'I find it strange that her Majesty should be offended withal.' Perhaps Elizabeth had taken offence because she had not been consulted, but he reasoned that he was not of sufficient status for his children's marriages to warrant such attention: indeed, 'it may be thought a presumption for me to trouble her Majesty with a private marriage between a free gentleman of equal calling with my daughter'. He had hoped that years of faithful service would have merited 'grace and favour at her hands', and that she would have 'countenanced this match with her gracious and princely good-liking'. Walsingham decided that he would have to stand up for himself: he asked Hatton (who had already provided an 'honourable and friendly defence' of the marriage), if the queen should raise the matter, to 'let her understand that you learn generally that the match is held for concluded, and withal to let her know how just cause I shall have to find myself aggrieved if her Majesty shall show her mislike thereof'.[21] Elizabeth was evidently not impressed by Walsingham's aggrievement. Her displeasure was still apparent in mid-April, when Roger Manners reported to his father that 'I have been with Mr Secretary who is somewhat troubled that her Majesty conceives no better of the marriage of his daughter with Sir Philip Sidney, but I hope shortly all will be well.'[22] By early May, however, the danger had passed, and Manners could report that 'Her Majesty passes over the offence taken with Mr Sidney concerning his marriage.'[23]

One intriguing result of Elizabeth's displeasure is hinted at in a letter to Mary, Queen of Scots, prompted by the French ambassador in London, Castelnau. The writer hinted that he hoped to persuade Philip Sidney to become a good servant of the Scottish queen, because Walsingham and Leicester had incurred great 'jalousie a ceste Reyne' because of their marriage negotiations for Philip.[24] Even now, it seems, Elizabeth worried about power pacts among her chief counsellors, and Walsingham and Leicester were two of the greatest of all. What Philip's marriage to Frances brought about, at least in the eyes of outsiders, was a tightening of links between Walsingham and Leicester; despite the Protestant credentials of these two, they might be provoked into seeking a new sovereign if Elizabeth remained obstructive.

Once all the misunderstandings were resolved, the marriage was finally celebrated on Friday 21 September 1583.[25] By now, Philip's status was somewhat enhanced by the fact that he had been knighted – a long overdue consequence of Casimir nominating him as his proxy in 1579 for the bestowing of his Order of the Garter: before the ceremony took place at Windsor in February 1583, Elizabeth had no option but to dub Philip. He was quickly absorbed into the Walsingham circle. Among the marriage articles was an item that 'the said Sir Francis is well contented and will undertake to pay or discharge the debts of the said Sir Philip so far as shall amount unto £1,500, and will allow to the said Sir Philip and Mrs Frances and their servants their diet if they will take it with him and in his house'.[26] In practice this meant that the Sidneys never set up house by themselves, but usually lodged with the Walsinghams, either in Walsingham House or Barn Elms (in the light of this, Thomas Moffet's idealised portrait of Philip as 'the head of a household' seems rather strained).[27] This enforced domestic arrangement made Philip's links with Sir Francis even closer.

Like so many marriages between people of their rank, that of Philip and Frances was one that started as a mutually beneficial arrangement between families; in this case, it appears that in its three years' duration, and perhaps despite their domestic arrangements, a real affection emerged between the two. Philip's mother had devoted her life to facilitating the complex political career of her husband – and not merely on the level of domestic housekeeping, but through active intervention at court. It seems reasonable to assume that, in time, Philip expected Frances to adopt just such a function: by 1586, she was identified as a patron of printed works – Jaques Le Moyne's pictorial work *La Clef des Champs* was dedicated to her in that year – which suggests that she was starting to possess her own public profile.[28] Moffet hints that there were concerns about the newly-weds' apparent inability to reproduce as promptly as they might have liked. He tells how he, in Philip's presence, 'deplored this slight infertility in his wife', and Philip, 'judging the matter fairly and weighing it according to its importance, answered that the inconvenience of sterility ought to be mitigated by a convenient practice, and ought to be accepted as in accord with the divine will, which alone brings anything to pass'.[29] As it was, the couple waited only two years for an heir, so Moffet's concern might have been a little excessive.

With closer links to Walsingham, Philip's name was now advanced more regularly for important political and military positions in England. In March 1583, his friend Edward Dyer spoke of Philip as a possible Captain of the Isle of Wight to replace Sir Edward Horsey, whose reputation had been dogged by the increasing piracy based on the island. 'It is so generally spoken that Sir Philip Sidney is Captain of the Isle that I know not what to believe,' wrote Dyer (who wanted the post himself) to Walsingham, but nothing came of the rumour.[30]

However, by this point Philip's ambitions lay in another family business – the Ordnance, which was under the control of his uncle, the Earl of Warwick. In January 1583, Warwick approached the queen with a plan to make his nephew joint master of the Ordnance. 'Her Majesty yields gracious hearing unto it,' Philip assured Burghley, while soliciting his support.[31] On 14 February, Walsingham requested the Solicitor General to draw up a joint patency for Philip and Warwick, but also begged him 'that for some considerations you will keep this matter secret, and give especial charge unto your clerk that shall engross the book, to use the same in like sort' – the secrecy perhaps suggesting that Philip's involvement might be seen as politically sensitive.[32] Philip was still petitioning Burghley in July, but as the year progressed, the prospect of a joint patency receded.[33] Instead, he was finally rewarded with a subordinate appointment as one of the 'inferior officers' under Warwick.

Although it was a junior position, it gave Philip a foothold in an institution that was crucial for any type of military or navigational planning. Based in the White Tower of the Tower of London, the Ordnance drew on some of the finest scientific thinking of its day; its keeper, for example, was the mathematician and engineer Thomas Bedwell. One of Philip's first tasks was to oversee the urgent repairs being undertaken at Dover Harbour, England's most important port on the south coast, and a natural Achilles' heel for prospective invaders. Here he was able to draw on the multifarious talents of the geographer, astronomer and surveyor Thomas Digges, son of the famed mathematician Leonard Digges; indeed, Philip seems to have delegated much of the hands-on work to other men,[34] concerning himself instead with reorganising the Ordnance Office's administration.[35] What interested him most about the Ordnance was not its daily operation, but the possibilities that access to its resources might afford.

Philip's official political career in England progressed only slowly, with his public persona being one of cultured courtier rather than important politician. But, unknown to many, the two often came together and Philip seems to have taken full political advantage of situations that were, to most eyes, banally 'cultural'. For example, in May 1583, the learned Polish prince Albert Laski visited England. After being entertained by Leicester, he proceeded to Oxford with the French ambassador Castelnau and Castelnau's current house guest, the Italian writer Giordano Bruno. Philip, who had met Laski in Venice nine years earlier, joined the company and witnessed Bruno's controversial public disputation with the rector of Lincoln College. George Abbot, then at Balliol, wrote of how Bruno 'got up into the highest place of our best and most renowed school, stripping up his sleeves like some juggler . . . he undertook among very many other matters to set on foot the opinion of Copernicus, that the earth did go round, and the heavens did stand still; whereas in truth it was his own head which rather did run round, and his brain did not stand still.' Bruno, for his part, complained:

> The wretched doctor who was put forward as the leader of the
> Academy on that grave occasion came to a halt fifteen times over fifteen
> syllogisms, like a chicken amongst stubble. Learn how roughly and
> rudely that pig behaved and with what patience and humanity the
> Nolan [Bruno's title for himself] replied, showing himself to be indeed
> a Neapolitan, born and bred beneath a kindlier sky. Hear how they
> made him leave off his public lectures on the immortality of the soul
> and on the quintuple sphere.[36]

On 15 June, Laski and his entourage moved on to visit John Dee at his house in Mortlake. As Dee noted jubilantly in his diary, 'He had in his company Lord Russell, Sir Philip Sidney, and other gentlemen: he was rowed by the Queen's men, he had the barge covered with the Queen's cloth, the Queen's trumpeters, &c. He came of purpose to do me honour, for which God be praised!' Indeed, the meeting was such a success that Dee would later accompany Laski back to Poland.[37]

Despite his contempt for the Oxford academics, Bruno seems to have approved of Philip, whom he regarded as a friend – when they met, he informed Philip that he had heard good things about him, both in Italy and in France. Over the next two years, Bruno dedicated to Philip two printed works in Italian: *Spaccio de la bestia trionfante* in 1584 and *De gl'heroici furori* in 1585. These dedications imply a friendship that was both political and literary. Bruno's *Spaccio* was designed to promote the alleged friendship of Henri III for England, disclaiming any love on the part of the French king for Spain or the Catholic League – its dedication to Philip effectively identified Philip publicly (whether with his consent or not) with Henri's plans. *De gl'heroici furori* implies that Bruno knew of Philip's *Astrophil and Stella*. In a series of dialogues, Bruno debates the nature of true love in a blistering attack on the false values of Petrarchan love poetry. 'Truly (most noble knight),' he declared as an opening gambit, 'it is the mark of a low, beastly and filthy mind to be always studying and gazing and giving one's most careful thought to the beauty of a female body . . .' Dedicating this opinion to a man who had spent months of his life studying and gazing and giving his most careful thought to Stella might be thought rather misplaced, but Bruno knew what he was doing. He dedicated the book to Philip, he explained, 'because the Italian likes to talk with someone who can understand. The poetry in the book is under the criticism and protection of a poet; the philosophy is nakedly revealed to so clear an intellect as yours; and the heroic matters are directed to a heroic and noble mind, with which you have shown yourself to be endowed.' He concluded by assuring Philip that he was not including in his attack ladies of Philip's acquaintance, since they were 'nymphs, goddesses of heavenly substance'. The dedication ends with a sonnet to the ladies of England, who are, he says knowingly, '*stelle*' [stars].[38]

During these years Philip's own literary endeavours became wide-ranging: in fact, the only thing most had in common was that they remained unfinished. One exception was 'Two Pastorals', in which he celebrated his friendship with Fulke Greville and Edward Dyer; providing a new spin on the classical commonplace of 'one mind in bodies twain', this friendship was 'one mind in bodies three'. Thomas Moffet endorsed the picture of Greville and Dyer as close friends at this time, adding to the circle Henry Brouncker (who had accompanied Philip to Prague in 1577) and 'those golden peacocks of the realm', the Earl of Essex and Willoughby, as 'his special companions'. According to Moffet, Philip explained his shunning of 'other nobles belonging to important families and factions' by saying, 'The pious and learned ought to be followed, even if they droop; the impious ought to be shunned although they flourish; with none ought one to live familiarly except those who shine and excel in antique morality, deep learning, and proved faith.'[39]

The piety that Philip expected of his familiar friends extended into his new literary endeavours. He now turned his attention – as did many godly Protestants – to the Psalms and embarked on an ambitious new English rendering. He was not interested in providing a scholarly translation: he referred not to the original Hebrew text, nor to the Vulgate Latin, but to Clément Marot and Théodore de Beze's 1560 French metrical versions and the English prose psalter appended to the Book of Common Prayer.[40] He planned to write each psalm in a different stanzaic form – and succeeded in finishing forty-three. But it was his sister Mary who completed the translation.

There were other projects, which have not survived. According to contemporary accounts, Philip started to translate *La semaine ou création du monde* by the French Huguenot poet Guillaume de Salluste, Sieur du Bartas, a verse account of the creation in seven books, the first part of which had been published in 1578.[41] Perhaps aware of this, du Bartas praised Philip in the *Seconde semaine*, published in April 1584: Sir Nicholas Bacon, Sir Thomas More and 'le Milor Cydné' were singled out as the 'firm pillars' of the English language.[42] Literary and political endeavours overlapped: du Bartas, now at the court of Henri of Navarre, solicited Philip, and the young Francis Bacon, to present his letters to the queen: as he wrote to Francis' brother Anthony in September 1584, 'I have asked Monsieur de Niort, minister at La Rochelle, to send to your brother and de Cydné a letter I've written to the Queen . . . I thought that my letters would be more reliably delivered by yourselves, and furthermore that I should consult you as to whether they were suitable to send to her Majesty.'[43] It seems that Philip was seen by the Navarre court as a worthwhile correspondent: in March 1585, Henri de Navarre sent letters (via his counsellor Du Pin and the English intermediary Anthony Bacon) to the English court, as Bacon described to Walsingham: 'Namely one to her Majesty, your honour, my Lord Chancellor, my Lord Treasurer, my Lord of Bedford, Leicester, Chamberlain, Sir Philip Sidney, Sir Francis Drake, Mr Raleigh, Mr Waad, all from the king.'[44]

According to Greville, Philip also 'most excellently translated among divers other notable works Monsieur Du Plessis' book against atheism, which is since done by another' – a reference to the English version of Du Plessis' *De la vérité de la religion chrestienne*, published in 1587 as *A Worke concerning the Trewnesse of the Christian Religion*. The title page states that it was 'begun to be translated into English by Sir Philip Sidney Knight, and at his request finished by Arthur Golding'. Golding himself assured Leicester that 'it was his [Philip's] pleasure to commit the performance of this piece of service . . . unto my charge; declaring unto me how it was his meaning, that the same being accomplished should be dedicated unto your Honour'. However, it is now thought that the version published in 1587, despite bearing Philip's name, was entirely Golding's work.[45]

All these projects point in the same direction: to an English Protestant literature that took its lead from continental models, but strove to create something new. Although completed by others after Philip's death the end products lack the inventiveness that characterises all Philip's 'finished' work. They may demonstrate what Philip could have achieved had he lived longer; alternatively, in their range and unfinished state, they may indicate that he was finding it increasingly difficult to complete any literary work.

Philip spent more of his energies, and focused them to better effect, on his *Arcadia*, to which he returned compulsively during the 1580s. Taking his original material, he reworked it, striving for a more sophisticated piece of work. The chronology of the story was played with, many of the songs were cut, new characters were introduced (including one, an idealised, virtuous lover named Argalus, that has been seen as autobiographical) and the rhetoric pushed even further. He provided the heroic adventures for his princes that he had only cursorily gestured towards in his original version. In Greville's words, 'His intent and scope was to turn the barren philosophy precepts into pregnant images of life . . . to limn out such exact pictures of every posture in the mind that any man . . . might (as in a glass) see how to set a good countenance upon all the discountenance of adversity, and a stay upon the exorbitant smilings of chance'.[46] It was a long, slow process, and by 1585 he had only got as far as redrafting the first two books, and was working on the third. He was halfway through a fight scene – indeed, halfway through a sentence – when he broke off work, at a date that we cannot establish. Had he been allowed to finish (if, indeed, he would ever have considered it finished), this 'New' *Arcadia* would have been a more ambitious, elaborate and high-flown work than its predecessor. In that, it reflected the growing aspirations of its creator in other pursuits.

In the early summer of 1584, within a period of just a few weeks, two deaths knocked European politics off-balance. On 31 May 1584, Anjou died after an illness of some months, probably tuberculosis contracted during his childhood.[47] Although his potential as husband to Elizabeth – or as serious military force in the Low Countries – was long past, his death meant that there was no Valois heir to replace the childless Henri III, whose own health was fast deteriorating. Next in line was the Huguenot Henri de Navarre, but his accession to the throne of a predominantly Catholic country would threaten civil war in France. On 29 June, an even sharper blow was struck when William of Orange succumbed to a second assassination attempt, this one by Balthasar Gérard at Delft. For the Low Countries, their last proper defence against Spain was gone. No man could provide the focus for resistance that Orange had done. St Aldegonde wrote to Walsingham calmly stating that now only outside assistance – from England or from France – could save the Low Countries from complete Spanish domination.

When the news of Orange's death arrived from Middelburg, Elizabeth was spurred into action. She had already determined to send Philip to the French court to console the king and the queen mother on the death of Anjou. 'But now,' wrote Walsingham to the English ambassador in Paris, Sir Edward Stafford on 6 July, 'she means to hasten his departure, and I think he will set out in five or six days.' In fact, Philip's instructions were drawn up on 8 July, and he set out just two days later.[48] A report on Philip's appointment sent to the French king by his London ambassador Castelnau serves as a useful reminder of how Philip was still perceived abroad as intimately connected to most of the upper échelon of English society:

He is the son of a father who has been viceroy in Ireland, and nephew of the earls of Sussex, Leicester and of Warwick, of Bedford and the Countess of Sussex, brother-in-law of the Earl of Pembroke, and related to the highest-ranking in England. He has married the only daughter and heiress of Walsingham, in the hope of being one day one of the greatest lords of this kingdom. He will be accompanied by the Earl of Essex, by the second son of England's Lord Treasurer [Burghley], the eldest son of milord Cobham, and several other well-born gentleman, to the number of 65 horses, and must leave towards the end of this week.

Castelnau was not without his own agenda in taking up Philip: he had been in contact with both Leicester and Philip for several months and was keen himself to facilitate French involvement in the Low Countries.[49]

Philip was commanded by Elizabeth to tell Henri that while the occasion demanded that she condole him on his loss, 'yet if it be considered how just cause we ourself have of grief having lost so dear a friend as the duke, his brother, was unto us (whereof no prince could give more notable and evident arguments to the world of the great and singular goodwill and love he bare us) it will then appear that as we are inclined to perform the one, so shall we be found altogether unfit for the other, having more need to receive comfort than apt to comfort others.' Henri and his mother Cathérine de Médicis should be made aware in no uncertain terms that Orange's death posed a serious threat to their own interests. If Henri refused to provide 'present assistance' to 'those poor afflicted people of the Low Countries', they would 'not be able to hold out'. If the Low Countries capitulated to their occupiers, then Philip of Spain – with the support of the Vatican and a number of princes in Austria – would reign supreme in Europe. 'What increase of treasure and strength by sea he is grown unto by the possession of the kingdom of Portugal all men of judgement both see and fear,' Philip was to point out. 'He lacketh only the quiet possession of the Low Countries to make him the most absolute monarch that ever was in this part of the world.'

Typically, however, Elizabeth stopped short of providing details of the kind of aid England might provide. Philip was not allowed 'to descend into particularities how this Spanish greatness may be prevented', but was to talk in only 'general words' to 'assure him that he shall find us ready to do anything that may stand with our honour'. Indeed, if Henri showed willing, Philip was to draw back, pointing out that Elizabeth had found him changeable and cold in previous negotiations, so she had not bothered on this occasion to send anyone with the power to treat. Philip was to report back to the queen for fresh instructions, and to apply for extended authority, only if the French king displayed a disposition 'to proceed effectually in the matter'.[50]

Once again, Philip had been given a high-level diplomatic mission, only to be rendered completely impotent by his instructions. What made this mission even worse was that he had to deal with the French queen mother, a woman he had called 'Jezebel' in his much-circulated letter to the queen, and to condole on the death of a man who had openly despised him. The irony was made worse by the fact that, as with all diplomatic missions, the funds made available to him (£3 6s. 8d. per diem for 'diet', with an advance of £300)[51] would scarcely make a dent in the costs of the elaborate journey, and there was no prospect of reward in kind for such services. When Philip was first named as a possible envoy, Walsingham noted that 'his friends, in this time of hard consideration of service, wish him rid of the burden'.[52]

But Philip's chagrin was soon to turn even sourer. Receiving his instructions from the queen, he set out immediately for Gravesend.[53] The first carriages were already on their way across the Channel when Philip received a message from Sir Edward Stafford. The French king, he told him, was travelling to Lyons, but his entourage was not sufficiently splendid 'to receive an ambassador'. More to the point, Stafford continued, Henri had already stopped mourning for his brother – presumably Henri's sly dig at the fact that Elizabeth had waited over a month (indeed until Orange's death) before sending condolences. Henri therefore asked for 'the stay of Mr Sidney' until he returned, which would be at the end of September – some three months away. Philip promptly returned to London.[54] Henri, realising the gravity of his *faux pas*, quickly despatched an official named Fourrier to add his apologies to those of the beleaguered French ambassador Castelnau, but the damage was done. When Fourrier expressed the French king's desire that Philip's envoy might 'proceed' when he returned from Lyons, Elizabeth coldly replied that she had sent Philip to do Henri honour, 'but since he did not like to have him go over, she was for her part well content to stay him'.

As for sending him over later, 'she saw no cause thereof'. Although Castelnau stayed in contact with Philip, he was unable to resuscitate the mission.[55]

Nobody came out of this diplomatic blunder well. While the behaviour of the French merely fulfilled francophobic English expectations, the conduct of Stafford also provoked negative comment. In the confines of her bedchamber, Elizabeth let it be known that she was offended with him, knowing full well that his mother, the Mistress of her Wardrobe, would pass the message on to Stafford, as she promptly did. Stafford was therefore suspicious when he received a letter from Philip that seemed inexplicably jolly in the circumstances:

> Sir, The cause of my sending at this time, this bearer Mr Burnam will tell you. Only let me salute you in the kindest manner that one near friend can do another. I would gladly know how you and your noble lady do, and what you do in this absence of the king. We are here all *solito*. Methinks you should do well to begin betimes to demand something of her Majesty as might be found fit for you. And let folks chafe as well when you ask, as when you do not.[56]

Now, Stafford knew, was precisely the worst time 'to demand something of her Majesty'. He wrote to Burghley, expressing his worries about Philip: 'The gentleman I love very well, and if he had not been at a bad school, which may corrupt any good nature, I could trust him well, but all these things hanging together, I am more than half afraid that he is made a stale [snare] to take a bird withal, and that his counsel would make her [the Queen] rather worse than better.'[57] Philip's 'bad school', in Stafford's eyes, had as its schoolmaster the Earl of Leicester. Stafford had ample personal reason to be suspicious of Leicester: his wife, Douglas Sheffield, had been Leicester's mistress and had borne him a son.

It is not clear from Stafford's accusation whether Philip was in fact attempting to set him up, but it is quite possible. As the year progressed Philip was increasingly keen to defend his Dudley connections. He penned an answer to a scurrilous pamphlet entitled *The Copy of a Letter written by a Master of Art of Cambridge to his friend in London . . . about the present state, and some proceedings of the Earl of Leicester and his friends in London* (later known as *Leicester's Commonwealth*), which appeared during the year. This anonymous work, couched in the form of a conversation between four gentlemen, set out to attack Leicester's power. Walsingham's intelligence network informed him that the author was Thomas Morgan, agent of Mary, Queen of Scots, in collaboration with three Catholic exiles in France – Charles Arundel, Sir Thomas Tresham and Lord Paget. In later years, however, it has been argued that Stafford might have had a hand in it, which puts a different spin on Philip's run-in with him.[58] Philip's short defence was never published, and probably little circulated, but it does suggest a new willingness to be allied with his uncle, and in fact Philip *did* have good cause to associate himself with Leicester at this point: as the embassy débâcle came to an end, Leicester's son and heir Robert died at Wanstead on 19 July, 'being at the age of three years and somewhat more'.[59] Sir Philip Sidney was once again the prospective heir of the Earls of Leicester and Warwick.

The autumn of 1584 saw a flurry of family business. On 23 September, Robert Sidney married at St Dennets. Robert owed his marriage to brother-in-law Pembroke, who had brokered a match with the rich Glamorgan heiress Barbara Gamage, in the face of several rival suitors. Not only did Pembroke persuade Barbara's guardian Sir Edward Stradling to approve the match (and even to host the ceremony), but also to support his own election as a knight of the shire of Glamorgan. By 1585, when Simon Robson dedicated his book *The Choice of Change* to Pembroke, Philip and Robert Sidney, they were, as he put it, 'linked & united together in an indissoluble band of amity & fraternity'.[60] Philip and Frances, and presumably Robert and Barbara, then travelled on to Wilton, where their sister Mary was once again pregnant, and their mother already in residence. It was a visit of mixed fortunes: on 14 October, baby Katherine Herbert celebrated her first birthday, and then died the following day – 'a child of promised much excellency if she might have lived', as Philip's mother wrote in the Sidney family psalter. On 16 October, Mary gave birth to her second son; on the 17th, Katherine was buried in Wilton Church. Within days, the baby boy had been baptised and named Philip after his uncle and godfather, the other sponsors being his uncle Robert and his grandmother Lady Sidney.[61] It was a reminder of the high mortality rate of infants – and a signal to Philip and Frances that they needed to start a family soon.

Indeed, Philip's public persona had ceased to be that of the bachelor courtier. On 6 December 1584, Philip joined a team of ten married men in a Westminster sword fight against ten bachelors. This time his marital status placed him in opposition to his usual allies – Greville, Denny, Henry Brouncker – with whom he had led the response to Sir Henry Lee in the Accession Day Tilt (which did not consider marital status) at Westminster less than a month earlier.[62] Philip was no longer the beardless young man in the Veronese portrait.

As it became obvious that Elizabeth would never bear a child to succeed her, English politicians looked increasingly towards the North, and to the young and vulnerable Scottish king, James VI, who was now under the control of the charismatic Earl of Arran. In the spring of 1584, a group of Scottish Protestant noblemen had attempted to seize the king, and failed, their leaders – the Earls of Mar, Angus and Glamis – fleeing to England. In December 1584, James sent the Master of Grey to the English court, ostensibly to demand the extradition of the refugee earls. As with so many diplomatic missions, however, the declared purpose masked another, opposed purpose. Grey informed Elizabeth that Arran's influence was rapidly waning and tried to persuade her to enter into a league with James for the purposes of mutual defence and the preservation of Protestantism. James wanted a pension, a bulwark against the claims of his mother that she should take a part in his government and – although here he knew he was aiming high – recognition as Elizabeth's successor.

Philip had long been interested in Scottish affairs: as far back as 1575 he had initiated a friendship with Sir John Seton, while attending Elizabeth on her summer progress, and in July 1583 he had instructed his secretary Stephen Lesieur to write to Archibald Douglas sending his regards, and enquiring how affairs were progressing in Scotland.[63] When, in April 1585, Philip's old friend from Vienna, Edward Wotton, was despatched to Edinburgh to negotiate the terms of the treaty, Philip took it upon himself to co-ordinate operations at the English court, keeping in contact with Wotton, getting friendly with the Master of Grey and footing the bill for much of the exiles' entertainment ('The burden of the charges of entertaining the Scottish lords will light upon Sir Philip Sidney,' Walsingham told Wotton).[64] When Elizabeth predictably quibbled about the £5,000 per annum pension proposed by James, Philip attempted to secure it, and even determined (with Walsingham) to raise the sum among their friends if need be.

On 23 May 1585, Walsingham forwarded a letter to Wotton from Philip, based on 'an advice delivered unto him by Mr Douglas touching the offer of a pension which you are directed to make unto the king'.[65] A few weeks later, he wrote:

> We are grown here to such an extreme kind of nearness as I see no hope
> to get the Master of Grey any relief from hence. I have already
> furnished him with £2,100, delivered unto him, notwithstanding, as a
> thing proceeding from her Majesty, for that otherwise he would not
> have accepted thereof. Sir Philip Sidney hath moved the earl of
> Leicester to be content to yield some present support until her Majesty
> may be wrought to make more accompt of the matter than presently she
> doth, but he yieldeth a deaf ear.[66]

Clearly in this area Philip was acting with Walsingham rather than with Leicester: a sign of a certain distancing from his uncle.

By September 1585, Walsingham was forced to admit that his labour would not bear fruit. Elizabeth refused to write to Grey, and would not consider giving James his pension. The impetus had been lost without the presence of its principal advocate, as Thomas Milles reported: 'Sir Philip Sidney is little at the court, and all men, as it seemeth, are weary.'[67] Walsingham concurred: 'The poor earl of Angus and earl of Mar receive here little comfort otherwise than from poor Sir Philip Sidney, so as our course is to alienate all the world from us.'[68] If Philip had lived, he would have been recognised as a pioneer in Anglo-Scottish relations, which worked through the next two decades to ensure that young King James won the English crown, and kept England Protestant.

However, Philip was destined instead to be remembered for his intervention in the Low Countries. In March 1585, Henri III finally put an end to months of uncertainty by rejecting the Dutch envoys' offer of sovereignty. Much as he was drawn to the thought of annexing the Low Countries, he could not risk acting as a protector to a Protestant power: that would only weaken his always tentative support at home. Henri's decision made the need for English support even more pressing. The Dutch ambassador in London, Ortel, threw himself into negotiations with Walsingham, Leicester and Burghley, and directly with the queen. He was soon joined by a formal deputation, once again offering sovereignty to Elizabeth, which once again she rejected. This time however she held out a promise of men and money, in return for three key ports (Flushing, Brill and Enckhuysen), to be held by the English as security ('cautionary towns'). It was a high price to pay, and there was a lengthy stand-off.

Philip was at the heart of these negotiations, although not in any official capacity. The Dutch envoys, including Janus Dousa and Dominicus Baudius and, from the autumn onwards, Paulus Melissus and Georgius Benedicti, were all poets as well as diplomats, and they were naturally drawn to the English knight with his similar interests and sympathetic politics.[69] In his autobiography, Baudius recalled how towards the end of June 1585, 'he accompanied the splendid legation which the States then sent to Queen Elizabeth, there made the acquaintance of many men of renowned fame and dignity, but was of all most dear to Philip Sidney'.[70] Benedicti wrote two complimentary verses on Sidney and published them in his *De rebvs gestis Illustriss, Principis Guilielmi* the following year.[71] Dousa, who had visited the English court in 1584, this time brought a copy of his *Petroniuis Arbiter*, and gave it to Philip, with a new ode to him.[72] In November, Baudius wrote to the Leiden scholar Justus Lipsius to extol his new patron, to whom he had been introduced via Dousa and Daniel Rogers: 'I leave out all the others, but this one man I must speak about . . . I am received into the *familia* of the illustrious knight Sir Philip Sidney. Should I, to you, bring to mind his wisdom, kindness, and his other gifts?'[73]

Throughout the uncertainty of the summer, only one prospect was deemed a safe bet: that Sir Philip Sidney would lead men to the Low Countries. In mid-July, Lord Talbot described the news as 'more uncertain than the weather . . . Every one may guess as he list, and I for my poor part believe that some five or six thousand footmen shall be sent, and no horsemen, although Sir Philip Sidney be already so far prepared to take the charge of five hundred.'[74]

On 25 August, Elizabeth despatched William Davison to Holland and Zeeland with the assurance that she would meet their demands for 5,000 foot and 1,000 horsemen, when she 'shall understand that they are content to deliver into her hands the towns of Flushing and Brill. It is thought they will make no difficulty,' commented Walsingham, 'if my Lord of Leicester may have the charge of the army and Sir Philip Sidney of Flushing.'[75] Indeed, the Dutch agreed to all of Elizabeth's conditions, but now it was her turn to be unsure. She demanded further that Flushing and Brill should be garrisoned from the troop numbers already negotiated. The Dutch agreed. Still she hesitated, now alleging uncertainty about who should go. It had been generally assumed that her choice would be Leicester, as the Dutch desired; now she thought perhaps Lord Grey would be a better choice. Leicester reported to Walsingham that the queen had 'used very pitiful words' to him, telling him that she feared she would not live, and did not want him to go.[76]

But while Elizabeth ultimately resolved that Leicester should go, she was even less amenable to the Dutch request that Philip Sidney fill the governorship of Flushing. In August she decided that he would not go. It was a decision that almost changed the course of Philip's life, and of English history.

Of all the events in Philip Sidney's life, his flight from court in August 1585 is the most disputed. It seems that, disappointed by his non-appointment to Flushing, he intended to join Sir Francis Drake's voyage to the West Indies — although preparations seem to have been under way for some time, and this latest disappointment merely forced the issue. Much of our knowledge of this rests on Fulke Greville's word, which is usually best taken with a considerable pinch of salt — or at least plenty of supporting evidence. In this case, little has been available. Greville described Philip's next move as 'an expedition of his own projecting; wherein he fashioned the whole body, with purpose to become head of it himself'. Drake's journey to the West Indies was to embark from Plymouth in September 1585.[77] According to Greville, 'The project was contrived between themselves in this manner; that both should equally be governors, when they had left the shore of *England*; but while things were a preparing at home, Sir *Fran.* was to bear the name, and by the credit of Sir *Phil.* have all particularly abundantly supplied.' The story seems too sensational to be believed, but from the evidence of a few scattered pieces of paper we can perhaps start to give Greville the benefit of the doubt.

Philip's flight to Plymouth needs to be seen in the context of a long-standing interest in colonial exploration. As early as the mid-1570s, Philip, along with Edward Dyer and John Dee, had been fascinated by the prospect of a possible Northwest Passage, and had invested heavily in Martin Frobisher's missions. Philip would have read French Huguenot tracts on the possibilities of colonialism.[78] Ironically, however, his first major involvement with a colonial venture had been a Roman Catholic initiative. In early 1582 his Oxford contemporary Richard Hakluyt dedicated his *Divers voyages touching the discouerie of America* to 'the right worshipful and most virtuous gentleman master Philip Sidney esquire'.[79] Hakluyt painted a picture of boundless possibilities for his nation. The time for Portugal and Spain was past: 'I conceive great hope, that the time approacheth and now is, that we of England may share and part stakes (if we will ourselves) both with the Spaniard and the Portingale in part of America, and other regions as yet undiscovered.' Prisons were filled with able-bodied men who would be better put to work founding new English colonies. Hakluyt believed that 'we might not only for the present time take possession of that good land, but also in short space by God's grace find out that short and easy passage by the Northwest, which we have hitherto

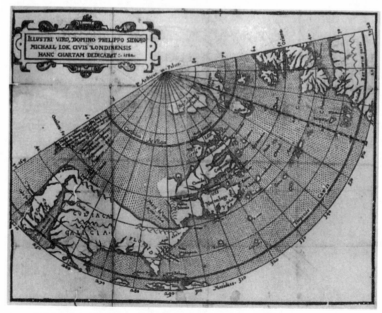

10. Michael Lok's map of the New World from Hakluyt's *Divers voyages*, 1582, dedicated to Philip Sidney.

so long desired, and whereof we have many good and more than probable conjectures: a few whereof I think it not amiss to set down, although your worship know them as well as myself'.

Hakluyt did not have to do much to revive Philip's interest in the New World, never quite extinguished by Languet's lukewarm reaction to the Frobisher mission. So he was primed when another plan was put to him. Sir Humphrey Gilbert had hit on the ingenious scheme of selling the rights to (as yet undiscovered and unsecured) lands, which he held by letters patent. Early customers included John Dee, who in September 1580 purchased all the land north of fifty degrees latitude.[80] But in 1581 Gilbert found a new clientele: English Catholics. The impetus lay in the recent relatively harsh statute against recusants, which had been enacted in the 1581 government. Nonconformity was now being fined at the rate of twenty pounds per month, an unsustainable penalty for all but the very richest (it was this move that had prompted Lady Kytson's appeal to a sympathetic Philip Sidney). Less affluent English Catholics, in the same dilemma as the Huguenots in France, saw a possible way out in the speculative colonial ventures being undertaken in the name of England. On this occasion, Sir Humphrey Gilbert was in charge of the venture: the would-be Catholic colonists were Sir Thomas Gerrard and Sir George Peckham, who had both already been imprisoned for their beliefs.

As early as 19 April 1582, one of Burghley's correspondents, 'P.H.', informed him in 'secret advertisements' that 'there is muttering among the papists that Sir Humphrey Gilbert goeth to seek a new found land, Sir George Peckham and Sir Thomas Gerrard goeth with him. I have heard it said among the papists, that they hope it will prove the best journey for England that was made these forty years.'[81] On 26 April, the Spanish ambassador in London, Bernardino da Mendoza, received intelligence that Gilbert was fitting out three ships to go to Florida and settle there. 'When he asked for the Queen's assistance he was answered in Council that he might go, and, that when he had landed and fortified, the Queen would send ten thousand men to conquer the territory and safeguard the port.'[82]

On 6 June, Gilbert entered into an agreement with Peckham and Gerrard, and a further agreement with Peckham alone; three days later, the three men agreed another contract. On 7 July, Philip was granted some three million acres of undiscovered lands in North America. While

Gerrard and Peckham received similar amounts in exchange for disbursing 'divers sums of money . . . as principal adventurers with the said Sir Humphrey towards his now intended voyage for discovery and habiting of certain parts of America', Philip's grant was substantively different. In the agreement he was not financially committed but promised 'that he . . . shall do his best endeavour to procure and obtain her Majesty's leave and good liking that all those who have or shall adventure with the said Sir Humphrey, Sir Thomas Gerrard and Sir George Peckham knights, the said Philip or any of them into the said country . . . may freely pass into those countries there to remain.'[83] In other words, while Gerrard and Peckham could put up the funds, it was up to Gilbert and Philip to ensure that the queen was well disposed towards the venture – and particularly that she would allow those involved to return to England if they pleased.[84]

As so often happened, the real ramifications of this paperwork were promptly recognised by Mendoza. On 11 July, his report opened with this news:

> As I wrote to your majesty some days since, Ongi Gilberto [Mendoza's phonetic attempt at Humphrey Gilbert] was fitting out several ships for a settlement in Florida and as this was not only prejudicial to your majesty but also to the English Catholics as giving advantage to heretics, Walsingham put it secretly to two spendthrift Catholic gentlemen who have some land that if they helped Ongi Gilberto in his expedition, they would escape losing life and property, by asking the Queen to allow them, in consideration for this service, to live in those parts with freedom of conscience and enjoy the use of their property in England – for which purpose they might rely on Philip Sidney.[85]

Walsingham later circulated a letter to potential investors: 'I am of opinion you shall do well to hearken to such offers as Sir Philip Sidney and Sir George Peckham will make unto you who have sufficient authority by and under her Majesty's letters patent to perform th'effect of your desire.'[86] In July 1583, Walsingham invested £115 of his own money, and Sidney drafted 10 per cent of his own grant (some 30,000 acres) to Peckham to furnish a ship for a forthcoming expedition.[87]

The involvement of the noted Protestants Sir Francis Walsingham and Sir Philip Sidney in this Catholic colonial venture might seem bewildering. But it points to a practical dilemma that Philip was continually addressing both in his political life and in his writings: was he first and foremost a Protestant, or an Englishman? This venture suggests that now his Englishness was being prioritised: it might take Catholic money, but it was worth the compromise if it allowed England to compete in the New World with Spain and Portugal.

Philip's interest in the New World was constant, even if he seems not to have developed a coherent plan for forwarding that interest. During the 1584 Parliament, Philip was a keen supporter of Ralegh's Virginia Bill, serving on the committee that debated it. In July 1584, he had dropped a hint in a letter to Sir Edward Stafford that he himself could be lured westward. 'Her Majesty seems affected to deal in the Low Country matters, but I think nothing will come of it. We are half persuaded to enter into the journey of Sir Humphrey Gilbert very eagerly; whereunto your Hakluyt [Stafford's chaplain] hath served for a very good trumpet.' On 12 August 1585, the first governor of Virginia, Ralph Lane, wrote to Philip with a more concrete proposal: 'If her Majesty at any time find herself burthened with the King of Spain, we have by our dwelling upon the island of St. John and Hispaniola for the space of five weeks so discovered the forces thereof, with the infinite riches of the same, as that I find it an attempt most honourable, feasible and profitable, and only fit for yourself to be chief commander in.'[88]

Clearly, Philip knew better than to ask for official permission to join Lane's, Gilbert's, or any other, mission. The reasons for this, Greville explains, were first, that Philip knew he stood no chance of persuading the queen or her Privy Council to let him take command of an employment that was 'so remote, and of so hazardous a nature' and for which he had no obvious previous experience; and second, that 'while it passed unknown, he knew it would pass without interruption; and when it was done, presumed the success would put envy and all her agents to silence'.[89]

Hence the secret deal with Sir Francis Drake. One lure for Drake, continued Greville, was that Philip possessed influential friends who 'would add both weight, and fashion to his ambition; and consequently either with, or without Sir Philip's company, yield unexpected ease, and honour to him in this voyage'. Meanwhile, Philip's main use to Drake was his position in the Ordnance. On 21 July 1585, Philip was finally named Master of the Ordnance, jointly with his uncle Ambrose, Earl of Warwick. Various entries in the State Papers at the Public Record Office testify to Philip's active involvement in preparations for Drake's mission during the summer months: in July, powder and munitions were delivered to Drake, by force of a letter directed to the Office of Ordnance, signed by Leicester, Walsingham and Philip;[90] sometime in 1585 there were 'stores and materials delivered out of the Ordnance office by order of Sir Phil. Sidney';[91] in July, a survey was carried out noting 'the natures of munitions most needful to be provided; showing the quantities of those remaining in store and the supply required'.[92] Sir Philip's actions began to give cause for concern. In August 1585, Walsingham's attention was drawn to 'a warrant under the hand of Sir Philip Sidney touching the passing of certain Iron Ordinance'; it was pointed out to Walsingham that the relevant official 'had not as yet seen her Majesty's warrant which is wont to be drawn unto him: and without that he cannot assent unto the passing of the same knowing how angry her Majesty hath been at the passing of such supply' in the past.[93] This suggests that Philip was now acting without the knowledge of Walsingham.

According to Greville, Philip was also active in choosing the officers and commanders to fulfil the diverse demands of service by land and sea. Indeed, according to a list of the 'Names of Ships & number of men in each, with Sir Francis Drake', the *Sea Dragon* was originally to be captained by William Hawkins the elder, 'but at the request of Sir Philip Sidney and Master Greville, Captain Henry White is now placed there and Master Hawkins appointed by the General to be another Lieutenant for him in his own ship'.[94] This was the same Harry White who had been Philip's close personal servant since he set off for Paris in May 1572.

The fleet set off from Woolwich for Plymouth. At Plymouth, according to Greville, Drake 'vowed and resolved' that when all was ready, and they were just waiting for a favourable wind, a 'watchword' would be despatched to Philip at court; indeed, very soon, 'a letter comes post for Sir Philip, as if the whole fleet stayed only for him, and the wind'. At the same time, intelligence reached the court that Dom Antonio was sailing once again towards England and planned to land at Plymouth. It was the ideal excuse. 'Sir Philip turning occasion into wisdom, puts himself into the employment of conducting up this king; and under that veil leaves the Court without suspicion'. He took with him Greville, 'to be his loving, and beloved *Achates* in this journey', and the pair were 'feasted the first night by Sir Francis, with a great deal of outward pomp and compliment'.

The fleet was a magnificent sight: the biggest expedition to leave English shores in a century, involving some 2,300 men in all. The queen had provided the two largest ships, on one of which (the 600-ton *Elizabeth Bonaventura*) Drake himself was to sail. Nineteen ships were provided by city merchants, eager to gamble on this venture. Among the men waiting to sail were Walsingham's son-in-law Christopher Carleill, an experienced soldier and sailor, Martin Frobisher and Francis Drake's brother Thomas. Amidst all the 'pomp and compliment', however, Greville became suspicious of their genial host, as he was 'observing the countenance of this gallant mariner more exactly than Sir Philip's leisure served him to do'. That night, as Philip and Greville lay in bed together, Greville told him of the 'discountenance and depression' he had discerned in Sir Francis – almost 'as if our coming were both beyond his expectation, and desire'. Philip was not easily convinced, but as it became increasingly evident that the ships were not even close to being ready and Drake evinced 'some sparks of false fire', Philip came round to Greville's way of thinking.

For days, time seemed to stand still. Dom Antonio did not appear; the fleet seemed to 'go further from our desires', despite frantic letters from court urging its departure. 'It may be the leaden feet, and nimble thoughts of Sir Francis wrought in the day, and unwrought by night; while he watched an opportunity to discover us, without being discovered.' Drake's method of 'discovering' – which effectively meant 'shopping' – his would-be fellow sailors was to let it be known at court what was going on; a few days later, according to Greville, 'a post steals up to the Court, upon whose arrival an alarum is presently taken'.

Drake's intelligence provoked the expected fevered reaction at the highest level. Vice Chamberlain Sir Christopher Hatton was ordered to write three letters: 'one to [Philip] himself to command his immediate return, the other to Sir Francis to forbid him the receiving of him in his fleet, the third to the Mayor of Plymouth to write him to see this performed accordingly; and that if they were already gone, some bark should be sent after with the letters'. The letters were sent by one Hyts, a former servant of Lady Drury. Four miles out of Plymouth, however, according to Sir John Stanhope, Hyts was 'surprised by four mariners, and his letters taken from him; the which being opened and read were sent him again'.[95] Stanhope does not identify the culprit, but Greville had a good idea who it was. As he tells it: 'This errand being partly advertised to Sir Philip beforehand, was intercepted upon the way; his letters taken from him by two resolute soldiers in mariner's apparel; brought instantly to Sir Philip, opened, and read.' Although he does not explicitly say so, Greville clearly implies that Philip ordered the interception himself.[96]

On 7 September, Dom Antonio finally arrived in Plymouth[97] and was entertained with Philip by Drake's wife, Lady Elizabeth, at their Devon estate,[98] while his servant Pryme was sent up to court bearing letters from both Antonio and Philip. According to the Spanish ambassador Mendoza, 'Dom Antonio had written to the Queen, saying that, in order to bear company with Philip Sidney he wished to embark on the fleet, whereat she scoffed greatly, as did also her ambassador in conversation with a friend of his who told me of it. From this it may be concluded that the going of Dom Antonio in the fleet was not with the Queen's connivance.'[99] There were confused reports at court. 'Now,' wrote Sir John Stanhope, 'it is said Sir Philip never meant to go, but stayeth there to see the ships set forth.' This news convinced few, he continued. 'Yet the bruit runneth on stilts in London and amongst many courtiers that Sir Francis is gone and Sir Philip too.'[100]

Certainly those closest to Philip believed he would go. Walsingham despaired of his impetuous son-in-law. On 13 September, he lamented to William Davison:

> Sir Philip Sidney hath taken a very hard resolution to accompany Sir
> Francis Drake in this voyage, moved hereunto for that he saw her
> Majesty disposed to commit the charge of Flushing to some other,
> which he reputed would fall out greatly to his disgrace to see another
> preferred before him, both for birth and judgement inferior unto him.
> This resolution is greatly to the grief of Sir Philip's friends, but to none
> more than myself. I know her Majesty would easily have been induced
> to have placed him in Flushing, but he despaired hereof, and the
> disgrace that he doubted he should receive hath carried him into a

desperate course. There is some order taken for his stay, but I fear it will not take place; and yet I pray you make me no author of this unpleasant news.

PS: If it shall please God to incline his heart to stay I will not fail to advertise you with speed.[101]

Walsingham here does not display any knowledge of his son-in-law's premeditation and gives the same reason that Mendoza, now stuck in Paris, forwarded to the King of Spain: that Philip 'had left in despair to embark on Drake's fleet in consequence of the Queen's having refused him the governorship of Flushing, for which he had asked'.[102] Commentators have cited Walsingham's letter as evidence that Greville must have invented the long-time planning of the Sidney/Drake project, but as Greville himself writes, Philip 'over-shoots his father-in-law then Secretary of Estate in his own bow' – by keeping his plans secret even from the greatest intelligence-gatherer of his age, Elizabeth's spymaster Walsingham.

The fleet finally sailed on Tuesday 14 September. From a journal kept by Christopher Carleill and Edward Powell, now badly mutilated but still extant in the Cotton manuscripts collection, we know that Philip and Fulke Greville were in fact aboard Drake's own command, the *Elizabeth Bonaventura*, as it left the shore. The journal gives us these tantalising hints: 'with the whole fleet about eight of the clock . . . [a]n hour's sailing or two Sir Philip Sidney with . . . [S]idney, Master Fulke Greville, Master Richard Drake and oth[er] . . . us aboard the admiral, they went to the shore & we plied . . .'[103] Philip and Greville, it appears, were on the *Elizabeth Bonaventura* as she sailed, but were then taken off for some reason and returned to shore.

According to Greville, he and Philip were taken off the ship because a second messenger had arrived: 'a more imperial mandate, carefully conveyed, and delivered to himself by a peer of this realm; carrying with it in the one hand grace, the other thunder'. The grace was 'an offer of an instant employment under his uncle, then going General into the Low Countries'. Philip, he alleged, 'would gladly have demurred', but on reflection 'duty of obedience' won the day. But the thunder was that it spelled the end of Philip's 'heroical design of invading, and possessing

America', which no other man, according to Greville, could have pulled off.[104]

Greville was sent back to Basingstoke to escort Dom Antonio to Osterley, for which he received twenty pounds in expenses — a far cry from the treasure troves of the Caribbean.[105] On 21 September, Philip had an audience with the queen, who, according to Sir John Stanhope, 'receiveth it for a truth from himself that he never meant to go'.[106] Such at least was the public treatment of this episode, with any misunderstandings cleared up and Philip smoothly rehabilitated to royal favour and prestigious military command in the Low Countries. In private, however, Elizabeth knew that something far more threatening had been averted.

And she needed Philip to go to Flushing to buy her goodwill — and time — from the States General, where tensions were rising. Without Leicester, there was no leader. Since the assassination of William of Orange, the only contender had been Phillips Marnix, Sieur de St Aldegonde, external burgomaster of Antwerp; now, however, he lay under popular suspicion that he had betrayed his city to Parma, leader of the Spanish forces, and was under an effective house-arrest: 'a man greatly suspected but by no man charged'. His only wish was to have his cause referred to Leicester. Delay was dangerous. 'The Enemy', as Philip invariably called Parma, was threatening Ostend, Sluis, Bergen and Bomel. While waiting for Leicester, the people had elected Maurice of Nassau, William of Orange's eighteen-year-old son, as governor of Holland and Zeeland, but it seemed that Maurice would be happy to depend wholly on Leicester's authority. 'I think truly,' Philip later wrote to Leicester with hindsight, 'if my coming had been longer delayed some alteration would have followed, for the truth is the people is weary of war, and if they do not see such a course taken as may be likely to defend them they will in a sudden give over the cause.'[107]

The great mission, so long hoped and planned for, now had to be scrambled together in haste.[108] Philip's last few weeks were spent consulting with his political allies on policy, frantically attempting to levy soldiers in Wales, and rounding up horses — a practical vindication of Jean Sturm's calls for England to become self-sufficient in the provision of cavalry.[109] Philip called up William Temple, a Cambridge fellow who had dedicated a book of Ramist scholarship to him, to serve as his secretary.[110] Philip's letters patents authorising his posting to Flushing were issued on 9 November, but even these recalled how close he was to losing the governorship: the draft copies contain erasures where the name of Sir Thomas Cecil had originally been.[111] By 10 November, he was at Gravesend, from where he sent a cipher alphabet to the queen, a token of future service, assuring her that 'your pleasure is my only boldness'.[112]

It was poor timing domestically. In November 1585, Frances Sidney gave birth to the couple's first child, a daughter.[113] Moffet tells how Philip 'warmly greeted the little girl . . . no less gratefully and lovingly than he would have if she had taken the sex, as well as her descent, from himself. What more delightful to Philip than that face? What could be granted more charming than that daughter? What had he ever heard with a better will than that he had been made a father and that a little girl had opened the way for a son who would be his heir.' That 'heard' betrays the fact that Philip had already left by the time his daughter was born; he probably never met her.[114]

Perhaps in return for Philip's co-operation, the queen consented to bestow a particular favour on his family. She agreed to act as godmother for his daughter, who was accordingly baptised Elizabeth on 20 November at the church of St Olave's in Hart Street, just around the corner from the Walsinghams' house, where Lady Frances was living.[115] From an entry in his account book showing that he paid six pounds to the nurse and midwife, it seems likely that Leicester was the godfather.[116] Scipio Gentili provided a verse tribute on Elizabeth's birth, entitled *Nereus, sive de natali Elizabethæ illustriss. Phillippi Sydnaei filiae*, in which the sea-god Nereus, the most truthful god, prophesies the infant's future.[117] The honour done to Elizabeth Sidney indicates the new, unaccustomed prestige of her father.

Even with their preferred candidate Philip Sidney promised as governor of Flushing, the Dutch were suspicious of the queen, and with good reason. Elizabeth knew that sending an official English force to the Low Countries meant that she was at war with Spain. It was in recognition of the gravity of the decision that she decided to publish her rationale as *A Declaration of the Causes moving the Queen of England to give aid to the defence of the people afflicted and oppressed in the Low Countries*, available in English, Dutch, French and Italian. However, still top of her priorities was England's continued trade with Antwerp. Now that she had Flushing (which commanded all trade to Antwerp on the River Schelde) she was, ironically, better equipped to negotiate a peaceful settlement with Spain.[118] Some of her closest advisers, of course, were not so pragmatically minded and Elizabeth had to treat secretly with Parma's agents in London until Walsingham's intelligence network uncovered them.

Philip heard these rumours, but tried to counter them with the good news that Maurice of Nassau, who was hereditary seignior and proprietor of Flushing, had acquiesced in the temporary transfer of the port to the English. He was further cheered when, just before sailing, he received a message from Maurice imploring Philip to think of him as a brother and companion in arms – an ironic invitation, given that nine years earlier Philip had almost become Maurice's brother-in-law by marrying his sister Marie.

Philip set sail on 18 November. He was perhaps lucky to miss the letter that the commander of Flushing, William Davison, sent to him two days earlier:

> Your long stay doth very much amaze and trouble us, and the more in that we can hear nothing in the meantime of your proceedings. It is a shame to think how things are handled. Of three or four months the companies have been here they have not had above one month's pay, many of them are already wasted with hunger's miseries, and but for the straining of mine own poor credit had been at this time utterly broken and disordered.[119]

The new governor of Flushing had his work cut out for him.

Philip Sidney

Sir Henry Sidney

Robert Dudley, Earl of Leicester

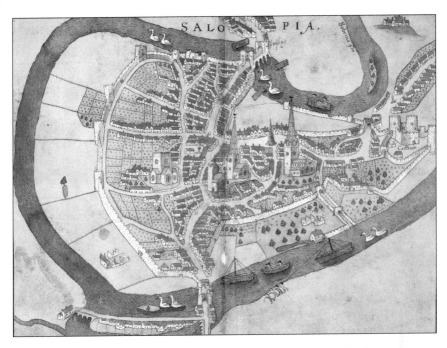

(*Above*) Shrewsbury in the late sixteenth century (*Below*) Shrewsbury School's register recording Philip's entry alongside Fulke Greville and James Harrington, 1564

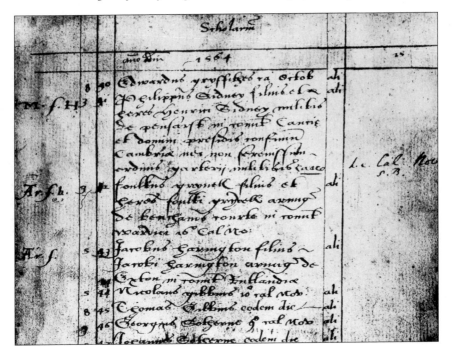

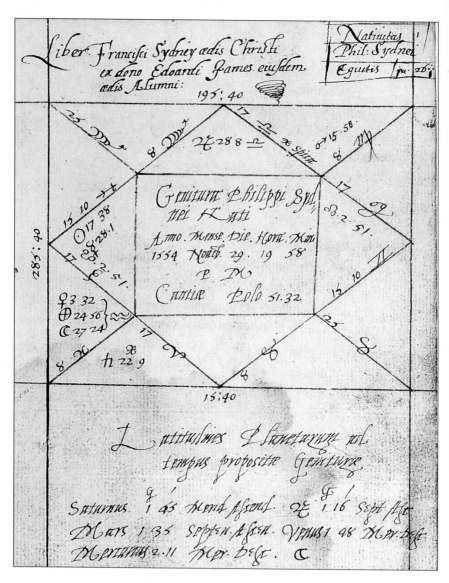

Philip Sidney's horoscope, cast in 1570

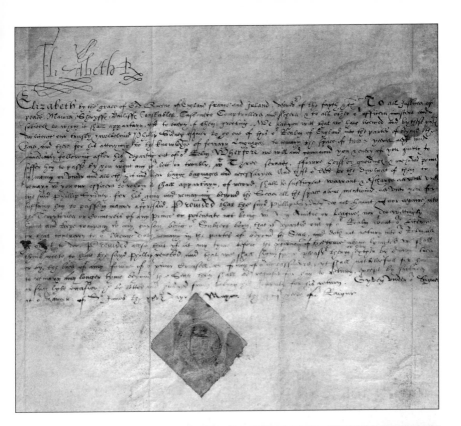

Philip Sidney's passport to
travel on the continent, 1572

Hubert Languet

The St Bartholomew's Day Massacre, 1572

The title page of the third edition of the *Countess of
Pembroke's Arcadia*, with Sidney emblems

A miniature of Mary Herbert,
née Sidney, Countess of Pembroke,
by Nicholas Hilliard

(*Above*) Sir Philip Sidney and Prince Maurice of Nassau surprise the town of Axel

(*Below*) Zutphen in 1586

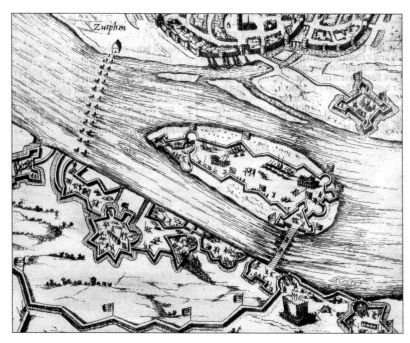

CHAPTER ELEVEN

The Great Work in Hand

P HILIP'S ENTRY INTO Flushing could not have been less auspicious.[1] At the last minute his trusted right-hand man Fulke Greville, appointed by Leicester to the command of a cornet, had been forbidden to go by the queen. No explanation was forthcoming, but it must have seemed that this was an uncanny repetition of his recall in 1578, when he had tried to reach Casimir's troops – that this, as then, was an oblique slur on Philip. On top of this, the promised Welsh forces were not yet mustered: Philip had to leave without them.

Arriving on Thursday 18 November 1585, accompanied by his brother Robert, a small personal retinue, and some 200 soldiers, Philip was immediately reminded of the Low Countries' habitually abysmal weather as strong winds and driving rain prevented him from dropping anchor in the town of Flushing itself. Even in good weather, the area was a desolate place, as the English traveller Richard Smith had commented twenty years earlier: 'Zeeland is a country lying very low so that the sea lieth above it round about, being defended from drowning of the sea only by a certain bank that is of a great height. It is but a small island for that the better part of the country hath been drowned by the sea, as appeareth by the churches and other things that are to be seen in the sea.'[2] Philip's ship had to be diverted to the fort of Ramekins. From there, he and his entourage were forced to wade through three miles of mud before arriving, bedraggled and very late, in Flushing – 'as dirty a walk as ever poor governor entered his charge withal', he remarked to Leicester.[3]

The planned welcome was subdued: in the words of one onlooker, 'The captains with their soldiers and the rest of the town received him in such manner as the time would permit.'[4] Philip was, however, as another observed slyly, 'the welcomer that he brought money'.[5] He was handed a letter of welcome from the States General, the Low Countries' assembly in The Hague, which made special mention of the 'good welcome' that the Dutch deputies had received from him in London.[6] As his men dispersed in lodgings all over Flushing, Philip made his home in the house of local merchant and magistrate Jacques Gelée, 'one of good reckoning among the inhabitants there'. Gelée's hospitality was not entirely altruistic: in return, he assured himself of Philip's support when he left for London in December to pursue a law case against some English merchants.[7]

On the following Sunday (21st), Philip dined at the State House in Middelburg, was 'very honourably entertained' by the States of Zeeland, and took his oath, returning the following day to receive the States' oath to Elizabeth as queen and to Sidney as governor of Flushing.[8] Although the ritual ran smoothly, Philip could already see the utter decay of the materials with which he had to work. According to William Borlas, reporting to Walsingham, the town was 'in some place to be very weak and the garrison to be very small for so great a town, for that there is almost two hundred of the soldiers sick in the hospital, and I think a thousand to be too few for so great a town'.[9] Writing to Leicester, Philip deemed the garrison 'far too weak to command by authority, which is pity for how great a jewel this is to the crown of England and the Queen's safety I need not write it to your lordship who knows it so well, yet I must needs say the better I know it the more I find the preciousness of it'.[10]

Philip had with him men he had worked with before, and whom he trusted. Thomas Digges, who had spent much of the period 1582–4 working on repairs to Dover Harbour for the Ordnance, had been appointed his muster-master; Philip sent him to work inspecting the Flushing fortifications, despatching brother Robert to Ostend to do the same there.[11] Their analysis was devastating. Digges reported 'that surely the rampiers and bulwarks were delivered in very bad case, the barriers in many places fallen to ground, the sentinel and *cours de garde* horse badly repaired and most beastly defiled in most loathsome manner, by whose fault I will not say, the ordinary in very bad case having neither good caring nor platforms'. Put in layman's terms, with the current state of fortification it would be 'utterly impossible with this garrison to hold it [Flushing] against any royal force'.[12] Treasurer Richard Huddlestone observed the Flushing men to be 'the worst accommodated of all our soldiers, amongst a people of a froward and perverse disposition'.[13] Flushing's bailiff Edward Burnham put it bluntly: 'If anything should fall out between the townsmen and us, we are likelier to be governed than that Sir Philip should govern them. To prevent the practices of such as stand ill-affected it were good to reinforce it [the garrison].'[14]

The Low Countries 1586

Despite all these hindrances, Philip was guardedly optimistic about his reception: 'I find the people very glad of me, and promise myself as much surety in keeping this town as the popular goodwill gotten by light hopes . . . may breed me.' But the situation demanded immediate action: 'All will be lost if government be not presently used.' Philip quietly bolstered each company of soldiers, rather than creating a new one, 'for fear of breeding jealousies in this people which is carried more by shows than substance'.[15] In consultation with Edward Norris and William Davison, he investigated ways of mustering forces and then paying them, although he soon found himself forced to borrow £300 'at usance' [interest] from one Hans Barnard.[16] Any decision of moment was put off until Leicester's arrival, for which Philip was extremely eager: 'your Lordship's coming is here longed for as Messiah's is of the Jews . . . Good my Lord haste away, if you do come, for all things considered, I had rather you came not at all than came not quickly, for only by your own presence those courses may be stopped which if they run on will be past remedy.'[17]

As it turned out, Philip had little enough time to take stock. Word came that La Motte, the governor of Gravelines, who was loyal to the Spanish, had arrived at the coastal town of Blankenburg, midway between Ostend and Sluys, with a sizeable force intent on seizing Ostend. Philip had particular interest in Ostend: an old friend, Captain Errington, was governor there and had already confided to Philip that he feared for the town, with its majority Catholic population and a current dearth of food and munitions. Philip decided to take action. He sent messengers to the States of Zeeland and to Count Hohenloe, the general of the Dutch forces, urging them to supply munitions and acquire more armour. Robert Sidney and three other captains were despatched to meet La Motte, who in the event laid siege to Ostend, only to withdraw unexpectedly a few days later.[18] Robert was horrified with what he saw. The Ostend garrison had laid waste to the surrounding countryside, as he wrote to Leicester: 'Almost for twenty miles riding every way there is never a house standing nor never a man out of a walled town to be seen.' There had been no pay for the last four months, and everything was in short supply: 'No victuals in store for above twenty days; if a soldier should break his pike or his halbert not any here to furnish him; of powder not 12,000 weight whereof five is not serviceable, all our victual must come from Flushing and out of Holland, and that is very dear.'

Robert assured his uncle that 'there cannot be more hate received than the Governor and Dutch captains here bear the States. Your Lordship's coming is wonderfully looked and wished for everywhere.'[19]

At last the Messiah came.[20] Leicester landed in Flushing on Friday 10 December, to the sound of 'all the shot of great ordnance', to be greeted by Maurice and William of Nassau, Philip, Davison and the town burgomasters and magistrates. The earl's retinue was enormous, travelling on fifty vessels in two parties: Leicester was 'guarded in his own person by fifty archers with bows and arrows, fifty halberders, and fifty gunners'.[21] His retinue comprised the cream of young English nobility – among them the Earl of Essex (brother of Penelope Rich), the Lords North, Audley and Willoughby, Sir William Russell, Sir Thomas Shirley, Sir Arthur Basset, Sir Walter Waller, Sir Gervais Clifton and Philip's younger brother Thomas, now sixteen – alongside 3,000 soldiers. Spanish newswriters reported worriedly that Sir William Stanley and Sir Henry Harrington had 1,500 men each from Ireland; and the Master of Gray 600 more from Scotland. It seemed that at last the English queen was in earnest.[22] Leicester was escorted with considerable pomp by the soldiers to his lodgings in the town house, 'passing honourably entertained', in John Stow's account, with 'ringing of bells, and making of bonfires after their manner, which is to fix great pitch barrels on the tops of high poles, and then to fire them'.[23]

The welcome was formalised the following day in an oration by Councillor of State Adolf van Meetkercke, who discoursed on what he regarded as the natural links between England and the Low Countries, notably their closely related languages. Unfortunately, in order to be comprehensible to the mixed audience, van Meetkercke was forced to speak in French.[24] That small glitch demonstrated a gulf between the English forces and their hosts that was to grow more evident as time went on, and which no amount of good will was able to extinguish. The interactions of the English with their hosts in the Low Countries made explicit all kinds of differences – in themselves minor, but cumulatively enough to undermine the illusion of unity. Even Christmas caused problems: the Dutch, in common with the rest of mainland Europe, had adopted the pope's new calendar, which effectively placed them ten days 'ahead' of England. Five days after Leicester arrived (on the English

10 December), the Dutch celebrated the birth of Christ; the English followed suit ten days later, underlining their resistance to adopting local practice (the 'Romish computation', as they put it). For the moment, however, all was co-operation. Leicester used the day, as he informed the Privy Council, 'to acquaint myself thoroughly of the state of the garrison and to give such direction to my nephew Philip for the supply and reinforcing thereof as I deemed expedient'.[25] In John Stow's account, 'According to his accustomed disposition he demeaned himself so humbly, that he purchased to himself no less love and good liking than among the English.'[26]

And among the English Leicester was at the peak of his powers. He had his patent from the queen read out loud to his followers, 'exhorting them all to be obedient', according to Edward Burnham, 'to forget the delicacies of England, and to betake themselves to military discipline as well in deed as in show, and instead of fine fare and good lodging to resolve himself to hardness'. If anyone wished to leave now, they could. No one did. 'They were very well satisfied and all cried "God save the Queen and my lord of Leicester." ' Burnham also realised that Leicester's arrival meant that Philip no longer would see governing Flushing as his top priority: 'As far as I can see,' Burnham mused to Walsingham, 'it will be a month or five weeks before Sir Philip returns to his government'.[27]

Philip indeed spent the next few weeks at Leicester's side as he made his way to The Hague, where he was to meet the States General. Their journey was nothing short of a royal progress. Even a routine inspection of the English force on Saturday 11 December at the castle of Ramekins gave occasion for a display of strength and loyalty: 'Returning again to their ships, [the English] were presented on the top of the walls in the front of the sea with fifty pike men very bravely furnished, having their English ancients displayed, with triumph of shot, sound of trumpets and drums near two hours together.'

Travelling largely on water, they called in at Middelburg, Williamstaede, Dordrecht, Rotterdam and Delft. The reception everywhere was both formally extravagant and popularly rapturous. Leicester commented delightedly on 'the love and affection I find in this people of Middelburg to my sovereign, and the good will and desire they show to do me honour for her Majesty's sake'.[28] The sheer scale of their welcome stunned the earl: even 'the worst of these towns presented me with fifteen hundred shot [soldiers armed with muskets] and armed men, at the least, and did conduct me from town to town with six and seven hundred shot'. At Middelburg, in a banner hung over the gate of the English house, were emblazoned the queen's arms, under which were Leicester's on one side and 'the arms of the States and their houses' on the other, all linked by a chain, and fastened to the English arms, with the legend underneath: '*Quos Deus coniunxit, homo non separet* [What God has joined, let no man put asunder].'

The highlight of the journey came at Delft. Leicester enthused to Walsingham:

This town is another London almost for beauty and fairness, and have used me most honourably, as these bearers can tell you; with the greatest shows that ever I saw. They met me along the river as I came [with] five hundred shot two miles off; at my landing there was not so few as fifteen hundred shot more, standing in a row from my landing till I came to my lodging, which was near a long mile. By the way in the great marketplace, they had set a squadron, at the least of eight hundred or a thousand pikes, all armed, which was a marvelous fair sight, and tall able personages as ever I saw. There was such a noise, both here, at Rotterdam, and Dordrecht, in crying, 'God save Queen Elizabeth,' as if she had been in Cheapside, with the most hearty countenances that ever I saw; and therefore, whatsoever hath been said to her Majesty, I believe she never bestowed her favour upon more thankful people than these countries of Holland. For the States dare not but be Queen Elizabeth's, for, by the living God, if there should fall but the least unkindness, through their default, the people would kill them, for these towns will take no direction but from the queen of England, I assure you. And if her Majesty had not taken them at this need, but forsaken them, she had lost them for ever and ever, and now hath she them, if she will keep them, as the citizens of London, in all love and affection.[29]

Leicester's letters home provide a vivid record of his extraordinary reception, but they also fulfilled a vital propaganda function: to assure the queen that she had made the right decision in sending him, and to persuade her to maintain and even increase her support. Leicester would not, he wrote to Walsingham, let messengers pass:

without letting you know where I am, and how greatly her Majesty is in all places reverenced and honoured, of all sorts of people, from highest to the lowest, assuring themselves already, now they have her Majesty's good countenance, to beat all the Spaniards out of their country again. Never was there people I think in that jollity that these be. I could be content to lose a limb that [in order that] her majesty did see these countries and towns as I have. She would then think a whole subsidy well spent, but only to have the good assurance and commandment of a few of these towns. I think there be not the like places again for England to be found.[30]

As Walsingham replied encouragingly, the reception 'ought to move her Majesty to like the better of the action, and to countenance the same in such sort as may both encourage your lordship and increase the love and goodwill towards her, of those well affected people'.[31]

Finally the party arrived on 28 December in The Hague, where Leicester was officially welcomed by Dr Leoninus, chancellor of Gueldres for the States General, and Dr Menin, councillor of Dordrecht for the States of Holland.[32] One commentator wrote that not even when Charles V made his entry had there been a spectacle this lavish. Now, however, serious negotiations had to get under way. The States General met with Leicester on 1 January 1586. His physician John James captured the moment: 'In the morning the whole company of the States that were abiding at the Hague, came to his Excellency to some matter of importance, whom he took in his bedchamber and there heard them privately in respect of some unlooked for matter which he was secretly told at that instance they had openly to offer him.'[33]

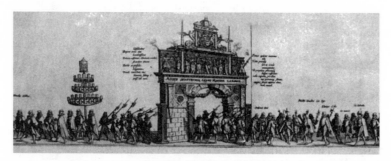

12. Leicester entering The Hague in glory, December 1585.

In fact the 'unlooked for matter' was to offer Leicester the civil and military government of the States: Zeeland, Holland, Friesland and Utrecht. As Lord North wrote:

> They put under his commandment all governors, colonels, admirals, captains and other officers whatsoever; they offered the profits of all the demesnes, the ordinary taxes which those people pay that contribute both to the enemy and them for their peace. They offered 200,000 florins a month for this whole year to come . . . toward the maintenance of the wars, with many other dignities and honours; thus much or more I think have been offered to Monsieur [Anjou] before. My lord gave them great thanks for their great offers and prayed them to digest it in writing, which, when he had considered, he would shape them answer.[34]

Leicester was not prepared simply to accept. Instead, he withdrew to Leiden, ten miles away, and left the negotiations to North, Davison, Clark and Philip. On 7 January, Philip and the others met six deputies of the States General and spent the next three days hammering out some of the technicalities of the agreement. Talks were suspended on Sunday evening, because Philip had to conduct a muster of the cavalry – suggesting that his presence was considered vital to the negotiations – but on Monday morning discussion turned to what form Leicester's proposed authority should take.

For Philip Sidney, it was a historic moment. Finally he was able to bring to bear his years of scholarship. His conversations with Hubert Languet and his directed reading with Gabriel Harvey had prepared him well to put the lessons of the past into present-day practice. Addressing the assembled negotiators, he declared (in a Dutch account) that 'he had learnt from histories [*de historien*] that when the state of the Republic of Rome had been in utter peril or danger, as the Netherlands nowadays are, which we [the Dutch] fully acknowledge, it had been necessary to create a dictatorship [*tot creatie van een dictateur*], with absolute power and disposition over everything concerning the prosperity of the country, without any instruction, limitation or restriction'.[35] Here, in the clearest language, was the philosophy that Philip had discussed so many times with Languet, which formed the basis of the questioning in such tracts as *Vindiciae, contra tyrannos*.

Leicester kept his distance from these debates, mustering some of his forces on 10 January and, from Leiden, calling a fast throughout Holland, Gelderland and Friesland for the 12th, as a display of piety. It was kept 'with great zeal': Leicester himself, in Stow's words, ostentatiously spent 'that day till night with hearing of preaching, reading and singing of Psalms: neither he nor his eating any thing till night'.[36] Meanwhile Davison pressed for better offers, ostensibly 'so that Her Majesty would be better contented'.[37] It was only on 14 January that Leicester, still in Leiden, accepted the offer of 'the rule and government general'.[38] He was sworn in shortly before noon on Tuesday 25 January, as Governor General of the United Provinces and Cities of the Low Countries; all the States present swore faith and obedience to him, in the presence of Dom Immanuell, Dom Antonio's son who had arrived the previous day, the Counts Maurice of Nassau and de Hohenloe and most of the noblemen of the country.[39]

But glory in the Low Countries would not necessarily translate into acclaim at home. Lord North slipped a mention of the States General's offer to Leicester into a letter to Burghley on 2 January, lessening the blow by stating that 'I do not see his Lordship minded as yet to accept it, or if he do I suppose he will have laid down plainly and certainly how and which way this liberal offer may have performance.'[40] On the 14th, Leicester himself wrote to tell Burghley that he had been persuaded to accept the governorship by the States, who had assured him that this was the only proper thing to do; in his own mind, Leicester was sure that he 'did never see greater probability of assured good success', and claimed to 'like the matter twenty times better' than he had done when in England. He did not, however, intend to explain himself further: once the oath was sworn, and the agreement sealed, Davison would be despatched to Elizabeth to give an account of the negotiations (from which of course Leicester had strategically kept himself aloof).[41] Davison was not enamoured of this latest duty and wrote ahead to beg Walsingham to dissuade Elizabeth from turning impulsively against him, before hearing him out.[42]

In accepting the governorship general, Leicester had crossed a line. He knew well that he had disobeyed the queen's strict instructions, which she had elaborated in private conversations with him. She had given him a military title – Lieutenant General of the English forces in the Low

Countries: his political position in the Low Countries was meant to be purely advisory. As she had made clear in her instructions, Elizabeth did not want sovereignty over the Low Countries, but Leicester in accepting this new role had effectively made her sovereign. Leicester was to reiterate that 'although she would not take so much upon her as to command them in such absolute sort', she nevertheless expected them to 'show themselves forward to use the advice of her Majesty to be delivered unto them by her lieutenant to work amongst them a fair unity and concurrence for their own defence'. If they failed to do so, 'her Majesty would think her favours unworthily bestowed upon them'. For his part, Leicester was 'to offer all his lordship's travail, care and endeavour, to understand their estates, and to give them advice, from time to time, in that which may be for the surety of their estate and her Majesty's honour'.[43]

But Leicester knew what he was doing. Even before leaving England, he had written a memorandum concerning 'What government is requisite to be appointed to him that shall be their governor'. The minute started:

> First that he have as much authority as the prince of Orange had, or any other governor or captain general hath had heretofore.
> That there be as much allowance by the states for the said governor as the prince had, with all offices appertainant.
> That the general contributions & collections for the expense of the war be appointed at his disposition.
> That there be a certain number of the best sort of persons appointed for counsellors of estate.[44]

It is clear also that Philip was aware that Leicester was flying in the face of the queen's orders. The instructions to Leicester were public documents, widely circulated: even if Philip had not been supplied with a copy for his information, he was in constant contact with Walsingham and several other privy councillors, all of whom had access to them. Arguing for Leicester as dictator of the Low Countries at The Hague, Philip fulfilled the ultimate duty for the Dudleys.

Philip stayed on with Leicester in Leiden, waiting for the storm to break in England. On 17 January, Walsingham wrote to tell Leicester that 'her Majesty is offended with the title of "excellency" given to his

Lordship, and therefore it is likely that she will mislike of the authority that the States have given him over them'.[45] Leicester replied, unperturbed:

> Some flying tale hath been told me here, that her Majesty should mislike with the name of 'excellency'. Surely I know the great increase it hath given me, but that I had the same at all strangers' hands that ever came into England, since I was made by her Majesty an earl, and abroad where she hath sent me. If I had delighted, or would have received titles, I refused a title higher than 'excellency', as Mr Da[vison], if you ask him, will tell ye.[46]

An official complaint was despatched from England on 26 January: a letter from the Privy Council, which expressed the royal anger, demanded that her favourite give back his commission and serve, as she had commanded, as her Lieutenant General.[47] When word came officially, the jokes stopped. Now, Leicester told Walsingham, he was 'not only grieved but wounded to the heart. For it is more than death unto me, that her majesty should be thus ready to interpret always hardly of my service, specially before it might please her to understand my reasons for that I do.'[48]

Leicester had delayed sending Davison to England for some weeks – Davison reached London only on 13 February. Even then he, with the help of Walsingham and Burghley, could do little good. Elizabeth wanted to humiliate Leicester by forcing him publicly to resign his governorship. Her determination was only exacerbated by whispers that Leicester's countess, her cousin Lettice, was about to join her husband in the Low Countries and set up a court more magnificent than Elizabeth's own. On 10 February, the queen charged Sir Thomas Heneage with delivering to Leicester the following devastating letter, which she had Walsingham draft:

> How contemptuously we conceive ourself to have been used by you, you shall by this bearer understand, whom we have expressly sent unto you to charge you withal. We could never have imagined (had we not seen it fall out in experience) that a man raised up by ourself, and extraordinarily favoured by us above any other subject of this land,

would have in so contemptible a sort broken our commandment in a cause that so greatly toucheth us in honour; whereof, although you have showed yourself to make but little accompt [account] in most undutiful a sort, you may not therefore think that we have so little care of the reparation thereof as we mind to pass so great a wrong in silence unredressed: and therefore our express pleasure and commandment is that, all delays and excuses laid apart, you do presently upon the duty of your allegiance, obey and fulfil whatsoever the bearer hereof shall direct you to do in our name: whereof fail you not as you will answer the contrary at your uttermost peril.[49]

Coming after almost thirty years of close liaison, written to the man she had once seriously considered marrying, this letter expressed Elizabeth's fiercest anger at what she saw as unjustifiable disobedience to her crown.

Leicester was not the only one wounded. Walsingham told him that the queen 'had put on a very hard conceit' of Philip, and hinted that she might move to recall him.[50] Davison had found Walsingham 'utterly discomforted with her majesty's hard opinion and course against the cause', and reported that Walsingham told him that Elizabeth 'had threatened Sir Philip Sidney and myself as principal actors and persuaders thereof for which it seems we owe our thanks to some with your lordship [Leicester]'.[51]

'Some with your lordship' was probably Davison's way of letting Leicester know that he knew exactly where the rumours had started – with His Excellency himself. Leicester assured both Elizabeth and the Privy Council that he had been a victim of the persuasions of Davison and others, and that he was deeply aggrieved by Davison's inadequate defence of him in England. In his defence Davison commented that Leicester needed no persuasion – 'let Sir Philip Sidney and others witness' – and (less convincingly) that only Leicester knew that the queen had forbidden him to accept the post.[52]

Philip wrote to let Davison know that Leicester 'thinks great unkindness in you, being advertised from thence, that you greatly disclaim from his defence which now your absence from Court seems much to confirm'. But Philip was not Leicester, and he had a different view. 'But of your faith I will make no doubt while I live, only I think you answered not the point of her Majesty's mislike, for you answered only upon the necessity, but should have argued withal upon the nature which is not absolute as her Majesty took it. Well a great blow is stricken, things went on beyond expectation, I doubt me hardly to be redressed.'[53] Philip was here attempting a difficult balancing act – being seen to support Leicester while in fact subtly undermining him. On 20 July, Philip wrote to reassure Davison of his personal support: 'For yourself cousin assure yourself any way that I can testify my assured friendship toward you I will. Ground upon it for I will not fail you and so I leave you to God's blessed protection.' He signed the letter 'Your loving friend and cousin' and addressed it 'To my especial good friend and cousin Mr Davison'.[54]

After a brief trip to Flushing, Philip was back in Leiden with Leicester, by 28 February.[55] However, he was soon to leave again since Leicester now selected Philip to plead his cause with Sir Thomas Heneage, whose arrival with the letter from the queen was imminent. So by 3 March Philip found himself in Middelburg, welcoming Heneage,[56] accompanying him on a four-day journey to Haarlem[57] and preparing him for the complexities of the Low Countries – he wrote to the Antwerp printer Christopher Plantin requesting the 'most up-to-date and best edition' of Ortelius' maps for Heneage to use.[58] By now, Heneage's mission had lost some of its bite. Due to unfavourable winds the envoy had been unable to sail for a fortnight; in the meantime, the Privy Council had stood firm behind Leicester, Burghley had tendered his resignation and the queen had been forced to soften Heneage's original instructions. None the less, when the royal envoy did arrive, Philip was not impressed with him. 'Sir Thomas Heneage,' he wrote to Burghley, 'hath with as much honesty in my opinion done as much hurt as any man this twelve-month hath done with naughtiness.' But he was not despondent: 'I hope in God when her Majesty finds the truth of things her graciousness will not utterly overthrow a cause so behoveful and costly unto her, but that is beyond my office. I only cry for Flushing and crave your favour, which I will deserve with my service.'[59]

Although Elizabeth soon declared herself adequately appeased, the damage had been done to Leicester in the Low Countries.[60] The temporary lack of confidence shown by his sovereign unnerved the Dutch, who started murmuring about their Governor General's regime. Leicester had unwisely surrounded himself with advisers who shared his beliefs, all militant Protestants. As such they failed to represent the more moderate members of the States General, and prompted a backlash. Leicester saw his political initiatives routinely delayed, a jealous hold kept on the privileges of the States General, and Dutch (which Leicester did not speak) proclaimed the official language of government. Matters worsened when Leicester published a strict new edict banning trading with the enemy. His firmly held political and religious ideals underlying the edict did not square with the financial realities of trade in the Low Countries. Put crudely, the war against the enemy was funded by trade with the enemy, and any attack on such trade was bound to be unpopular. Opposition to the edict was immediate and forceful: the day after the placard was displayed, Leicester confided to Walsingham that for the first time he heard the States General 'bussing' against him – a punning reference to the opposition co-ordinated by the councillor Paul Buys, one of Leicester's own appointments, whom he had come to despise.[61] An alliance of politicians and merchants ensured that the edict was sabotaged: Leicester was forced to attenuate it four months later.

Leicester's second blunder occurred when he tried to enforce his own Calvinist beliefs on his new population. It was quite acceptable for Leicester to possess Puritan credentials: Geoffrey Whitney, the emblemist, called him 'a zealous favourer of the gospel and of the godly preachers thereof',[62] and the printed account of his entries were dedicated to 'the most religious prince'. It was another matter altogether for him to force his beliefs on his new people. Leicester's letters testify that for him this was an overriding priority: 'Since our arrival in the Netherlands no concern has been as near to our heart as the honour of God, the question of the Christian religion, and the unity of the churches and congregations.'[63] He was delighted to note that the inhabitants of Utrecht, 'who were lately the worst of all these provinces', now 'begin exceedingly to increase in religion' (by which he always meant *the* religion), which he took as a sign that within six months 'these provinces will be equal with any country for religion'.[64] As a reward, he attempted to move the new university from Leiden to Utrecht and appointed an orthodox magistrate in the city.[65] He perhaps misunderstood Utrecht's motivation for this display of godly fervour, which was a strategy to raise their profile in relation to Holland and Zeeland rather than an out-pouring of inner faith. Against the wishes of the States General, he called for a general synod, to be held in The Hague in June. The synod decided on a very orthodox church ordinance, which was guaranteed not to appeal to the non-Calvinist Protestants, let alone the Catholics. The States General opted not to ratify the ordinance, and some of Leicester's more liberal followers were horrified at the move.

These simmering resentments made themselves felt in personal satire against the earl, who was, it was said, spending lavishly 'all for his own private causes'. A scurrilous print showed Leicester milking a Dutch cow until she bled.[66] Ironically, the print was far from the truth. Elizabeth was characteristically withholding funds, forcing Leicester to dig deeper into his own pocket: within the first three months, the earl calculated, he had 'spent and laid out for her Majesty's service above £11,000 sterling already'.[67] In March he was 'driven to borrow' £4,000 from the merchants of Middelburg to pay the troops at Utrecht and to pay for his own journey.[68] Leicester attempted to raise revenue, with a 'secret offer' designed to yield £30–40,000 per annum by permitting rose nobles to be minted in the Low Countries, only to face opposition from both London and The Hague – as Burghley pointed out, as soon as their nature was known, the coins' value would plummet.[69] 'Forget not money, money' pleaded the postscript of one of Leicester's letters.[70]

Elizabeth required Leicester to remain militarily inactive – at precisely the moment when he reckoned his chances were good – so that she could

13. Leicester milking the Dutch cow.

pursue secret peace negotiations with France. Indeed, Walsingham had to relay to Leicester the queen's instruction that 'if you shall see no cause to the contrary', he should inform the States General that 'certain overtures for peace are daily made unto her', which she would not pursue without their approval; Leicester's task was to ensure that the States General did not form a 'jealous conceit' that she was in any way alienated from them.[71] Leicester persisted in looking on the bright side, believing that popularity with 'the honest councillors and the common people' would see him through.[72] Those around him were more astute. The financial expert Horatio Palavicino wrote in cipher to Walsingham that Leicester's strength was no match for the burden he was under.[73] Eventually, even Leicester's optimism started to slide.

Philip also faced financial difficulties. Although the States General found £20,000 to maintain their forces, it fell far short of what was required. Philip appealed to the Privy Council for funds to erect barracks, to prevent a worsening of tension between the soldiers and local inhabitants. In theory Elizabeth approved of the plan, but proposed that the burghers should be persuaded to build new houses or rent out vacant properties — and Leicester would have to finance it, since 'her Majesty's charges do daily increase beyond her expectation'. Only once these measures had been exhausted might the queen step in to help, wrote the clerk to the Privy Council to Philip. Then he was told to strike that last sentence out. The queen would not be financing this initiative.[74]

Philip was very blunt about the implications of the queen's refusal. 'If the queen pay not her soldiers she must lose her garrisons there is no doubt thereof. But no man living shall be able to say the fault is in me . . . It hath been a costly beginning unto me this war, by reason I had nothing proportioned unto it, my servants unexperienced and myself every way unfurnished, and no helps, but hereafter if the war continue I shall pass much better through with it.'[75] According to the Catholic intelligencer Thomas Morgan, Philip had to spend time in March in Germany on a recruitment drive, 'to draw some from thence to assist the Huguenots'.[76]

By 24 March, matters had reached a head. Philip wrote to Walsingham acknowledging 'the discomfort' that his actions were causing at home, but refusing to regret the situation. It is a remarkable letter, presenting a rare portrait of Philip as a driven man. He is able to discount the queen's lack of co-operation because she is only a tool of the Almighty – if she fails, then other sources will be found:

> I had before cast my count of danger, want and disgrace, and before God sir it is true that in my heart the love of the cause so far overbalance them all that with God's grace they shall never make me weary of my resolution. If her Majesty were the fountain [i.e. the source] I would fear considering what I daily find that we should wax dry, but she is but a means whom God useth and I know not whether I am deceived but I am faithfully persuaded that if she should withdraw herself other springs would rise to help this action. For methinks I see the great work indeed in hand, against the abusers of the world, wherein it is no greater fault to have confidence in man's power, than it is too hastily to despair of God's work. I think a wise and constant man ought never to grieve while he doth play as a man may say his own part, truly though others be out, but if himself leave his hold because other mariners will be idle he will hardly forgive himself his own fault. For me I can not promise of my own course . . . because I know there is a higher power that must uphold me or else I shall fall, but certainly I trust, I shall not by other men's wants be drawn from myself.[77]

Although he hoped not to be 'drawn from myself', Philip's actions were perforce largely in Leicester's control. Still needing to prove himself in battle, Philip became annoyed at Leicester's policy of inaction: 'The enemy stirs of every side, and your side must not be idle, for if it be, it quickly loseth reputation.' At Davison's instigation ('more your persuasion than any desire in me,' claimed Philip), Leicester had appointed his nephew colonel of the Zeeland regiment, and by late January garrison gossip had it that Philip might well be made governor of all the Isles.[78] The latter never came to pass, perhaps because of the open resentment of Count Hohenloe, Paul Buys and Barneveldt. Hohenloe (or 'Hollok' as Philip called him) 'caused a many-handed supplication to be made that no stranger might have any regiment but presently after with all the same hands protested they meant it not by me to whom they wished all honour etc.' Paul Buys, he punned, 'hath too many busses [buzzes] in his head, such as you shall find he will be to God and man about one pitch'. Only 'the Count Maurice showed himself constantly kind toward me therein.'[79] As far as Philip was concerned, Leicester had some of the right instincts, but seemed incapable of following through on them. Philip would have to create opportunities for himself.

Both the Spanish forces, led by Parma, and those of the States General, led by Leicester, were bent on capturing those fortified towns that controlled the trade routes, which meant those towns on the principal rivers. At this point, Parma held Antwerp and other cities along the Schelde; but Philip, of course, held Flushing, which effectively controlled access to that river.[80] As Thomas Digges put it:

> In Holland, Zeeland and Utrecht the enemy had clearly nothing; in Friesland also nothing saving that the city of Groningen and that part of the country called Omelands [Ommelanden] were wholly his: in Gelderland and Zutphen he had a good part: in Brabant the Estates had but Bergen-op-Zoom, St Ghertrudenburg, Huesden, Grave and Wau Castle with the fort of Lillo: in Flanders they had Sluys and Ostend and the forts of Terneuse, the Dole, Lyskenshooke and St Anthony's Hook; all the rest were the enemy's together with all the other of the seventeen provinces.[81]

The situation was as confusing as it sounds, and highly changeable: no sooner was one flashpoint resolved than another emerged.

Top on Parma's wish-list was Grave, the easternmost stronghold of the States General on the River Maas. As early as 2 February, Philip had appealed to Leicester to be allowed to besiege Spanish-held Steenbergen, in order to detract Parma from besieging Grave. Three weeks later, he was mustering troops at Bergen-op-Zoom in preparation for such a siege, but was overtaken by events. Marbois, the governor of Wau Castle, told La Fergie, the governor of Steenbergen, that he would resign his castle to the Spanish forces when La Fergie entered the gates. When La Fergie led his men to the castle, however, at midnight on Saturday 26 February, he 'was received with a whole volley of shot whereby he himself was slain and five more of his company, and the sixth sore wounded and taken, the rest threw away their armour and fled'. Marbois had apprised Philip of the scheme, hoping that Philip would lay in wait at Steenbergen and 'interrupt th'enemy' as they left or returned. Philip promptly led 1,000 men from Bergen to Steenbergen, but found that he had missed the enemy going out, and after the fiasco at Wau castle the Steenbergen troops were suspicious enough not to return to base. But Philip refused to give up easily and stayed outside Steenbergen all through Sunday and Monday until ten o'clock, hoping to be able to launch an assault on the town, 'but he could do no good', recorded John James, 'by reason that the moat about the town was frozen too hard for them to pass by their boat, but not hard enough to bear them. So they were forced to depart without further success.'[82]

Steenbergen was a rare exception. Without military action to absorb his attentions, Philip spent time in more familiar pursuits. He consolidated a friendship with the great scholar Justus Lipsius. While Philip had been in The Hague, debating the necessity of Leicester's dictatorship, Leicester had been to hear Lipsius lecture on Tacitus' *Agricola* on 3 March.[83] According to Dusseldorpius, Leicester – who had been accompanied by Dom Immanuel and other noblemen – invited Lipsius to a meal at his lodgings in the sacred monastery of St Barbara, where he 'banqueted his way through the holy days of Lent at a table exceedingly well-furnished with meats'.[84] In return, Lipsius inscribed a copy of his most popular work *De constantia* to Leicester.[85]

In April, Lipsius also met Philip, who was lodging on the same street in Leiden. He was impressed by the young Englishman. 'The earl himself, and Sidney, too, we have had with us; the *princeps* is indeed an honourable, benign, heroic man: the other, his kinsman, son of his sister, has remarkable prudence and wisdom.'[86] To Dousa, a long-time Sidney admirer, Lipsius remarked, 'Blessed is England in this, that its nobility is truly noble, educated as it is in studies of *virtus* and *doctrina*.'[87] With Lipsius, Philip enjoyed the level of academic conversation that he remembered from his days with Languet and the Camerarius brothers. Together they debated another sticking point of European unity – the correct pronunciation of Latin. 'You ask me in earnest, illustrious Philip Sidney, what I think about the pronunciation of Latin – whether this "German manner" which we now use is the true one, or some other, which (like so many things) has died out long ago and since laid hidden under the darkness of ignorance and ancientness. It is a delicate and subtle question.' This debate was presumably prompted by Philip's knowledge that Lipsius had just completed an entire book on the subject, *De recta pronunciatione Latinae linguae dialogus*. When Lipsius came to publish the work later in the year, he dedicated it to his new English friend, 'O bright star of Britannia', to whom, he declared, 'the very gods . . . have refused nothing':

> Do I refer to excellencies of appearance? You have been created both
> for physical strength and elegance. Of your mind? You are most erudite,
> and wit and judgement abound in you. Hardly anything is wanting in
> you that Nature and Fortune can provide. Indeed, you are gifted: the
> more so because you do not abuse it, like the majority of that
> aristocracy, and turn it to ambition and pomp, but you make it
> contribute, where you can, to yourself and to the common weal. And
> this privately and publicly, in gown and in armour: with that lively force
> of mind everywhere sufficient, you are the favourite of Mars and never
> desert the rites of Sophia and the Muses. What Archilogus once
> proudly asserted, you can say with still better reason:
>
>> Although I am the servant and admirer of the god of war,
>> I yet retain the famous gifts of the Muses.[88]

Philip Sidney now had a dual persona, soldier and poet: Lipsius clearly hoped that, despite the lure of battle, the 'famous gifts of the Muses' would win the day.

This dual persona presented new, practical problems however, as shown when later in the year, Lipsius' printer Christopher Plantin sent two copies of the treatise to the canon Nicolas Oudart. In one copy, he wrote, he had cut away part of the title page – which gave the author, the title and the legend '*Ad V. Illustrem Philippvm Sidneivm, Eqvitem*' – and the fulsome dedicatory epistle; although he had left the other copy intact, he begged Oudart not to reveal to anyone what those parts contained. The name of the dedicatee, he claimed, had been printed against his will and he had begged Lipsius not to tolerate such things in the future. Indeed, a copy of the book now in the Museum Plantin-Moretus in Antwerp, which carries a handwritten *approbatio* by the censor Laurentius Nagelmaker, is missing half its title page and the dedication in just this manner. It is a salutary reminder that, for all his prestige in the international scholarly community, his military action meant that Philip's name was now anathema in the Spanish-occupied regions of the Low Countries.[89]

Domestic concerns also intruded into Philip's military life. He had been attracted to Bergen-op-Zoom, he told Walsingham: 'For Bergen-op-Zoom I delighted in it I confess because it was near the enemy, but especially having a very fair house in it and an excellent air I destined it for my wife.' Clearly, Philip meant to bring Frances over to join him and Bergen seemed a suitably domestic spot. Interestingly, he gave up the idea. Realising 'how apt the Queen is to interpret every thing to my disadvantage, I have resigned it to my Lord Willoughby, my very friend and indeed a valiant and frank gentleman, and fit for that place. Therefore I pray you know that so much of my regality is fallen. I understand I am called very ambitious and proud at home, but certainly if they knew my heart they would not altogether so judge me.' He felt that he had to pay attention not merely to political and military matters in the Low Countries, but to reactions at home. He was also unsure as to whether Lady Frances should travel over: 'I know not what to say to my wife's coming till you resolve better for if you run a strange course I may take such a one [house] here as will not be fit for any of the feminine gender.'

News from home, arriving on 13 May, forced the issue.[90] Sir Henry had died eight days earlier, in the bishop's palace at Worcester, 'of a kind of cold palsy by reason of an extreme cold he took upon the water in his passage and remove by barge between Bewdley and Worcester not long after he had been purged'.[91] He was just fifty-six years old. As the eldest son, Sir Philip felt he had to set his father's estate in order and immediately applied to the queen for leave of absence from his governorship. (Ever the practical horseman, he also enquired of Walsingham whether some of his father's 'serviceable horses' might be shipped over, 'to serve in my cornet, which, though already it be in the field, full and fair, yet would I have those to supply the want, of some such as I would take out to serve my private use that whether I be there, or no, yet my cornet may always be full as it ought.'[92])

Unexpectedly, the queen rejected Philip's request: a Spanish intelligence report from London notes that he had 'been pressing the queen urgently to let him return to England, but his petition has been firmly refused, and his wife has therefore made ready to join him'.[93] Philip missed his father's elaborate funeral.[94] Sir Henry's remains were divided: his entrails were buried in the Dean's Chapel of Worcester Cathedral; his heart was taken in a small leaden urn to the parish church of Ludlow, where it was buried in the oratory near to the monument to Philip's sister Ambrosia.[95] On 15 June a six-day funeral procession of some 140 horsemen, fellow councillors, friends, kinsmen and servants accompanied the corpse from Worcester through Chipping Norton, Oxford and Kingston to Penshurst, where he was buried on 21 June.[96] As the Spanish intelligencer reported, the only comfort to Philip from his father's death was that it settled the question of where his wife should be — Frances joined Philip at Flushing towards the end of June.[97]

In quick succession came more sad news. After years of supporting Sir Henry, 'the old Lady Sidney, widow' — already an invalid and a semi-recluse — died in London, probably at the Walsinghams' house, on 9 August, outliving her husband by just three months. Her body was carried on 22 August from St Olave's in Hart Street down to Penshurst, where she was buried next to Sir Henry.[98] According to Thomas Moffet, this news came to Philip with the additional information that his sister Mary was ill and not expected to recover (although ultimately she did).

With this triple blow, Philip mused on the likely outcome of the campaign. 'We shall have a sore war upon us this summer, wherein if appointment had been kept and these disgraces forborne which have greatly weakened us we had been victorious.'[99] Within six months he was to know just how weak they had become.

CHAPTER TWELVE

The Very Hope of Our Age

W ITH HIS NEW-FOUND official status, Philip found himself in a novel dilemma. Previously he had been naturally associated with Leicester, but he had been able, if necessary, to distinguish himself successfully from his uncle. Now, despite being recognised for his own worth, he was serving under Leicester and his actions were to a great extent dictated by Leicester's policy. As 1586 progressed, however, Philip tried to forge his own way. It was a strategy that would inevitably lead to conflict.

Parma had not given up hopes of winning Grave, but throughout April and May, despite repeated Spanish assaults, the town stayed firm. And then, on 7 June, to the States General's surprise and horror, Grave's young governor, Hemart, surrendered. Leicester wrote to Walsingham, still reeling with shock: 'The best fortified place thoroughly of all these provinces, none like it, being full-manned, victualled, and stored with all manner of artillery and munition, having but three hours' battery laid to it, and a show of an assault upon Thursday last in the morning, gave it up at afternoon.'[1] Hemart claimed to have been swayed by civilian entreaties, although many were quick to jump to less favourable conclusions, including Lord North: 'The best that can be made of it was most vile cowardice mixed with such negligence as is unspeakable in the time of that siege.'[2] Philip sat on the court-martial at Utrecht on 17 June that sentenced Hemart, and several of his captains, to death by decapitation the following day.[3]

While the firm action taken against Hemart was intended to apportion blame and punish it, the incident itself was another blow to Leicester's leadership. An Antwerp writer later alleged that Hemart and his men 'had done no treason, nor made any secret confederacy with the enemy' and that they had yielded the town only 'through a certain youthful want of skill in military service'. Leicester's harsh response, he continued, 'turned away the hearts of many noblemen and inhabitants there from him'.[4] This controversy did nothing to help Leicester's morale. In just four months his energy was sapped, his dreams shattered. As early as March, he had left a lavish reception in Haarlem to write to

Walsingham of how it would 'glad me to be rid of this heavy high calling, and wish me at my poor cottage again, if any I shall find'.[5] Even as he joined his troops in the field for the summer campaign, on 18 May, he had lamented to Walsingham, 'I am weary, indeed I am weary, Mr Secretary.'[6] Now his assumption that Grave could defend itself appeared misguided at best, murderously reckless at worst. While he looked for a speedy recall, however, his friends feared that he would never be welcome back in England: as his brother wrote, 'have great care of yourself, I mean for your safety, and if she [the queen] will needs revoke you, to the overthrowing of the cause, if I were as you, if I could not be assured there, I would go to the furthest part of Christendom rather than ever come into England again'.[7] England was not an available option: Leicester, and by extension Philip, had to win the day in the Low Countries.

Having conquered Grave, the way to Gelderland was now open to Parma; if he successfully attacked Bommelerwaard (the region between the Rivers Maas and Waal), then he would be at liberty to launch an invasion into Holland. This had to be avoided at all costs. Leicester therefore diverted part of his army to Bommelerwaard, using the remainder to strengthen Arnhem and its neighbouring towns. When Parma appeared to be approaching the area, reaching Venlo, Leicester's captains Martin Schenk and Roger Williams were sent with 150 lancers to get there first. Reaching Parma's camp at midnight, they quickly despatched the sentinels and the guards on Parma's own tent – rumour spread that Schenk had the audacity to pistol-whip the duke himself. It was a rare moment of triumph: in Lord North's words, 'While night lasted, they were kings in the camp and did what they would.'[8] But the escapade had to end: the camp (numbering some 2,000) pursued the intruders, killing and wounding about fifty men. Even so, concluded North, it was 'a notable enterprise and most marvellous scape'. In late June, however, Venlo capitulated to Parma's forces.

Through July Parma turned his attentions to Nuys on the Rhine. Leicester was nowhere to be seen. He was under massive pressure from the queen to cut costs: among her schemes, she demanded that he should reduce the two bands headed by Sidney and Sir Thomas Cecil to the 5,000 footmen mentioned in the contract between herself and the States. After all she had, as she reminded him, yielded to tolerate his title of 'Excellency'.[9] Lacking any support from home, Leicester's authority in the field began to wane. The originally malleable Count Maurice of Nassau was by now wholly alienated from Leicester and had spent the spring in Middelburg, talking with St Aldegonde. Leicester's own general of troops, Sir John Norris, was openly contemptuous, advocating an aggressive campaign. Finally, on 13 July, Sir William Pelham arrived and was named Lord Marshal, much to the annoyance of Norris and Count Hohenloe. Leicester planned to go into battle, but, as Thomas Doyley commented, 'I know not how the Count Hollock, the Lord Marshal, or Sir John Norris . . . can brook one to command or be commanded of the other.'[10] The entire English force was riven with disputes, quarrels and factions: as Sir Thomas Cecil lamented to his father, 'Our affairs here be such, as that which we conclude over night is broken in the morning. We agree not one with another but we are divided in many factions, so as if the enemy were as strong as we are factious and unresolute I think we should make shipwreck of the cause this summer.'[11]

In stark contrast, in late June Philip had finally seen some encouraging (if brief) action, taking the initiative rather than waiting for his uncle to dole out glory. Together with Hohenloe, brother Robert and some other captains, he overthrew a cornet of horse belonging to the garrison at Breda on 30 June; Hohenloe and Robert Sidney also captured thirty horsemen serving the governor of Breda, including one Captain Walsh.[12] As Sir Lewis Lewkenor told the story, Walsh was infamous – 'there is scarcely any one in England that professeth arms, but knew both him and his fortunes'. After leaving the English, Walsh decided to become 'a private soldier' (that is, a mercenary) and found employment 'under Canullo de Mount's company of horsemen in the garrison of Breda'. 'Issuing one day forth of the town', Walsh 'was upon the plains near adjoining encountered and defeated by Sir Philip Sidney's company of English lances, and among the rest Captain Walsh in two places [was] grievously wounded, and taken prisoner.' He was taken into Holland, where Leicester immediately ordered that Walsh be hanged. According to Lewkenor, however, 'Sir Philip Sidney (being full of true honour) earnestly entreated my lord for his pardon', arguing that he knew Walsh to be valiant and that (his present action excepted) he 'had ever borne a dutiful regard towards her majesty'. Philip obtained Walsh's pardon and the reprieved man went on to serve under Leicester (again as a mercenary).[13] Some, however, viewed this leniency as uncalled-for after the intransigence shown to Hemart.[14] Whatever the merits of Walsh's case, this minor exchange between the Governor General and the governor of Flushing suggests that Philip was willing to contradict his uncle; that he saw different ways of leading, which he believed might work better than Leicester's.

In July came another chance for Philip to shine. Count Maurice forwarded to Leicester information about the defences of the Flemish town of Axel and sketched a plan of attack.[15] The entire mission was to be kept secret: at Maurice's insistence, however, Leicester informed Philip – again, the Dutch trusted the nephew over the uncle. Philip was sent to reconnoitre, and reported back that he believed the plan could succeed. During the night of 6 July, Philip and his Zeeland regiment joined Willoughby with 500 men at Flushing. They rowed up the Schelde to within three miles of Axel, where they were joined by Maurice. John Stow tells of how Philip, a mile away from their destination, made a speech to the soldiers – which, to the modern reader, might eerily prefigure Shakespeare's Henry V before Agincourt:

> He declared what cause they had in hand, as God's cause, under, and
> for whom they fought, for her Majesty; whom they knew so well to be
> so good unto them, that he needed not to show, against whom they
> fought, men of false religion, enemies to God and his church: against
> Antichrist, and against a people whose unkindness both in nature and
> in life did so excel, that God would not leave them unpunished:
> further, he persuaded them that they were Englishmen, whose valour
> the world feared and commended, and that now they should not, either
> fear death or peril whatsoever, both for that their service, they ought
> [owed] to their Prince, and further, for the honour of their country,
> and credit to themselves. Again, the people whom they fought for were
> their neighbours, always friends, and wellwillers to Englishmen. And
> further, that no man should do any service worth the noting, but he
> himself would speak to the uttermost to prefer him to his wished
> purpose.

This oration, according to Stow, 'did so link the minds of the people that they desired rather to die in that service than to live in the contrary'.[16]

They reached Axel shortly after midnight. Thirty or forty soldiers swam across the moat with ladders, scaled the wall, killed the sleeping guards and opened the gates. The men inside the garrison either fled or were killed. Philip was, according to some, the prime mover: Leicester told Walsingham that Philip 'with his bands had the leading and entering the town, which was notably handled'. He placed a guard in the market-place, while the soldiers (both English and Dutch) exterminated the entire garrison and four neighbouring sconces, incurring only one non-fatal casualty. Maurice also pierced the dykes, destroying huge amounts of property. Philip's heroics were not popular with the States of Zeeland, which balked at having to finance yet another new garrison: only when Leicester angrily commanded it were 800 men provided under Colonel Piron.

The Axel campaign was quickly exploited by Leicester, who made sure in letters home that the significance of the action was known – 'this town of Axel is of very great importance; we shall have way to get at Antwerp and Bruges by it'.[17] He also ensured that his nephew's involvement was played up, ironically enough, given that it was Maurice (not Leicester) who had insisted on Philip's involvement. Leicester, whatever his failings as a military leader, clearly saw the value of Philip's actions after the event. In Greville's account, Philip becomes a brilliant strategist, reviving classical manoeuvres:

> how like a soldier did he behave himself, first, in contriving, then in executing, the surprise of Axel, where he revived that ancient and severe discipline of order and silence in their march and after their entrance into the town, placed a band of choice soldiers to make a stand in the marketplace, for security to the rest that were forced to wander up and down by direction of commanders, and, when the service was done, rewarded that obedience of discipline in every one, liberally, out of his own purse.[18]

But the governor of Brill, Sir Thomas Cecil, wrote that 'the plot was laid as I understand by Monsieur Byrd, Governor of Turneux, not far off Axel', and that it was Byrd, rather than Philip, who first entered the garrison. In Sir Thomas' version Axel contained only 150 men, 'most of them Almains, and but two Spaniards';[19] in Leicester's version some 600, 'as I hear'. Whatever the truth of the matter, there was no doubt that the incident provided a much-needed boost to morale: even Sir Thomas wrote to his father, 'since the loss of Grave and Venlo your Lordship will not think with what faces they looked upon us. This hath made us somewhat to lift up our heads.'

Another chance came with Gravelines, a key Spanish stronghold in northern Flanders.[20] Philip received intelligence from a group of Walloon captains, headed by Captain Nicholas Marchaunt, that they had contrived to corrupt a sergeant, a corporal and various other men inside the Gravelines garrison, who promised to hand the town over to Sidney. Philip was understandably wary, particularly since Gravelines was under the control of La Motte, an experienced commander who seemed unlikely to change sides. He therefore sent Marchaunt into the town for a fortnight, in order to win over men. On 16 July, Philip cast anchor before Gravelines and exchanged pre-agreed signals with men inside the walls. This should have led to the appearance of hostages whom Marchaunt was pledged to deliver. Instead, only a corporal and one of Marchaunt's servants appeared, bearing a letter assuring Philip of the continued success of the plan: both town and garrison were his. Philip remained unconvinced and sent in a captain, who again supported Marchaunt's claim.

Finally, Philip sent in a small force – just twenty-six men, then forty more under Lieutenant Browne. He was wise not to send more. The garrison fell on the Englishmen and forced them with gunshot back to the waterside. Others, attempting to flee, were ambushed by horsemen. Philip opened fire from his vessel, before returning at speed to Flushing. However, as Thomas Doyley wrote to Burghley, he fled 'having left 44 men behind him'.[21] The fate of these men became notorious. Sir Lewis Lewkenor wrote angrily of 'how cruelly and tyrannously' the Spanish inside Gravelines used

those poor men of ours that were sent before to discover it. All were safe, according to promise, whom they had received into their gates with friendly salutations, and entertained a good space in the town, in the end when they saw the success of the enterprise answered not their bloody, traiterous, and unmanly expectation, they disarmed and unclothed them in the marketplace, and, finally, like cruel butchers, and not like honourable soldiers, murdered them every one.[22]

Philip wrote to Davison resignedly: 'The long practice of Graveling which was brought unto us is proved a flat treason I think even in them that dealt with us. The circumstances I leave to Burnet [the messenger], who yet thinks better of the practicers then I do.'[23] Some thought Philip foolish: Sir Roger Williams, usually a faithful Leicester adherent, believed it unthinkable that a senior officer in the Spanish forces like La Motte would ever defect.[24] Leicester had believed in Philip, writing to Walsingham the day before he heard the news: 'God, I trust, hath given [Philip] blessed success, and then we are fully quit with our enemies and her Majesty as good a place as Calais.'[25] William Knollys, however, thought Leicester as gullible as his nephew: he exhibited 'that too much trust [which] had like to have beguiled us [at Gravelines]', he reported to Burghley.[26] It was left to Greville posthumously to turn the incident into another display of Sidneian heroism: 'How providently, again, did he preserve the lives and honour of our English army at that enterprise of Gravelines?'[27]

Despite the patchy success of his military endeavours, Philip was still Leicester's nephew and it was to him that Justus Lipsius turned for help in dealing with a situation of Leicester's making. Lipsius had become increasingly unhappy at Leiden, constantly threatening to leave, citing his ill health.[28] Just a few days before his attempt to resign, Lipsius travelled to Utrecht to see Philip. He missed him 'by a few hours', but forwarded a letter to him. 'The war now keeps you occupied; but neither learning nor politics must be neglected,' he opened. 'Learning' concerned Lipsius' hostility to Leicester's intervention into university politics. The Governor General had taken it upon himself to appoint a new professor at Leiden in complete disregard of the university's curators. 'Politics' concerned the fate of Paul Buys. An advocate of the States of Holland for many years until 1584, Buys had been one of Leicester's own appointments to the Council of State in January 1586. It soon became apparent, however, that Buys' ambition matched Leicester's own and he made a point of opposing many of the governor's initiatives. In mid-July, with Leicester's tacit approval, the burghers of Utrecht removed Buys from the Council and held him in close confinement.[29] Lipsius did not approve, as he told Philip:

To you I prophesy (and wish it were to prove untrue) that these rapid torrents are leading us into internal strife. If your rule had complete control, their faults would be less dangerous – obviously they do not see which places may be open in your stronghold. That you will have free and firm use of the reins of government, that I approve of and do recommend; but only if it is done with moderation and with a certain ease. In so sick a body, will you cure everything in a few months? A diet is required . . . I pray you to consider and act accordingly.[30]

Philip replied sympathetically to this critique of English policy, promising to help Buys and reiterating his proposal that Lipsius should 'depart to that other place . . . I know that you would be very welcome to our queen and to many others, yea to all others.' Since the queen would be involved, it seems likely that Philip was offering Lipsius a chair at an English university.[31] In the event, Lipsius did not move to England, but in this matter – as in so much during the course of the year – Philip was identified as an alternative locus of power to Leicester and took advantage of this subtly to distance himself from Leicester's regime.

On his return to Flushing, Philip found that the situation there had seriously deteriorated. He sent, in his postbag of 14 August 1586, impassioned missives to Burghley, Walsingham and the Privy Council, in all of which a newly desperate tone is evident. Burnham was despatched to inform the Privy Council of 'the weak store of all sort of necessary munition that both this town [Flushing] and the castle of Ramekins have'. He had tried the States General for funds 'to the uttermost', but without success – partly because they believed that Flushing 'more toucheth her Majesty because it is her pawn', but 'principally because they have ever present occasion to employ both all they have and indeed much more upon the places nearest to the enemy'. No matter what effort he made:

I nor all that be here, can perform the service we owe to her Majesty without such merely necessary things. I will neither speak of the consequence of the place, nor of any quantity, your lordships can better judge, I do only protest to your honours that I think it very likely we shall have occasion to use it, and till then it may be kept by some officer appointed by her Majesty never one grain of it to be used for no service till it be for the last point of extremity. There is nothing will keep these people in better order than that they see we are strong.[32]

To Burghley, Philip personalised the plea by pointing out that when Burnham told him 'in what case for all sort of munition we are in this town . . . I think Sir Thomas Cecil [Burghley's son] be in the like'. He appealed to Burghley, since:

the places [Flushing and the Brill] are of so great moment. If we be turned over to the States it is as good as nothing, and it shall be no loss to her Majesty to have some store under an officer of her own, whom it shall please her, not to be spent but upon urgent necessity. The garrison is weak, the people by these cross fortunes crossly disposed, and this is the conclusion: if these two places be kept her Majesty hath worth her money in all extremities, if they should be lost none of the rest would hold a day.[33]

Philip asked Walsingham to 'labour for me or rather for her Majesty in it': 'She need be discouraged with no thing while she keeps these principal sea places – nay I think it were hard to say whether it were not better for us to embrace no more but we do still make camps and straight again mar them for want of means, and so lose our money to no purpose, where if we would gall him [Parma] now in Friesland now in Flanders he should have no leisure to lie before towns as he doth.'[34]

In a second letter to Walsingham on the same day, his complaints finally came to the point and for the first time Philip explicitly distanced himself from Leicester:

I assure you sir this night we were at a fair plunge to have lost all for want of it [money]. We are now four months behind, a thing unsupportable in this place. To complain of my lord of Leicester you know I may not but this is the case: if once the soldiers fall to a thorough mutiny this town [Flushing] is lost in all likelihood. I did never think our nation had been so apt to go to the enemy as I find them. If this place might possibly have some peculiar care of it, it should well deserve it, for in fine this island, if once her Majesty would make herself sure of it, is well worth all the charge her Majesty hath even been at in this cause, and all the king of Spain's force should never be able to recover it though all the rest were lost, and without it should be never able to invade England. I have already gotten in a Dutch company at my commandment and into Campheer so as with no great matter I could make her Majesty sure of this isle, if this town were well provided both with men and munition.[35]

This plan comes directly from Philip – he is suggesting to Walsingham that he himself be provided with supplies, so that he can bypass Leicester's less-than-satisfactory control.

What might have come to a showdown between Philip and Leicester was averted – funds finally came through late in August. Neuss fell to Parma on 4 August, and the threat now shifted to Gelderland and Overijssel. Philip rejoined Leicester as he pitched camp near Amerongen, and was intimately involved in the planning of the next phase. Determined to relieve Berck on the Rhine from Parma's siege, Philip decided to assault Doesburg, a high-walled stronghold moated with deep ditches, manned by about 300 Walloons sent by Parma in addition to about 500 citizens. Leicester sent Hohenloe and Philip with 500 cavalry and 800 footmen at night, 'to discover and beset the city about', before joining them himself. Two days later, during a ten-hour battery, Leicester forced two breaches in the town wall. Philip begged Leicester to let him lead the assault, but the earl gave one breach to Hohenloe (leading Germans and Scots) and the other to Norris (with English and Zeelander troops) – a diplomatic decision perhaps or a move designed to limit Philip's profile? In the event, Doesburg surrendered just as the men were about to enter, although that did not prevent the soldiers from pillaging the town, against orders. Norris tried to restrain the pillagers (many of them from Sir William Stanley's regiment); Philip, understanding the soldiers' tense state, resented this.[36]

After Doesburg, the next target had to be Zutphen, defended by two allegedly invincible forts. Zutphen lay on the east or right bank of the River Ijssel and was held by the Spanish, under the veteran colonel Don Francisco Verdugo, marshal of the Spanish army; on the opposite bank were the two infamous forts that Hohenloe had besieged for ten months two years earlier, with 11,000 foot and 3,000 cavalry. He was unsuccessful then, and Leicester assumed that the forts, under the control of Parma's

14. Zutphen.

man Taxis, were still impregnable. None the less he decided to lay siege to both the town and the forts, hoping to lure over Parma, who was besieging Berck on the Rhine. On Tuesday 13 September, Leicester moved camp to a hillside within a mile of Zutphen.[37] To co-ordinate his forces, he manoeuvred boats to form a bridge across the river. Norris pitched camp in Warnsfeld churchyard about a mile east of Zutphen, taking with him Philip and Count Louis William of Nassau. Leicester was stationed on the west side of the river, in order to attack the forts. Meanwhile, Parma realised that he had to revictual Zutphen, which had been under siege for some weeks. He therefore sent a train of some 500 carts bearing provisions for three months, with an escort of 600 horsemen. Verdugo was instructed to have 1,000 men prepared to come to the aid of the provisions train if Leicester's forces attempted to stop the convoy.

Leicester sensed another problem at Deventer, only six miles away, whose support for his regime had at best been equivocal. While trenches were built around Zutphen and its forts, Leicester – accompanied by Philip, a cornet of horse and 400 footmen – marched into Deventer. They had been there two days when news came that Spanish forces had been sighted in the vicinity of Zutphen. Abandoning their retinue in Deventer, Leicester and Philip galloped back to the camp at Zutphen. Presumably Philip spent the next few days supervising the completion of the trench-building: the single letter we have of Philip's from the camp, dated 22 September 1586, merely recommends its bearer, 'Richard Smith her Majesty's old servant', to Secretary Walsingham.[38]

On the evening of Wednesday 21 September, after a day spent putting the finishing touches to the trenches, English soldiers intercepted Parma's messenger to Verdugo and learned of the convoy. Leicester ordered Sir John Norris to prepare an ambush for what he expected would be a nominal force: while the main body of soldiers was camped on the other side of the river, Norris had 200 horsemen of his own, and 300 of Stanley's footsoldiers able to meet the convoy between Zutphen and Warnsveld.

As Thursday dawned, some of the English commanders camped near the forts crossed the river with fifty or sixty men to join Norris. It seems that this decision was taken against Leicester's orders: he complained to Burghley that they went 'unwares to me . . . I was offended when I knew it, but could not fetch them back.' (Later, when the skirmish at Zutphen started to gain importance, however, Leicester would change his tune: to Walsingham he alleged, 'I was the appointer of all that went forth.'[39]) Thick mist hindered them for a while, but eventually they found Norris' camp, where they were warmly welcomed. Unbeknownst to them, the incoming Spanish force under Marques del Vasto, loaded with supplies, was now close by and had thrown up its own entrenchments, waiting for a helpful sally from the gates of Zutphen.

Suddenly the fog lifted. Into view came the victual wagons surrounded by a Spanish force of 3,000 foot soldiers and at least 1,500 horsemen. There was no time to rethink: the English forces advanced. The English horsemen charged the Spanish cavalry, driving them over their line of pikemen and back over their own trenches. They could go no further, as musket shot from the Spanish trenches forced them back. Quickly reforming, the English charged again, once more forcing the Spaniards back behind their musketry, once more being repelled by musket shot.

Great bravery was reported on the part of the English. The Italian Count Annibale Gonzago ('a man of great account' in John James' estimation) was mortally wounded by Sir Thomas Perrot. The Albanian cavalry leader Captain George Crescia was unhorsed by Willoughby and taken prisoner; Willoughby caused great suffering with his curtle-axe. The commander of the provisions convoy, the Marquis del Vasto, was said to be in danger of his life. Stanley came through unscathed, although his horse was shot eight times. Lord North, convalescing after being wounded, demanded to be lifted back on to his horse, and went into battle. The Spaniards cried that Sir William Russell was more like a devil than a man.

The third charge threw the Spanish cavalry into disarray, but once again the English had to face the musket shot. The battle lasted for some ninety minutes before Norris rode to Leicester and urged him to provide more men: 'Be merry, for you have had this day the honourablest day that ever you had, for a handful of your men have driven the enemy three times to retreat this one day.' Leicester, however, refused to withdraw any more men from other positions to act as reinforcements; as Verdugo let 2,000 more troops out from the gates of Zutphen, Norris retreated across the river. English losses were twenty-two footsoldiers and twelve or thirteen calvary. Spanish losses were estimated at 250–300. Despite Norris' claims, it was a hollow victory: after the exhilarating battle, the enemy convoy simply rolled into Zutphen.[40]

Among the wounded was Sir Philip Sidney. His horse had been killed under him on the second charge. Unfazed by the loss, he had secured a replacement and on the third charge rode right through the Spanish lines. As he turned to retreat, however, he was struck by a musket ball from the trenches. The wounding of Sidney is the stuff of myth: allegedly, seeing that his fellow-in-arms Sir William Pelham lacked thigh armour (cuisses), Philip had taken his own off as a mark of solidarity. It makes a great story, but military expert John Smythe, writing in 1590, blamed his wounding on the new trend of under-arming in warfare. Officers serving on horseback, he complained, think themselves 'very well armed with some kind of headpiece, a collar, a deformed high and long-bellied breast, and a back at the proof; but as for pouldrons, vambraces, gauntlets, tasses, cuisses, and greves, they hold all for superfluous. The imitating of which their unsoldierlike and fond arming, cost the noble and worthy gentleman Sir Philip Sidney his life, by not wearing his cuisses.' It seems that Philip was a victim of the meeting of two new vogues: the English love of light armour, and the

Spanish use of muskets in battle. The bullet lodged three fingers above the left knee, and shattered the bone: as Smythe remarked sadly, 'In the opinion of divers gentlemen that saw him hurt with a musket shot, if he had that day worn his cuisses, the bullet had not broken his thigh bone, by reason that the chief force of the bullet (before the blow) was in a manner past'.[41]

According to Greville, as Philip was led from the battlefield he passed by Leicester, who told him how much he regretted his wounding. Philip allegedly replied, 'Oh my Lord, this have I done to do your honour and her Majesty service.' It is one of dozens of stories that Zutphen gave rise to, each telling us as much about their teller as about Philip. According to George Gifford, one of Leicester's chaplains, Philip had his own interpretation of events. 'Being come back into the camp, and lying in a tent, he lift up his eyes to heaven not imputing it to chance; but with full resolution affirmed that God did send the bullet and commanded it to strike him.'[42] According to Stow, Russell was in tears, saying, 'O noble Philip, there was never man attained hurt more honourably than ye have done, nor any served like unto you.'[43] Most famous of all is the story told by Greville of how Philip declined a drink of water, giving it instead to a common wounded soldier – a story that seems to owe more to Greville's classical reading than to the events at Zutphen.[44]

Philip was taken in Leicester's barge down the Ijssel to Arnhem, twenty miles south of Zutphen, where he was lodged in the house of a judge's widow named Madame Gruithuissens, and given medical treatment.[45] In a hurried postscript to a letter to Burghley, probably written on the 24th, Leicester described Philip's injury as 'a very dangerous wound, the [thigh] bone being broke in pieces'; Philip, however, he reported, 'is of good comfort, and the surgeons are in good hope of his life, if no ill accident come, as yet there is not. He slept this last night four hours together, and did eat with good appetite afterward. I pray God save his life, and I care not how lame he be.'[46]

Chief among the physicians was Dr John James, who had joined Leicester's household the previous year. James held doctorates from both Trinity College, Cambridge, and the new University of Leiden, where he was the first English student. James' journal, which survives in manuscript in the British Library's collection, provides us with a usefully pragmatic account with which to balance the more idealised (or just fanciful) versions of these days.[47]

With gunshot wounds, the question was usually whether or not to cauterise: Ambroise Paré, who had treated Coligny, was inclined against, arguing that such wounds were not venomous. William Clowes, who served in the Low Countries and whose surgeon's chest carried the Dudley crest, was convinced that 'there be mo [more] killed by . . . wicked practices [in surgery] than there are many times slain by the sword of the enemy'. Two years later, he put into print the results of his expertise as *A Proved Practice for All Young Chirugeons, Concerning Burnings with Gunpowder and Wounds Made with Gunshot, Sword, Halberd, Pike, Lance, or Such Other*. Philip was lucky enough to have Clowes attending him, rather than the likes of Franciscus Arcaus, who also published his advice in 1588, prescribing for such wounds 'the blood of a maid of nineteen or twenty years old, which must be drawn the moon being at the full, the sign in Virgo, and the sun in Pisces'.[48]

Philip was wounded on 22 September 1586. Leicester held back from informing Walsingham of his son-in-law's condition for five days:

> My grief was so great for the hurt of your son, my dear nephew and son also, as I would not increase yours by the discomfort thereof; but seeing this is the sixth day after his hurt, and having received from the surgeons a most comfortable letter of their very good hope they have now of him, albeit yester-evening he grew heavy and into a fever, about two o'clock he fell to exceeding good rest, and after his sleep found himself very well, and free from any ague at all, and was dressed, and did find much more ease than at any time since he was hurt, and his wound very fair, with the greatest amendment that is possible for the time, and with as good tokens. I do but beg his life of God, beseeching for his mercy's sake to grant it. My hope is now very good.[49]

The following day Leicester wrote, 'I have received great comfort and hope, from time to time, specially this day, being the seventh day, from his surgeons and physicians . . . the Lord giveth me good cause to hope of his merciful dealing in granting life to our dear son to remain with us, for he hath all good accidents that may be wished.'[50]

Leicester was broadcasting an emphatically positive picture for consumption back home. On the ground in Arnhem, the grapevine prognosis was far less sanguine. From Deventer on 25 September, the minister Bernhardus Vezekius wrote to Dr James to tell him that, 'The rumour about the wound of the illustrious and noble lord Sidney has greatly upset us, and from your letter I learn that he is not yet sure to recover: but we pray God that He will restore his honour to his former health, and long preserve him for us and our churches.'[51] By 28 September, Leoninus and Killigrew sadly reported to the States General that Philip was 'very dangerously wounded'.[52]

Leicester visited Arnhem on the 29th and was probably still there when Philip drew up his will on the 30th, naming Leicester as one of its supervisors, alongside the Earls of Warwick, Pembroke and Huntingdon and Sir Francis Walsingham, with Lady Frances as executrix. It was on either the 29th or 30th that Philip called for the preacher George Gifford, who remained with Philip 'for the space of seventeen or eighteen days before his death' committing his memories to paper in 'a brief note'. While much of his narrative is a highly conventional account of the art of dying well, some details seem realistic.[53]

Leicester was still giving out confident news of Philip's recovery on 2 October. 'Good Mr Secretary,' he wrote to Walsingham, 'I trust now you shall have longer enjoying of your son, for all the worst days be past, as both surgeons and physicians have informed me, and he amends as well as is possible in this time, and himself finds it (for he sleeps and rests well and hath a good stomach to eat) without fear, or any distemper at all.' Four days later, the earl reiterated that Sir Philip was 'well amending as ever any man hath done for so short time. He feeleth no grief now but his long lying, which he must suffer.' By now Lady Frances had arrived at Arnhem (presumably from Flushing) and on Friday 7th, after breakfast, Leicester visited the couple once again, before returning to the camp at Deventer.[54]

On 12 October 1586, when Martine brought official news of Zutphen to the English court (where previously, Heneage informed Leicester, 'but very uncertain and false rumours were brought hither of your conflict with the Spaniards, and of the great valour and grievous hurt of your noble nephew'), the queen sent a bearer to carry 'her gracious letters of her highness' own hand to comfort him [Sidney] and to bring her word again how he doth as soon as he can'.[55] Meanwhile the noble nephew was weakening. After his uncle left him Philip's condition deteriorated, as Fulke Greville recounted, in a second-hand but convincingly vivid account:

> Now after the sixteenth day was past, and the very shoulder-bones of this delicate patient worn through his skin with constant and obedient posturing of his body to [the physicians'] art, he, judiciously observing the pangs his wound stang him with by fits, together with many other symptoms of decay, few or none of recovery, he began rather to submit his body to these artists than any further to believe in them. During which suspense he one morning, lifting up the clothes for change and ease of his body, smelt some extraordinary noisome savour about him differing from oils and salves as he conceived, and, either out of natural delicacy, or at least care not to offend others, grew a little troubled with it; which they that sat by perceiving, besought him to let them know what sudden indisposition he felt. Sir Philip ingenuously told it, and desired them as ingenuously to confess whether they felt any such noisome thing or no. They all protested against it upon their credits, whence Sir Philip presently gave this severe doom upon himself, that it was inward mortification; and a welcome messenger of death.[56]

The surgeons' vain attempts to extract the bullet had left Philip with even greater wounds, prone to infection; gangrene had presumably set in, although perhaps it had not been detected as anything more than grotesque bedsores. Thomas Moffet alleged that a doctor from Bergen had 'opened and pulled apart . . . the stitched edges of the muscles', but was unable to get hold of the bullet. At this late stage, the only option was amputation. None of the accounts by Philip's followers mention amputation, perhaps out of consideration for their friend and master's reputation, but one Spanish report asserted that Philip's 'thigh' had been 'cut off in consequence of his hurt'.[57] Suggestively, George Whetstone later compared Sidney in his fortitude to Caius Marius who 'smiled while his thigh was a cutting off'.[58]

Perhaps it was at this time that, according to Gifford, Philip, weakening, 'therefore gathered he should die'. He did not fear death, he insisted, 'but he feared that being a man of a strong and sound heart and in his flourishing years, the pangs of death would be so grievous that he should lose his understanding'. This fear, apparently, remained with him, no matter what Gifford or anyone else said to reassure him.

On 15 October, Leicester hurried back to Arnhem, 'partly in respect of his own health finding himself somewhat acrased [ill] by the bad air of Deventer and partly to see Sir Philip Sidney'. Dr James wrote that by this time Philip 'began to grow weaker of his hurt, and the worse by means of a fever lately fallen upon him'.[59] Despite his fever and physical weakness, however, Philip remained active. Edmund Molyneux later alleged that during these days 'he wrote a large epistle to Belerius a learned divine, in very pure and eloquent Latin (in like sort as many times he had done before to some great ones (upon occasions) and to others of learning and quality) the copy thereof was not long after, for the excellency of the phrase, and pithiness of the matter, brought to her Majesty's view'.[60] Presumably the letter was religious in content. It is slightly suspicious that such a celebrated piece of writing should not have been preserved for posterity (by Molyneux, for example, given his record), but there is evidence that Philip remained mentally active until his dying day.

On Sunday 16 October, the Leiden poet Baudius arrived at Arnhem bearing letters from Janus Dousa to Philip and Dr James – letters that evidently contained some new plan, although it is not clear what. 'Sidney was too ill to read your letter,' Baudius reported to Dousa. 'We have told him the whole matter as well as we could. What of it? We have agreed, and one cannot find him more willing to grant. And so he immediately orders that young man to be sent in (whom I remember to have seen with you, very witty and well-educated) and tells him to prepare a letter of personal commendation to the earl.'[61] As it happened Leicester arrived that same day, making the letter-writing superfluous: the unidentified 'young man' could present the case to Leicester himself. Baudius reported that, this notwithstanding, 'I shall deal with Sidney, that he may mention your business when the earl comes to visit him officially, and I am certain that he will do as I ask.'[62] Even in his present condition, Philip's influence with his uncle was a prized political commodity.

In fact, Philip did manage to pen one letter that day, his last known writing, 'leaning upon a pillow in his bed', according to Molyneux. The letter was to the uncle of Dr Gisbert Enerwitz, the elderly Dutchman Johan Wier, now physician to the Duke of Cleves, who had worked on treatments for skin infections and fever. Philip knew that his attending physicians had exhausted their repertoire; he needed a specialist, and fast. It was an uncharacteristically unguarded, scrawled letter (in Latin), reflecting the state of mind of a man in extreme pain and distress: 'My Wier, come, come, I am in danger of my life and I want you. I shall never be ungrateful, neither living nor dead. I can [write] no more but I strenuously beg you to hurry. Farewell. From Arnhem.'[63] Dr Enerwitz hurried off to deliver the letter, but in his professional opinion, having attended Philip for three days, doubted whether the patient would live to see Wier. He added to Philip's letter:

> He was in a fair way of healing but three days ago fever supervened and he has become weaker, wherefore he has earnestly besought me to write and ask you to come and tend him in his weakness. I have told the gentleman that you are laid up with an infirmity, that you are displeased with me and moreover overwhelmed with business. Nevertheless he feels confident you will come if you are not prevented by weakness. He has written the above lines in bed with his own hand and asked me to write also, which I could not refuse. I pray you to come, your trouble will not go unrewarded.[64]

To the end indeed, Philip remembered his duties towards his physicians, adding a codicil to his will bequeathing 'to Isert the bone-setter, twenty pounds', and topping up bequests to four surgeons (Goodridge, Kelly, Adrian and John).[65]

On the night of 16–17 October, as the Monday dawn approached, Gifford asked Philip how he was. 'I feel myself more weak,' he replied. 'I had this night a trouble in my mind,' he added, 'for examining myself, methought I had not a sure hold in Christ. After I had continued in this perplexity a while, observe how strangely God did deliver me — for indeed it was a strange deliverance that I had! There came to my remembrance a vanity wherein I had taken delight, whereof I had not rid myself. It was my Lady Rich. But I rid myself of it, and presently my joy and comfort returned within few hours.' If Gifford is telling the truth, then this might confirm that Astrophil was indeed in love with Stella. If it is a piece of poetic licence on Gifford's part, then it shows just how profoundly Philip Sidney's posthumous literary persona was to impinge on memories of his life.

As Philip returned yet again to his fear that he would lose his reason, Gifford tried to allay his qualms. Philip seemed reassured, and 'with a cheerful and smiling countenance put forth his hand, and clapped me softly on the cheek'. Then he lifted up his eyes and hands, exclaiming, 'I would not change my joy for the empire of the world.'

The final hours were difficult. For three or four hours he called to be read the word of God, and answered if 'it was not grievous unto him'. He asked the meaning of any difficult passage. If the reading were interrupted, he would call out, 'I pray you speak still to me', and he responded to the speeches by raising up his hands and eyes. Gifford also recalled that at his bedside was 'a learned man which could speak no English'; Philip 'spake to him in Latin', saying 'that goodly men in time of extreme afflictions, did comfort and support themselves with the remembrance of their former life, in which they had glorified God. It is not so in me, I have no comfort that way. All things in my former life have been vain, vain, vain.'

Although speech was painful, Philip exhorted his brothers Robert and Thomas 'in an affectionated manner' with various instructions, 'and namely to learn by him that all things here are vanity'. When he could no longer speak, he gestured that he still wanted to be spoken to, and became distressed if speech stopped. As Gifford recorded:

> When he was so far changed, that his eyes were shut up, his breath seemed to come but even from the upper part of his breast; his hands so cold that all natural heat and life seemed utterly gone out of them, we supposed that his senses and understanding had failed, and that it was to no purpose to speak any longer to him. But it was far otherwise. For I said thus unto him, 'Sir, if you hear what we say let us by some other means know it, and if you still have your inward joy and consolation in God, hold up your hands.' With that he lifted up his hand and stretched it forth on high, which we thought he could scarcely have moved . . . After this, requiring of him to lift up his hands to God that we might see that his heart did still pray to the Almighty, he lifted both his hands, and set them together at his breast and held them upwards after the manner of those which make humble petition; and so his hands remained, and were so still that they would have so continued standing up but that we took them the one from the other.[66]

Philip Sidney died at Arnhem at 2 p.m. on Monday 17 October 1586. He was thirty-one years old.

Over the coming months, lavish testimonials to Philip were ten a penny. But the first to be written was perhaps the most eloquent. Dr James wrote in his journal during the evening of 17 October:

> This afternoon about two o'clock, the most virtuous and honourable gentleman Sir Philip Sidney, Lord Governor of Vlissingen [Flushing] being clean worn away with weakness (all strength of nature failing to continue longer life in him) departed in wonderful perfect memory even to the last gasp, and in so good and godly a mind, as they that were present stood astonished, in doubt whether they should receive greater comfort of the manner of his death, or grief for the loss of so rare a gentleman and so accomplished with all kind of virtue and true nobility, as few ages have ever brought forth his equal, and the very hope of our age seemeth to be utterly extinguished in him.[67]

Epilogue

LEICESTER'S GOVERNORSHIP OF the Netherlands ended in failure. He returned to England in December 1587 and died on 4 September 1588.

SIR ROBERT SIDNEY succeeded as Earl of Leicester on his uncle's death. He also filled Philip's role as Governor of Flushing and built an impressive London home which gave his name to Leicester Square. He died in 1626.

THOMAS SIDNEY died in the Netherlands in 1595, aged twenty-six.

LADY FRANCES SIDNEY was pregnant at the time of Philip's death, but appears to have miscarried in December 1586. She secretly married Philip's friend Robert Devereux, Earl of Essex, in 1590. Eight pregnancies (although only three surviving children) followed before Essex was executed for treason in 1601. The widowed Frances then made a third marriage to the Earl of Clanrickarde. She died in 1632.

LADY MARY, THE COUNTESS OF PEMBROKE, 'completed' some of Philip's unfinished writings and co-ordinated the publication of his work. His *Arcadia* thus became known for all time as *The Countess of Pembroke's Arcadia*.

FULKE GREVILLE aided the Countess in her editorial endeavours and wrote his life of Sidney, planned as a dedication to an edition of his own writings, which he seems to have taken up only after Philip's death. He never married and was stabbed to death by a manservant in 1628.

Notes

The following abbreviations are used in the notes; bibliographical information is confined to the bibliography:

EW	(Sir) Edward Waterhouse
FW	(Sir) Francis Walsingham
HL	Hubert Languet
HS	(Sir) Henry Sidney
JC	Joachim Camerarius
MDS	Lady Mary Dudley, later Lady Sidney
MS	Mary Sidney Herbert, Countess of Pembroke
PC	Privy Council
PS	(Sir) Philip Sidney
RD	Robert Dudley, Earl of Leicester
RS	(Sir) Robert Sidney
TS	Sir Thomas Smith
TW	(Sir) Thomas Wilson
WC	Sir William Cecil, later Lord Burghley
WD	William Davison
APC	*Acts of the Privy Council*
Arcana	Hubert Languet, *Arcana secvli decimi sexti, Hvberti Langveti . . . epistolae secretae ad . . . Avgvstum Sax. dvcem*
BL	British Library, London
BN	Bibliothèque Nationale, Paris
Bodl.	Bodleian Library, Oxford
Bruce	*Correspondence of Robert Dudley, earl of Leycester, during his government of the Low Countries, in the years 1585 and 1586*, ed. John Bruce
Brugmans	H. Brugmans, *Correspondentie van Robert Dudley graaf van Leycester en andere documenten betreffende zijn gouvernement-generaal in de Nederlanden 1585–1588*
C	Hubert Languet, *Ad Joachimum Camerarium patrem, & Ioachim Camerarium, filium, medicum, scriptae Epistolae*, ed. Ludovicus Camerarius [epistle no. followed by sig. ref.]
Carew	*Calendar of the Carew Manuscripts preserved in the Archiepiscopal Library at Lambeth 1575–1588*, ed. J.S. Brewer and William Butler
Chéruel	A. Chéruel, *Marie Stuart et Catherine de Médicis: étude historique sur les relations de la France et de l'Écosse*

CSPD	*Calendar of State Papers*, Domestic
CSPF	*Calendar of State Papers*, Foreign
CSPI	*Calendar of State Papers*, Irish
CSP Rome	*Calendar of State Papers*, Rome
CSPS	*Calendar of State Papers*, Spanish
CSP Scotland	*Calendar of State Papers*, Scotland
CKS	Centre for Kentish Studies, Maidstone, Kent
Collins	Arthur Collins, *Letters and Memorials of State . . . Written and collected by Sir Henry Sydney [et al.]*
Collins, 'Memoirs'	Arthur Collins, 'Memoirs', in Collins [see above]
Devereux	Devereux, Walter Bourchier, ed., *Lives and Letters of the Devereux, earls of Essex, in the reigns of Elizabeth, James I., and Charles I. 1540–1646*
Digges	Dudley Digges, *The Compleat Ambassador: or two Treaties of the Intended Marriage of Qu: Elizabeth Of Glorious Memory*
DNB	*Dictionary of National Biography*, ed. Leslie Stephen and Stephen Lee
DP	*The Defence of Poesie*
EHR	*English Historical Review*
F	Albert Feuillerat, ed., *The Complete Works of Philip Sidney* [epistle no. followed by volume and page ref.]
FSL	Folger Shakespeare Library, Washington DC
Greville, 'Dedication'	Fulke Greville, 'A Dedication to Sir Philip Sidney', in *The Prose Works of Fulke Greville, Lord Brooke*, ed. John Gouws
Hasler	P.W. Hasler, ed., *The House of Commons 1558–1603*
HLQ	*Huntington Library Quarterly*
HMC	Historical Manuscripts Commission
HMCD	HMC, *Report on the Manuscripts of Lord de L'Isle & Dudley Preserved at Penshurst Place*
HMCR	HMC, *The Manuscripts of his Grace the Duke of Rutland . . . preserved at Belvoir Castle*
HMCS	HMC, *Calendar of the Manuscripts of the Most Hon. The Marquis of Salisbury, K.G. . . . preserved at Hatfield House, Hertfordshire*
JWCI	*Journal of the Warburg and Courtauld Institutes*
L	Hubert Languet, *Epistolae politicae et historicae. Scriptae quondam ad illustrem, & generosum dominum Philippum Sydnaeum* [epistle no. followed by sig. ref.]
Lettenhove	Kervyn de Lettenhove, Joseph, Baron de, ed., *Relations politiques des Pays-Bas et de l'Angleterre*
'Memoir'	'Sir Henry Sidney's memoir of his government of Ireland, 1583', *The Ulster Journal of Archæology* 3 (1855) 33–52, 85–99 and 336–57; 5 (1857), 299–323; 8 (1860), 179–95

MP	*Miscellaneous Prose of Sir Philip Sidney*, ed. Katherine Duncan-Jones and Jan van Dorsten
Moffet, *Nobilis*	Thomas Moffet, *Nobilis or A View of the Life and Death of a Sidney and Lessus Lugubris*, trans./ed. Virgil B. Heltzel and Hoyt H. Hudson
NA	Philip Sidney, *The Countess of Pembroke's Arcadia (The New Arcadia)*, ed. Victor Skretkowicz
Nicollier-De Weck	Béatrice Nicollier-De Weck, *Hubert Languet (1518–1581): un réseau politique international de Melanchthon à Guillaume d'Orange*
NQ	*Notes and Queries*
OA	Philip Sidney, *The Countess of Pembroke's Arcadia (The Old Arcadia)*, ed. Jean Robertson
Osborn	James M. Osborn, *Young Philip Sidney 1572–1577*
PMLA	*Publications of the Modern Language Association of America*
Ringler	*The Poems of Sir Philip Sidney*, ed. William A. Ringler, Jr.
PRO	Public Record Office, London
SJ	*Sidney Journal*
SNJ	*Sidney Newsletter and Journal*
SP	State Papers
TCC	Trinity College, Cambridge
van Dorsten, *Poets*	J.A. van Dorsten, *Poets, Patrons, and Professors: Sir Philip Sidney, Daniel Rogers, and the Leiden humanists*
Wallace	Malcolm William Wallace, *The Life of Sir Philip Sidney*
Wright	Wright, Thomas, ed., *Queen Elizabeth and her Times, a series of original letters*

INTRODUCTION

1 Aubrey, *Brief Lives*, ed. Dick, 280.

2 Lant, *Sequitur celebritas et pompa funebris.*

3 Holinshed, *Chronicles*, 3: 1555; see also Greville, 'Dedication', 85.

4 *Academiae Cantabrigiensis Lachyrmæ tvmvlo Nobilissimi Equitis, D. Philippi Sidneij Sacratæ*, ed. Neville; *Exeqviæ illvstrissimi eqvitis, D. Philippi Sidnaei, gratissimæ memoriæ ac nomini impensæ*, ed. Gager; *Peplvs illvstrissimi viri D. Philippi Sidnaei svpremis honoribvs dicatvs*, ed. Lloyd; D[ay], *Vpon the life and death of the most worthy, and thrise renowned knight, Sir Phillip Sidney*; Phillip, *The Life and Death of Sir Philip Sidney, late Lord gouernour of Flvshing*; Churchyard, *The Epitaph of Sir Phillip Sidney Knight, lately Lord Gouernour of Flushing*; W[hetstone], *Sir Phillip Sidney, his honorable life, his valiant death, and true vertues.*

5 For the publishing of PS's works, see Woudhuysen, *Sir Philip Sidney and the Circulation of Manuscripts 1558–1640.*

6 Greville, 'Dedication'; Moffet, *Nobilis.*

7 *CSPD 1581–1590*, 90.

8 Greville, 'Dedication', 10–11.

Notes

1: A Dudley in Blood

1 Sidney family psalter. TCC MS R.17.2, fo. 6a. These entries, dating from 1529 to 1584 on a calendar preceding the psalter, were probably entered *en masse* c. 1583–4, but the precise wording of this entry suggests that it was transcribed from another, contemporary source. On the psalter, see James, *The Western Manuscripts in the library of Trinity College, Cambridge*, 2: 410–1.

2 Holinshed, *Chronicles*, 3: 1548.

3 'Memoir' 8: 192–3. For Edward's household, see Jordan, *Edward VI: The Young King: The protectorship of the duke of Somerset*, 38. For HS's appointment as a gentleman of the bedchamber, see Edward VI's chronicle, 18 April 1550. *The Chronicle and Political Papers of King Edward VI*, ed. Jordan, 25.

4 Northumberland to PC, 4 June 1552, Otford. *CSPD 1547–1553*, 239. Edward VI's chronicle, 11 October 1551. Jordan, *Chronicle*, 86. For Northumberland, see Jordan, *Edward VI: The Threshold of Power*; Beer, *Northumberland*; Loades, *John Dudley Duke of Northumberland*.

5 Heylyn, *Ecclesia Restaurata*, U2ʳ–Y4ᵛ at U4ʳ. See Chapman, *Lady Jane Grey: October 1537–February 1554*, 90.

6 Davey, *The Nine Days' Queen: Lady Jane Grey and her Times*, ed. Hume, 250–1.

7 MacCulloch, ed./trans., 'The *Vitae Mariae Reginae Angliae* of Robert Wingfield of Brantham', 262.

8 Northampton to Sir John Mason, 8 June 1551. *CSPF 1547–1553*, 122–3. Northampton et al. to PC, 17 June 1551, Nantes. *CSPF 1547–1553*, 146.

9 Warrant to Sir John Williams to pay HS £200, 27 December 1552, Greenwich. *APC 1552–1554*, 196. Sir William Pickering to WC, 17 January 1553, Paris. *CSPF 1547–1553*, 238. Pickering to PC, 17 January 1553, Paris. *CSPF 1547–1553*, 238.

10 Northumberland to WC, 28 December 1552. *CSPD 1547–1553*, 284. In 1552, Thomas Hoby, occupied in Paris with translating Baldessar Castiglione's *The Courtier* into English, allegedly sent HS an *Epitome of the Italian Tongue*. Wallace, 16–17.

11 On Philip of Spain, see Kamen, *Philip of Spain*.

12 Proclamation announcing articles of marriage with Philip of Spain, 14 January 1554, Westminster. *Tudor Royal Proclamations*, ed. Hughes and Larkin, 2: 24–5.

13 Philip II to Simon Renard, 16 February 1554. *CSPS January–July 1554*, 104. See Loades, 'Philip II and the government of England'.

14 On Penshurst, see Dollman and Jobbins, *An Analysis of Ancient Domestic Architecture*, vol. 2, unpaginated pp. 3–7 of notes; Sidney, *Historical Guide to Penshurst Place*; Wayne, *Penshurst: The Semiotics of Place and the Poetics of History*; [Oliphant], *Penshurst Place and Gardens*; Jonson, *Workes*, Zzz 2–Zzz 3.

15 Sidney family psalter. TCC MS R.17.2, fo. 4a.

16 'Memoir' 8: 192.

17 Holinshed, *Chronicles*, 2: 150.

18 Quoted in Anon., *Penshurst Place*, 3.

19 Sidney, *Historical Guide*, 8–9.

20 On Jane Dormer, see *DNB* 15: 245–7; Clifford, *The Life of Jane Dormer Duchess of Feria transcribed by E.E. Estcourt*, ed. Stevenson. According to Clifford (writing c. 1640), two of HS's sisters, Mabel and Elizabeth, noted 'for their rare virtue and zeal in Catholic religion', had served in Mary's household (see Clifford, *Life of Jane Dormer*, 13, 62–3). However, HS's four sisters were named Mary, Lucy, Anne and Frances, and there is no mention of any Sidney sister in the official records: see Merton, 'The women who served Queen Mary and Queen Elizabeth: Ladies, gentlewomen and maids of the Privy Chamber, 1553–1603'.

21 Last will and testament of the Duchess of Northumberland, 1554. Collins, 'Memoirs' 1: 33–6 at 34.

22 McCoy, 'From the Tower to the tiltyard: Robert Dudley's return to glory'; Adams, 'The Dudley Clientèle, 1553–1563'.

23 Collins, 'Memoirs' 1: 37.

24 HS's passport to the kings of the Romans and of Bohemia, n.d.: *CSPD 1553–1558*, 98 (bis). Allowance to HS, 6 May 1555, Hampton Court. *APC 1554–1556*, 126.

25 'Memoir' 8: 193.

26 'Memoir' 8: 193. For Sussex's deputyship, see Brady, *The Chief Governors: The rise and fall of reform government in Tudor Ireland 1536–1588*, ch. 3.

27 'Record of payment to certain ministers under Henry Sidney, to 19 July 1557, at Athlone'. CKS U1475 O25/1.

28 Sidney family psalter. TCC MS R.17.2, fos 5b, 6a.

29 PS to Robert Walker, 22 February 1577. CKS U1475 F26/5; F26 (3: 104).

30 PS's horoscope, 1570. Bodl. Ashmole MS 356(5); trans. Osborn, 518.

31 HMCD 1: 240.

32 Moffet, *Nobilis*, 71.

33 Bodl. Ashmole MS 356(5); trans. Osborn, 518.

34 Moffet, *Nobilis*, 70–1; *Astrophil and Stella*, sonnet 11, Ringler, 170.

35 For the early years of Elizabeth's reign see MacCaffrey, *The Shaping of the Elizabethan Regime*. For WC's 'old room' see Sir John Alen to WC, 16 December 1558, Dublin. *CSPI 1509–1573*, 151.

36 Rodrigeuz-Salgado and Adams, eds, 'The count of Feria's dispatch to Philip II of 14 November 1558'.

37 Wilson, *Sweet Robin: A Biography of Robert Dudley, Earl of Leicester 1533–1588*, 78–81. See also Kendall, *Robert Dudley Earl of Leicester*; Haynes, *The White Bear: Robert Dudley, The Elizabethan Earl of Leicester*.

38 On Ambrose Dudley see *DNB* 16: 97–8.

39 See 'Coronation Roll', PRO LC 2/4/3, fo. 104, cit. Merton, 'Women who served Mary and Elizabeth'.

40 Robert Beale, 'A Treatise of the Office of a Councellor and Principall Secretarie to her Majestie', printed in Read, *Mr Secretary Walsingham and the policy of Queen Elizabeth*, 1: 423–43 at 437. See Wright, 'A change in direction: the ramifications of a female household, 1558–1603'; Merton, 'Women who served Mary and Elizabeth'.

41 [Unknown] to Sir Thomas Challoner, 25 November 1559, Westminster. *CSPF 1559–1560*, 137.

42 Challoner to WC, 1 December 1559, Brussels. *CSPF 1559–1560*, 154.

43 Sir Nicholas Throckmorton to Elizabeth, and Throckmorton to WC, both 20 February 1560, Blois. *CSPF 1559–1560*, 390, 391.

44 BL Lansdowne MS 94, fo. 29 cit. Wilson, *Sweet Robin*, 97.

45 Feria to Philip II, 18 April 1559, London. *CSPS 1558–1567*, 57–8.

46 De Quadra to Philip II, 13 December 1559, London. *CSPS 1558–1567*, 118. Henry Killigrew to Throckmorton, 10 October 1560, London. *CSPF 1560–1561*, 350.

47 Richard Lord Rich and Thomas Mildmay to WC, 13 August 1560, and enclosure. *CSPD 1547–1580*, 21.

48 Quoted in Wright, 'A change in direction', 169.

49 De Quadra to Philip II, 13 November 1559, n.p.. *CSPS 1558–1567*, 113–14.

50 MacCaffrey, *Shaping*, 73.

51 De Quadra to the Duchess of Parma, 7 September 1559, London. *CSPS 1558–1567*, 95–6.

52 De Quadra to the Bishop of Arras, 7 September 1559, London. *CSPS 1558–1567*, 96.

53 De Quadra to Alba, 2 October 1559, London. *CSPS 1558–1567*, 98–102. See also de Quadra to Philip II, 5 October 1559, London. *CSPS 1558–1567*, 105; de Quadra to Ferdinand, 16 October 1559, London. *CSPS 1558–1567*, 107.

54 De Quadra to Philip II, 13 November 1559. *CSPS 1558–1567*, 111.

55 De Quadra to Philip II, 18 November 1559, London. *CSPS 1558–1567*, 115–16.

56 For this campaign, see MacCaffrey, *Shaping*, 77–85.

57 WC to Throckmorton, 8 May 1561, Greenwich. *CSPF 1561–2*, 104.

58 De Quadra to Philip II, 5 May 1561, London. *CSPS 1558–1567*, 203.

59 HL to Mordeisen, 16 June 1561, Antwerp. *Arcana*, pt 2, ep. 47, p. 117; trans. Chamberlin, *Elizabeth and Leycester*, 93.

60 On Warwick, see *DNB* 16: 97–8.

61 CKS U1475 F1.

62 Geoffrey Fenton to MDS, 22 June 1567, Paris, in Fenton, *Certaine Tragical Discourses writen out of Frenche and Latin*, ¶.v.ʳ.

63 The report of Ahasverus Allinga, 30 January 1564, London. As rendered in von Klarwill, *Queen Elizabeth and Some Foreigners*, trans. North, 180–99 at 190.

64 Memorandum by WC, [1567]. *A Collection of State Papers . . . Now remaining at Hatfield House*, ed. Haynes, 444; dated by Haynes April 1566.

65 Holinshed, *Chronicles*, 3: 1550.

66 HS to PS, [1566?]. Collins 1: 8–9.

67 'Defence of the Earl of Leicester'. *MP*, 134–9.

2: YOUR SON AND MY SCHOLAR

1 Williams, *The Council in the Marches of Wales under Elizabeth I*. For Hyddye, see 'The Account Book of William Poughnull and Richard Farr bailiffs and John Holland chamberlain 26 October 3 Elizabeth', fo. 12a [entry for 13 October 1562], pr. in Ludlow Historical Research Group, *Ludlow Bailiffs' Accounts 1561–2*, 15.

2 Campion, in *The Histories of Ireland*, ed. Ware, M3ᵛ.

3 Churchyard, *The Worthines of Wales*, J3ʳ⁻ᵛ.

4 Powel, *The historie of Cambria, now called Wales*, ¶.iij.ᵛ, ¶.iiij.ʳ.

5 Barber, 'England II: Monarchs, Ministers, and Maps, 1550–1625', 67.

6 Owen and Blakeway, *A History of Shrewsbury*, 1: 354, 355, 356–7, 371–2 and 372 n.1.

7 HS to Elizabeth, 1 November 1560. PRO SP 12/14 art. 38. Elizabeth to Winchester, 2 November 1560. PRO SP 12/14/39, both *CSPD 1547–1580*, 163 and cit. Williams, *Council in the Marches*, 129.

8 'Accounts of the household in Wales', 1559–62. CKS U1475 O61.

9 Instructions to HS, 15 July 1562. Haynes, *State Papers*, 391–3.

10 Randolph to WC, 4 August 1562, Berwick. *CSPF 1562*, 206–7.

11 Challoner to WC, 20 July 1563, Madrid. *CSPF 1563*, 468.

12 MDS to Cockrane, 22 July 1573. CKS U1500 C1/3.

13 'Memoir', 8: 191–2 quoting Psalm 102.6. See also Merton, 'Women who served Mary and Elizabeth', 89.

14 In December 1565, HS reported that he and his wife had passed thirty days 'flitting' from place to place on the coast. HS to WC, 17 December 1565, Beaumaris. PRO SP 63/15 art. 66. In a service held by Adam Loftus, Archbishop of Dublin, at St Patrick's around Easter 1567, MDS was a communicant. Loftus to WC, 25 January 1568, Dublin. PRO SP 63/23 art. 18.

15 On 4 May 1570, HS asked 'to have his wife sent over'. HS to PC, 4 May 1570, Dublin. PRO SP 63/30 art. 50. On 21 June 1570, he urged EW 'to hasten the arrival of Lady Sidney'. HS to EW, 28 May 1570, Dublin Castle. PRO SP 63/30 art. 55.1.

16 *Autobiographical Tracts of Dr. John Dee, Warden of the College of Manchester*, ed. Crossley, 11. On Dee and the Dudleys, see French, *John Dee: The World of an Elizabethan Magus*, 126–7.

17 *Astrophil and Stella*, sonnet 63, Ringler, 196.

18 Moffet, *Nobilis*, 71–2.

19 CKS U 1475 A54 [2], A33/3 and A4/4.

20 HS to Lady Mildred Cecil, 2 October 1569, Dublin. HMCS 1: 439.

21 Camden, *Britain, or A Chorographicall Description of the most flourishing Kingdomes, England,*

Scotland, and Ireland, and the Ilands adioyning, out of the depth of Antiqvitie, trans. Holland, Ddd2ᵛ.

22 CKS U1475 Q31/1–21 and Q32/1–3. For the prolonged challenges to these posts, see Wallace 28–33. The legal documents already describe PS as 'scholaris', but his official education did not begin until November of that year.

23 Guzman de Silva to Philip II, 21 November 1564, London. *CSPS 1558–1567*, 393.

24 Williams, *Council in the Marches*, 258.

25 On Shrewsbury, see Champion, *Everyday Life in Tudor Shrewsbury*; Coulton, 'The establishment of Protestantism in a provincial town: a study of Shrewsbury in the sixteenth century'; Collinson, 'The Shearmen's Tree and the Preacher: The strange death of Merry England in Shrewsbury and beyond'.

26 Bentham to Parker, 11 April 1561. 'The Letter-Book of Thomas Bentham, Bishop of Coventry and Lichfield', ed. O'Day and Berlatsky, 210–11.

27 I follow Oldham in identifying Ashton as the St John's scholar, rather than the Trinity College, Cambridge fellow. Oldham, *Headmasters of Shrewsbury School 1552–1908*, 9–10.

28 On Shrewsbury School see also Rimmer and Adnitt, *A History of Shrewsbury School from the Blakeway MSS . . . and many other sources*; Fisher, *Annals of Shrewsbury School*, rev. Hill; Oldham, *Headmasters*, 9–15; Baldwin, *William Shakspere's Small Latine & Lesse Greeke*, 1: 388–92. I am also indebted to discussions with Warren Boutcher: see his related 'Pilgrimage to Parnassus: Local intellectual traditions, humanist education and the cultural geography of sixteenth-century England'.

29 Camden, *Britain*, Ddd2ᵛ.

30 Shrewsbury School Register, pr. as Calvert, ed., *Shrewsbury School Regestum Scholarum 1562–1635. Admittances and Readmittances*, 15.

31 CKS U1475 A35.

32 Champion, *Tudor Shrewsbury*, 38.

33 On Leigh, see Hasler 2: 457; Champion, *Tudor Shrewsbury*, 72–3. I am extremely grateful to Mr James Lawson, Taylor Librarian and Archivist at Shrewsbury School, for his advice on the significance of Leigh.

34 PRO E.133/1/36, cit. Bowden, *The Wool Trade in Tudor and Stuart England*, 92.

35 Champion, *Tudor Shrewsbury*, 41.

36 School Ordinances and Bailiff's Ordinances: Baker, *History of the College of St John the Evangelist, Cambridge*, ed. Mayor, 405–13; Rimmer and Adnitt, *History of Shrewsbury School*, 46–52; Scott, *Notes from the Records of St John's College Cambridge*.

37 Rimmer and Adnitt, *History of Shrewsbury School*, 52.

38 Leighton, ed., 'Early chronicles of Shrewsbury 1372–1603'. See also Somerset, ed., *Shropshire*, 1: 204, 207–11.

39 Matteo Bandello, *Histoires Tragiques*, trans. François de Belleforest (1559), [PS's copy] in Canterbury, King's School, Walpole Collection. See Robertson, 'Sidney and Bandello'.

40 Fenton, *Certaine Tragical Discourses*, ¶ ij.ʳ– ¶ vi.ʳ. For the opposite view, see Hadfield, 'Sidney's comments on history in *An Apology for Poetry* and Geoffrey Fenton's *Tragicall Discourses*: a note', 50.

41 HS and MDS to PS [1566?]. Collins 1: 8–9.

42 *A Very Godly letter made, by the right Honourable Sir Henry Sidney* . . . (1591).

43 Moffet, *Nobilis*, 72–3.

44 Greville, 'Dedication', 5.

45 Marshall's accounts, CKS U1475 A35, pr. in Wallace as Appendix I (405–23). For the Ordinances, see note 36 above.

46 See Pacheco to Philip II, 2 September 1565, London. *CSPS 1558–1567*, 473–4. See also Guzman de Silva, 24 September 1565, London. *CSPS 1558–1567*, 481.

47 'Memoir' 8: 191.

48 See Fitzwilliam to WC, 18 March 1571, St Sepulchre's. PRO SP 63/31 art. 28: '[the bearer is] going aboard with my L. Deputy his children to the sea.'

49 CKS U1475 A35; Wallace, 411, 412.

50 'At the christening of a son of Mr Leigh's who beareth his name given to midwife 20d. and to the nurse 10d. and more money was offered to the mother but it would not be taken . . . my Lady Newport being godmother'. CKS U1475 A35; Wallace, 413.

51 An earlier attempt at this journey in late July had also included his host George Leigh and schoolfellow Edward Onslowe.

52 Duncan-Jones, *Sir Philip Sidney Courtier Poet*, 34.

53 *Letters of Thomas Wood, Puritan, 1566–1577*, ed. Collinson, 13.

54 Gúzman de Silva to Philip II, 12 December 1566. *CSPS 1558–1567*, 605.

55 William Rowe to RD, Frankfurt. Quoted in Hannay, *Philip's Phoenix: Mary Sidney, Countess of Pembroke*, 18.

56 Dop, *Eliza's Knights: Soldiers, poets, and puritans in the Netherlands 1572–1586*, 9, 157.

57 Ringler, xvii.

58 Bodl. Ashmole MS 356(5); trans. Osborn, 519.

59 Gray's Inn Admissions Register, fo. 572. Foster, *The Register of Admissions to Gray's Inn, 1521–1889*, col. 37. Duncan-Jones gives 1566/7 but admissions from that period are on fo. 563, including the Earl of Oxford on 1 February 1566/7.

60 Cooper, *Thesavrvs Lingvae Romanæ & Britannicæ*. On Cooper see Rosenberg, *Leicester Patron of Letters*, 125–8; McConica, ed., *History of the University of Oxford*, vol. 3, *The Collegiate University*, 233 n. 1, 367–8.

61 Wood, *Athenae Oxonienses*, 1: 609–11.

62 PS to WC, 26 February 1570, Oxford. BL Lansdowne MS 12, art. 50; F3 (3: 76–7).

63 RD to Mathew Parker, 3 March 1570. Quoted in Wallace, 102.

64 Moffet, *Nobilis*, 84.

65 McConica, *History of the University of Oxford*, 3: 693–5.

66 PS to WC, 26 February 1570, Oxford. BL Lansdowne MS 12, art. 50; F3 (3: 76–7).

Wood asserts that Thornton succeeded Day as canon in 1567 (*Athenae* 3: 922).

67 Wood, *Athenae* 4: 225. There is no independent evidence to support the Puritan controversialist Nathaniel Baxter's claim that he was Philip's tutor. See B[axter], *Sir Philip Sydneys Ouránia, That is, Endimions Song and Tragedie, Containing all Philosophie*, N^v; *DNB* 3: 428–9.

68 Ringler, xviii.

69 PS to RS, 18 October 1580, Leicester House. CKS U1475 C7/8; F92 (3: 132).

70 [Hakluyt], *Divers voyages touching the discouerie of America, and the Ilands adiacent vnto the same*, ¶ – ¶ 4^r.

71 BL Cotton MS Appendix LXII, fo. 4a, cit. Wallace 310 n. 72. Wallace, 102.

72 On Allen, see Foster, 'Thomas Allen (1540–1632), Gloucester Hall and the survival of Catholicism in post-Reformation Oxford'.

73 Moffet, *Nobilis*, 76.

74 Carew, *The Svrvey of Cornwall*, Dd 2^v.

75 Bodl. Ashmole MS 356(5); trans. Osborn, 15–16.

76 PS to WC, 8 July 1569, Oxford. BL Lansdowne 11, art. 77; F2 (3: 75–6); trans. Wallace, 94–5. See also PS to WC, 12 March 1569, Oxford. PRO SP 12/49 art. 63; F1 (3: 75); trans. Fox-Bourne, *Memoir*, 34.

77 HS to Lady Cecil, 26 October 1569, Dublin Castle. HMCS 1: 439.

78 WC to HS, 3 September 1568, Wallingford. PRO SP 63/25 art. 75.

79 WC to HS, 10 August 1568, Brickhill. PRO SP 63/25, art. 63.

80 HS to WC, 8 August 1568, Salop. CKS U1475 C1, fo. 136a.

81 HS to WC, 30 November 1568, Maryboroughe. CKS U1475 C1, fo. 140a.

82 WC to HS, 6 January 1569, n.p. PRO SP 63/27, art. 2.

83 WC to HS, 2 February 1569, Hampton Court. PRO SP 63/27 art. 17.

84 HS to WC, 7 April 1569, The Newry. HMCS 1: 404–5.

85 Statement of value of HS's lands, 1568. BL Lansdowne MS 10, fos. 187a–192a. Settlements for the proposed marriage of Philip Sidney and Anne, daughter of Sir Wm Cecil, 6 August 1569. HMCS 1: 415–16.

86 Thomas to WC, 24 October 1569, Dublin. PRO SP 63/29 art. 69.

87 Nicholas White to WC, 27 October 1569, Dublin. PRO SP 63/29 art. 74.

88 HS to WC, 14 February 1570, Dublin Castle. CKS U1475 C1, fo. 143a.

89 On Oxford see *DNB* 58: 225–9.

90 J. Lord St John to Rutland, 28 July 1571, n.p. HMCR 1: 94.

91 Fitzwilliam to WC, 19 August 1571, St Sepulchre's. *CSPI 1509–73*, 454.

92 WC to Rutland, 15 August 1571, Hatfield. HMCR 1: 95.

93 Beckingsale, *Burghley: Tudor Statesman*, 290–1.

94 On HS's Lord Deputyships, see 'Memoir', *passim*; Campion, *Histories of Ireland*, L3^v–M3^v; Lynam, 'Sir Henry Sidney'; Brady, *Chief Governors*, chs. 4–7. For relevant correspondence, see Ó Laidhin, ed., *Sidney State Papers 1565–70*. On PS and Ireland, see Maley, 'Sir Philip Sidney and Ireland'.

95 HS to Elizabeth, 20 April 1567, Kilmaynham. Collins 1: 18–31 at 24.

96 HS to RD, 28 June 1566, Kilmaynham. Collins 1: 14–15 at 14.

97 HS to RD, 5 September 1566, Drogheda. HMC, *Report on the Pepys Manuscripts preserved at Magdalene College, Cambridge*, 89–90.

98 Campion, *Histories of Ireland*, L4ᵛ; 'Memoir' 3: 44.

99 Account by HS's physician, c. February 1568. PRO SP 15/14 art. 6, cit. Brady, *Chief Governors*, 127.

100 HS to WC, 24 February 1569, Dublin Castle. Collins 1: 43–4 at 43.

101 'Memoir' 3: 347.

102 Brady, 'Court, castle and country', 29. See also Maley, *Salvaging Spenser*, ch. 5. For the 1541 Act see Curtis and McDowell, eds, *Irish Historical Documents, 1172–1922*. 77.

103 Derricke, *The Image of Irelande, with a discourse of Woodkarne*, plate 12, discussed in Hadfield and Maley, 'Introduction: Irish representatives and English alternatives', 13.

104 Greville, 'Dedication', 5.

105 Elizabeth to HS, 19 August 1570, Tuddington. *Sidney State Papers 1565–70*, 137.

106 Campion, *Histories of Ireland*, M3ᵛ; 'Memoir' 5: 308.

107 CKS U1475 A53.

108 W[hetstone], *Sir Phillip Sidney, his honorable life*, B2ʳ. Laurence Humphreys, 'Ad vtramqve academiam, Philippi Sidnæi vmbra', in *Exeqviæ illvstrissimi eqvitis, D. Philippi Sidnaei*, *4ᵛ. See Wallace, 105–7 and Buxton, *Sir Philip Sidney and the English Renaissance*, 43, for the Cambridge hypothesis, countered by Boas, *Sir Philip Sidney, Representative Elizabethan*, 21–2.

109 Dee, *Autobiographical Tracts*, 11. French speculates on this: see French, *John Dee*, 127.

3: Young and Raw

1 Instructions for Lincoln, 25 May 1572, St James. Digges, 206–11. Licence for PS, 25 May 1572, St James. New College, Oxford MS 328–2, fo. 40; Buxton and Juel-Jensen, 'Sir Philip Sidney's first passport rediscovered'.

2 For Bryskett, see *DNB* 7: 168–9; superseded by Plomer and Cross, *The Life and Correspondence of Lodowick Bryskett*; Jones, 'Lodowick Bryskett and his family'.

3 Br[yskett], *A Discovrse of Civill Life*, C4ᵛ–Dʳ.

4 HMCD 1: 413.

5 Fitzwilliam to WC, 7 April 1571. PRO SP 12/32 art. 3.

6 'Names of the Lords and Gentlemen who attended the Earl of Lincoln into France, 1557 (sic)'. HMCS 1: 146. See also Bell, *A Handlist of British Diplomatic Representatives 1509–1688*, 91–2.

7 This account drawn from Smith to WC, 18 June 1572, Louvre. BL Cotton MS Vespasian F. vi, fo. 93; in *Original Letters, illustrative of English history*, ed. Ellis, 3: 12–22.

8 On FW, see Stählin, *Sir Francis Walsingham und seine Zeit*; Read, *Mr Secretary Walsingham*.

9   RD to FW, 26 May 1572, Court. BL Lansdowne MS 117, fo. 159b.

10 FW to RD, 17 October 1572, Paris BL Cotton MS Vespasian. F. vi., fo. 189a.

11 WC to FW, n.d. (before 5 July 1572), n.p. Digges, 218.

12 FW to WC, 22 June 1572, Paris. *CSPF 1572–1574*, 135.

13 FW to WC, 20 June 1572, Paris. Digges, 213.

14 For HL, see Chevreul, *Étude sur le XVIᵉ siècle: Hubert Languet,* now superseded by Nicollier-De Weck. For Beale's registration at Wittenberg in May 1560, see *Album Academiae Vitebergensis ab A. Ch. MDII usque ad A. MDCII,* vol. 2, ed. Hartwig, p. 4 [col. a, line 37]. HL was in Wittenberg in October–November 1560, see HL to Mordeisen, 6 October 1560, Wittenberg (*Arcana* pt 2, ep. 29, p. 65); 5 November 1560 (*Arcana* pt 2, ep. 31, p. 69) and 27 November 1560 (*Arcana* pt 2, ep. 32, p. 78), all from Wittenberg. Nicollier-De Weck, 501–2. On Beale, see Patricia Brewerton, 'Paper Trails: Re-reading Robert Beale as Clerk to the Privy Council'.

15 *Journal of Sir Francis Walsingham, from Dec. 1570 to April 1583,* ed. Martin, entry for 18 January 1571 (p.3); see also entries for 4 and 7 June 1571 (p. 8), 26 June 1571 (p. 9), 4 July 1571 (p. 9).

16 HL sent reports of his audience with Charles IX and Cathérine de Médicis on 25 June 1572 not only to Augustus, but also to the Palatine minister Ehem, who sent it on to William of Hesse. Nicollier-De Weck 273 and n. 2.

17 PS to RD, 23 March 1573, Frankfurt. F6 (3: 79).

18 Walsingham, *Journal,* entries for 19 and 26 December 1571 (pp. 1, 3). For Ramus, see Ong, *Ramus: Method, and the Decay of Dialogue.*

19 Ramus, *Commentariorum de Religione Christiana, Libri quatuor* (1577), ed. de Banos, √4ʳ, trans. Buxton, *Sidney and the English Renaissance,* 46.

20 On Wechel, see Evans, *The Wechel Presses.*

21 See HL to JC, 19 June 1571, Paris. C46 (F9ᵛ). HL to JC, 2 July 1571, Paris. C47 (F9 ᵛ).

22 Wolf, *Lucas Geizkoffler und seine Selbstbiographie 1550–1620,* 34. My attention was drawn to this work by Osborn.

23 See Brüning to PS, 31 October 1575, Padua. Yale Osborn MS f a 14, fos 90–1.

24 Wolf, *Geizkoffler,* 56.

25 See Hay, *The Life of Robert Sidney Earl of Leicester (1563–1626),* 32–7.

26 Wolf, *Geizkoffler,* 33.

27 Anonymous newsletter, 18 July 1572, Antwerp. Lettenhove 6: 459–60 at 460.

28 FW to Mr Brocket, 10 August 1572, BL Cotton MS Vespasian F.vi, fo. 122.

29 FW to WC, 10 August 1572, Paris. Digges, 233.

30 Bryskett, *Discovrse,* X3ᵛ–X4ʳ.

31 *Histoire universelle de Jacques–Auguste de Thou,* 6: 374.

32 [Goulart], *Mémoires de l'estat de France sovs Charles IX,* 1:Ij viij.ᵛ.

33 Camden, *Annales rerum Anglicarvm, et Hibernicarvm, regnante Elizabetha, ad annum salvtis M.D.LXXXIX,* Gg 2ᵛ, trans. as *The Historie of the most Renowned and Victorious Princesse Elizabeth, Late Queene of England,* Ggᵛ.

34 Greville, 'Dedication', 20.
35 Wolf, *Geizkofler*, 39.
36 De Serres, *The Three Partes of Commentaries, Containing the whole and perfect discourse of the Ciuil warres of Fraunce*, trans. Timme, 'Fyrst parte', 9.
37 De Serres, *Commentaries*, 'Tenth book', C^v–C.ij.^r.
38 *Mémoires de Maximilien de Bethune, duc de Sully, principal ministre de Henry le Grand*, 1: 20; trans. as *Memoirs of Maximilian de Bethune, duke of Sully, prime minister to Henry the Great*, 1: 18–19.
39 Wolf, *Geizkofler*, 34.
40 On the massacre, see Noguères, *La Saint-Barthélemy 24 août 1572*, trans. Engel as *The Massacre of Saint Bartholomew*; Sutherland, *The Massacre of St Bartholomew and the European conflict 1559–1572*; Kingdon, *Myths about the St. Bartholomew's Day Massacres 1572–1576*.
41 Read, *Walsingham*, 1: 219–20; Kingdon, *Myths*, 28.
42 FW to TS, 24 September 1572, Paris. Digges, 254–5.
43 Wolf, *Geizkofler*, 37–8; trans. Osborn, 64–5.
44 De Serres, *Commentaries*, 'Tenth book', C.iiij.^v.
45 Charles IX to La Mothe Fénélon, 27 August 1572, Paris. *Correspondance diplomatique de Bertrande de Salignac de la Mothe Fénélon*, ed. Teulet, 7: 330.
46 Stählin rejects the latter part of Zuñiga's story: Stählin, *Walsingham und seine Zeit*, 1: 530–1.
47 FW to TS, 27 August 1572, Paris. Digges, 238.
48 FW to TS, 2 September 1572, Paris. Digges, 239.
49 TS to FW, 12 September 1572, Woodstock. Digges, 252–3.
50 Bizari, *Senatus populique genuensis rerum domi fori gestorum historiae*, 562. On Bizari, see Firpo, *Pietro Bizzarri*; Osborn, 'Sidney and Pietro Bizari'.
51 Fox, abridged by Bright, *An Abridgement of the Bookes of Acts and Monuments of the Chvrch*, ¶3^v–¶4^r. On Bright, see Carlton, *Timothie Bright Doctor of Phisicke*; Keynes, *Dr Timothie Bright 1550–1615*, 1–21; Brewerton, 'Crossing boundaries: the career of a sixteenth-century physician'.
52 This paragraph is based on Noguères, *Massacre of Saint Bartholomew*, 100–1. Noguères does not cite his source.
53 Bright, *In physicam Gvlielmi Adolphi Scribonii . . . Animaduersiones*, ¶ ij^r.
54 Bright, *In physicam Scribonii animaduersiones*, ¶ iij[v].
55 Ong, *Ramus*, 28–9.
56 *Mémoires et Correspondance de Du Plessis-Mornay*, ed. Vaudoré and Auguys, 1: 71–2. 'M. de Morvillier' is Jean de Morvillier (1506–77) who was Garde des Sceaux, 1568–70. See also Wolf, *Geizkofler*, 53, 56, 65.
57 *A Letter to Queen Elizabeth, MP*.
58 See, for example, Hunt, 'Consorting with Catholics', 25–6.
59 TS to FW, 12 September 1572, Woodstock. Digges, 253.

60 TS to FW, 12 September 1572, Woodstock. Digges, 252–3.

61 WC, RD, F. Knollys, TS and James Croft to FW, 9 September [1572]. Digges, 246–50.

62 RD to FW, 11 September [1572]. BL Lansdowne MS 117, fo. 198a.

4: AN EXTRAORDINARY YOUNG MAN

1 Nicollier-De Weck, 279.

2 Clasen, *Palatinate in European History*, 3, 6, 12.

3 FW to RD, 17 October 1572. BL Cotton MS Vespasian F. vi, fo. 189a. The flawed copy is in Digges, 273.

4 The confusion arises from Watson's date of admission. An early commentator writes, 'John Watson M.D. admitted Dean of Winch. feb^r. 14. 1572[/3]. on the death of Fran. Newton. yet I think Watson occurrs Dean 16. Febr. 1570'. BL Lansdowne MS 981, fo. 101a; see also Le Neve, *Fasti Ecclesiae Anglicanae*, 3: 2; *DNB*, 60: 13–14. Venn and Venn, *Alumni Cantabrigienses*, pt 1, 3: 252, also date Newton's death to 1572.

5 Digges, 250, 251.

6 PS to RS, 1579? F38 (3: 125–6).

7 Estienne, ed., *Herodian historiarum libri VIII*, ¶ ij.$^{r-v}$.

8 Estienne, *The Frankfort Book Fair*.

9 Greville, 'Dedication', 6.

10 Benzing, *Buchdruckerlexicon des 16. Jahrhunderts*, 57.

11 Strong and van Dorsten, *Leicester's Triumph*, 9; see also Read, *Walsingham*, 1: 151–5.

12 PS to RD, 23 March 1573, Frankfurt. F6 (3: 78–9).

13 PS to William Blunt, 20 March 1573, Frankfurt. F5 (3: 78).

14 PS to RD, 23 March 1573, Frankfurt. F6 (3: 79).

15 'A note of sundry payments for Mr. Philip Sidney' [1573]. CKS U1475 A10/24.

16 Ascham, *The Scholemaster*. For PS and double translation, see HL to PS, 1 January 1574, Vienna. L8 (A11^r–A12^v). PS to HL, 15 January 1573, Padua. F10 (3: 82–3).

17 Mentioned in HL to PS, 4 June 1574, Vienna. L32 (E2^r–E3^r).

18 Koszul, 'Les Sidney et Strasbourg'; Schmidt, *La vie et les travaux de Jean Sturm*; Chrisman, *Lay Culture, Learned Culture*; Spitz and Tinsley, *Johann Sturm on Education*.

19 Bell, *Handlist of British Diplomatic Representatives*, 133.

20 WC to Sturm, 18 July 1573, London. *Zürich Letters (second series)*, ed. Robinson, 216–17. See also WC to Sturm, 15 September 1572, Woodstock. *Ibid.*, 210–11.

21 Sir John Wolley to Sturm, 24 July 1573, Orpington. *Zürich Letters (second series)*, 220–1.

22 *Novum Testamentum*, ed. Estienne, *.ii.^{r}.

23 Estienne, *Herodiani historiarum libri VIII*; trans. Buxton, *Sidney and the English Renaissance*, 57–8.

24 Nicollier-De Weck, 295. Seven years later, HS would try to engage Lingelsheim as tutor to PS's younger brother RS.
25 HL to Beale, 7 September 1573, Vienna. BL Egerton MS 1693, fo. 11b; trans. van Dorsten, *Poets*, 31.
26 HL to PS, 1 May 1574, Vienna. L27 (D6ᵛ).
27 Bizari to Vulcob, 15 October 1573, Augusta. Yale Osborn MS f a 14, fos 4–5; Firpo, *Pietro Bizzarri*, 239–42 at 242. On Bochetel, see *Dictionnaire de biographie française*, ed. Balteau *et al.*, 6: 749–50.
28 On Abondio, see Dworschak, *Antonio Abondio, medaglista e ceroplasta*.
29 According to PS to HL, 19 December 1573, Venice. F8 (3: 81). It may be that 'Raichel' is a misreading for Dr Johannes Aichholtz, Professor of Medicine at Vienna, with whom de l'Écluse lodged. See Osborn, 100.
30 This meal has been dated to Nuremberg in late April 1577, but HL was not in Nuremberg at this time. See Höltgen, 'Why are there no wolves in England?'
31 Philip Camerarius, *Operæ*, 1: S2ʳ–S4ʳ; for an incomplete English translation, see *The Living Librarie*, trans. Molle, Kᵛ–K3ʳ. See also Höltgen, 'Why are there no wolves?'
32 *OA*, 254–9.
33 Hertford MS, fo. 42ff; van Dorsten, *Poets*, app. I no. 4; trans. van Dorsten, *Poets*, 62–7 at 65.
34 Joachim Camerarius, *Vita Philippi Melanchthonis*, O11ʳ, trans. in Bayle, *A General Dictionary*, trans. Bernard *et al.*, 6: 629 n.[A].
35 Bayle, *General Dictionary*, 6: 631 n.[G] citing Thuanus, *De vita sua*, bk 2, 1176.
36 Brutus, *Vindiciae, contra tyrannos* (1579). The most recent edition is ed./trans. George Garnett (1994).
37 Brutus, *Vindiciae*, ed. Garnett, 9, 8.
38 HL to PS, 22 January 1574, Vienna. L11 (B3ᵛ).
39 HL to PS, 22 January 1574, Vienna. L11 (B4ʳ).
40 PS to HL, 19 December 1573, Venice. F8 (3: 81).
41 PS to HL, 19 December 1573, Venice. F8 (3: 80–1).
42 HL to PS, 1 January 1574, Vienna. L8 (A11ʳ–A12ᵛ). PS to HL, 15 January 1574, Padua. F10 (3: 83).
43 PS to HL, 4 February 1574, Padua. F11 (3: 84).
44 HL to PS, 28 January 1574, Vienna. L12 (B5ᵛ).
45 PS to HL, 4 February 1574, Padua. F11 (3: 84).
46 HL to PS, 1 January 1574, Vienna. L8 (A12ʳ).
47 PS to HL, 4 February 1574, Padua. F11 (3: 84).
48 PS to Denny, 22 May 1580, Wilton. Bodl. MS Don.d.152; pr. Buxton, 'An Elizabethan reading-list', 343–4.
49 HL to PS, 22 January 1574, Vienna. L11 (B3ᵛ).
50 PS to HL, 4 February 1574, Padua. F11 (3: 84).

5: The Company of Wise Men

1 Róna, 'Sir Philip Sidney and Hungary', 46. There is no evidence to support Róna's claim (47–8) that PS accompanied Charles de l'Écluse on this journey; indeed, de l'Écluse left Antwerp for Vienna on 10 September, not reaching Vienna until early November. See Osborn, 'Sidney and Pietro Bizari', 352. See also Gál, 'Sir Philip Sidney's guide to Hungary'.

2 HL to PS, 22 September 1573, Vienna. L1 (A^{r-v}).

3 HL to PS, 10 March 1575, Prague. L41 (F5–F6^v).

4 HL to PS, 12 August 1577, Frankfurt. L58 (I9^r). HL to PS, 31 March 1578, Frankfurt. L66 (K12^v).

5 Marshall's accounts. CKS U1475 A35.

6 DP. MP, 118.

7 Puttenham, The Arte of Poesie, 83.

8 Holinshed, Chronicles, 1: 162.

9 HL to PS, 28 January 1574, Vienna. L12 (B5^v).

10 On Monau, see Nicollier-De Weck 332–3 n. 96. Jacob Monau to HL, 12 March 1574, Padua. BN MS lat. 8583, fo. 130, cit. Nicollier-De Weck, 559.

11 See Venice, Consiglio dei Dieci, no. 78, fo. 127; Osborn, 166.

12 Receipt signed by PS for money received from Thomaso Balbani on his letter of credit from Vetturelli, 6 November 1573, Venice. CKS U1475 F26/8.

13 PS to RS [1579?]. F28 (3: 127).

14 HL to PS, 12 December 1573, Vienna. L5 (A6^r).

15 On Hanau, see Nicollier-De Weck, 340 n. 145.

16 HL to PS, 4 December 1573, Vienna. L4 (A4^v).

17 HL to PS, 7 January 1574, Vienna. L9 (B^r).

18 HL to PS, 7 January 1574, Vienna. L9 (B^v). HL to PS, 5 February 1574, Vienna. L13 (B7^v–B8^r). On Delius, see Nicollier-De Weck, 341 n. 150; for his letters to Languet during this period, see Delius to HL, 9 February 1574, Padua, and 10 April 1574, Venice, cit. Nicollier-De Weck, 557, 561. On Le Goulx, ibid, 341 n. 151; for his correspondence with Languet: Le Goulx to HL, 21 January 1574 and 11 February 1574, Padua and 10 April 1574, 13 April 1574, Venice, cit. Nicollier-De Weck, 556, 557, 561. For Welsperg, see Nicollier-De Weck, 277 n. 17; correspondence: HL to Welsberg, 22 October 1573, Vienna, Welsperg to HL, 10 December 1573, Padua, HL to Welsperg, 15 January 1574, Vienna, Welsperg to HL, 10 February [1574], [Padua] and 1 June 1574, Padua, cit. Nicollier-De Weck, 551, 553, 555, 557, 564. All this correspondence remains unpublished, in the BN (MS lat. 8583), and the Hessisches Staatsarchiv, Marburg.

19 HL to PS, 15 January 1574, Vienna. L10 (B2^r).

20 PS to HL, 19 December 1573, Venice. F8 (3: 80–1).

21 HL to PS, 15 January 1574, Vienna. L10 (B2^r).

22 HL to PS, 5 March 1574, Vienna. L17 (C2^v).

23 HL to PS, 28 January 1574, Vienna. L12 (B5^r). HL to PS, 22 January 1574, Vienna. L11 (B3^v).

24 Yeames, 'Grand Tour', 106. From PS's letters we know that on 5, 19 and 25 December 1573 he was in Venice. On 15 January and 4, 11 and 26 February 1574 he was in Padua, as he was on 15 April. On 29 April, the Venice Consiglio di Dieci granted him a licence. He was in Padua on 7 May, Venice on 18 June.

25 Woolfson, *Padua and the Tudors*.

26 See HL to Slavata, 22 October 1573 and 19 February 1574, Vienna. Hruby, *Etudiants tchèques aux écoles protestantes de l'Europe occidentale*, # 134, 213–14. On Slavata, see Nicollier-De Weck, 332 n. 95.

27 On Solms, see Osborn, 260–70; Nicollier-De Weck, 356.

28 Padua, Archivio di Stato, Notarile, 5007, fos 26a–7b. I am grateful to Jonathan Woolfson for providing me with a copy of this document.

29 See PRO SP 12/105, fo. 105 for Hart and Wendon as fugitives.

30 Woolfson, *Padua and the Tudors*, 243, 282.

31 PS to HL, 15 April 1574, Venice. F14 (3: 87–90).

32 See references to Windsor in Zündelin to PS, 3 May 1574, Venice. Yale Osborn MS fa. 14, fo. 17.

33 For Windsor's correspondence with Sussex in the early–mid 1570s see BL Cotton MS Titus B. ii, fos 395, 397, 400, 403, 405–6, 407, 409, 410–11, 412, 413, 415, 417–18, 419, 420–1, and BL Cotton MS Titus B. vii, fos 188, 190, 195, 197, 198, 200, 202, 203–9. The former collection also includes a letter demonstrating an earlier link: Windsor to Sussex, 12 November 1565, Warwickshire. BL Cotton MS Titus B. ii., fo. 399a–b.

34 Windsor to Elizabeth, 24 June 1572, the Spa. HMCS 2: 53–4.

35 Zündelin to PS, 20 June 1574, Venice. Yale Osborn MS fa. 14, fo. 30.

36 HL to PS, 10 March 1575, Prague. L41 (F5^r–F6^v).

37 Licence for PS, 25 May 1572, St James. New College, Oxford MS 328–2, fo. 40; Buxton and Juel-Jensen, 'Sidney's first passport rediscovered', 42–6.

38 Guaras to Philip II, 1574. BL Additional MS 28263, fo. 2, cit. Duncan-Jones, *Courtier Poet*, 88.

39 Report by a chronicler of the German nation, Eucharius Seefrid of Ottengen, in German nation's Acta 1574, Vatican Library, Italia II, Veneto 2, I, (15) pp. 181–2. This account is based on Osborn, 196–7.

40 Clemente Parretti to WC, 28 September 1575, Venice. HMCS, 2: 114.

41 Venice, Archivio di Stato, Consiglio dei Dieci, Parti Communi, R. 31, c. 127r and Capi del Consiglio dei Dieci: Lettere, fil 75, pr. Osborn, 523.

42 HL to PS, 18 March 1574, Vienna. L19 (C5^r–C6^r). HL to PS, 23 April 1574, Vienna. L26 (D4^v–D5^v).

43 HL to PS, 26 March 1574, Vienna. L20 (C7^r).

44 HL to PS, 1 January 1574, Vienna. L8 (A12^r).

45 See Rosand, 'Dialogues and apologies: Sidney and Venice', 238; Judson, *Sidney's Appearance: a study in Elizabethan portraiture*, 23–7.

46 HL to PS, 22 January 1574, Vienna. L11 (B4^v).

47 PS to HL, 4 February 1574, Padua. F11 (3: 84–5).

48 Rosand, 'Sidney and Venice', 241. See also Rosand, *Painting in Cinquecento Venice*, 118–23 and 224 nn. 44–9; Fehl and Perry, 'Painting and the Inquisition at Venice'; Muraro, 'Un celebre ritratto'; Kuin, 'New light on the Veronese portrait of Sir Philip Sidney', 33–4, and illustrations.

49 HL to PS, 23 April 1574, Vienna. L26 (D4^v–D6^v).

50 HL to PS, 11 June 1574, Vienna. L33 (E4^r).

51 HL to PS, 6 June 1575, Prague. L44 (F11^v).

52 Hertford MS, fo. 216; van Dorsten, *Poets*, app. I, no. 3; trans. van Dorsten, *Poets*, 55–6.

53 See Kuin, 'New light on the Veronese portrait', *passim*; *idem*, 'Languet and the Veronese portrait of Sidney: Antwerp findings'.

54 De Banos, in his ed. Ramus, *Commentariorum de Religione Christiana* (1577), √4^v.

55 Moffet, *Nobilis*, 71; Jonson, *Conversations with Drummond*, cit. Judson, *Sidney's Appearance*, 16; Aubrey, *Brief Lives*, ed. Dick, 278.

56 Strong, *Gloriana: The Portraits of Queen Elizabeth I*, 23–4.

57 PS to HL, June 1574, Venice. F19 (3: 97).

58 HL to PS, 28 June and 2 July 1574, Vienna. L36 and 37 (E10^v–E11^r, E11^v–E12^r).

59 Osborn, 219. Perrot to PS, 27 August 1574, Venice. Yale Osborn MS f. a 14 fos 32–33a; trans. Osborn, 231. On Henri in Venice, see Champion, *Henri III*, chs 3 and 4.

60 Castelnau to Henri III, 28 July 1584, London. Chéruel, 313–18 at 317. Osborn himself points up the anomaly of PS's familiarity with Henri's entourage: see Osborn, 232.

61 PS to HL, 18 June 1574, Venice. F19 (3: 97–8). PS to RD, 27 November 1574, Vienna. BL Cotton MS Galba B. xi, fo. 337a–b; F20 (3: 98–100).

62 See Lobbet to PS, 1 June 1574, Strasburg. Yale Osborn MS fa. 14, fo. 26, on his decision to leave. HL to PS, 17 July 1574, Vienna. L39 (F3^r) on his illness. HL to PS, 24 July 1574, Vienna. L40 (F3^v–F5^r), on the friends leaving. Accerbo Vetturelli to HS, 21 October 1574. BL Additional MS 17650, fo. 2. HS had deposited £135 with Vetturelli on 28 June 1574; see receipt by John Lupovini, Vetturelli's agent. CKS U1475 F26/8.

63 [Bryskett], 'A pastorall Aeglogue upon the death of Sir Phillip Sidney Knight, &c.', in Spenser, *Colin Clovts Come home Againe*, H2^r–H4^v at H3^v.

64 See Lobbet to PS, 5 October 1574, Strasburg. Yale Osborn MS fa. 14, fo. 38. HL to PS, 12 June 1575, Prague. L45 (F12^r–G3^v). For HL's lodging with Lingelsheim see Nicollier-De Weck, 295. See also van Dorsten, 'Sidney and Languet'.

65 Zündelin to PS, 6 September 1574, Venice. Yale Osborn MS fa. 14, fo. 34.

66 PS's will. *MP*, 147–52 at 149.

67 *DP*. *MP*, 73.

68 Sturm to Elizabeth, 15 March 1584, Nordheim. *CSPF 1583–1584*, 405–6.

69 Clifford, *The Schoole of Horsmanship*, ¶.ii.ʳ.

70 Przezdziecki, *Diplomatic Ventures and Adventures: Some experience of British envoys at the Court of Poland*, 27–9; van Dorsten, 'Sidney and Languet', 217–18; Zamoyski, *The Polish Way*, 126–8.

71 HL to André Dudith, 10 October 1574, Vienna. Costil, *André Dudith: humaniste hongrois*, 147; trans. Osborn, 246.

72 Stafford, *The Gvide of Honovr* (1634), A7ʳ; Naunton, *Fragmenta Regalia* (1641), C3ʳ–C4ᵛ. The story is also raised in Matthew, *A Collection of Letters* (1660), B6ᵛ. I am grateful to Sharon Zink (Queen Mary and Westfield College, London) for this last reference. See Wilson, *Sir Philip Sidney*, 319–20. The fullest surveys of the material to date are Zins, 'Philip Sidney a Polska', and 'Poeta Philip Sidney - Anglieski pretendent do tronu Polskiego?'

73 Zündelin to PS, 27 November 1574, Venice. Yale Osborn MS fa. 14, fos 45–46a.

74 PS to RD, 27 November 1574, Vienna. BL Cotton MS Galba B. xi, fo. 370; F20 (3: 98–100).

75 PS to WC, 17 December 1574, Vienna. F21 (3: 100–2).

76 Lobbet to PS, 7 December 1574, Strasburg. Yale Osborn MS fa. 14, fo. 47.

77 HL to Augustus, 1 March 1575, Prague. *Arcana* I, pt 2, ep. 29 (K2ʳ).

78 PS to Jordan, 2 March 1575, Prague. F22 (3: 102). HL to PS, 24 May 1579. HL to JC, 9 March 1575, Prague. C24 (K3ʳ–K4ᵛ).

79 PS to Jordan, 2 March 1575, Prague. F22 (3: 102).

80 '*Imperator his diebus eum ad se accersiuit & valde clementer accepit.*' HL to Augustus, 1 March 1575, Prague. *Arcana* I, pt 2, ep. 29 (K2ʳ).

81 Andreas Paull to HL, 28 October 1574, Dresden. BN MS lat. 8583, fo. 91–94 quoted Nicollier-De Weck, 338 n.131.

82 See HL to Jean de Glaubourg, 8 March 1575, Prague. Harvard College Library, Houghton collection, accession *51M–135; pr. and trans. Bond, 'A letter of Languet about Sidney'. See also Nicollier-De Weck, 73.

83 HL to PS, 10 March 1575, Prague. L41 (F5ʳ–F6ᵛ). See HL to Wittengenstein, recommending PS, 12 March 1575, Prague. L43 (F8ʳ–F9ʳ).

84 HL to PS, 10 March 1575, Prague. L41 (F5ʳ⁻ᵛ).

85 HL to PS, 13 March 1575, Prague. L42 (F7ᵛ).

86 HL to PS, 10 March 1575, Prague. L41 (F5ʳ–F6ᵛ).

87 HL to PS, 13 March 1575, Prague. L42 (F7ᵛ).

88 Augustus to HL, 4 January 1575. Peifer, *Epistolae*, 192–3; Nicollier-De Weck, 349.

89 Lobbet to PS, 6 April 1575, Strasburg. Yale Osborn MS fa. 14, fo. 61.

90 'Instructions for Thomas Wilkes sent to the Count Palatine', 16 February 1575

[draft by WC]. *CSPF 1575–1577*, 17. Osborn identifies the book as *De tribus impostoribus* (1575) attributed to J.M. Lucas (Osborn, 304 n.1).

91 Lobbet to PS, 7 April 1575, Strasbourg. Yale Osborn MS fa. 14, fo. 63.

92 PS to Hanau, 3 May 1575, Antwerp. Staatsarchiv Marburg/Lahn 86 Hanau α831 no. 2; trans. Osborn, 308.

93 HL to PS, 10 March 1575, Prague. L41 (F6ʳ).

94 'Tomorrow I leave for England.' PS to Hanau, 3 May 1575, Antwerp. Staatsarchiv Marburg/Lahn 86 Hanau α831 no. 2; trans. Osborn, 308.

6: BORN FOR COMMAND

1 Lobbet to PS, 31 May 1575, Strasburg. Yale Osborn MS fa. 14, fo. 65; Osborn, 319.

2 Lobbet to PS, 22 November 1575, Strasburg. Yale Osborn MS fa. 14, fos 92–93a; trans. Osborn, 384.

3 De Banos to PS, 19 September 1575, Frankfurt. Yale Osborn MS fa. 14, fo. 81; trans. Osborn, 360.

4 De Banos to PS, 19 March 1576, Frankfurt. BL Additional MS 15914, fo. 27a; trans. Osborn, 416–17.

5 De Banos to PS, 24 April 1576, Frankfurt. BL Additional MS 15914, fo. 28; trans. Osborn, 424. De Banos to PS, 19 March 1576, Frankfurt [address]. BL Additional MS 15914, fo. 28b.

6 Ramus, *Commentariorum de Religione Christiana, Libri quatuor*, ed. de Banos (1576); a 2. For extant copies of the 1576 edition, see Ong, *Ramus and Talon Inventory*, 391; see also Waddington, *Ramus*, 469. The dedication is identical in the 1577 and 1583 editions.

7 FW to HS, 15 May 1575, London. Collins 1: 69–70.

8 Guzman de Silva to Philip II, 10 July 1568, London. *CSPS 1568–79*, 50–1. On Elizabeth's progresses, see Dovey, *An Elizabethan Progress*.

9 PS's credit note to Richard Rodway, 8 August 1575. CKS U1475 F26/9.

10 MDS to Molyneux, 1 September 1574, Chiswick. Collins 1: 66–7 at 67.

11 MDS to WC, 12 September 1573, Limehouse. BL Lansdowne MS 17, fo. 41a.

12 MDS to Sussex, 1 February 1573, St Anthony's. BL Cotton MS Vesp. F. xii, fo. 179a.

13 MDS to Sussex, n.d. BL Cotton MS Titus B. ii., fo. 302a.

14 MDS to WC, 2 May 1572. PRO SP 63/36, art. 14.

15 MDS to John Cockeram, 'Tuesday after St Barts' day, 1573', Greenwich. BL Additional MS 15914, fo. 12.

16 Möller to PS, 17 July 1575, Prague. BL Additional MS 15914, fo. 19a.

17 For biographical details on MS, see Hannay, *Philip's Phoenix*; *Collected Works of Mary Sidney Herbert*, ed. Hannay *et al.*, 1: 1–21.

18 Elizabeth to HS, [February 1575]. PRO SP 12 Warrant Book 1: 83, cit. Wallace, 149–50.

19 RD to WC, 28 June 1575, Grafton. Wright 2: 11–12.

20 Gascoigne, *The Princely Pleasures at the Courte at Kenelwoorth*; Laneham, *A Letter*. Both were reprinted in *The Progresses and Public Processions of Queen Elizabeth*, ed. Nichols (1823). On the 'Laneham' publication, see Griffin, 'The breaking of the giants', 4–5.

21 On Dyer, see Sargent, *At the Court of Queen Elizabeth*; Duncan-Jones, *Courtier Poet*, 101–6; May, 'Sir Edward Dyer'.

22 MDS to Molyneux, 1 September 1574, Chiswick. CKS U1475 C7/6; Collins 1: 66–7 at 67.

23 Fraunce, *Shepheardes logike*, BL Additional MS 34361; Monardes, *Simplicivm medicamentorvm ex novo orbe delatorvm*, ed. de l'Écluse, A2ʳ⁻ᵛ.

24 Watson, *The ΕΚΑΤΟΜΠΑΘΙΑ or Passionate Centurie of Loue*, [leaf] 2ʳ⁻ᵛ.

25 Harvey, *Three proper, and wittie, familiar Letters*, D.iiij.ʳ.

26 Whitney, *A Choice of Emblemes*, b2ᵛ–b3ʳ.

27 CKS U1475 E93.

28 Nichols, *Progresses*, 1: 544–5.

29 Owen and Blakeway, *A History of Shrewsbury*, 1: 360.

30 Osborn, 374.

31 HS's will, 20 August 1575. *The Third Report of the Royal Commission on Historical Manuscripts*, Appendix, 199.

32 HMCD 1: 269.

33 Hay, *Life of Robert Sidney*, 21–2.

34 *The Queenes Majesties entertainment at Woodstocke* (1585); *The Queen's Majesty's Entertainment at Woodstock, 1575*, ed. Pollard. On Lee, see Chambers, *Sir Henry Lee*.

35 Heliodorus, *An Æthopian historie written in Greeke*, trans. Underdowne.

36 For the presentation copy see BL Royal MS 18 A. XLVIII; on Gascoigne, see Prouty, *George Gascoigne*.

37 FSL X.d.271, discussed in Woudhuysen, 'A "lost" Sidney document'. Robert Walker's accounts confirm that £100 was paid to PS 'for the fee of cupbearer for three years' (1575–8). See HMCD 1: 249.

38 Phillips, 'George Buchanan and the Sidney circle'. PS to Buchanan, ? October 1579, Court, demonstrates that they had not met or corresponded previously. *The Warrender Papers*, ed. Cameron, 1: 146.

39 Seton to PS, 2 September 1575, Seton. Yale Osborn MS fa. 14, fo. 76; Osborn, 355–6. On 6 September 1575 Lord Seton wrote to the queen thanking her for favours shown to his son during this visit to her court. Seton to Elizabeth, 6 September 1575, Seton. *CSPF 1575–1577*, 125.

40` 'The Christening of Elizabeth the first daughter of the Lord Russell . . .' BL Hargrave MS 497, fos 57a–59b; on PS's involvement, see fos 58b–59a.

41 HL to PS, 13 August 1575, Prague. L46 (G3ᵛ). HL to PS, 21 June 1575, Prague. L45 (F12ᵛ).

42 HL to PS, 13 August 1575, Prague. L46 (G3ᵛ).

43 Zündelin to PS, 20 June and 23 October 1575, Venice. Yale Osborn MS fa. 14, fos 69–70b, 88; Osborn, 339–43, 374–6. De Banos to PS, 30 June 1575, Antwerp. BL Additional MS 18675, fo. 4a–b; trans. Osborn, 333–6. De Banos to PS, 19 September and 17 October 1575, Frankfurt. Yale Osborn MS fa. 14, fos 81, 87; Osborn, 360–2, 368. Lobbet to PS, 5 and 25 July, 30 August and 5 September 1575, Strasburg. Yale Osborn MS fa. 14, fos 71, 73, 75, 78; Osborn, 336–8, 352–4, 354–5, 356–8. Moller to PS, 17 July 1575, Prague. BL Additional MS 15914, 19–20; trans. Osborn, 350–2.

44 Lobbet to PS, 14 February 1576. Yale Osborn MS fa. 14, fos 104–105a; trans. Osborn, 409.

45 HL to PS, 17 March 1576, Vienna. L52 (H7^v–H8^r).

46 PS to HL, 21 April 1576, London. BN MS lat. 8583, fos 32–3; trans. Osborn, 420–1.

47 Achille de Harley to FW, 3 March 1576, Paris. Osborn, 412 [source not given].

48 PS to HL, 21 April 1576, London. BN MS lat. 8583, fos 32–3; trans. Osborn, 420–1.

49 PS to HL, 21 April 1576, London. BN MS lat. 8583, fos 32–3; trans. Osborn, 420–1.

50 Dee, *General and Rare Memorials*, A^v.

51 Gilbert, *A Discourse of a Discovery for a new Passage to Catania*.

52 Sargent, *At the Court of Queen Elizabeth*, 40–1. This area of PS's life has been best treated by Kuin, 'Querre-Muhau: Sir Philip Sidney and the New World'.

53 Hertford MS, fo. 221; van Dorsten, *Poets*, app. I.1; trans. van Dorsten, *Poets*, 39.

54 On Essex, see Devereux 1: 11–162; *DNB* 14: 443–7; Brady, *Chief Governors*.

55 EW to HS, 21 March 1576, Court. Collins, 1: 168–70 at 168.

56 Antonio de Guaras [to Gabriel de Zayas?], 5 December 1575, London. *CSPS 1568–1579*, 511.

57 Richard Broughton to Richard Bagot, 26 August 1576, n.p. Devereux, 1: 136–7.

58 FW to HS, 17 July 1576, St James's. Collins, 1: 123–4 at 123.

59 William Gerrarde to FW, 11 July 1576, Dublin; PC to HS, 10 July 1576, St James's; FW to HS, 24 July 1576, Whitehall. PRO SP 63/56 arts. 11, 7; *CSPI 1574–1585*, 97 (*bis*); Collins 1: 124–5 at 124.

60 HS to PC, 15 August 1576, Dublin Castle. Collins 1: 125–6 at 126.

61 HS to Privy Council, 9 July 1576, Queen's Castle of Athlone. Collins 1: 121.

62 HS to PC, 20 September 1576, Galway. CKS U1475 C1, fos 40a–41b; Collins 1: 128–30 at 129, 130. See also Baker, 'Off the map: charting uncertainty in Renaissance Ireland', 76–7.

63 'Memoir', 5: 314. On Grace O'Malley, see Chambers, *Granuaile: The Life and Times of Grace O'Malley c. 1530–1603*.

64 'Discourse on Irish affairs', *MP*, 11.

65 *DP*, *MP*, 75–6.

66 HL to PS, 13 August 1576, Ratisbon. L54 (H12^v).

67 PS to Robert Walker, 4 November 1576, Greenwich. CKS U1475 F26/2; F24 (3: 103).

68 HL to PS, 13 August 1576, Ratisbon. L54 (H12ᵛ).

69 HS to RD, 4 February 1577, Dundalk. Collins, 1: 88–9 at 88.

70 Thomas, Earl of Ormond to HS, 6 September 1576, Kilkenny. Collins, 1: 128.

71 EW to HS, 9 September 1576, Dublin. CKS U1475 C3/3.

72 Anonymous account of Essex's death, [c. 1576]. Thomas Hearne, 'Editoris præfatio' in Camden, *Annales rerum Anglicarum et Hibernicum regnante Elizabetha*, ed. Hearne, 1: LXXXIX–XCVIII at XCIII.

73 Essex to Elizabeth, 20 September 1576, Dublin. Devereux, 1: 142.

74 Essex to WC, 21 September 1576, Dublin. Devereux, 1: 144.

75 'Memoir', 5: 314.

76 [Unknown] to the Bishop of Meath, [22 September 1576], n.p. PRO SP 63/56, art. 35; *CSPI 1574–1585*, 99.

77 On Penelope Rich, see Freedman, *Poor Penelope*.

78 See Nicholas Poyntz, Richard Berkeley, Thomas Throckmorton, Giles Poyntz to Berkeley, 26 October 1573. Fox Bourne, *Sir Philip Sidney*, 55–6.

79 Anonymous account of Essex's death, [c. 1576]. Hearne, 'Editoris præfatio', XCIII.

80 EW to HS, 14 November 1576, Chartley. Collins, 1: 147–8 at 147.

81 HS to FW, 20 October 1576, Dublin Castle. Collins, 1: 140–2.

82 See HS to WC, 20 September 1576, Galway. PRO SP 63/56 art. 32; *CSPI 1574–1585*, 99. This cannot prove that PS *did* in fact continue directly to England after Essex's death, but it was clearly HS's intention that he should.

7: SECRET COMBINATIONS

1 See Louthan, *The quest for compromise*, ch. 8.

2 Crato, *Oratio fvnebris de Diuo Maxæmiliano II imperatore*, A8ᵛ.

3 HL to Augustus, 18 October 1576, Ratisbon. *Arcana*, I, ep. 94 (Hhᵛ–Hh 2ʳ).

4 Clasen, *The Palatinate in European History*, 19–20.

5 Robert Colshill to WC, 1 November 1576, Cologne. *CSPF 1575–1577*, 411.

6 Elizabeth to Rudolf II, [1576]. *CSPF 1575–1577*, 471.

7 Gentili, *De Legationibus, libri tres*, Qᵛ; trans. Laing, 2: 171.

8 See HL to Augustus, 5 January 1577, Prague. *Arcana*, I pt 2, ep. 104 (Llᵛ).

9 HL to Augustus, 8 February 1577, Prague; 23 February 1577, Prague. *Arcana*, I pt 2, eps 106, 108 (Ll 4ʳ, Mm 3ᵛ).

10 Nicollier-De Weck, 377–80.

11 PS was at Leicester House on 8 February 1577. See PS to WC, 8 February 1577, Leicester House. F25 (3: 104).

12 Titus Livius, *Romanae historiae principis, decades tres* (Basle, 1555), h 5ʳ, now in Princeton University Library, deposit of Lucius Wilmerding, Jr. See Jardine and Grafton, '"Studied for action": how Gabriel Harvey read his Livy', 36, from which these transcriptions and translations are taken.

13 Harvey's Livy, aaʳ; Jardine and Grafton, '"Studied for action"', 38.

14 *Private Diary of Dr. John Dee*, ed. Halliwell, 2.

15 Moffet, *Nobilis*, 75–6.

16 For this aspect of Dee's expertise, see Sherman, *John Dee: The Politics of Reading and Writing in the Renaissance*.

17 PS's instructions, 7 February 1577. BL Harley MS 36, fos 232a–235a.

18 Greville, 'Dedication', 25.

19 Thomas Screven to Rutland, 16 February 1577, London. HMCR, 1: 111. On Brouncker, see Moffet, *Nobilis*, 126–8.

20 Collins, 'Memoirs', 1: 100.

21 TW [to FW], 5 March 1577, Brussels. *CSPF 1575–1577*, 541.

22 TW to FW, 10 March 1577, Brussels. *CSPF 1575–1577*, 543.

23 Greville, 'Dedication', 20.

24 Don John to Elizabeth, 7 March 1577, Louvain. *CSPF 1575–1577*, 542.

25 PS to FW, 22 March 1577, Frankfurt. F27 (3: 105–7).

26 PS's instructions, 7 February 1577. BL Harley MS 36, fos 232b–233a.

27 PS to FW, 22 March 1577, Frankfurt. F27 (3: 105–7).

28 Moffet, *Nobilis*, 81.

29 See John Delfino, bishop of Torcello, to Ptomely Galli, cardinal of Como, 6 April 1577, Prague. *CSP Rome 1572–1578*, 300.

30 Demetz, *Prague in Black and Gold*, 179.

31 PS to de l'Écluse, 8 April 1577, Prague. Gömöri, 'Philip Sidney's letter to Charles L'Écluse in 1577', corrected in Kuin, 'Sir Philip Sidney's letter to Charles de l'Écluse in 1577: a rectification'; trans. Osborn, 462.

32 De l'Écluse to JC, 12 April 1577, Vienna. Hunger, *Charles de l'Écluse (Carolus Clusius)*, 340–1.

33 See Delfino to Galli, 24 April 1577, Prague. *CSP Rome 1572–1578*, 301–2.

34 PS to FW, 22 March 1577, Heidelberg. F27 (3: 107).

35 On Rudolf see Evans, *Rudolf II and his World*; Demetz, *Prague in Black and Gold*, ch. 5, especially 179–82.

36 Newsletter, 13 April 1577, Prague. *CSP Rome 1572–1578*, 301. See also Newsletter, 20 April 1577, Prague. *CSP Rome 1572–1578*, 301.

37 PS to FW, 3 May 1577, Heidelberg. BL Cotton MS Galba B. xi, fo. 330a; F29 (3: 109–14).

38 Moffet, *Nobilis*, 81.

39 PS to FW, 3 May 1577, Heidelberg. BL Cotton MS Galba B. xi, fos 330b, 331a; F29 (3: 109–14).

40 The debate on this meeting has been completely circumscribed by the account by Simpson, *Edmund Campion*, 114–17. Simpson's selective paraphrases of writings by Persons and Fitzherbert are quoted *verbatim* (as if they were the originals) by later scholars, including the fullest, most recent attempt: Duncan-Jones, 'Sir Philip

Sidney's debt to Edmund Campion'.

41 Campion to John Bavand, n.d. [1577]. The original, in Latin, is at Stonyhurst College, Anglia I/4a; this trans., Simpson, *Campion*, 123.

42 Sir Thomas Tresham, notes for his defence, 1581. BL Additional MS 39830, fo. 48a, quoted *in extenso* in Reynolds, *Campion and Parsons*, 137.

43 Thomas Fitzherbert [to unknown], 1 February 1628, as rendered in Simpson, *Campion*, 115–16.

44 Robert Persons, as rendered in Simpson, *Campion*, 115.

45 For the letter, see Rudolf to Elizabeth, 14 April 1577, Prague. *CSPF 1575–1577*, 558. For the gifts, John Delfino, bishop of Torcello, to Ptolomey Galli, Cardinal of Como, 20 April 1577, Prague. *CSP Rome 1572–1578*, 301; also Moffet, *Nobilis*, 81–2.

46 Moffet, *Nobilis*, 81.

47 PS to the Camerarius brothers, 1 January 1579, Court at London. F Addendum (3: 183–4).

48 PS to FW, 3 May 1577, Heidelberg. BL Cotton MS Galba B. xi, fo. 331b; F29 (3: 109–14). I have followed Feuillerat's reconstruction.

49 Ludwig to Elizabeth, 1 May 1577, 'In Castro Novo' (i.e. in the New Castle at Baden?) *CSPF 1575–1577*, 573. See Osborn, 474 n. 9.

50 HL to JC, 9 April 1577, Frankfurt. C29 (K8^v–K9^v); and 22 September 1577, Frankfurt, C31 (K11^r–K12^v) . HL was still in Prague on 13 March, but by 31 March had reached Frankfurt. See inventory of letters, Nicollier-De Weck, 589.

51 HL to Augustus, 7 April 1577 and 8 June 1577, Frankfurt. *Arcana*, I, eps. 114 and unnumbered letter (between 114 and 115), Oo^v–Oo2^r, Oo 2^{r-v}. 'Languetus ist gestert abont kommen.' Weyer and Beutterich to Casimir, 3 May 1577, Heidelberg. *Briefe des Pfalzgrafen Johann Casimir mit verwandten schriftstücken*, ed. von Bezold, 1: 268.

52 PS to FW, 3 May 1577, Heidelberg. BL Cotton MS Galba B. xi, fo. 331b; F29 (3: 109–14).

53 HL to Marnix, 15 June 1577, Frankfurt. *Marnixi Epistulae*, ed. Gerlo and De Smet, 2: 89–93 at 91–2. See also HL to JC, 17 June 1577. C30 (K8^v–K10^r).

54 See Casimir to PS, 12 June 1577, Neustat. *CSPF 1575–1577*, 599–600.

55 PS to FW, 3 May 1577, Heidelberg. BL Cotton MS Galba B. xi, fo. 331b; F29 (3: 109–14).

56 Casimir to PC, 8 May 1577, Lauterburg. *CSPF 1575–1577*, 575.

57 Hesse to Elizabeth, 20 May 1577, Cassel. *CSPF 1575–1577*, 580.

58 See PS to Hesse, 13 May 1577, Frankfurt. F30 (3: 114–15).

59 HL to PS, 14 June 1577, Frankfurt. L56 (I5^v).

60 PS to HL, 1 October 1577, Court. F31 (3: 116).

61 HL to PS, 28 November 1577, Frankfurt. L62 (K5^r).

62 HL mentions being absent several times from Frankfurt: see HL to PS, 15 July 1577, Frankfurt. L57 (I6^r–I8^v); Nicollier-De Weck, 238 n.35.

63 HL to JC, 22 September 1577, Frankfurt. C31 (K11^r–K12^v).

64 HL to PS, 15 July 1577, Frankfurt. L57 (I6^v).

65 HL to PS, 14 June 1577, Frankfurt. L56 (I5^v).

66 HL to PS, 15 July 1577, Frankfurt. L57 (I6^v).

67 HL to PS, 15 July 1577, Frankfurt. L57 (I6^v).

68 HL to PS, 15 July 1577, Frankfurt. L57 (I6^r–I8^v).

69 HL to PS, 15 July 1577, Frankfurt. L57 (I7^{r-v}).

70 HL to PS, 23 September 1577, Frankfurt. L59 (I9^v).

71 HL to PS, 9 October 1577, Frankfurt. L60 (I10^v).

72 HL to PS, 28 November 1577, Frankfurt. L62 (K5^r). On Brandenburg, see Hoefer, *Nouvelle Biographie Universelle*, 7: 246.

73 HL to PS, 14 June 1577, Frankfurt. L56 (I4^v).

74 HL to JC, 17 June 1577, Frankfurt. C30 (K10^r).

75 RD to Orange, 8 May 1577, Greenwich. BL Cotton MS Galba C. vi, pt 1, fo. 45; Lettenhove 9: 294 (ep. 3418). See also RD to the Princess of Orange, 8 May 1577, Greenwich. BL Cotton MS Galba C. vi, pt 1, fo. 45; Lettenhove 9: 295 (ep. 3419).

76 TW to FW, 24 May 1577, Antwerp. Lettenhove 9: 307 (ep. 3426). TW to WC, 28 May 1577, Antwerp. Lettenhove 9: 508 (ep. 3427). On this incident generally, see also Kuin, 'The Middelburg weekend: More light on the proposed marriage between Philip Sidney and Marie of Nassau'.

77 Fuller, *The Profane State*, Kkk2^r.

78 Greville, 'Dedication',

79 BL Cotton MS Galba C.vi, fos 51a–54a; Lettenhove 9: 310–14. For the authorship debate, see Osborn, 482.

80 Orange to Elizabeth, 11 June 1577, Dordrecht. Lettenhove 9: 522 (ep. 3435).

81 Daniel Rogers to FW, 20 July 1577, Horn. *CSPF 1577–1578*, 22.

82 Antonio de Guaras to Don John, 1 June 1577, London. Lettenhove 9: 316–17 (ep. 3431).

83 The following discussion is based on Kuin, 'The Middelburg weekend'.

84 'Certain Sonnets', no. 23; Ringler, 151–2.

85 EW to HS, 10 June 1577, Greenwich. Collins 1: 193.

86 FW to HS, 10 June 1577, Greenwich. CKS U1475 C2/15; Collins 1: 193.

87 Daneau, *Geographiæ Poeticæ*, ¶ 2^r.

88 Greville, 'Dedication', 27.

89 Paulus Melissus [Paul Schede], 'Ad Philippvm Sydnevm, Elisabethæ reginæ Angliæ ad Rom. imp. legatvm', in *Melissi Schediasmata poetica*, 2nd edn (1586), R.v.^{r}–R.vi.^{r} (1: 265); trans. van Dorsten, *Poets*, 50.

90 See Melissus to FW, 19 February 1586, London. *CSPD 1581–1590*, 307.

91 Bizari, *Senatus populique Genuensis rerum domi forisque gestarum historiae*, Bb3^r (569); trans. Osborn, 495 n. 50.

92 Gentili, *De legationibus*, T^v; trans. Laing, 2: 201.

93 TW to FW, 11 June 1577, Brussels. Lettenhove 9: 344 (ep. 3445).

94 'Heads of a Treaty', June 1577. *CSPF 1575–1577*, 492–3.

95 Instructions for Daniel Rogers, 22 June 1577. Lettenhove 9: 357.

96 Elizabeth to Casimir, 23 June 1577, Greenwich. *CSPF 1575–1577*, 603.

97 Elizabeth to Orange, 24 June 1577, Greenwich. *CSPF 1575–1577*, 603.

98 Rogers to FW, 20 July 1577, Hoorn. *CSPF 1577–1578*, 22.

99 Rogers to FW, 24 July 1577, Enckhuyzen. *CSPF 1577–1578*, 26–9.

100 HL to PS, 12 August 1577, Frankfurt. L58 (I8ᵛ–I9ʳ).

101 HL to Augustus, 23 September 1577, Frankfurt. *Arcana*, I, ep. 123 (Rr 4ᵛ).

102 Beale to FW, 11 October 1577, Frankfurt. *CSPF 1577–1578*, 242–7.

103 FW to Rogers, 31 October 1577, Windsor. *CSPF 1577–1578*, 293–5.

104 PS to HL, 1 October 1577, Court. F31 (116–18).

105 PS to HL, 10 October 1577, Court. F31 (3: 116–17).

106 See HL to PS, 23 September 1577, Frankfurt. L59 (I10ʳ).

107 PS to HL, 10 March 1578, F3: 121. FW, 2 November 1577. *CSPF 1577–1578*, 303. HL to Beale, 31 March 1578, Frankfurt. BL Egerton MS 1693, fo. 21.

108 PS to HL, 1 March 1578. F33 (3: 119–21).

109 Mendoza to Philip II, 12 April 1578, London. *Correspondencia de Felipe II con sus embajadores en la corte de Inglaterra 1558 á 1584*, 4: 217; *CSPS 1568–1579*, 575.

8: THE PERFECT COURTIER

1 Elizabeth to HS, 17 July 1577. LPL MS 628/275, cit. Brady, *Chief Governors*, 152.

2 HS to RD, August 1577, Newry. CKS U1475 C1, fo. 84a.

3 HS to PS, March 1577, Dublin Castle. CKS U1475 C1, fo. 57a–b.

4 On the 'cess' dispute, see 'Memoir', 8: 181–3; Holinshed, *Chronicles*, 2: 144–6; MP, 3–7; Brady, *The Chief Governors*, 146–58 and ch. 6; Maley, *Salvaging Spenser*, 27–8.

5 EW to HS, 16 September 1577, Oatlands. Collins 1: 227.

6 EW to HS, 30 September 1577, Windsor Castle. Collins 1: 228.

7 'Discourse on Irish Affairs', MP 8–12.

8 Elizabeth to HS, 1 November 1577, Windsor Castle. *Carew* 2: 117.

9 HS to Grey, 17 September 1580, Denbigh. CKS U1475 C5/24; Collins 1: 279–83 at 281.

10 Fenton to RD, 1580. PRO SP 63/76 art. 19, cit. MacCarthy-Morrogh, *The Munster Plantation*, 26.

11 PS to HS, 25 April 1578. CKS U1475 Z53/23 (Collins' transcript); F35 (3: 122–3).

12 PS to Molyneux, 31 May 1578, Court. CKS U1475 Z53/24 (Collins' transcript); Collins 1: 256.

13 Molyneux to PS, 1 July 1578, Dublin Castle. Collins 1: 256.

14 PS to Molyneux, 10 April 1581, Baynards Castle. Collins 1: 293. Molyneux to PS, 28 April 1581, Salop. Collins 1: 293–4.

15 Holinshed, *Chronicles*, 2: 150.

16 'Memoir', 8: 183.

17 Jenyson to WC, 26 January 1587, Dublin Castle. *CSPI 1586–1588*, 246.

18 These tributes are taken from Wallace, 194.

19 HS to Grey, 17 September 1580. Collins 1: 280.

20 Aubrey, *Brief Lives*, ed. Dick, 138.

21 Richard Brackinbury to Rutland, 12 December 1576, Court. HMCR 1: 110.

22 HS to RD, 4 February 1577. CKS U1475 C7/3; Collins 1: 89.

23 Sidney family psalter. TCC MS R.17.2. fo. 2b.

24 HS to RD, 19 May 1577, Kilmaynham. *Carew*, 80–3.

25 HS to FW, 16 September 1577. PRO SP 63/59 art. 15; *CSPI 1574–1585*, 121.

26 See Pembroke's receipt: BL Additional MS 15552, fo. 1; Edward Pakenham, 'A Book of all my receipts of money, payments and allowances out of the same since November, 1577', BL Additional MS 17520, fo. 12.

27 Hannay, *Philip's Phoenix*, 41–2.

28 On the Pembrokes at Wilton, see Wilkinson, *Wilton House Guide*, 80–8; Crawley, *Twelve Centuries of Wilton House*; Brennan, *Literary Patronage in the English Renaissance*.

29 'Certain Sonnets', no. 22; Ringler, 149.

30 Aubrey, *Brief Lives*, 220.

31 Brennan, *Literary Patronage*, 42.

32 WD to RD, 3 October 1577, Brussels. BL Cotton MS Galba C. vi, pt 1, fo. 45; Lettenhove 9: 555 (ep. 3585).

33 HL to PS, 26 December 1577, Frankfurt. L61 (302–6).

34 PS to HL, 1 March 1578. F33 (3: 119–21).

35 Casimir to PS, 25 April 1578, Lautern. *CSPF 1577–1578*, 638.

36 'Certain requests of Duke Casimir proposed to D. Rogers to declare them further to her Majesty.' May [?] 1578. *CSPF 1577–1578*, 731.

37 [Unknown] to FW, [April] 1578, *CSP Scotland 1574–1581*, 286

38 Mendoza to Zayas, 13 June 1578, London. *CSPS 1568–1579*, 595.

39 PC to PS, 5 June 1578. *APC 1577–1578*, 240.

40 *The Lady of May. MP*, 21–32, discussed at 13–20.

41 FW to WD, 11 May 1578. *CSPF 1577–1578*, 671.

42 For important interpretations, see Orgel, 'Sidney's experiment in pastoral'; Montrose, 'Celebration and insinuation'; Cooper, *Pastoral*, 149–51; Axton, 'The Tudor mask and Elizabethan court drama'; Berry, 'Sidney's May Game for the Queen'.

43 Berry, 'Sidney's May Game', 257.

44 RD to Hatton, 9 July 1578, Buxton. BL Additional MS 15891, fo. 56b.

45 HS to RD, 1 August 1578, BL Cotton Titus B. xiii, fo. 25, cit. Wallace, 200. See also HS to PS, 1 August 1578. Collins 1: 392.

46 Harvey, *Gratulationum Valdinensium Libri Quatuor*, K.iiij.ʳ⁻ᵛ.

47 Bodl. Rawl. MS D. 345, discussed in Duncan-Jones, *Courtier Poet*, 155.

48 RD to FW, 7 August 1578, Bury. *CSPF 1578–1579*, 121.

49 Greville, 'Dedication', 87.

50 TW, writing to RD at Wilton, asks him to salute Warwick, Pembroke and MDS. TW to RD, 9 November 1578, Court at Richmond. Wright, 2: 95.

51 See Worden, *The Sound of Virtue*, 84–6. On Anjou, see Holt, *The Duke of Anjou and the Politique Struggle during the Wars of Religion.*

52 On these marriage negotiations, see especially Doran, *Monarchy and Matrimony.*

53 Mendoza to Philip II, 31 December 1578, London. *CSPF 1578–1579*, 624.

54 Nicollier-De Weck, 404.

55 Mendoza to Zayas, 19 January 1579, London. *CSPF 1578–1579*, 632.

56 Nichols, *Progresses*, 2: 277.

57 HS's account book, BL Additional MS 17520, fo. 12.

58 Greville, 'Dedication', 7.

59 HL to Augustus, 17 February 1579, Dover. *Arcana*, I, pt 2, ep. 172, p. 774.

60 HL to PS, 27 February 1579, Flushing. L74 (M^r–M2^r).

61 Gilpin to FW, 27 December 1580. *CSPF 1579–1580*, 527.

62 *Apologie ou defense de tres illustre prince Guillaume . . . prince d'Orange.*

63 HL to Buchanan, 20 February 1581, Delft. Buchanan, *Epistolae*, 81–4 at 83. HL to Beale, 15 February 1581 and 22 April 1581. BL Egerton MS 1693, fos 46, 48.

64 Camden, *Historie of Elizabeth* (1630), Mm^v.

65 RD to WD, 26 February [1579], n.p. BL Harley MS 285, fos 77a, 77b.

66 Gilbert Talbot to Shrewsbury, May 1579. Lodge, *Illustrations of British History, Biography, and Manners*, 2: 156.

67 Doran, *Monarchy and Matrimony*, 250 n.41.

68 Camden, *Historie of Elizabeth* (1630), Mm4^r.

69 Mary, Queen of Scots to Archbishop of Glasgow, 4 July 1579. Froude, *History of England*, 10: 493.

70 Mendoza to Philip II, 6 July 1579, London. *CSPS 1568–1579*, 681–2.

71 Greville, 'Dedication', 37–41.

72 HL to PS, 14 October 1579. Ward, *The Seventeenth Earl of Oxford 1550–1604*, 164–77.

73 Greville, 'Dedication', 37–41.

74 PS to Hatton, 28 August 1579, n.p. BL Additional MS 15891, fo. 34b; F39 (3: 128).

75 Mendoza to Philip II, 25 August 1579. *CSPS 1568–1579*, 693.

76 Stubbs, *Discoverie of a Gaping Gulf*; see Berry, ed., *John Stubb's 'Gaping Gulf' with Letters and other relevant documents*, and *MP*, 36.

77 *A Letter to Queen Elizabeth. MP*, 46–57. This argument based on *MP*, 44–5.

78 HL to PS, 22 October 1580, Antwerp. L21 (C8^v–C10^r).

79 For copies, see list in *MP*, 37–8.

80 HL to PS, 12 March 1580, Antwerp. L89 (O4^v–O6^r). HL to PS, 22 October 1580, Antwerp. L21 (C8^v–C10^r).

81 Greville, 'Dedication', 16–17.

82 Fabianus Niphus to Dannewitz, 14 January 1580, London. *CSPF 1579–1580*, 130.

83 HL to PS, 14 November 1579, Antwerp. L83 (N6^v).

9: FANCY, TOY AND FICTION

1 Spenser, *The Shepheardes Calender*, title page; Harvey, *Three proper, and wittie, familiar Letters*; idem, *Two other, very commendable Letters, of the same mens writing*, G.iij.^{v}, G.iiij^r., H.ij.^{v}.

2 Harvey, *Three Letters*, E.ij.^{v}, F.v.^{r}.

3 Harvey, *Three Letters*, D.iiij.^{r}; Drant, *Praesvl*; for PS's nota, see Ringler, 391.

4 Sidney family psalter. TCC MS R. 17.2, fo. 2b.

5 PS to RD, 2 August 1580, Clarinton. F41 (3: 129).

6 PS to RD, 2 August 1580, Clarinton. F41 (3: 129).

7 PS to RD, 2 August 1580, Clarinton. F41 (3: 129).

8 'A Dialogue betweene two shepherds', Ringler, 343–4; see also Ringler, 517.

9 Aubrey, *Brief Lives*, 138. On Mary's patronage, see Brennan, *Literary Patronage*, xii, 11–12.

10 *OA*, 3.

11 Holinshed, *Chronicles*, 3: 1554.

12 *OA*, 3.

13 Puttenham, *Arte of English Poesie*, F.iiij.

14 *DP. MP*, 121, 94.

15 Webbe, *A Discourse of English Poetrie*, B3^v.

16 *DP. MP*, 112.

17 *DP. MP*, 112. W[hetstone], *Sir Phillip Sidney, his honorable life*, B2^v.

18 Brennan, *Literary Patronage*, 43.

19 Holinshed, *Chronicles*, 3: 1554.

20 Dean, 'Henry Oxinder's key (1628) to *The Countess of Pembroke's Arcadia*'; Marenco, *Arcadia Puritana*; Weiner, *Sir Philip Sidney and the Poetics of Protestantism*; Worden, *The Sound of Virtue*.

21 My reading here is inspired by the work of Lorna Hutson: see 'Fortunate travelers: reading for the plot in sixteenth-century England' and *The Usurer's Daughter*.

22 See Duncan-Jones, 'Sidney's personal *imprese*'.

23 Holinshed, *Chronicles*, 3: 1555.

24 Von Bülow, trans., 'Journey through England and Scotland made by Lupold von Wedel', 236.

25 Duncan-Jones, 'Sidney's personal *imprese*'.

26 [Camden], *Remaines of a Greater Worke, Concerning Britaine*, Z3^v; Buxton, *Sidney and the English Renaissance*, 149. The reference is to Ovid, *Metamorphoses*, 13: 141.

27 Fraunce, *Symbolicæ philosophiæ liber quartus et ultimus*, ed. Manning, trans. Hann, 49. The original is CKS U1475 Z16.

28 Fraunce, *Symbolicæ philosophiæ*, 176. The reference is to Homer, *Iliad*, 1: 262.

29 *NA*, 353.

30 Nichols, *Progresses*, 2: 301; see also Montrose, 'Celebration and insinuation', 28.

31 See Feuillerat ed., *Documents relating to the Office of the Revels in the time of Elizabeth*, 336; Young, *Tudor and Jacobean Tournaments*, 202.

32 *DNB* 28: 52–4.

33 'Blue' required 'that whoso hurteth horse with spear or sword shall lose the honour and his pledge.' No other speaker at the joust mentions horses. See Duncan-Jones, *Courtier Poet*, 203.

34 Hasler 3: 382–4.

35 Simon Adams' discovery was first made known in Duncan-Jones, 'Sir Philip Sidney's debt to Edmund Campion', 95 and n. 34.

36 [Camden], *Remaines*, Z3ᵛ. This fits Stow's assertion that when Denbigh died on 19 July 1584, he was 'of the age of three years and somewhat more'. Stow, *Annales of England*, Jiii 4ʳ (1191).

37 W[hetstone], *Sir Philip Sidney*, B3*.

38 Brennan, *Literary Patronage*, 43–4.

39 Stow, *Annales*, Hhhh6ʳ⁻ᵛ (1179–80).

40 Some of the materials were 'Collected, gathered, penned and published by Henry Goldwel, Gen.' in *A briefe declaratio[n] of the shews, deuices, speeches, and inuentions done and performed*; rpt. in Nichols, *Progresses*, 2: 312–29. See also Feuillerat, *Documents*, 340–4; Young, *Tudor and Jacobean Tournaments*, 203.

41 See Council, '*O Dea Certe*: The allegory of *The Fortress of Perfect Beauty*'; Montrose, 'Celebration and insinuation', 23–30; Doran, *Monarchy and Matrimony*, 180–1.

42 Goldwell, *Briefe declaration*, A.viᵛ–A.viiʳ.

43 Thomas Milles to WD, 19 May 1581. PRO SP 12/149 art. 10a, cit. Council, '*O Dea Certe*', 331.

44 *Astrophil and Stella*, sonnet 41; Ringler, 185.

45 Ringler, 437–8; for the Countess' gift to the Queen on this occasion, see Nichols, *Progresses*, 2: 389.

46 Huntingdon to WC, 10 March 1581, Newcastle. Quoted in Wallace, 246.

47 Sidney family psalter. TCC MS R.17.2, fo. 5b.

48 Ringler, 444–5. See also BL MS Lansdowne 885, fo. 86b.

49 Ringler, 175, 438–42; Duncan-Jones, 'Sidney, Stella and Lady Rich'.

50 *Astrophil and Stella*, sonnet 37; Ringler, 183.

51 Thomas Nashe, 'Preface' to *Syr P.S. His Astrophel and Stella* (1591), A3ʳ.

52 This correspondence is in the Teyler Museum, Haarlem, MS Hotomaniora; see P.J. Blok ed., 'Correspondance inédite de Robert Dudley . . . et de François et Jean Hotman', ep. 108.

53 Dom Antonio to PS, 13 May [1581], Tunis. CKS U1475 F26/7; trans. Collins, 1: 294.

54 PS to RS, 18 October 1580, Leicester House. CKS U1475 C7/8; F42 (3: 130–3 at 133).

55 Dom Antonio to PS, 13 May [1581], Tunis. CKS U1475 F26/7; trans. Collins, 1: 294.

56 Wilson, *Sweet Robin*, 237–8.

57 Mendoza to Philip II, 10 September 1581, London. Fernandez de Navarrete, *Coleccion de Documentos Inéditos*, 92: 110–12; *CSPS 1580–1586*, 171–2. Mendoza names 'Milord Habart y Phelipe Sigdine': Hume renders 'Habart' as 'Howard', but 'Herbert' [i.e. Pembroke] seems more likely.

58 PS to Hatton, 26 September 1581, Dover. BL Addit. MS 15891, fo. 64a; F47 (3: 135–6).

59 PS to WC, 10 October 1581, London. Hatfield House Cecil MS 12/13; F48 (3: 136–7).

60 See McGrath and Rowe, 'The recusancy of Sir Thomas Cornwallis'.

61 PS to RD, 15 December 1581, Salisbury. F54 (3: 140–1).

62 Doran, *Monarchy and Matrimony*.

63 Mendoza to Philip II, 24 November 1581, London. *CSPS 1580–1586*, 226.

64 Nichols, *Progresses*, 2: 344.

65 Nichols, *Progresses*, 2: 346.

66 Nichols, *Progresses*, 2: 343–8, 350.

67 William Herle to RD, 3 March 1581, Antwerp. *CSPF 1581–1582*, 514.

68 Herle to FW, 28 April 1582, Antwerp. *CSPF 1581–1582*, 665.

69 HL to Crato, 27 June 1581, Antwerp. Bibl. Ste-Geneviève MS 1456, fo. 407; BN Dupuy MS 797, p. 348, cit. Nicollier-De Weck, 447.

70 Du Plessis-Mornay, *Mémoires*, 1: 27.

71 See Kuin, 'Languet and the Veronese portrait of Sidney'.

10: HEROICAL DESIGNS

1 Antonio d'Avigna to FW and PS, 6 December 1583. *CSPF 1583–1584*, 260–1.

2 Sebastiano Pardini to PS, 21 February 1581, Paris. *CSPF 1581–1582*, 71.

3 François Perrot de Mezières to FW, 20/30 June 1584, Bièvres. *CSPF 1583–1584*, 559.

4 Alfaranti de Viçose, Sieur d'Alfeyran to FG, 20 April 1582, Antwerp. *CSPF 1581–1582*, 633.

5 Frederich Schwartz von Ruissingen to FW, 31 January 1580, Antwerp. *CSPF 1579–1580*, 144.

6 Charles de Fremyn to Davison, 19 July 1579, Antwerp. *CSPF 1579–1580*, 19. Fremyn to FW, 7/17 July 1583, Antwerp. *CSPF 1583–1584*, 11.

7 Fremyn to FW, 10 April 1582, Antwerp. *CSPF 1581–1582*, 624–5. Similar sentiments were voiced by Viçose, Sieur d'Alfeyran, an intimate of Anjou. See note 4 above.

8 *Herodiani historiae libri VIII*, ed. Estienne.

9 Franciscus Junius to PS, 1 July 1580, Otterburg, in his *Grammatica Hebraeae Linguae*, A.ij.ʳ⁻ᵛ; trans. van Dorsten, 'Sidney and Franciscus Junius the elder', 2–4. Wechel also reprinted Ramus, *Commentariorum de Religione Christiana*, ed. de Banos (1583).

10 Monardes, *Simplicium medicamentorum historiae liber tertius*, ed. de l'Écluse.

11 Daneau, *Geographiæ Poeticæ.*

12 See Scipio Gentili, *Paraphrasis aliqvot psalmorvm Davidis, carmine heroico; idem, In XXV. Davidis psalmos epicæ paraphrases;* Alberico Gentili, *De legationibus, libri tres.* On the Scipios, see Buxton, *Sidney and the English Renaissance*, 156–8.

13 Derricke, *The Image of Irelande*, a.ij.ʳ–a.iij.ᵛ. This work was in fact completed three years earlier; the dedication is dated 16 June 1578, Dublin.

14 'Certain special notes to be imparted to Mr. Philip Sidney, in the handwriting of Edm. Molyneux, esq; and signed by Sir Henry Sidney, 27 April 1582.' CKS U1475 C7/4; Collins, 1: 295–6.

15 Longleat, Dudley MSS, box 3, no. 56 cit. Hammer, *The Polarisation of Elizabethan Politics*, 52 and n. 66.

16 Petition of John Wickerson to FW, February? 1583. PRO SP 12/158, art. 85; *CSPD 1581–1590*, 98.

17 Denny to FW, 6 October 1581, Powerscourt. PRO SP 63/86, art. 15, cit. Wallace, 275; *CSPI 1574–1585*, 323. PS to FW, 17 December 1581, Wilton. PRO SP 12/150, art. 85; F51 (139).

18 WC to FW, 10 February 1583, Westminster. PRO SP 12/158, art. 62, cit. Wallace, 291; *CSPD 1581–1590*, 95.

19 Lobbet to FW, ?19 May 1583, Strasburg. *CSPF 1583*, 355.

20 'Memoir', 3: 37.

21 FW to Hatton, 19 March 1583, Barn Elms. BL Additional MS 15891, fos 104b–105a.

22 Manners to Rutland, 20 April 1583, The Savoy. HMCR 1: 149.

23 Manners to Rutland, 7 May 1583, Court. HMCR 1: 150.

24 [Castelnau] to Mary, Queen of Scots, 12 June 1583, London. HMCS 3: 3.

25 Sidney family psalter. TCC MS R.17.2, fo. 5a.

26 Marriage articles between PS and Frances Walsingham. HMCD 1: 272–3; see Baughan, 'Sir Philip Sidney and the matchmakers', 519.

27 Moffet, *Nobilis*, 84.

28 Le Moyne, *La Clef des Champs*, dedicated 'A Madame, Madame De Sidney', 26 March 1586.

29 Moffet, *Nobilis*, 85.

30 Dyer to FW, 27 March 1583, PRO SP 12/159, art. 47, cit. Wallace, 288; *CSPD 1581–1590*, 103.

31 PS to WC, 27 January 1583, Court. BL Harley MS 6993, fo. 25; F57 (3: 142–3).

32 FW to Sir Thomas Egerton, 14 February 1583, Richmond. *The Egerton Papers*, ed. Collier, 92.

33 PS to WC, 20 July 1583, Ramsbury. BL Lansdowne MS 39, art. 29; F58 (3: 143).

34 See Thomas Digges to FW, 8 June 1584. PRO SP 12/171, art. 13; *CSPD 1581–1590*, 180. Memorial by FW for Dover Haven, ?4 July 1584. PRO SP 12/172, arts 12, 13, 14; *CSPD 1581–1590*, 189. Minet, 'Some unpublished plans of Dover Harbour'.

35 'Certain Orders set down for the government of the office of the Ordnance by Ambrose, Earl of Warwick, to be observed by the inferior officers', 1584? PRO SP 12/175, art. 97; *CSPD 1581–1590*, 220–1.

36 Abbot, *The reasons which Doctour Hill Hath Brought, for the Upholding of Papistry . . . Unmasked*, 88–9, cit. McNulty, 'Bruno at Oxford', 302–3. Bruno, *La cena de le Ceneri*, G7; trans. Yates, *Giordano Bruno and the Hermetic Tradition*, 207. See also Bossy, *Giordano Bruno and the Embassy Affair*, 22–5.

37 Dee, *Diary*, 20. See also *idem, Autobiographical Tracts*, 13.

38 Bruno, *Spaccio de la bestia trionfante; idem, De gl'heroici furori*; translations from the discussion by Buxton, *Sidney and the English Renaissance*, 160–7.

39 Moffet, *Nobilis*, 82–3.

40 Clement Marot and Théodore de Bèze, *Pseaumes de David, mis en rhythme françoise*.

41 For evidence of this see Ringler, 339.

42 Du Bartas, *Seconde semaine*, pt I, bk 6, ll. 611–18, in *The Works of Guillaume de Salluste Sieur du Bartas*, ed. Holmes *et al.*

43 Du Bartas to Anthony Bacon, 12 September 1584, Montauban. BL Cotton MS Nero B. vi, fo. 288; pr. in *Works*, ed. Holmes *et al.*, 1: 201, where the recipient is misidentified as Francis Bacon.

44 Anthony Bacon to FW, 19 March 1585, Montauban. PRO SP 78/3, fo. 161–2 (art. 54); *CSPF 1584–1585*, 334–5. On English-Navarrese relations see Jardine and Stewart, *Hostage to Fortune: The troubled life of Francis Bacon 1561–1626*, chs 3 and 4.

45 FG to FW, [1586?]. *CSPD 1581–90*, 369. Golding, *A Worke concerning the Trewnesse of the Christian Religion*, *4ʳ. For the authorship debate, see *MP*, 155–7.

46 Greville, 'Dedication', 10–11.

47 Holt, *Anjou*, 209.

48 FW to Stafford, 6 July 1584. *CSPF 1583–1584*, 594. Instructions for PS, 8 July 1584. BL Cotton MS Galba E.vi, fo. 241; *CSPF 1583–1584*, 601–2. Castlenau wrote that PS, 'nephew of the Earl of Leicester', was the proposed envoy on 6 July 1584. See Castelnau to Henri III, 16 July 1584, London. Chéruel, 304–11 at 309.

49 Castelnau to Henri, 7/17 July 1584, London. Chéruel, 311–13 at 312.

50 Instructions for PS, 8 July 1584. BL Cotton MS Galba E. vi, fo. 241. For Castelnau's intelligence on PS's instructions, see Castelnau to Henri III, 17 July 1584, London. Chéruel, 311–13.

51 PRO E. 403/2559, fo. 271a, first cit. in Duncan-Jones, *Courtier Poet*, 258.

52 FW to Stafford, 2 July 1584, Court. *CSPF 1583–1584*, 579.

53 See Gilbert Talbot to Lord North, 8 July 1584. BL Additional MS 34079, fo. 17.

54 Hunsdon to WD, 28 July 1584, Berwick. *CSP Scotland 1584–1585*, 242.

55 FW to Stafford, 29 July 1584. *CSPF 1583–1584*, 645–6.

56 PS to Stafford, 21 July 1584, Court. CKS U1475 Z53/30; F62 (3: 145).

57 Stafford to WC, 11 August 1584, Paris. *CSPF 1584–5*, 19–20.

58 *Copy of a Letter*; Leimon and Parker, 'Treason and plot in Elizabethan diplomacy', 1142–3.

59 Stow, *Annales of England*, 1191.

60 See *Stradling Correspondence*, ed. Traherne; Williams, *Council*, 243–5; Robson, *The Choice of Change*, A2^r; Sidney family psalter. TCC MS R.17.2, fo. 5a; Brennan, *Literary Patronage*, 49–50.

61 Sidney family psalter. TCC MS R.17.2, fo. 5b.

62 Young, *Tudor and Jacobean Tournaments*, 48–9, 160; Bodl. Ashmole MS 845, fo. 16a, cit. Duncan-Jones, *Courtier Poet*, 271.

63 Lesieur to Archibald Douglas, 29 July 1583, Ramsbury. HMCS, 3: 8.

64 FW to Wotton, 10 September 1585, Court. *The Hamilton Papers*, ed. Bain, 2: 697.

65 FW to Wotton, 23 May 1585, Barn Elms. *Hamilton Papers*, 2: 643.

66 FW to Wotton, 18 June 1585. *Hamilton Papers*, 2: 654.

67 Thomas Milles to Wotton, 14 August 1585, London. *Hamilton Papers*, 2: 678.

68 FW to Wotton, 4 September 1585, Court. *Hamilton Papers*, 2: 694. This reading relies on Bain's identification of ciphers: see *ibid.*, 2: xxxvi.

69 Van Dorsten, *Poets*, 79.

70 Baudius, *Epistolarum centuriae tres*,*6^v; van Dorsten, *Poets*, appendix II, no. 47; trans. van Dorsten, *Poets*, 81.

71 Benedicti, *De rebvs gestis Illustriss. Principis Guilielmi, Comitis Nassovij, &c. Lib. II*, C8^r, D3^v.

72 Dousa, *Odarum Britannicarum liber*, C3^{r-v}; trans. van Dorsten, *Poets*, 82.

73 Baudius to Lipsius, [November/December 1585, Flushing]. Leiden University Library, MS BPL 885; pr. van Dorsten, *Poets*, appendix II, no. 53; trans. van Dorsten, *Poets*, 94.

74 Talbot to Shrewsbury, 14 July 1585, Court. HMCR, 1: 177.

75 FW to Wotton, 26 August 1585, Barn Elms. *Hamilton Papers*, 2: 685.

76 RD to FW, 21 September, 24 September 1585. *CSPD 1581–1590*, 267, 268.

77 On Drake's mission, see especially Keeler ed., *Sir Francis Drake's West Indian Voyage*. Also: Corbett, *Drake and the Tudor Navy*, vol. 2; Lloyd, *Sir Francis Drake*, ch. 6; Sugden, *Sir Francis Drake*, ch. 14; Cummins, *Francis Drake*, 133–59.

78 On Huguenot colonialism see the ongoing work of Frank Lestringant: *Le huguenot et le sauvage*; *Mapping the Renaissance World*, trans. Fausset; *L'expérience huguenote au Nouveau Monde (XVIe siècle)*.

79 [Hakluyt], *Divers voyages touching the discouerie of America*, ¶–¶^{4}.

80 Dee, *Diary*, 8.

81 P.H. [to WC?], 19 April 1582. PRO SP 12/153, art. 14; Quinn, ed., *The Voyages and Colonising Enterprises of Sir Humphrey Gilbert*, 2: 243.

82 Mendoza to Philip II, 26 April 1582. Fernandez de Navarrete, *Documentos Inéditos*,

92: 358; Quinn, *Gilbert*, 2: 244. Gilbert was still fitting out the ships on 4 and 21 May 1582. Fernandez de Navarrete, *Documentos*, 92: 371, 389–91; Quinn, *Gilbert*, 2: 245.

83 Quinn, *Gilbert*, 2: 264–5.

84 Kuin, 'Sidney and the New World', 573.

85 Mendoza to Philip II, 11 July 1582, London. Fernandez de Navarrete, *Documentos*, 92: 396–7.

86 FW [after 1 January 1583?]. PRO SP 12/165, art. 35 (draft); Quinn, *Gilbert*, 2: 376.

87 PS, July 1583? PRO SP 12/161, art. 44 (draft); Quinn, *Gilbert*, 2: 377–8.

88 On the 1584 parliament, see Hasler. PS to Stafford, 21 July 1584, Court. F62 (3: 145). Ralph Lane to PS, 12 August 1585. PRO CO 1/1, fos 15–16, printed in Wallace, 319. This letter probably did not reach PS before he left for Plymouth.

89 Greville, 'Dedication', 42. The following account is taken from *ibid.*, 42–6.

90 'Note of the powder and munitions delivered to Sir Francis Drake', July 1585. PRO SP 12/180, art. 56; *CSPD 1581–1590*, 255.

91 PRO SP 12/180, art. 57; *CSPD 1581–1590*, 255.

92 PRO SP 12/180, art. 58; *CSPD 1581–1590*, 255. See also PRO SP 12/180, arts 51 and 52 (29 and 30 July 1585).

93 Robert Beale to FW, 29 August 1585, Barnet. PRO SP 12/181, art. 72.

94 FSL MS L.b.344, fo. 2, quoted in Keeler, *Drake's West Indian Voyage*, 48–9.

95 Stanhope to Rutland, 12 September 1585, Nonesuch. HMCR, 1: 178.

96 Some commentators have identified Drake as the commissioner. See Thomson, *Sir Francis Drake*, 175: 'On balance it seems likely that the business was engineered in the fleet . . . The outrage is quite in Drake's style.'

97 Corporation of Plymouth Records. *Ninth Report of the Royal Commission on Historical Manuscripts*, pt 1, 278, cit. Corbett, *Drake and the Tudor Navy*, 2: 19.

98 'The only news he sent was that Dom Antonio was in the county of Devonshire . . . in a house belonging to Drake, with Philip Sidney.' Mendoza to Philip II, 8 October 1585, Paris. *CSPS 1580–1586*, 550.

99 Mendoza to Philip II, 8 October 1585, Paris. *CSPS 1580–1586*, 550.

100 Stanhope to Rutland, 12 September 1585. HMCR, 1: 178.

101 FW to WD, 13 September 1585, Court. PRO SP 84/3, art. 73; *CSPF 1585–1586*, 23–4.

102 Mendoza to Philip II, 8 October 1585, Paris. *CSPS 1580–1586*, 550.

103 'The Record kept aboard the Ship *Tiger* by Christopher Carleill and Edward Powell, 13 September 1585 to 14 April 1586', BL Cotton MS Otho E. viii, fos 229–34 at 229; Keeler, *Drake's West Indian Voyage*, 69–106 at 70.

104 Greville, 'Dedication', 46.

105 'Mr. Grevill was sent back from Basingstoke to fetch Don Antonio, who is to lie at Osterley when he comes.' Stanhope to Rutland, 21 September 1585. HMCR, 1: 180. PRO E 351/542, fo. 78b, records a payment to Greville for riding post with

his servants by royal command, from Norwich to Plymouth, to attend on Dom Antonio, 8 October 1585, cit. Rebholz, *The Life of Fulke Greville*, 73.

106 Stanhope to Rutland, 21 September 1585. HMCR, 1: 180.

107 PS to RD, 22 November 1585, Flushing. BL Cotton MS Galba C.vii, fo. 213; F66 (148, 149).

108 By 30 September, Roger Williams knew PS was coming, advising him to 'place a substantial lieutenant in your town and yourself with the army general of the cavalry'. Williams to PS, 30 September 1585, Bergen-op-Zoom. PRO SP 84/3, fo. 203a. WD to PS, 17 October 1585, Middelburg. PRO SP 84/4, art. 56.

109 Manners to Rutland, 10 November 1585, The Savoy. HMCR, 1: 181. PS to Sir Moyle Finch, 20 December 1585, Flushing. F76 (3: 156). FW to Sir Edward Stradling, 11 January 1586. *Stradling Correspondence*, ed. Traherne, 31.

110 Ramus, *Dialecticae libri dvo, scholiis G. Tempelli Cantabrigiensis illustrati*, ¶ ij^r–¶ iiij^v. Temple later wrote a Latin analysis of PS's then unpublished *Defence of Poesie*: see *William Temple's 'Analysis' of Sir Philip Sidney's 'Apology for Poetry'*, ed./tr. Webster.

111 Letters patent. PRO SP 84/5, fos 4 and 5 [drafts], 39; discussed, Wallace, 332–3 n. 4.

112 PS to Elizabeth, 10 November [1585], Gravesend. F65 (3: 147).

113 Elizabeth Sidney's date of birth has never been satisfactorily established: Hunter gives 31 January 1583/4 in his *Chorus Vatum*, but the date of the baptism would make this unlikely. BL Additional MS 24490, art. 18. In March 1600, RS's correspondent Rowland Whyte refers to Elizabeth reaching the age of twenty-one 'which will not be yet these 6 years', which would place her birth more logically in 1585. Rowland Whyte to RS, 3 March 1600. Collins, 2: 7, 174; see also 83, 120.

114 Moffet, *Nobilis*, 85.

115 '1585, November 20, the daughter of Sir Philip Sidney, Knight.' Bannerman, *Registers of St Olave, Hart Street, London, 1563–1700*.

116 BL Harley MS 1641, fo. 36; Christ Church, Oxford, Evelyn MS 258b, fo. 335a, pr. in Adams ed., *Household Accounts and Disbursement Books of Robert Dudley, Earl of Leicester*, 335.

117 Scipio Gentili, *Nereus, sive de natali Elizabethæ illustriss. Phillippi Sydnaei filiae*. See Buxton, *Sidney and the English Renaissance*, 158.

118 See FW to WC, 26 October 1585, Court. PRO SP 12/183, art. 56; *CSPD 1581–1590*, 280.

119 WD to PS, 16 November 1585, Flushing. PRO SP 84/5, art. 75. On WD, see *DNB* 14: 179–82.

11: The Great Work in Hand

1 On RD's Netherlands campaign, see: [Digges], *A Briefe Report of the Militarie Services done in the Low Covntries, by the Erle of Leicester*; Stow, *Annales of England*; Bor, *Oorsprongk,*

begin, en vervolgh der Nederlandsche oorlogen, beroerten, en borgerlyke oneenigheden; Strong and van Dorsten, *Leicester's Triumph;* Wilson, *Queen Elizabeth and the Revolt of the Netherlands;* Parker, *The Dutch Revolt;* Oosterhoff, *Leicester and the Netherlands 1586–1587.* Much of the relevant correspondence has been printed in Bruce and Brugmans. On PS in the Netherlands, see Poort, '"The desired and destined successor": A chronology of Sir Philip Sidney's activities 1585–1586'.

2 Diary by Richard Smith. Yeames, 'The Grand Tour of an Elizabethan', 92.

3 PS to RD, 22 November 1585, Flushing. BL Cotton MS Galba C.viii, fo. 191a; F66 (147–9).

4 Borlas to FW, 23 November 1585, Flushing. PRO SP 84/5, art. 57.

5 Doyley to FW, Wright, 2: 270.

6 The Hague, Rikjsarchief, Archives of the States General, 11910, fo. 295.

7 PS to FW, 15 December 1585, Middelburg. PRO SP 84/5, fo. 214; F 74 (3: 155). RD also recommended him to FW: see RD to FW, 13 December 1585, Middelburg. PRO SP 84/5, art. 111; *CSPF 1585–1586,* 213.

8 Borlas to FW, 23 November 1585, Flushing. PRO SP 84/5, art. 57; *CSPF 1585–1586,* 176–7.

9 Borlas to FW, 23 November 1585, Flushing. PRO SP 84/5, art. 57; *CSPF 1585–1586,* 176–7.

10 PS to RD, 22 November 1585, Flushing, BL Cotton MS Galba C.viii, fo. 191a; F66 (3: 147–9).

11 Thomas Digges to FW, 2 December 1585, n.p. PRO SP 84/5, art. 83a; *CSPF 1585–1586,* 192. On Digges, see Webb, 'The mathematical and military works of Thomas Digges, with an account of his life'.

12 Digges to FW, 23 November 1585, Flushing. PRO SP 84/5, art. 58; *CSPF 1585–1586,* 177.

13 Capt. Richard Huddlestone to WC, 21 January 1586, The Hague. PRO SP 84/6, art. 37; *CSPF 1585–1586,* 310–11.

14 Burnham to FW, 27 December 1585 [Flushing]. PRO SP 84/5, art. 149; *CSPF 1585–1586,* 245–6.

15 PS to RD, 22 November 1585, Flushing, BL Cotton MS Galba C.viii, fo. 191a, 192b, 191a; F66 (3: 147–9).

16 Norris to FW, 28 November 1585, Flushing. PRO SP 84/5, art. 64; *CSPF 1585–1586,* 180. PS to FW, 1 December 1585, Middelburg. BL Harley MS 286, fo. 72a; F69 (3: 150–1).

17 PS to RD, 22 November 1585, Flushing, BL Cotton MS Galba C.viii, fos 191b, 191b–192a; F66 (3: 147–9).

18 Digges to FW, 2 December 1585, n.p. PRO SP 84/5, art. 83; *CSPF 1585–1586,* 191–2.

19 RS to RD, 29 November 1585, Ostend. PRO SP 84/5, art. 69; *CSPF 1585–1586,* 184–6.

20 This account is based on Dr John James, 'Journal of Leicester's expedition to the Netherlands, 10 December o.s. 1585–23 November o.s. 1586', BL Additional MS 48014, fos 149a–164b. This work is cited in Duncan-Jones, *Courtier Poet*. I am grateful to Patricia Brewerton for allowing me to quote from her unpublished transcription. On Leicester's arrival, see esp. Strong and van Dorsten, *Leicester's Triumph*.

21 Stow, *Annales*, Kkkk2ᵛ.

22 Newsletter, December 1585. *CSPS 1580–1586*, 553–4.

23 Stow, *Annales*, Kkkk2ᵛ.

24 Oration of Adolf Meetkercke, 11/21 December 1585, Flushing. PRO SP 84/5, art. 106; *CSPF 1585–1586*, 209.

25 RD to PC, 14/24 December 1585, Middelburg. PRO SP 84/5, art. 112; *CSPF 1585–1586*, 213–14.

26 Stow, *Annales*, Kkkk2ᵛ.

27 Burnham to FW, 27 December 1585, Delft. PRO SP 84/5, art. 149; *CSPF 1585–1586*, 246.

28 RD to WC, 17/27 December 1585, Middelburg. BL Lansdowne MS 45, fo. 86a; Bruce, 28.

29 RD to FW, 26 December/5 January 1585/6, Delft. BL Harley MS 285, fo. 172a–b; Bruce, 31–2.

30 RD to FW, 26 December/5 January 1585/6, Delft. BL Harley MS 285, fo. 171a; Bruce, 30.

31 FW to RD, [replying to 26 December/5 January 1585/6], n.p. BL Harley MS 285, fo. 152a; Bruce, 35.

32 Speech by Dr Leoninus, 28 December/7 January 1585/6, The Hague. PRO SP 84/5, arts. 155–6. Speech by Dr Menin, 28 December/7 January 1585/6, The Hague. PRO SP 84/5, art. 157; *CSPF 1585–1586*, 249.

33 James' journal, 1 January 1586. BL Additional MS 48014, fo. 150a–b.

34 North to WC, 2 January 1586, The Hague. PRO SP 84/6, art 3; *CSPF 1585–1586*, 277–8.

35 'Verslag der Onderhandelingen tusschen Leycester en de afgevaardigden der Staten-Generaal', 7/17–16/26 January 1586, The Hague. Brugmans, 31–62 at 46 (10/20 January 1586), trans. Poort, '"Desired and destined successor"', 29.

36 Stow, *Annales*, Kkkk5ʳ.

37 'Verslag der Onderhandelingen', 11/21 January 1586. Brugmans, 55.

38 'Verslag der Onderhandelingen', 14/24 January 1586. Brugmans, 60.

39 James' journal, 25 January 1586. BL Additional MS 48014, fo. 152a.

40 North to WC, 2 January 1586, The Hague. PRO SP 84/6, art. 3; *CSPF 1585–1586*, 277–8.

41 RD to WC, 14/24 January 1586, Leiden. BL Harley MS 285, fo. 176; Bruce, 60, 63.

Notes

42 WD to FW, 16/26 January 1586, Leiden. PRO SP 84/6, art. 28; *CSPF 1585–1586*, 303.

43 'Instruccions for the Erle of Leicester. Nouemb. [1585]'. BL Cotton MS Galba C.viii, fo. 193a–b at 193b; Bruce, 12–15 at 15. See also 'Abstracts of the Earle of Leycesters Instruccons appointed by her Majestie to be her Leftenant of her forces in the low contreys', December 1585. BL Cotton MS Galba C.viii, fo. 109b–110b.

44 Minute by RD, [1585]. BL Harley MS 285, fo. 144a; Bruce, 20.

45 Heads of letter from [FW] to RD, 17/27 January 1586. PRO SP 84/6, art. 29; *CSPF 1585–1586*, 303.

46 RD to FW, 7 February [1586], The Hague. BL Harley MS 285, fo. 200b; Bruce, 94.

47 PC to RD, 26 January/5 February 1586, Court at Greenwich. PRO SP 84/3, arts. 53–4; *CSPF 1585–1586*, 322–4.

48 RD to FW, 8 February 1586, The Hague. BL Harley MS 285, fo. 202a; Bruce, 99.

49 Elizabeth to RD, 10 February 1586. BL Cotton MS Galba C.viii, fo. 27b; Bruce, 110.

50 FW to RD, 28 March 1586, Court. BL Cotton MS Galba C.viii, fo. 66; Bruce, 192.

51 WD to RD, 17 February 1585, London. BL Cotton MS Galba C.ix, fo. 82a; Bruce, 118.

52 WD's marginal comments on RD to FW, 10 March 1586, Haarlem. BL Harley MS 285, fo. 230; Bruce, 168.

53 PS to WD, 19 March 1586, Amsterdam. BL Harley MS 285, fo. 293a; F87 (3: 165).

54 PS to WD, 20 July 1586, Flushing. BL Harley MS 285, fo. 243a [address 244b]; F105 (3: 177–8).

55 By 18 February, PS was in Flushing: see Gecommitteerde Raden van Zeeland to PS, 18/28 February 1586. Brugmans, 85 ('Nous entendons le retour de vostre seigneurie à Vlissingues . . .'). For Leiden, see Strong and van Dorsten, *Leicester's Triumph*, app. 2; van Dorsten, *Poets*, 115.

56 PS to FW, 3/13 March 1586, Middelburg. PRO SP 84/7, art. 3; F84 (3: 164).

57 Doyley to WC, 16 April 1586, Utrecht. PRO SP 84/7, art. 98; *CSPF 1585–1586*, 556–8.

58 PS to Plantin, 28 March/7 April 1586, Utrecht. Harvard bMS Eng. 870 (6); Bond, 'A letter from Sir Philip Sidney to Christopher Plantin'.

59 PS to WC, 18 March 1586, Amsterdam. PRO SP 84/7, art. 37; F86 (3: 165).

60 Elizabeth to RD, 1 April 1586, Greenwich. PRO SP 84/7, art. 75; Bruce, 209.

61 RD to FW, 5 April 1586, Utrecht. Bruce, 216.

62 Whitney, *A Choice of Emblemes,* * 3ʳ.

63 RD to Adolf van Nieuwaar, 8/18 May 1586, Utrecht. Brugmans, 138–9; trans. Dop, *Eliza's Knights*, 164.

64 RD to FW, 27 February 1586, The Hague. BL Harley MS 285, fo. 222b; Bruce, 141.

65 van Dorsten, *Poets*, 126–30.

66 Strong and van Dorsten, *Leicester's Triumph*, fig. 2.

67 RD to FW, 9 March 1586, Haarlem. BL Harley MS 285, fo. 225b; Bruce, 166.

68 RD to PC, 27 March 1586, Utrecht. BL Harley MS 285, fo. 234a–b; Bruce, 190.

69 WC to RD, 6 March 1586, Greenwich. BL Cotton MS Galba C.ix, fo. 116b; Bruce, 153.

70 RD to FW, 24 February 1586, Hague. BL Harley MS 285, fo. 218a; Bruce, 137.

71 FW to RD, 21 April 1586, Court. BL Cotton MS Galba C.ix, fos 183b, 184a; Bruce, 231–2.

72 RD to FW, 21 February 1586, n.p. BL Harley MS 285, fo. 214; Bruce, 130.

73 Palavicino to FW, 2 April 1586, n.p. *CSPF 1585–1586*, 516.

74 PC to PS, 2 March 1586, n.p. PRO SP 84/7, arts 1 (draft) and 2 (endorsed 10 March 1586); *CSPF 1585–1586*, 407–8.

75 PS to FW, 24 March 1586, Utrecht. BL Harley MS 287, art. 1; F89 (166–8).

76 Thomas Morgan to Mary, Queen of Scots, 31 March 1586. HMCS, 3: 137.

77 PS to FW, 24 March 1586, Utrecht. BL Harley MS 287, art. 1; F89 (166–8).

78 PS to RD, 19 February 1586, Flushing. BL Cotton MS Galba C.ix, fo. 93b; F81 (3: 161–2). Capt Wylsford to FW, 26 January 1586. PRO SP 84/6, art. 55; *CSPF 1585–1586*, 324–5.

79 PS to WD, 24 February 1586, Flushing. BL Cotton MS Galba C.ix, fo. 75; F82 (162–3).

80 Motley, *History of the United Netherlands*, 2: 1.

81 [Digges], *Briefe Report*.

82 James' journal, 5 March 1586. BL Additional MS 48014, fo. 153b; Doyley to WC, 16 April 1586, Utrecht. PRO SP 84/7, art. 98; *CSPF 1585–1586*, 556–8. See also 'News from sundry parts', 24 March 1586. *CSPF 1585–1586*, 484.

83 James' journal, 3 March 1586. BL Additional MS 48014, fo. 153a.

84 Franciscus Dusseldorpius, *Annales*, ed. R. Fruin, in *Werken, uitgegeven door het historisch genottschap*, 3.i (The Hague, 1893), 209–10; van Dorsten, *Poets*, app. II, no. 67; trans. van Dorsten, *Poets*, 117.

85 'A Loan Exhibition depicting the Reign of Queen Elizabeth', 1933, no. 368. [catalogue] cit. van Dorsten, *Poets*, 118.

86 Lipsius to H. Ranzonius, 5 April 1586, Leiden. François and Jean Hotman, *Epistolae*, Iiiᵛ–Iii 2ʳ (442–3), trans. van Dorsten, *Poets*, 118.

87 Lipsius to Dousa, 1 September 1585, Leiden. BL Burney MS 370, fo. 35; van Dorsten, *Poets*, app. II no. 4; trans. van Dorsten, *Poets*, 118.

88 Lipsius to PS, 17 March 1586, Leiden. Dedicatory epistle to *De recta pronvnciatione*; van Dorsten, *Poets*, app. II, no. 69; trans. van Dorsten, *Poets*, 119.

89 Plantin to Nicolas Oudart, 8 October 1586, Antwerp. *Correspondance de Christophe Plantin*, ed. Dénuce, 8: 58–60. See also Voet with Voet-Gisolle, *The Plantin Press (1558–1589): A Bibliography*, 3: 1380–2. For the copy, see Museum Plantin-Moretus, Antwerp, R 15.3.

90 Thomas Doyley to WC, 24 May 1586, Arnhem. PRO SP 84/8, art. 41; *CSPF 1585–1586*, 666–9.

91 Holinshed, *Chronicles*, 3: 1548. Stow dates the death as 1 May: see Stow, *Annales*, LIll 2ʳ.

92 PS to FW, 26 May 1586, Arnhem. PRO SP 84/8, art. 49; F102 (3: 176).

93 Unsigned advices from London, 24 June 1586. *CSPS 1580–1586*, 585.

94 On the funeral, see Wallace, 361.

95 The urn was rediscovered over two centuries later in the garden of Edward Coleman Esq. of Leominster in Herefordshire, inscribed: 'Her. Lih. The./Hart. of Syr./Henry. Sydney. L.P. Anno./Domini. 1586.' Wallace, 361 n.2.

96 See 'Chardges and expenses in fetchinge of the corps of Sir H. Sydney knight of the Order deceased from the cittie of Worcester to his Mannor of Penshurst' [9–21 June 1586]. BL Lansdowne MS 50, fos 191a–193a. For the burial date, see Stow, *Annales*, LIll2ʳ.

97 'I am presently going toward Flushing whence I hear that your daughter is very well and merry.' PS to FW, 28 June 1586, Utrecht. PRO SP 84/8, art. 131; F104 (3: 177).

98 Entry under 22 August 1586. Bannerman, *Registers of St. Olave*.

99 PS to FW, 24 March 1586, Utrecht. BL Harley MS 287, art. 1; F89 (3: 168).

12: THE VERY HOPE OF OUR AGE

1 RD to FW, 31 May 1586, n.p. Bruce, 284–5.

2 North to WC, 16 June 1586, Utrecht. PRO SP 84/8, art. 93; *CSPF 1586–1587*, 18–20.

3 Doyley to WC, 24 June 1586, Utrecht. PRO SP 84/8, art. 117; *CSPF 1586–1587*, 48–50.

4 [E.M. of Antwerp], *A Trve discovrse historicall, of the svcceeding governovrs in the Netherlands*, trans. T.C. and Ric. Ro., N2ᵛ.

5 RD to FW, 9 March 1586, Haarlem. BL Harley MS 285, fo. 225; Bruce, 167.

6 RD to FW, 8 May 1586, Arnhem. Bruce, 263.

7 Warwick to RD, 6 March 1586, n.p. BL Cotton MS Galba C.ix, fo. 113; Bruce, 151.

8 Doyley to WC, 24 June 1586, Utrecht. PRO SP 84/8, art. 117; *CSPF 1586–1587*, 48–50.

9 'A memorial for Mr Atye', 20 June 1586. PRO SP 84/8, art. 110; *CSPF 1586–1587*, 41–2.

10 Doyley to WC, 8 August 1586, Utrecht. PRO SP 84/9, art. 75; *CSPF 1585–1586*, 116–17.

11 Thomas Cecil to WC, 21 July 1586, The Hague. PRO SP 84/9, art. 43; *CSPF 1585–1586*, 98.

12 Stow, *Annales*, 731.

13 [Lewkenor], *The Estate of English Fvgitives vnder the King of Spaine and his ministers*, C4^v.

14 [E.M.], *Discovrse*, N2^v.

15 For competing accounts of Axel, see RD to Elizabeth, 8 July 1586, Utrecht. PRO SP 84/9, art. 9; *CSPF 1586–1587*, 75–6. RD to FW, 8 July 1586, n.p. Bruce, 337. RD to WC, 9/19 July 1586, Utrecht. PRO SP 84/9, art. 13; *CSPF 1586–1587*, 81. Thomas Cecil to WC, 8/18 July 1586, Utrecht. PRO SP 84/9, art. 10; *CSPF 1586–1587*, 77; Stow, *Annales*, Mmmm6^v–Mmmm7^r; [Lewkenor], *Discovrse*, D2$^{r–v}$; Dop, *Eliza's Knights*, 174–5.

16 Stow, *Annales*, Mmmm6^v–Mmmm7.

17 RD to FW, 11 July 1586, n.p. Bruce, 346.

18 Greville, 'Dedication', 72.

19 Thomas Cecil to WC, 8/18 July 1586, Utrecht. PRO SP 84/9, art. 10; *CSPF 1586–1587*, 77.

20 On Gravelines, see 'A Discourse of the enterprise of Graveling', 23 July 1586. PRO SP 84/9, art. 46; *CSPF 1586–1587*, 99–100. Thomas Doyley to WC, 8 August 1586, Utrecht. PRO SP 84/9, art. 75; *CSPF 1586–1587*, 115–17.

21 Doyley to WC, 8 August 1586. PRO SP 84/9, art. 75; *CSPF 1586–1587*, 115–16.

22 Lewkenor, *Discovrse*, G2^r.

23 PS to WD, 20 July 1586, Flushing. BL Harley MS 285, fo. 243a; F105 (3: 177–8).

24 Williams, 6 March 1588, BL Lansdowne MS 58, fo. 162–3, cit. Dop, *Eliza's Knights*, 175.

25 RD to FW, 18 July 1586, Brill. PRO SP 84/9, art. 31; *CSPF 1586–1587*, 92.

26 William Knollys to WC, end of July 1586. PRO SP 84/9, art. 65; *CSPF 1586–1587*, 111.

27 Greville, 'Dedication', 72.

28 On this incident see van Dorsten, *Poets*, 148–51.

29 See Oosterhoof, *Leicester and the Netherlands*, 111–14.

30 Lipsius to PS, 30 August 1586, Utrecht. *Præstantium ac eruditorum virorum epistolæ ecclesiasticæ et theologicæ*, ed. Limborch; trans. van Dorsten, *Poets*, 148–50.

31 PS to Lipsius, 14 September 1586, Deventer. Leiden University Libr., MS. Lips. 4; F 112 (3: 182); trans. van Dorsten, *Poets*, 130–1.

32 PS to PC, 14 August 1586, Flushing. PRO SP 84/9, art. 89; F107 (3: 178–9).

33 PS to WC, 14 August 1586, Flushing. BL Stowe MS 150, fo. 50a–b; F110 (3: 181).

34 PS to FW, 14 August 1586, Flushing. PRO SP 84/9, art. 91; F108 (3: 179–80).

35 PS to FW, 14 August 1586, Flushing. PRO SP 84/9, art. 90; F109 (3: 180).

36 On Doesburg, see [E.M.], *Discovrse*, N2^v–N3^r.

37 On the skirmish at Zutphen, see RD to WC, [24] September 1586, camp before Zutphen. PRO SP 84/10, art. 23; *CSPF 1586–1587*, 165–6; [E.M.], *Discovrse*, N3^v–N4^v; Dop, *Eliza's Knights*, 1–6.

38 PS to FW, 22 September 1586, Zutphen. PRO SP 84/10, art. 19; F113 (3: 182–3).

39 RD to WC, [24] September 1586. PRO SP 84/10, art. 23; *CSPF 1586–1587*, 164–6.

RD to FW, 28 September 1586, n.p. Bruce, 416.

40 Indeed, one Dutch source has it that the convoy had completed the victualling mission and was on its way home. Van Dorsten, 'The final year', 21.

41 Smythe, *Certain Discourses . . . Concerning the formes and effects of diuers sorts of weapons, and other verie important matters Militarie*, B3ʳ.

42 Gifford, *The Maner of Sir Philip Sidneyes Death*, ed. Juel-Jensen.

43 Stow, *Annales*, 737.

44 Greville, 'Dedication', 77.

45 On PS's final days and funeral, see Beltz, 'Memorials of the last achievement, illness and death of Sir Philip Sidney'; Wallace, 380–97; van Dorsten, 'The final year'; Poort, '"The desired and destined successor"'; Duncan-Jones, *Courtier Poet*, 295–303.

46 RD to WC, [24] September 1586, camp before Zutphen. PRO SP 84/10, art. 23; *CSPF 1586–1587*, 165.

47 Van Dorsten, *Poets*, 59. James' journal, BL Additional MS 48014.

48 Hale, *The Art of War and Renaissance England*, 30–1.

49 RD to FW, 27 September 1586, camp before Zutphen. Bruce, 414–15. See also RD to WC, 27 September 1586, camp before Zutphen [postscript]. PRO SP 84/10, art. 30; *CSPF 1586–1587*, 168.

50 RD to FW, 28 September 1586, n.p. Bruce, 415.

51 Vezekius to James, 25 September/5 October 1586, Deventer. *Epistvlae et tractatvs cvm Reformationis tvm ecclesiae Londino-Batavae historiam illvstrantes (1544–1622)*, ed. Hessels, 814–15 at 814; trans. van Dorsten, *Poets*, 152.

52 Leoninus and Killigrew to the States General, 28 September/8 October 1586, Arnhem. Brugmans, 234–5.

53 Gifford, *Sidneyes Death*, B1.

54 James' journal, 7 October 1586. BL Additional MS 48014, fo. 163a.

55 Heneage to RD, 13 October 1586, court. BL Cotton MS Galba C. x, fo. 6; Bruce, 438. I have followed Bruce's reconstruction.

56 Greville, 'Dedication', 79–80.

57 Advices from Deventer, 9 November 1586. *CSPS 1580–1586*, 650.

58 W[hetstone], *Sir Phillip Sidney, his honorable life*, C2 and marginal note.

59 James' diary, 15 October 1586. BL Additional MS 48104, fo. 163a–b.

60 Holinshed, *Chronicles*, 3: 1555. Duncan-Jones suggests that 'Belerius' might be Pierre Beller, who translated Philo Judaeus; or Antwerp scholar-printer Jean Beller, who translated Thomas à Kempis' *Imitation of Christ. Courtier Poet*, 297–8.

61 D. Baudius to J. Dousa, 16/26 October 1586, Arnhem. BL Burney MS 371, fo. 123; van Dorsten, *Poets*, 218–19; trans. van Dorsten, *Poets*, 152. Van Dorsten dates this as September, but the mention of RD's visit suggests that the date on the letter is in fact correct.

62 Baudius to Dousa, 16/26 October 1586. BL Burney MS 371, fo. 123; van Dorsten,

Poets, 218–19; trans. van Dorsten, *Poets*, 152–3.

63 PS to Johan W. Wier, [15/25 October 1586], Arnhem. PRO SP 84/10, art. 73; F114 (3:183). For date see Beltz, 'Memorials'.

64 Gisbert Enerwitz to Wier, 15/25 October 1586, Arnhem. PRO SP 84/10, art. 73; *CSPF 1586–1587*, 202.

65 PS's will. *MP*, 152.

66 Gifford, *Sidneyes Death*, B4ʳ–B7ʳ.

67 James' diary, 17 October 1586. BL Additional MS 48104, fo. 163b. The scene is highly conventional, but see also Henry Archer to Sir Thomas Heneage, 23 October [1586], Utrecht: 'Sir Philip Sidney on Monday died, to the great heaviness of his excellency and our whole people here, but he died so godly as all wondered, and most praised God for it.' BL Harley MS 285, fo. 264; Bruce 480.

Bibliography

1. Manuscripts

Antwerp, Museum Plantin-Moretus
R 15.3 (mutilated copy of Lipsius, *De recta pronunciatione* [1586])

Cambridge, Trinity College
R.17.2 (Sidney family psalter)

Cambridge, MA, Harvard University, Houghton Library
MS Eng. 870
fms Eng 725
accession *51M-135

Canterbury, King's School
Walpole Collection
Matteo Bandello, *Histoires tragiques*, trans. François de Belleforest (PS's copy)

London, The British Library
Additional MSS
    15552, 15891, 15914, 17520, 17650, 18675, 24490, 28263, 34079, 34361, 39830, 48014
Burney MSS
    370, 371
Cotton MSS
    Galba B.xi, C.vi, C.vii, C.viii, C.ix, C.x, E.vi
    Nero B.vi
    Otho E. viii
    Titus B. ii, B. xiii
    Vespasian F.vi, F.xii
    Appendix LXII
Egerton MS 1693
Hargrave MS 497
Harley MSS
    36, 285, 286, 287, 1641, 6993
Lansdowne MSS
    10, 11, 12, 17, 39, 45, 50, 58, 94, 117, 885, 981
Royal MS 18 A. XLVIII
Stowe MS 150

London, Lambeth Palace Library
MS 628
MS 647

London, Public Record Office
CO1   Colonial
E.133, 351, 403   Exchequer
LC 2/4/3   Coronation Roll
SP 12   Domestic – Elizabeth
SP 15   Domestic – Addenda
SP 63   Ireland
SP 78   Foreign – France
SP 84   Foreign – Low Countries

Maidstone, Centre for Kentish Studies
U1475 A4, A10, A33, A35, A54
U1475 C1, C2, C3, C5, C7
U1475 E93
U1475 F1, F26
U1475 O25, O61
U1475 Q31, Q32
U1475, Z16, Z53
U1500 C1

New Haven CT, Yale University, Beinecke Rare Book and Manuscript Library
Osborn MS fa. 14

Oxford, Bodleian Library
Ashmole MSS
   356(5), 845
Don.d.152

Oxford, New College
MS 328-2

Padua, Archivio di Stato
Notarile 5007

Paris, Bibliothèque Nationale
Dupuy 797
lat. 8583

Bibliography

Princeton, NJ, Princeton University, Firestone Memorial Library
Deposits of Lucius Wilmerding, Jr:
Titus Livius, *Romanae historiae principis decades tres, cvm dimidia* (Basle: per Ioannes Heruagios, 1555) (Gabriel Harvey's copy)

Washington, DC, Folger Shakespeare Library
L.b.344
X.d.271

2. Calendars and printed editions of manuscript sources

State Papers

Domestic
Calendar of State Papers, Domestic Series, of the Reign of Edward VI, Mary, Elizabeth, 1547-1580, ed. Robert Lemon (London: Longmans, 1856)
Calendar of State Papers, Domestic Series, of the Reign of Edward VI, 1547-1553, preserved in the Public Record Office, ed. C.S. Knighton (London: HMSO, 1992)
Calendar of State Papers, Domestic Series, of the Reign of Mary I, 1553-1558, preserved in the Public Record Office, ed. C.S. Knighton (London: PRO, 1998)
Calendar of State Papers, Domestic Series, of the Reign of Elizabeth, 1581-1590, ed. Mary Anne Everett Green (London: Longmans, 1865)

Foreign
Calendar of State Papers, Foreign Series, of the Reign of Edward VI, 1547-1553, ed. William B. Turnbull (London: Longmans, 1861)
Calendar of State Papers, Foreign Series, of the Reign of Elizabeth (London: Longmans and HMSO, 1865-1936)
    1559-1560, ed. Joseph Stevenson (1865)
    1560-1561, ed. Joseph Stevenson (1865)
    1561-1562, ed. Joseph Stevenson (1866)
    1562, ed. Joseph Stevenson (1867)
    1563, ed. Joseph Stevenson (1869)
    1572-1574, ed. Allan James Crosby (1876)
    1575-1577, ed. Allan James Crosby (1880)
    1577-1578, ed. Arthur John Butler (1901)
    1578-1579, ed. Arthur John Butler (1903)
    1579-1580, ed. Arthur John Butler (1904)
    January 1581-April 1582, ed. Arthur John Butler (1907)
    May-December 1582, ed. Arthur John Butler (1909)
    January-June 1583 and Addenda, ed. Arthur John Butler (1913)

July 1583-July 1584, ed. Sophie Crawford Lomas (1916)
August 1584-August 1585, ed. Sophie Crawford Lomas (1916)
September 1585-May 1586, ed. Sophie Crawford Lomas (1921)
June 1586-March 1587, ed. Sophie Crawford Lomas and Allen B. Hinds (1927)

Ireland
Calendar of State Papers relating to Ireland, of the reigns of Henry VIII, Edward VI, Mary, and Elizabeth
(London: Longmans, 1860-77)
1509-1573, ed. Hans Claude Hamilton (1860)
1574-1585, ed. Hans Claude Hamilton (1867)
1586-1588, ed. Hans Claude Hamilton (1877)

Rome
*Calendar of State Papers Relating to English Affairs, preserved principally at Rome, in the Vatican Archives
and Library* (London: HMSO, 1916)
1572-1578, ed. J.M. Rigg

Scotland
Calendar of State Papers Relating to Scotland and Mary, Queen of Scots 1547-1603 (Edinburgh: HM
General Register House/HMSO, 1907-14)
Vol. 5 *1574-1581* ed. William K. Boyd
Vol. 7 *1584-1585* ed. William K. Boyd

Spain
*Calendar of Letters, Despatches, and State Papers Relating to the Negotiations between England and Spain,
January-July 1554*, ed. Royall Tyler (London: HMSO, 1949)
*Calendar of Letters and State Papers Relating to English Affairs, preserved principally in the archives of
Simancas*, ed. Martin A.S. Hume (London: HMSO, 1892-6)
Vol. 1 *Elizabeth 1558-1567* (1892)
Vol. 2 *Elizabeth 1568-1579* (1894)
Vol. 3 *Elizabeth 1580-1586* (1896)

Others

Acts of the Privy Council of England, ed. John Roche Dasent (London: HMSO, 1894-1907)
Vol. 4 *1552-1554* (1892)
Vol. 5 *1554-1556* (1893)
Vol. 10 *1577-1578* (1895)
Adams, Simon, ed., *Household Accounts and Disbursement Books of Robert Dudley, Earl of Leicester,
1558-1586*, Camden 5th ser., vol. 6 (Cambridge: Cambridge University Press for
the Royal Historical Society, 1995)

Bibliography

Aubrey, John, *Aubrey's Brief Lives*, ed. Oliver Lawson Dick (London: Secker & Warburg, 1958)

Bain, Joseph, ed., *The Hamilton Papers: Letters and Papers illustrating the political relations of England and Scotland in the XVIth century*, vol. 2 1543-1590 (Edinburgh: HM General Register House, 1892)

Bannerman, W.B., ed., *The registers of St Olave, Hart Street, London, 1563-1700* (London: Harleian Society, vol. 46, 1916)

Bateson, Mary, ed., 'A Collection of Original Letters from the Bishops to the Privy Council, 1564' (1893), *Camden Miscellany* 9 (1895)

Baudius, Dominicus, *Epistolarum centuriae tres* (Leiden, 1636)

Beale, Robert, 'A Treatise of the Office of a Councellor and Principall Secretarie to her Majestie', printed in Read, *Mr Secretary Walsingham*, 1: 423-43

Bentham, Thomas, 'The Letter-Book of Thomas Bentham, Bishop of Coventry and Lichfield', ed. Rosemary O'Day and Joel Berlatsky, *Camden Miscellany* 27 (1979), 113-238

Bethune, Maximilian, duc de Sully, *Memoires de Maximilien de Bethune, duc de Sully, principal ministre de Henry le Grand. Mis en order, avec des Remarques, par M.L.D.L.D.L.*, 3 vols (London, 1747)

Bethune, Maximilian, duc de Sully, *Memoirs of Maximilian de Bethune, duke of Sully, prime minister to Henry the Great*, 3 vols, 3rd edn (London: A. Millar, 1761)

Blok, P.J. ed., 'Correspondance inédite de Robert Dudley, comte de Leycester, et de François et Jean Hotman', *Archives du Musée Teyler*, 2nd ser., vol. 12 (Haarlem: Loosjes, 1911), 79-296

Bor, Peiter, *De Nederlandse Historien, Oorspongh, begin en vervolgh der Nederlandsche oorlogen, beroerten, en burgerlijke oneenigheden, 1555-1600*, 4 vols (Amsterdam, 1679-84)

Brewer, J.S. and William Bullon, eds, *Calendar of the Carew Manuscripts preserved in the Archiepiscopal Library at Lambeth 1575-1588* (London: Longmans, 1868)

Bruce, John, ed., *Correspondence of Robert Dudley, earl of Leycester, during his government of the Low Countries, in the years 1585 and 1586* (London: Camden Society, 1844)

Brugmans, H., ed., *Correspondentie van Robert Dudley graaf van Leycester en andere documenten betreffende zijn gouvernement-generaal in de Nederlanden, 1585-1588* (Utrecht, 1931)

Buchanan, George, *Georgij Buchanani Scoti ad Viros sui Seculi clarissimos Eorumque ad eundem, Epistolae* (London: D. Brown, 1711)

Calvert, E., ed., *Shrewsbury School Regestum Scholarum 1562-1635, Admittances and Readmittances. Transcribed from the original entries* (Shrewsbury: Adnitt & Naunton, 1892)

Cameron, Annie I., ed., *The Warrender Papers*, vol. 1 (Edinburgh: Edinburgh University Press for the Scottish Historical Society, 1931)

Chéruel, A., *Marie Stuart et Catherine de Médicis: étude historique sur les relations de la France et de l'Écosse* (Paris: L. Hachette, 1858)

Clifford, Henry, *The Life of Jane Dormer Duchess of Feria transcribed by E.E. Estcourt*, ed. Joseph Stevenson (London: Burns and Oates, 1887)

Collier, J. Payne, ed., *The Egerton Papers* (London: Camden Society, 1840)

Collins, Arthur, ed., *Letters and Memorials of State, in the Reigns of Queen Mary, Queen Elizabeth, King James, King Charles the First, Part of the Reign of King Charles the Second, and Oliver's Usurpation. Written and collected by Sir Henry Sydney . . . Sir Philip Sydney . . . Sir Robert Sydney . . . Robert, the second Earl of Leicester . . . Philip Lord Viscount Lisle*, 2 vols (London: T. Osborne, 1746)

Curtis, T.C. and R.B. McDowell, eds, *Irish Historical Documents, 1172-1922* (London: Methuen, 1943; 1977)

Dee, John, *Autobiographical Tracts of Dr. John Dee, Warden of the College of Manchester*, ed. James Crossley (Manchester: Chetham Society, 1851)

Dee, John, *The Private Diary of Dr. John Dee*, ed. James Orchard Halliwell (London: Camden Society, 1842)

Devereux, Walter Bouchier, ed., *Lives and Letters of the Devereux, earls of Essex, in the reigns of Elizabeth, James I., and Charles I. 1540-1646*, 2 vols, (London: John Murray, 1853)

Digges, Dudley, *The Compleat Ambassador: or two Treaties of the Intended Marriage of Qu: Elizabeth Of Glorious Memory* (London: Gabriel Bedell and Thomas Collins, 1655)

Du Plessis-Mornay, Philippe, *Mémoires et Correspondance de Du Plessis-Mornay*, ed. A.D. Vaudoré and P.R. Auguys, 12 vols (Paris: Treuttel & Würtz, 1824)

Dusseldorpius, Franciscus, *Annales*, ed. R. Fruin, in *Werken, uitgegeven door het historisch genottschap*, 3.i (The Hague, 1893)

Edward VI of England, *The Chronicle and Political Papers of King Edward VI*, ed. W.K. Jordan (London: George Allen and Unwin Ltd, 1966)

Ellis, Henry, ed., *Original Letters, illustrative of English history*, 2nd ser., 4 vols (London: Harding and Lepard, 1827)

Fernandez de Navarrete, Martin, ed., *Coleccion de Documentos Inéditos para la Historia de España* vol. 92 (Madrid: Ginesta Hermanos, 1988)

Feuillerat, Albert, ed., *Documents relating to the Office of the Revels in the time of Queen Elizabeth* (Louvain: A. Uystpruyst, 1908)

Foster, Joseph, ed., *The Register of Admissions to Gray's Inn, 1521-1889* (London: privately printed, 1889)

Fraunce, Abraham, *Symbolicæ philosophiæ liber quartus et ultimus*, ed. John Manning, trans. Estelle Haan (New York, NY: AMS Press, 1991)

Gifford, George, *The Maner of Sir Philip Sidneyes Death Written by his Chaplain M.G. Gifford*, ed. B.E. Juel-Jensen (Oxford: New Bodleian Library, 1959)

Hartwig, Otto, ed., *Album Academiae Vitebergensis ab A. Ch.MDII usque ad A. MDCII*, vol. 2 (Halle: Maximilian Niemeyer, 1894)

Haynes, Samuel, ed., *A Collection of State Papers, relating to affairs in the reigns of King Henry VIII, King Edward VI, Queen Mary, and Queen Elizabeth, From the year 1542 to 1570 . . . left by William Cecil Lord Burghley, and Now remaining at Hatfield House . . .* (London: William Bowyer, 1740)

Hessels, Joannes Henricus, ed., *Epistvlae et tractatvs Reformation tvm ecclesiae Londino-Batavae historiam illvstrantes (1544-1622) ex avtographis mandante ecclesia Londino-Batava* (Cambridge: typis Academiae, 1889)

Historical Manuscripts Commission, *Calendar of the Manuscripts of the Most Hon. The Marquis of Salisbury, K.G. . . . preserved at Hatfield House, Hertfordshire.* 24 vols (London: HMSO, 1883-1976)

Historical Manuscripts Commission, *Ninth Report of the Royal Commission on Historical Manuscripts,* pt 1 (London: HMSO, 1883)

Historical Manuscripts Commission, *Report on the Manuscript of Lord de L'Isle & Dudley Preserved at Penshurst Place,* 6 vols (London: HMSO, 1925–66)

Historical Manuscripts Commission, *Report on the Pepys Manuscripts preserved at Magdalene College, Cambridge,* (London: HMSO, 1911)

Historical Manuscripts Commission, *The Manuscripts of his Grace the Duke of Rutland . . . preserved at Belvoir Castle,* vol. 1 (London: HMSO, 1888)

Historical Manuscripts Commission, *The Third Report of the Royal Commission on Historical Manuscripts* (London: HMSO, 1872)

Hotman, François and Jean Hotman, *Francisci et Joannis Hotomanorum patris ac filii, et clarorum virorum ad eos Epistolae* (Amsterdam: apud Georgium Gallet, 1700)

Hughes, Paul L. and James F. Larkin, eds, *Tudor Royal Proclamations,* 3 vols (New Haven, CT: Yale University Press, 1964-1969)

[Hull, F.], *De L'Isle M.S.S.* Parts I-III (typescript catalogue, 1972)

James, Montague Rhodes, *The Western Manuscripts in the library of Trinity College, Cambridge: a descriptive catalogue,* vol. 2 (Cambridge: Cambridge University Press, 1901)

Johann Casimir, *Briefe des Pfalzgrafen Johann Casimir mit verwandten schriftstücken,* ed. Friedrich von Bezold, 3 vols (Munich: M. Rieger'sche Universitäts-Buchhandlung, 1882-1903)

Kervyn de Lettenhove, Joseph Baron de, ed., *Relations politiques des Pays-Bas et de l'Angleterre sous le règne de Philippe II,* 11 vols (Brussels: F. Hayez, 1882-1900)

Languet, Hubert, *Epistolae politicae et historicae. Scriptae quondam ad illustrem, & generosum dominum Philippum Sydnaeum* (Frankfurt: Gulielmi Fitzeri, 1633)

Languet, Hubert, *Epistolae, politicae et historicae ad Philippum Sydnaeum* (Leiden: Elzevir, 1646)

Languet, Hubert, *Ad Joachimum Camerarium patrem, & Ioachim Camerarium, filium, medicum, scriptae Epistolae,* ed. Ludovicus Camerarius (Groningen: typis Iohannis Nicoli, 1646)

Languet, Hubert, *Arcana secvli decimi sexti. Hvberti Langveti legati, dvm vivet, et consiliarii Saxonici epistolae secretae ad principem svvm Avgvstvm Sax. dvcem & S.R.I. septe, virvm* (Halae Hermvndvror: *impensis* Ioh. Friderici Zeitleri & Henr. Georgii Mvssellii, 1699)

Leighton, W.A., ed., 'Early chronicles of Shrewsbury 1372-1603', *Transactions of the Shropshire Archaeological Society* 3 (1880), 257-64

Limborch, Phillipus à, *Præstantium ac eruditorum virorum epistolæ ecclesiasticæ et theologicæ,* 2nd edn (Amsterdam: *apud* Henricum Wetsenium, 1684)

Lodge, Edmund, *Illustrations of British History, Biography, and Manners, in the Reigns of Henry VIII, Edward VI, Mary, Elizabeth, & James I,* 2nd edn, 3 vols (London: John Chudley, 1838)

Ludlow Historical Research Group, *Ludlow Bailiffs' Accounts 1561-2* (Ludlow, typescript, n.d.)

Marnix, Phillips van, de Sint-Aldegonde, *Marnixi Epistulae: de briefwisseling van Marnix van Sint-Aldegonde: Een kritishce uitgave*, ed. Aloïs Gerlo and Rudolf De Smet, 3 vols (Brussels: University Press, 1990-6)

Moffet, Thomas, *Nobilis or A View of the Life and Death of a Sidney and Lessus Lugubris*, trans./ed. Virgil B. Heltzel and Hoyt H. Hudson (San Marino, CA: The Huntington Library, 1940)

Nichols, John, ed., *The Progresses and Public Processions of Queen Elizabeth*, new edn, 3 vols (London: John Nichols, 1823)

Ó Laidhin, Tomás, ed., *Sidney State Papers 1565-70* (Dublin: Stationery Office for the Irish Manuscripts Commission, 1962)

Peifer, David, *Epistolae* (Iéna, 1708)

Philip II of Spain, *Correspondencia de Felipe II con sus embajadores en la córte de Inglaterra 1558 á 1584 (Archivo general de Simancas)*, vol. 4 [series vol. 91] (Madrid: M. Ginesta Hermanos, 1888)

Plantin, Christopher, *Correspondance de Christophe Plantin*, vol. 8, ed. J. Dénuce (Antwerp: De Groote Boekhandel and 'S Gravenhage: Martinus Nijhoff, 1918)

Robinson, Hastings, trans./ed.. *The Zurich Letters (second series), comprising the correspondence of several English bishops and others with some of the Helvetian reformers, during the reign of Queen Elizabeth*, 2 vols (Cambridge: Cambridge University Press, 1845)

Rodríguez-Salgado, M.J. and S. Adams, eds., 'The count of Feria's dispatch to Philip II of 14 November 1558', *Camden Miscellany* 28 (1984)

Salignac de la Mothe Fénélon, Bertrande de, *Correspondance diplomatique de Bertrande de Salignac de la Mothe Fénélon, ambassadeur de France en Angleterre de 1568 à 1575*, ed. A. Teulet, 7 vols (Paris: Panckoucke, 1838-40)

Scott, R.F., *Notes from the Records of St John's College Cambridge*, 3rd series ([Cambridge:] privately printed, 1906-13)

Sidney, Henry, 'Sir Henry Sidney's memoir of his government of Ireland, 1583' ed. H.R. Hore, *The Ulster Journal of Archaelogy* 3 (1855), 33-52; 5 (1857), 299-323; 8 (1860), 179-95

Somerset, J. Alan B., ed., *Shropshire*, 2 vols (Toronto: University of Toronto Press [Records of Early English Drama], 1994)

Stradling, Edward, *Stradling Correspondence: A series of letters written in the reign of Queen Elizabeth*, ed. John Montgomery Traherne (London: Longman et al., 1840)

Temple, William, *William Temple's 'Analysis' of Sir Philip Sidney's 'Apology for Poetry': an edition and translation*, ed./trans. John Webster (Binghamton, NY: Centre for Medieval & Early Renaissance Studies [Medieval & Renaissance Texts & Studies vol. 32], 1984)

Temple, William, *see also* Ramus, Petrus

von Bülow. Gottfried, trans., 'Journey through England and Scotland made by Lupold von Wedel in the years 1584 and 1585', *Transactions of the Royal Historical Society*, 2nd ser., vol. 9 (1895), 223-70

Walsingham, Francis, *Journal of Sir Francis Walsingham, from Dec. 1570 to April 1583*, ed. Charles Trice Martin in *The Camden Miscellany* 6 (London: Camden Society, 1871)

Wingfield, Robert, 'The *Vitae Mariae Reginae Angliae* of Robert Wingfield of Brantham', ed./trans. Diarmaid MacCulloch, *Camden Miscellany* 8 (London: Royal Historical Society [Camden 4th ser., vol. 29], 1984), 181-301

Wood, Thomas, *Letters of Thomas Wood, Puritan, 1566-1755*, ed. Patrick Collinson (London, 1960)

Wright, Thomas, ed., *Queen Elizabeth and her Times, a series of original letters*, 2 vols (London: Henry Colburn, 1838)

Yeames, A.H.S., 'The Grand Tour of an Elizabethan', *Papers of the British School at Rome* 7 (1914), 92-113

3. Editions of Philip Sidney's works cited

Syr P.S. His Astrophel and Stella (London: Thomas Newman, 1591)

The Correspondence of Sir Philip Sidney and Hubert Languet, ed. Steuart A. Pears (London: William Pickering, 1845)

The Compleat Works of Philip Sidney, 4 vols, ed. Albert Feuillerat (Cambridge: Cambridge University Press, 1923)

The Poems of Sir Philip Sidney, ed. William A. Ringler, Jr (Oxford: Clarendon Press, 1962)

Miscellaneous Prose of Sir Philip Sidney, ed. Katherine Duncan-Jones and Jan van Dorsten (Oxford: Clarendon Press, 1973)

The Countess of Pembroke's Arcadia (The Old Arcadia), ed. Jean Robertson (Oxford: Clarendon Press, 1973)

The Countess of Pembroke's Arcadia (The New Arcadia), ed. Victor Skretkowicz (Oxford: Clarendon Press, 1987)

4. Early printed texts (and later editions)

Abbot, George, *The reasons which Doctour Hill Hath Brought, for the Upholding of Papistry . . . Unmasked* (Oxford: Joseph Barnes, 1604)

Apologie ou defense de tres illustre prince Guillaume par la grace de Dieu prince d'Orange . . . presentee a Messieurs les Estats Generauls de Païs Bas (Leiden: Sylvius, 1581)

Ascham, Roger, *The Scholemaster* (London: John Daye, 1570)

B[axter], N[athaniel], *Sir Philip Sydneys Ourània, That is, Endimions Song and Tragedie, Containing all Philosophie* (London: Edward White, 1606)

Bayle, Pierre, *A General Dictionary, Historical and Critical*, trans. John Peter Bernard, Thomas Birch, John Lockman *et al.*, vol. 6 (London: James Bettenham, 1738)

Benedicti, Georgius, *De rebvs gestis Illustriss. Principis Guilielmi, Comitis Nassovij, &c. Lib. II.*

(Leiden: *ex officina* Ioannis Paetsij, 1586)

Bizari, Pietro, *Senatvs popvlisqve Genvensis rervm domi forisqve gestarvm historiae atqve annales* (Antwerp: Christopher Plantin, 1579)

Bor, Pieter, *Oorsprongk, begin, en vervolgh der Nederlansche oorlogen, beroerten, en borgerlyke oneenigheden*, rev. edn, 4 vols (Amsterdam: Joannes van Someren, Abraham Wolfgangh and Hendrick en Dirck Boom, 1679)

Bright, Timothy, *In physicam Gvlielmi Adolphi Scribonii, Post secundam editionem ab autore denuò copiossimè adauctam, & in III. Libros distinctam. Animaduersiones* (Cambridge: Thomas Thomas, 1584)

Bright, Timothy, *see also* Fox, John

Bruno, Giordano, *De gl'heroici fvrori* (Paris: Antonio Baio, i.e. London: John Charlewood, 1585)

Bruno, Giordano, *Le cena de le Ceneri* (London: John Charlewood, 1584)

Bruno, Giordano, *Spaccio de la bestia triofante* (Paris: [i.e. London: John Charlewood], 1584)

'Brutus, Stephanus Junius', *Vindiciae, contra tyrannos* (Basle, 1579)

'Brutus, Stephanus Junius', *Vindiciae, contra tyrannos: or, concerning the legitimate power of a prince over the people, and of the people over a prince*, ed./trans. George Garnett (Cambridge: Cambridge University Press, 1994)

Br[yskett], Lod[owick], *A Discourse of Civill Life: Containing the Ethike part of Morall Philosophie. Fit for the instructing of a Gentleman in the course of a vertuous life* (London: Edward Blount, 1606)

Bryskett, Lodowick, 'A Pastorall Aeglogue', in Edmund Spenser, *Colin Clout's Come Home Againe* (London: William Ponsonbie, 1595)

Camden, William, *Annales rervm Anglicarvm, et Hibernicarvm, regnante Elizabetha, ad annvm salvtis M.D.LXXXIX* (London: Simon Waterson, 1615)

Camden, William, *Annales rerum Anglicarum et Hibernicum regnante Elizabetha*, ed. Thomas Hearne, 3 vols ([Oxford], 1717)

Camden, William, *Britain, or A Chorographicall Description of the most flourishing Kingdomes, England, Scotland, and Ireland, and the Ilands adioyning, out of the depth of Antiqvitie*, trans. Philemon Holland (London: George Bishop & John Norton, 1610)

[Camden, William], *The Historie of the most Renowned and Victorious Princesse Elizabeth, Late Queene of England* (London: Benjamin Fisher, 1630)

Camden, William, *Remaines of a Greater Worke, Concerning Britaine, the inhabitants thereof, their Languages, Names, Surnames, Empreses, Wise speeches, Poësies, and Epitaphes* (London: Simon Waterson, 1605)

Camerarius, Joachim, *Vita Philippi Melanchthonis* (The Hague: Adrian Ulacq, 1609)

Camerarius, Philip, *Operae horarvm svbcisivarvm, meditationes historicae, avctiores quam antea editae*, 3 vols (Frankfurt: *typis* Ioannis Saurij, *impensis* Petri Kopffijm, 1592)

Camerarius, P[hilip], *The Living Librarie, or, Meditations and Observations Historicall, Natvral, Political, and Poetical*, trans. John Molle (London: Adam Islip, 1621)

Campion, Edmund, *et al.*, *The Histories of Ireland: The one written by Edmund Campion, the other*

Bibliography

by Meredith Hanmer Dr of Divinity, ed. James Ware (Dublin: Society of Stationers, 1633)

Carew, Richard, *The Survey of Cornwall* (London: Iohn Iaggard, 1602)

Churchyard, Thomas, *The Epitaph of Sir Phillip Sidney Knight, lately Lord Gouernour of Flushing* (London: Thomas Cadman, [1587])

Churchyard, Thomas, *The Worthines of Wales* (London: Thomas Cadman, 1587)

Clifford, Christopher, *The Schoole of Horsemanship* (London: Thomas Cadman, 1585)

Colaianne, A.J. and W.J. Godshalk, eds, *Elegies for Sir Philip Sidney (1587)* (Delmar, NY: Scholars' Fascimilies & Reprints, 1980)

Cooper, Thomas, *Thesavrvs Lingvae Romanæ & Britannicæ* (London: in aedibvs quondam Bertheleti, 1565)

The Copy of a Letter written by a Master of Art of Cambridge to his friend in London . . . about the present state, and some proceedings of the Earl of Leicester and his friends in London (n.p.: n.pub., 1584)

Crato von Crafftheim, Johannes, *Oratio fvnebris de Diuo Maxæmiliano II imperatore cæsare avgvsti, &c.* (Frankfurt: André Wechel, 1577)

Daneau, Lambert, *Geographiæ Poeticæ, Id est, Vniversæ Terræ descriptionis ex optimis ac vetustissimis quibusque Latinis Poetis libri quatuor: Quorum, Primus Europam: Secundus, Africam; Tertius, Asiam; Quartus, Mare universum, & Maris Insulas continet* ([Geneva]: apud Iacobum Stoer, 1580)

D[ay], A[ngel], *Vpon the life and death of the most worthy, and thrise renowned knight, Sir Philip Sidney* (London: Robert Waldegrave, [1587])

Dee, John, *General and Rare Memorials pertayning to the Perfect Arte of NAVIGATION* (London: John Day, 1577)

Derricke, John, *The Image of Irelande, with a discourse of Woodkarne* (London: John Day, 1581)

De Serres, Jean, *The Three Partes of Commentaries, Containing the whole and perfect discourse of the Ciuil warres of Fraunce*, trans. Thomas Timme (London, 1574)

De Thou, Jacques-Auguste, *Histoire universelle de Jacques-Auguste de Thou, Depuis 1543, jusque'en 1607. Traduite sur l'edition latine de Londres*, vol. 6 1570-1573 (London, 1734)

[Digges, Thomas], *A Briefe Report of the Militaire Services done in the Low Covntries, by the Erle of Leicester: written by one that serued in good place there in a letter to a friend of his* (London: Gregorie Seton, 1587)

Dousa, Janus, *Odarum Britannicarum liber* (Leiden, 1586)

Drant, Thomas, *Praesvl, Eiusdem Sylva* (London, 1576)

Du Bartas, Guillaume de Salluste, Sieur, *The Works of Guillaume de Salluste Sieur du Bartas: A critical edition*, 3 vols, ed. Urban Tigner Holmes Jr, John Coriden Lyons and Robert White Linker (Chapel Hill, NC: University of North Carolina Press, 1935-40)

Eick[ius], Arnold, *Elogium illvstrissimi principis, Roberti, comitis Leycestrii, Baronis de Denbigh, &c. Begliæ Gubernatoris Generalis. Recognitum & auctum. Ad serenissimam reginam Angliæ, Franciæ ac Hyberniæ, Elisabetham. Cum Elogio. Clarissimi viri, D. Philippi Sidnei, Vrbis Flissingæ præfecti. Seu De vera nobilitate* (n.p.: n.pub., n.d. [1585/6])

Estienne, Henri, ed., *The Frankfort Book Fair: The Francofordiense Emporium of Henri Estienne*, ed. James Westphall Thompson (Chicago, IL: The Caxton Club, 1911)

Estienne, Henri, ed., *Novum Testamentum. Obscuriorum vocum & quorundam loquendi generum accuratas partim suas partim aliorum interpetationes margini* (Paris: Henri Estienne, 1576)

Fenton, Geffray, *Certaine Tragical Discourses writen out of Frenche and Latin* (London: Thomas Marshe, 1567)

Fox, John, *An Abridgement of the Bookes of Acts and Monuments of the Chvrch*, abridged by Timothy Bright (London: Timothy Bright, 1589)

Fuller, Thomas, *The Holy State/The Profane State* (Cambridge: John Williams, 1642)

Gager, William, ed., *Exeqviæ illvstrissimi eqvitis, D. Philippi Sidnaei, gratissimæ memoriæ ac nomini impensæ* (Oxford: Joseph Barnes, 1587)

Gascoigne, George, *The Princely Pleasures at the Courte at Kenelwoorth, That is to saye, The Copies of all such Verses, Proses, or poetical inuentions, and Other Deuices of Pleasure, as were there deuised, and presented by sundry Gentlemen, before the Quene's Majestie, in the yeare 1575* (London: Richard Ihones, 1576)

Gentili, Alberico, *De Legationibus, libri tres* (London: Thomas Vautrollier, 1585)

Gentili, Alberico, *De Legationibus, libri tres*, trans. Gordon J. Laing, 2 vols (New York, NY: Oxford University Press, 1924)

Gentili, Scipio, *In XXV. Davidis psalmos epicæ paraphrases* (London: John Woolf, 1584)

Gentili, Scipio, *Nereus, sive de natali Elizabethæ illustriss, Phillippi Sydnaei filiæ* (London: John Wolfe, 1585)

Gentili, Scipio, *Paraphrasis aliqvot psalmorvm Davidis, carmine heroico* (London: Thomas Vautrollier, 1581)

Gilbert, Humphrey, *A Discourse of a Discovery for a New Passage to Catania* (London: R. Jones, 1576)

Gilpin, George, *see* Marnix, Phillips van, de Sint-Aldegonde

Golding, Arthur, *A Worke concerning the Trewnesse of the Christian Religion* (London: Thomas Cadman, 1587)

Goldwel, Henry, *A briefe declaratio[n] of the shews, deuices, speeches, and inientions done & performed before the Queenes Maiestie, & the French Ambassadours, at the most valiaunt and worthye Triumphe, attempted and executed on the Monday and Tuesday in Whitsun weeke last, Anno 1581* (London: Robert Waldegrave, 1581)

[Goulart, Simon], *Mémoires de l'estat de France sovs Charles IX*, 3 vols (Middelburg: Henry Wolf, 1578)

Greville, Fulke, *The Prose Works of Fulke Greville, Lord Brooke*, ed. John Gouws (Oxford: Clarendon Press, 1986)

[Hakluyt, Richard], *Divers voyages touching the discouerie of America, and the Ilands adiacent vnto the same, made first of all by our Englishmen, and afterward by the Frenchmen and Britons* (London: Thomas Woodcocke, 1582)

Hakluyt, Richard, *The Original Writings & Correspondence of the Two Richard Hakluyt*, ed. E.G.R.

Taylor, 2 vols (London: The Hakluyt Society [2nd ser., nos 76 and 77], 1935)

Harvey, Gabriel, *Gratulationum Valdinensium libri quatuor* (London: Henry Bynneman, 1578)

Harvey, Gabriel, *Three proper, and wittie, familiar Letters, lately passed betwene two Vniuersitie men: touching the Earthquake in Aprill last, and our English refourmed Versifying* (London: H. Bynneman, 1580)

Harvey, Gabriel, *Two other, very commendable Letters, of the same mens writing: both touching the foresaid Artificiall Versifying, and certain other Particulars* (London: H. Bynneman, 1580)

Heliodorus, *An Æthopian historie written in Greeke . . . Englished by T. Underdoune*, trans. Thomas Underdowne (London: Francis Coldocke, 1569)

Herbert, Mary Sidney, *The Collected Works of Mary Sidney Herbert Countess of Pembroke*, ed. Margaret P. Hannay, Noel J. Kinnamon and Michael G. Brennan, 2 vols (Oxford: Clarendon Press, 1998)

Herodian, *Herodiani historiae libri VIII*, ed. Henri Estienne (Paris: Henri Estienne, 1576)

Heylyn, Peter, *Ecclesia Restaurtata; or, The History of the Reformation of the Church of England* (London: H. Twyford, T. Dring, J. Place and W. Palmer, 1661)

Holinshed, Raphael *et al.*, *Chronicles*, 3 vols (London, 1587)

Jonson, Ben, *The Workes of Beniamin Jonson* (London: Will. Stansby, 1616)

Junius, Franciscus, *Grammatica Hebraeae Linguae* (Frankfurt: André Wechel, 1580)

Laneham, Robert, *A Letter Whearin part of the entertainment vntoo the Queenz maiesty, at Killingwoorth Castl, iz signified* (London, 1575)

Lant, Thomas, *Sequitur celebritas et pompa funebris* (London: graven in copper by D.T. de Brij, 1587)

Le Moyne, Jacques, *La Clef des Champs, pour troouer plusieurs Animaux, tant Bestes qu'Oyseaux, auec plusieurs Fleurs & Fruitz* (Blackfriars: Jacques le Moyne, 1586)

[Lewkenor, Lewis], *A Discovrse of the Vsage of the English Fvgitives, by the Spaniard* (London: John Drawater, 1595)

[Lewkenor, Lewis], *The Estate of English Fvgitives vnder the King of Spaine and his ministers* (London: John Drawater, 1595)

Lipsius, Justus, *De recta pronvnciatione Latinæ lingvæ dialogvs: Ad V. Illustrem Philippvm Sidneivm, Eqvitem* (Antwerp: Christopher Plantin, 1586)

Lloyd, John, ed., *Peplvs illvstrissimi viri D. Philippi Sidnaei svpremis honoribvs dicatvs* (Oxford: Joseph Barnes, 1587)

[M., E., of Antwerp], *A Trve discovrse historicall, of the svcceeding governovrs in the Netherlands*, trans. T.C. and Ric. Ro. (London: Matthew Lownes, 1602)

[Marnix, Phillips van, de Sint-Aldegondel], *The Bee hiue of the Romische Churche*, trans. George Gilpin (London: Thomas Dawson for Iohn Stell, 1579)

Marot, Clement and Théodore de Bèze, *Les CL. Pseaumes de David, mis en rhythme françoise* ([Geneva]: P. Dauantes, 1560)

Matthew, Tobie, *A Collection of Letters* (London: Henry Herringman, 1660)

Melissus, Paulus [Paul Schede], *Melissi Schediasmata poetica*, 2nd edn (Paris: Arnold Sittart, 1586)

Monardes, Nicolas, *Simplicium medicamentorum historiae liber tertius*, ed. Charles de l'Écluse (Antwerp: Christopher Plantin, 1582)

Naunton, Robert, *Fragmenta Regalia* (n.p.: n.pub., 1641)

Neville, Alexander, ed., *Academiae Cantabrigiensis Lachyrmæ tvmvlo Nobilissimi Equitis, D. Philippi Sidneij Sacratæ* (London: ex officina Ionnis Windet impensis Thomæ Chardi, 1587)

Peacham, Henry, *The Compleat Gentleman*, rev. edn (London, 1661)

Phillip, John, *The Life and Death of Sir Philip Sidney, late Lord gouernour of Flvshing* (London: Robert Waldegrave, 1587)

Powel, David, *The historie of Cambria, now called Wales* (London: Rafe Newberie & Henrie Denham, 1584)

Puttenham, George, *The Arte of Poesie* (London: John Field, 1587)

The Queenes Majesties at Entertainment Woodstocke (London: Thomas Cadman, 1585)

The Queenes Majesty's Entertainment at Woodstocke, 1575, ed. A.W. Pollard (Oxford, 1910)

Ramus, Petrus, *Commentariorum de Religione Christiana, Libri quatuor*, ed. Théophile de Banos (Frankfurt: André Wechel, 1577)

Ramus, Petrus, *Commentariorum de Religione Christiana, Libri quatuor eivsdem vita A Theophilo Banosio descripta* (Frankfurt: André Wechel, 1583)

Ramus, Petrus, *Commentariorum de Religione Christiana, Libri quatuor nunquam antea editi*, ed. Théophile de Banos (Frankfurt: André Wechel, 1576)

Ramus, Petrus, *Dialecticae libri dvo, scholiis G. Tempelli Cantabrigiensis illustrati* (Cambridge: Thomas Thomas, 1584)

Robson, Simon, *The Choice of Change* (London, 1585)

Sidney, Henry, *A Very Godly letter made, by the right Honourable Sir Henry Sidney, Knight of the most Noble order of the Garter, Lord deputie of Ireland, and Lord president of Wales. Now xxv. Yeeres past vnto Phillip Sidney his Sonne then of tender yeeres, at schoole in the towne of Shrowesbury with one M. Astone* (London: T. Dawson, 1591)

Smythe, John, *Certain Discourses . . . Concerning the formes and effects of diuers sorts of weapons, and other verie important matters Militarie* (London: Richard Johnes, 1590)

Spencer [i.e. Spenser], Ed[mund], *Colin Clovts Come home againe* (London: William Ponsonbie, 1595)

[Spenser, Edmund], *The Shepheardes Calender Conteyning twelve Ælogues proportionable to the twelve monethes* (London: Hugh Singleton, 1579)

Stafford, Antony, *The Gvide of Honovr, Or the Balance wherin she may weigh her Actions* (London: T. Slater, 1634)

Stow, John, *The Annales of England, faithfully collected out of the most autenticall Authors, Records, and other Monuments of Antiquitie, from the first inhabitation vntill this present yeare 1592* (London: Ralfe Newbery, 1592)

[Stubbs, John], *The Discoverie of a Gaping Gulf whereinto England is like to be swallowed by an other French mariage, if the Lord forbid not the banes, by letting her Maiestie see the sin and punishment thereof* (London: Hugh Singleton, 1579)

Stubbs, John, *John Stubb's 'Gaping Gulf' with Letters and other relevant documents*, ed. Lloyd E. Berry (Charlottesville, VA: University Press of Virginia for the Folger Shakespeare Library, 1968)

Watson, Thomas, *The EΚΑΤΟΜΠΑΘΙΑ or Passionate Centurie of Loue* (London: John Wolfe for Gabriell Cawood, 1581)

Webbe, William, *A Discourse of English Poetrie* (London: John Charlewood, 1586)

W[hetstone], G[eorge], *Sir Philip Sidney, his honorable life, his valiant death, and true vertues* (London: Thomas Cadman, 1587)

Whitney, Geffrey, *A Choice of Emblemes, and other devises* (Leiden: Christopher Plantin, 1586)

5. SECONDARY SOURCES

Adams, Simon, 'The Dudley clientèle, 1553-1563' in *The Tudor Nobility*, ed. G.W. Bernard (Manchester: Manchester University Press, 1992), 241-65

Anon., *Penshurst Place*, rev. edn (Woodchester, Glos.: Arthurs Press Ltd, n.d.)

Axton, Marie, 'The Tudor Mask and Elizabethan court drama' in *English Drama: Forms and development: Essays in honour of Muriel Clara Bradbrook*, ed. Marie Axton and Raymond Williams (Cambridge: Cambridge University Press, 1977), 37-42

Baker, David J., 'Off the map: charting uncertainty in Renaissance Ireland' in *Representing Ireland: Literature and the origins of conflict, 1534-1660*, ed. Brendan Bradshaw, Andrew Hadfield and Willy Maley (Cambridge: Cambridge University Press, 1993), 76-92

Baker, Thomas, *History of the College of St John the Evangelist, Cambridge*, ed. John E.B. Mayor, 2 vols (Cambridge: Cambridge University Press, 1869)

Baldwin, T.W., *William Shakespeare's Small Latine & Lesse Greeke*, 2 vols (Urbana, IL: University of Illinois Press, 1944)

Balteau, J. *et al*, eds., *Dictionnaire de biographie française* (Paris, 1933)

Barber, Peter, 'England II: Monarchs, Ministers, and Maps, 1550-1625' in *Monarchs, Ministers and Maps: The emergence of cartography as a tool of government in early modern Europe* (Chicago, IL: University of Chicago Press, 1992), 57-98

Baughan, Denver Ewing, 'Sir Philip Sidney and the matchmakers', *Modern Language Review* 33 (1938), 506-19

Beal, Peter, 'Poems by Sir Philip: The Ottley Manuscript'. *The Library*, 5th ser., 33 (1978), 284-95

Beckingsale, B.W., *Burghley: Tudor Statesman* (New York, NY: St Martin's Press, 1967)

Beer, Barrett L., *Northumberland: The Policial Career of John Dudley, Earl of Warwick and Duke of Northumberland* (Kent State University Press, 1973)

Bell, Gary M., *A Handlist of British Diplomatic Representatives 1509-1688* (London: Royal Historical Society, 1990)

Beltz, G.F., 'Memorials of the last achievement, illness and death of Sir Philip Sidney', *Archaeologia* 27 (1840), 31-3

Benzing, Josef, *Buchdruckerlexicon des 16. Jahrhunderts (Deutsches sprachgebiet)* (Frankfurt am Main: Vittorio Klostermann, 1952)

Berry, Edward, 'Sidney's May Game for the Queen', *Modern Philology* 86 (1989), 252-64

Boas, Frederick S., *Sir Philip Sidney, Representative Elizabethan* (London: Staple Press, 1955)

Bond, William H., 'A Letter from Sir Philip Sidney to Christopher Plantin', *Harvard Library Bulletin* 8 (1954), 233-5

Bond, William H., 'A letter of Languet about Sidney', *Harvard Library Bulletin* 9 (1955) 105-9

Bossy, John, *Giordano Bruno and the Embassy Affair* (New Haven, CT: Yale University Press, 1991)

Boutcher, Warren, 'Pilgrimage to Parnassus: Local intellectual traditions, humanist education and the cultural geography of sixteenth-century England', in *Pedagogy and Power: Rhetorics of classical learning*, ed. Yun Lee Too and Niall Livingstone (Cambridge: Cambridge University Press, 1998), 110–47

Bowden, Peter J., *The Wool Trade in Tudor and Stuart England* (London: Macmillan, 1962)

Brady, Ciaran, *The Chief Governors: The rise and fall of reform government in Tudor Ireland 1536-1588* (Cambridge: Cambridge University Press, 1994)

Brady, Ciaran, 'Court, castle and country: The framework of government in Tudor Ireland' in *Natives and Newcomers: Essays on the making of Irish colonial society 1534-1641*, ed. Ciaran Brady and Raymond Gillespie (Dublin: Irish Academic Press, 1986), 22-49

Brennan, Michael, *Literary Patronage in the English Renaissance: The Pembroke family* (London: Routledge, 1988)

Buxton, John, 'An Elizabethan reading-list: An Unpublished Letter from Sir Philip Sidney', *Times Literary Supplement*, 24 March 1972, 343-4

Buxton, John, *Sir Philip Sidney and the English Renaissance*, 2nd edn (London: Macmillan, 1964)

Buxton, John and Bent Juel-Jensen, 'Sir Philip Sidney's first passport rediscovered', *The Library*, 5th ser., 25 (1970), 42-6

Cannegieter, Dorothee and Diederike van Dorsten-Timmerman, *Sir Philip Sidney 1554-1586* (Zutphen: De Walburg Pers, 1986)

Carlton, William J., *Timothie Bright Doctor of Phisicke: A memoir of "The Father of Modern Shorthand"* (London: Elliot Stock, 1911)

Chamberlin, Frederick, *Elizabeth and Leycester* (New York, NY: Dodd, Mead & Company, 1939)

Chambers, Anne, *Granuaile: The Life and Times of Grace O'Malley c. 1530-1603* (Portmarnock, Co. Dublin: Wolfhound, 1979)

Chambers, E.K., *Sir Henry Lee: An Elizabethan Portrait* (Oxford: Clarendon Press, 1936)

Champion, Bill, *Everyday Life in Tudor Shrewsbury* (Shrewsbury: Shropshire Books, 1994)

Champion, Pierre, *Henri III roi de Pologne: Un séjour à Vienne, voyage en Italie, et retour en France 1574-1575* (Paris: Bernard Grasset, 1951)

Bibliography

Chapman, Hester W., *Lady Jane Grey: October 1537 – February 1554* (London: Jonathan Cape, 1962)

Chevreul, Henri, *Étude sur le XVIᵉ siècle: Hubert Languet* (Paris, 1852)

Chrisman, Miriam Usher, *Lay Culture, Learned Culture: Books and social change in Strasbourg, 1480-1599* (New Haven, CT and London: Yale University Press, 1982)

Clasen, Claus-Peter, *The Palatinate in European History 1559-1660* (Oxford: Basil Blackwell, 1963)

Collinson, Patrick, 'The Shearmen's Tree and the Preacher: The strange death of Merry England in Shrewsbury and beyond', in *The Reformation in English Towns 1500-1640*, ed. Patrick Collinson and John Craig (London: Macmillan, 1998), 205-20

Cooper, Helen, *Pastoral* (Ipswich: Brewer, 1977)

Corbett, Julian S., *Drake and the Tudor Navy: with a history of the rise of England as a maritime power*, 2 vols (London: Longmans, Green and Co., 1898)

Costil, Pierre, *André Dudith: humaniste hongrois 1533-1589: Sa vie, son œuvre et ses manuscrits grecs* (Paris: Société d'édition 'Les belles lettres', 1935)

Coulman, D., '"Spotted to be known"', *JWCI* 20 (1957), 179-80

Coulton, Barbara, 'The establishment of Protestantism in a provincial town: a study of Shrewsbury in the sixteenth century', *Sixteenth Century Journal* 27 (1996), 307-35

Council, Norman, '*O Dea Certe:* The allegory of *The Fortress of Perfect Beauty*', *HLQ* 39 (1976), 329-42

Crawley, Sylvia, *Twelve Centuries of Wilton House* (Westminster: Coates and Parker, n.d.)

Cummins, John, *Francis Drake: The Lives of a Hero* (London: Weidenfeld & Nicolson, 1995)

Davey, Richard, *The Nine Days' Queen: Lady Jane Grey and her Times*, ed. Martin Hume, 2nd edn (London: Methuen, 1910)

Dean, William, 'Henry Oxinder's key (1628) to *The Countess of Pembroke's Arcadia*: some facts and conjectures', *SNJ* 12/2 (1993), 14-21

Demetz, Peter, *Prague in Black and Gold: The History of a City* (London: Allen Lane, 1997)

Dictionary of National Biography, ed. Leslie Stephen and Stephen Lee, 63 vols (London: 1885-1900)

Dollman, F.T. and J.R. Jobbins, *An Analysis of Ancient Domestic Architecture*, 2 vols (London: Atchley & Co., J.R. Jobbins, and Joseph Masters, 1863–4)

Dop, Jan Albert, *Eliza's Knights: Soldiers, poets, and puritans in the Netherlands 1572-1586* (Alblasserdam: Remak, 1981)

Doran, Susan, *Monarchy and Matrimony: The courtships of Elizabeth I* (London: Routledge, 1996)

Dovey, Zillah, *An Elizabethan Progress: The Queen's Journey into East Anglia, 1578* (Far Thrupp, Glos.: Alan Sutton Publishing, 1996)

Duncan-Jones, Katherine, 'Sidney's personal *imprese*', *JWCI* 33 (1970), 321-4

Duncan-Jones, Katherine, 'Sidney, Stella and Lady Rich', in *Sir Philip Sidney: 1586 and the Creation of a Legend*, ed. van Dorsten *et al.* (Leiden: E.J. Brill/Leiden University Press for the Sir Thomas Browne Institute, 1986), 170–92

Duncan-Jones, Katherine, *Sir Philip Sidney Courtier Poet* (London: Hamish Hamilton, 1991)

Duncan-Jones, Katherine, 'Sir Philip Sidney's debt to Edmund Campion' in *The Reckoned Expense: Edmund Campion and the Early English Jesuits. Essays in celebration of the first centenary of Campion Hall, Oxford (1896-1996)*, ed. Thomas M. McCoog (Woodbridge, Suffolk: Boydell Press, 1996), 85–102

Dworschak, Fritz, *Antonio Abondio, Medaglista e Ceroplasta 1538-1591* (Trento, 1958)

Evans, R.J.W., *Rudolf II and his World: A study in intellectual history 1576-1612* (Oxford: Clarendon Press, 1973)

Evans, R.J.W., *The Wechel Presses: Humanism and Calvinism in Central Europe 1572-1627, Past and Present Supplement 2* (London: Past and Present Society, 1975)

Fehl, Philipp and Marilyn Perry, 'Painting and the Inquisition at Venice: three forgotten files' in *Interpretazioni Veneziane: studi di storia dell'arte in onore di Michelangelo Muraro*, ed. David Rosand (Venice: Arsenale, 1984), 371-83

Firpo, Massimo, *Pietro Bizzarri: Escule italiano del cinquecento* (Turin: G. Giappichelli, 1971)

Fisher, George William, *Annals of Shrewsbury School*, rev. J. Spencer Hill (London: Methuen & Co., 1899)

Foster, Michael, 'Thomas Allen (1540-1632), Gloucester Hall and the survival of Catholicism in post-Reformation Oxford', *Oxoniensia* 46 (1981), 99-128

Fox-Bourne, H.R., *Sir Philip Sidney: Type of English chivalry in the Elizabethan age* (New York, NY: G.P. Putnam's Sons, 1891)

Freedman, Sylvia, *Poor Penelope: Lady Penelope Rich, An Elizabethan Woman* (Abbotsbruck, Bucks: The Kensal Press, 1983)

French, Peter, *John Dee: The World of an Elizabethan Magus* (London: Routledge & Kegan Paul, 1972)

Froude, James Anthony, *History of England from the fall of Wolsey to the defeat of the Spanish Armada*, 12 vols (London: Longmans, 1875)

Gál, I., 'Sir Philip Sidney's guide to Hungary', *Hungarian Studies in English* 4 (1969), 53-64

Godshalk, William L., 'Note 211. A Sidney autograph', *The Book Collector* 13 (1964), 65

Gömöri, George, 'Philip Sidney's letter to Charles L'Écluse in 1577', *NQ* 242 (1997), 29-30

Griffin, Benjamin, 'The breaking of the giants: Historical drama in Coventry and London', *English Literary Renaissance* 29 (1999), 3-21

Hadfield, Andrew and Willy Maley, 'Introduction: Irish representatives and English alternatives' in *Representing Ireland: Literature and the origins of conflict, 1534-1660*, ed. Brendan Bradshaw, Andrew Hadfield and Willy Maley (Cambridge: Cambridge University Press, 1993), 1-23

Hadfield, Andrew, 'Sidney's comments on history in *An Apology for Poetry* and Geoffrey Fenton's *Tragicall Discourses*: a note', *SJ* 15/2 (Fall 1997), 48-51

Hale, John R., *The Art of War and Renaissance England* (Washington, DC: Folger Shakespeare Library, 1961)

Hammer, Paul E.J., *The Polarisation of Elizabethan Politics: The Political Career of Robert Devereux,*

Bibliography

2nd Earl of Essex, 1585-1597 (Cambridge: Cambridge University Press, 1999)

Hannay, Margaret, P., *Philip's Phoenix: Mary Sidney, Countess of Pembroke* (Oxford: Oxford University Press, 1990)

Hasler, P.W., ed., *The House of Commons 1558-1603*, 3 vols (London: History of Parliament Trust, 1981)

Hay, Millicent V., *The Life of Robert Sidney Earl of Leicester (1563-1626)* (Washington, DC: Folger Books, 1984)

Haynes, Alan, *The White Bear: Robert Dudley, The Elizabethan Earl of Leicester* (London: Peter Owen, 1987)

Hoefer, Johann Christian Ferdinand, *Nouvelle Biographie Universelle* (Paris: Firmin Didot, 1853)

Holt, Mack P., *The Duke of Anjou and the Politique Struggle during the Wars of Religion* (Cambridge: Cambridge University Press, 1986)

Höltgen, Karl Josef, 'Why are there no wolves in England?: Philip Camerarius and a German version of Sidney's Table Talk', *Anglia: Zietschrift für Englische Philologie* 99 (1981), 60-82

Howell, R., 'The Sidney circle and the Protestant cause in Elizabethan foreign policy', *Renaissance and Modern Studies* 19 (1975), 31-46

Hunger, F.W.T., *Charles de l'Écluse (Carolus Clusius): Nederlandsch Kruidkundige 1526-1609* ('S-Gravenhage: Martinus Nijhoff, 1943)

Hunt, Marvin, 'Consorting with Catholics: Sir Philip Sidney and "The Prayers of All Good Men"', *SNJ* 12 (1982), 21-8

Hutson, Lorna, 'Fortunate travelers: reading for the plot in sixteenth-century England', *Representations* 41 (1993), 83–103

Hutson, Lorna, *The Usurer's Daughter: Male friendship and fictions of women in sixteenth-century England* (London: Routledge, 1994)

Hruby, Frantisek, *Etudiants tchèques aux écoles protestantes de l'Europe occidentale à la fin du 16e et au début du 17e siècle: Documents* (Universita J.E. Purkyne v Brne, 1970)

Jardine, Lisa and Alan Stewart, *Hostage to Fortune: The troubled life of Francis Bacon 1561-1626* (London: Victor Gollancz, 1998)

Jardine, Lisa and Anthony Grafton, '"Studied for action": how Gabriel Harvey read his Livy'. *Past and Present* 129 (1990), 30-78

Jones, Deborah, 'Lodowick Bryskett and his family' in *Thomas Lodge and other Elizabethans*, ed. Charles J. Sisson (Cambridge, MA: Harvard University Press, 1933), 243-361

Jordan, W.K., *Edward VI: The Threshold of Power: The dominance of the duke of Northumberland* (London: Allen & Unwin, 1970)

Jordan, W.K., *Edward VI: The protectorship of the Duke of Somerset* (London: George Allen & Unwin, 1968)

Judson, Alexander C., *Sidney's Appearance: A Study in Elizabethan Portraiture* (Bloomington IN: Indiana University Press, 1958)

Kamen, Henry, *Philip of Spain* (New Haven, CT, and London: Yale University Press,

1997)

Keeler, Mary Frear, ed., *Sir Francis Drake's West Indian Voyage* (London: The Hakluyt Society, 1981)

Kendall, Alan, *Robert Dudley Earl of Leicester* (London: Cassell, 1980)

Keynes, Geoffrey, *Dr Timothie Bright 1550-1615: A Survey of his Life with a Bibliography of his Writings* (London: The Wellcome Historical Medical Library, 1962)

Kingdon, Robert M., *Myths about the St Bartholomew's Day Massacres 1572-1576* (Cambridge, MA, and London: Harvard University Press, 1988)

Koszul, A., 'Les Sidney et Strasbourg', *Bulletin de la faculté des lettres de Strasbourg* 17 (1938), 37-44

Kuin, Roger, 'Languet and the Veronese portrait of Sidney: Antwerp findings', *SJ* 15/2 (1997), 42-4

Kuin, Roger, 'New light on the Veronese portrait of Sir Philip Sidney', *SNJ* 15/1 (1997), 19-47

Kuin, Roger, 'Querre-Muhau: Sir Philip Sidney and the New World', *Renaissance Quarterly* 51 (1998), 549-85

Kuin, Roger, 'Sir Philip Sidney's letter to Charles de l'Écluse in 1577: a rectification', *NQ* 242 [n.s. 44] (1997), 469-70

Kuin, Roger, 'The Middleburg weekend: More light on the proposed marriage between Philip Sidney and Marie of Nassau', *SNJ* 12/2 (1993), 3-13

Leimon, M. and G. Parker, 'Treason and plot in Elizabethan diplomacy: the "fame of Sir Edward Stafford" revisited', *EHR* 111 (1996), 1134-58

Le Neve, John, *Fasti Ecclesiae Anglicanae*, ed. T. Duffus, 3 vols (Oxford: Oxford University Press, 1854)

Lestringant, Frank, *Le huguenot et le sauvage: l'Amérique et la controversie coloniale en France, au temps des guerres de religion, 1555-1589* (Paris: Amateurs de livres, 1990)

Lestringant, Frank, *L'expérience huguenote au Nouveau Monde (XVIe siècle)* (Geneva: Droz, 1996)

Lestringant, Frank, *Mapping the Renaissance World: The geographical imagination in an age of discovery*, trans. David Fausset (Cambridge: Polity, 1994)

Levy, Charles S., 'A supplementary inventory of Sir Philip Sidney's correspondence', *Modern Philology* 67 (1969-1970), 177-81

Levy, Charles S., 'The Sidney-Hanau correspondence', *ELR* 2 (1972), 19–28

Lloyd, Christopher, *Sir Francis Drake* (London: Faber 1957)

Loades, David, *John Dudley Duke of Northumberland 1504-1553* (Oxford: Clarendon Press, 1996)

Loades, David, 'Philip II and the government of England', in *Law and Government under the Tudors: Essays presented to Sir Geoffrey Elton, Regius Professor of Modern History in the University of Cambridge on the occasion of his retirement*, ed. Claire Cross, David Loades and J.J. Scarisbrick (Cambridge: Cambridge University Press, 1988), 177-94

Loades, David, *The Reign of Mary Tudor: Politics, government and religion in England 1553-1558*,

2nd edn (London: Longman, 1991)

Louthan, Howard, *The Quest for Compromise: Peacemakers in Counter-Reformation Vienna* (Cambridge: Cambridge University Press, 1997)

Lynam, E.W., 'Sir Henry Sidney', *Studies* 2 (1913), 185-203

MacCaffrey, Wallace T., *The Shaping of the Elizabethan Regime: Elizabethan Politics, 1558-1572* (Princeton, NJ: Princeton University Press, 1968)

MacCarthy-Morrogh, Michael, *The Munster Plantation: English migration to Southern Ireland 1583-1641* (Oxford: Clarendon Press, 1986)

McConica, James, ed., *The History of the University of Oxford*, vol. 3 *The Collegiate University* (Oxford: Clarendon Press, 1986)

McCoy, Richard C., 'From the Tower to the tiltyard: Robert Dudley's return to glory', *Historical Journal* 27 (1984), 425-35

McGrath, Patrick and Joy Rowe, 'The recusancy of Sir Thomas Cornwallis', *Proceedings of the Suffolk Institute of Archaeology* 28 (1961), 226-71

McMahon, A. Philip, 'Sir Philip Sidney's Letter to the Camerarii', *PMLA* 62 (1947), 83-95

McNulty, Robert, 'Bruno at Oxford', *Renaissance News* 13 (1960), 300-5

Maley, Willy, *Salvaging Spenser: Colonialism, culture and identity* (Basingstoke: Macmillan, 1997)

Maley, Willy, 'Sir Philip Sidney and Ireland', *Spenser Studies* 12 (1991), 223-7

Marenco, Franco, *Arcadia Puritana* (Bari: Adriatica, 1968)

May, Steven W., 'Sir Edward Dyer' in *Sixteenth-Century British Nondramatic Writers*, 2nd ser., ed. David A. Richards (Detroit: Bruccoli Clark [Dictionary of Literary Biography, vol. 136], 1994), 80-4

Minet, W., 'Some unpublished plans of Dover Harbour', *Archaeologia* 72 (1921), 184-224

Montrose, Louis Adrian, 'Celebration and insinuation: Sir Philip Sidney and the motives of Elizabethan courtship', *Renaissance Drama* n.s. 8 (1977), 3-36

Motley, John Lothrop, *History of the United Netherlands: from the death of William the Silent to the Twelve Year's Truce – 1609*, 4 vols (London: John Murray, 1867)

Muraro, Michelangelo, 'Un celebre ritratto: Sir Philip Sidney a Venezia nel 1574 sceglie Veronese per farsi ritrarre' in *Nuovi studi su Paolo Veronese*, ed. Massimo Gemin (Venice, 1990), 391-6

Nicollier-De Weck, Béatrice, *Hubert Languet (1518-1581): un réseau politique international de Melanchthon à Guillaume d'Orange* (Geneva: Droz [Travaux d'Humanisme et Renaissance, vol. 293], 1995)

Noguères, Henri, *La Saint-Barthélemy 24 août 1572* (Paris: Robert Laffont, 1959)

Noguères, Henri, *The Massacre of Saint Bartholomew*, trans. Claire Eliane Engel (London: Allen & Unwin, 1962)

Oldham, J.B., *Headmasters of Shrewsbury School 1552-1908* (Shrewsbury: Wilding and Son, 1937)

[Oliphant, Jane], *Penshurst Place and Gardens* (Tonbridge, Kent: Addax Heritage, 1993)

Ong, Walter J., *Ramus and Talon Inventory* (Cambridge, MA: Harvard University Press, 1958)

Ong, Walter J., *Ramus: Method, and the Decay of Dialogue* (Cambridge, MA: Harvard University Press, 1958)

Oosterhoff, F.G., *Leicester and the Netherlands 1586-1587* (Utrecht: HES Publishers, 1988)

Orgel, Stephen, 'Sidney's experiment in pastoral: *The Lady of May*', *JWCI* 26 (1963), 198-203

Osborn, James M., 'Sidney and Pietro Bizari', *Renaissance Quarterly* 24 (1971) 344-54

Osborn, James M., *Young Philip Sidney 1572-1577* (New Haven, CT, and London: Yale University Press, 1972)

Owen, H. and J.B. Blakeway, *A History of Shrewsbury*, 2 vols (London: Harding, Lepard & Co., 1825)

Parker, Geoffrey, *The Dutch Revolt*, rev. edn. (Harmondsworth: Penguin, 1988)

Phillips, James E., 'George Buchanan and the Sidney circle'. *HLQ* 12 (1948), 23-55

Plomer, H.R. and T.P. Cross, *The Life and Correspondence of Lodowick Bryskett* (Chicago, 1927)

Poort, Marjon, '"The desired and destined successor": A chronology of Sir Philip Sidney's activities 1585-1586', in *Sir Philip Sidney: 1586 and the Creation of a Legend*, ed. Van Dorsten *et al.* (Leiden: E.J. Brill/Leiden University Press for the Sir Thomas Browne Institute, 1986), 25-37

Prouty, C.T., *George Gascoigne* (New York, NY: Columbia University Press, 1942)

Przezdziecki, Renaud, *Diplomatic Ventures and Adventures: Some experience of British envoys at the Court of Poland* (London: The Polish Research Centre, 1953)

Quinn, David Beers, ed., *The Voyages and Colonising Enterprises of Sir Humphrey Gilbert*, 2 vols (London: Hakluyt Society, 1940)

Read, Conyers, *Mr Secretary Walsingham and the policy of Queen Elizabeth*, 3 vols (Oxford: Clarendon Press, 1925)

Rebholz, Ronald A., *The Life of Fulke Greville* (Oxford: Clarendon Press, 1971)

Reynolds, E.E., *Campion and Parsons: The Jesuit Mission of 1580-1* (London: Sheed and Ward, 1980)

Rimmer, Alfred and H.W. Adnitt, *A History of Shrewsbury School from the Blakeway MSS and many other sources* (Shrewsbury: Adnitt & Naunton, 1889)

Robertson, Jean, 'Sidney and Bandello'. *The Library*, 5th ser., 21 (1966), 326-8

Róna, E., 'Sir Philip Sidney and Hungary', *Annales Univeritatis Scientiaum Budapestinensis de Rolando Eötrös nominatae: Sectio Philologica* 2 (1960), 45-50

Rosand, David, 'Dialogues and apologies: Sidney and Venice', *Studies in Philology* 88 (1991), 236-49

Rosand, David, *Painting in Cinquecento Venice: Titian, Veronese, Tintoretto*, rev. edn (Cambridge: Cambridge University Press, 1997)

Rosenberg, Eleanor, *Leicester, Patron of Letters* (New York, NY: Columbia University Press, 1955)

Sargent, Ralph M., *At the Court of Queen Elizabeth: The life and lyrics of Sir Edward Dyer* (London: Oxford University Press, 1935)

Schmidt, Charles, *La vie et les traveaux de Jean Sturm, premier recteur du Gymnase et de l'Académie de Strasbourg* (Strasbourg: C.F. Schmidt, 1855)

Sherman, William H., *John Dee: The Politics of Reading and Writing in the Renaissance* (Amherst, MA: University of Massachusetts Press, 1995)

Sidney, Mary, *Historical Guide to Penshurst Place* (Tunbridge Wells: Goulden & Curry, 1903)

Simpson, Richard, *Edmund Campion: A Biography*, new edn (London: John Hodges, 1896)

Spitz, Lewis W. and Barbara Sher Tinsley, *Johann Sturm on Education: The Reformation and Humanist Learning* (St Louis, MO: Concordia Publishing House, 1995)

Stählin, Karl, *Sir Francis Walsingham und seine Zeit* (Heidelberg: Carl Winter's Universitätsbuchhandlung, 1908)

Stedelijk Museum Zutphen, *Sir Philip Sidney 1554-1586*, trans. Rosemary van Wengen-Shute (Zutphen: Stedelijk Museum, 1986)

Strong, Roy, *Gloriana: The Portraits of Queen Elizabeth I* (London: Thames and Hudson, 1987)

Strong, R.C. and J.A. van Dorsten, *Leicester's Triumph* (Leiden: Leiden University Press, and Oxford: Oxford University Press, for the Sir Thomas Browne Institute, 1964)

Stump, Donald V., Jerome S. Dees and C. Stuart Hunter, *Sir Philip Sidney: an annotated bibliography of texts and criticism (1584-1984)* (New York: G.K. Hall, 1994)

Sugden, John, *Sir Francis Drake* (London: Barrie & Jenkins, 1990)

Sutherland, N.M., *The Massacre of St Bartholomew and the European conflict 1559-1572* (London: Macmillan, 1973)

Thomson, George Malcolm, *Sir Francis Drake* (London: Secker & Warburg, 1972)

Upton, C.A., '"Speaking sorrow": The English university anthologies of 1587 on the death of Philip Sidney in the Low Countries' in *Academic Relations between the Low Countries and the British Isles 1450-1700*, ed. H. de Ridder-Symoens and J.M. Fletcher (Ghent, 1989), 131-41

van Dorsten, J.A., *Poets, Patrons, and Professors: Sir Philip Sidney, Daniel Rogers, and the Leiden humanists* (Leiden: Leiden University Press, and London: Oxford University Press for the Sir Thomas Browne Institute, 1962)

van Dorsten, Jan A., 'Sidney and Franciscus Junius the elder', *HLQ* 42 (1978-79), 1-13

van Dorsten, Jan A., 'Sidney and Languet', *HLQ* 29 (1966), 215-22

van Dorsten, Jan, Dominic Baker-Smith and Arthur F. Kinney, eds, *Sir Philip Sidney: 1586 and the Creation of a Legend* (Leiden: E.J. Brill/Leiden University Press for the Thomas Browne Institute, 1986)

van Dorsten, Jan, *see also* Strong, R.C.

Venn, John and J.A. Venn, *Alumni Cantabrigienses*, pt 1, 4 vols (Cambridge: Cambridge University Press, 1924)

Voet, Leon with Jenny Voet-Gisolle, *The Plantin Press (1558-1589): A bibliography of the works printed and published by Christopher Platin at Antwerp and Leiden*, 6 vols (Amsterdam: Von Hoeve, 1980-1983)

von Klarwill, Victor, *Queen Elizabeth and Some Foreigners*, trans. T.H. North (London: John Kane, 1928)

Waddington, Charles, *Ramus (Pierre de la Ramée): Sa vie, ses écrits et ses opinions* (Paris: Ch. Meyrueis, 1858)

Wallace, Malcolm William, *The Life of Sir Philip Sidney* (Cambridge: Cambridge University Press, 1915)

Ward, B.M., *The Seventeenth Earl of Oxford 1550-1604 from contemporary documents* (London: John Murray, 1928)

Watson, Elizabeth Porges, 'Introduction' to *Defence of Poesie, Astrophil and Stella and Other Writings* (London: Everyman, 1997), xxvii-lxii

Watson, George, ed., *The New Cambridge Bibliography of English Literature* (Cambridge: Cambridge University Press, 1974)

Wayne, Don E., *Penshurst: The Semiotics of Place and the Poetics of History* (London: Methuen, 1984)

Webb, H.J., 'The mathematical and military works of Thomas Digges, with an account of his life', *Modern Language Quarterly* 6 (1945), 389-400

Weiner, Andrew D., *Sir Philip Sidney and the Poetics of Protestantism: a study in contexts* (Minneapolis: University of Minnesota Press, 1978)

Wilkinson, Nevile R., *Wilton House Guide: A Handbook for visitors* (London: Chiswick Press, 1908)

Williams, Franklin B., Jr, *Index of Dedications and Commendatory Verses in English Books before 1641* (London: The Bibliographical Society, 1962)

Williams, Penry, *The Council in the Marches of Wales under Elizabeth I* (Cardiff: University of Wales Press, 1958)

Wilson, Charles, *Queen Elizabeth and the Revolt of the Netherlands* (London: Macmillan, 1970)

Wilson, Derek, *Sweet Robin: A Biography of Robert Dudley, Earl of Leicester 1533-1588* (London: Hamish Hamilton, 1981)

Wilson, Mona, *Sir Philip Sidney* (London: Duckworth, 1931)

Wolf, Adam, *Lucas Geizkofler und seine Selbstbiographie 1550-1620* (Vienna: Wilhelm Braumüller, 1873)

Wood, Anthony à, *Athenae Oxonienses*, 4 vols (London, 1813)

Woolfson, Jonathan, *Padua and the Tudors: English students in Italy, 1485-1603* (Toronto: University of Toronto Press, 1998)

Worden, Blair, *The Sound of Virtue: Philip Sidney's 'Arcadia' and Elizabethan Politics* (New Haven, CT: Yale University Press, 1996)

Woudhuysen, H.R., 'A "lost" Sidney document', *Bodleian Library Record* 13 (1990), 353-9

Woudhuysen, H.R., *Sir Philip Sidney and the Circulation of Manuscripts 1558-1640* (Oxford: Clarendon Press, 1996)

Wright, Pam, 'A change in direction: the ramifications of a female household, 1558-1603'

in *The English Court: from the Wars of the Roses to the Civil War*, ed. David Starkey *et al.*
(London: Longman, 1987), 147–72

Yates, Frances A., 'Elizabethan chivalry: the romance of the Accession Day tilts,' *JWCI*
(1957), 4–25

Yates, Frances A., *Giordano Bruno and the Hermetic Tradition* (London: Routledge & Kegan
Paul, 1964)

Young, Alan, *Tudor and Jacobean Tournaments* (London: George Philip, 1987)

Zamoyski, Adam, *The Polish Way: A thousand-year history of the Poles and their culture* (London:
John Murray, 1987)

Zandvoort, R.W., 'Sidney in Austria', *Weiner Beiträge zur Englischen Philologie* 66 (1958),
227–45

Zins, Henryk, 'Philip Sidney a Polska', *Kwartalnik Neofilologiczny* (1974), 147–57

Zins, Henryk, 'Poeta Philip Sidney – Anglieski pretendent do tronu Polskiego?', *Przeglad
Humanistyczny* 8 (1974), 83–95

6. Unpublished work

Brewerton, Patricia, 'Crossing boundaries: the career of a sixteenth-century physician',
paper, 1999.

Brewerton, Patricia, 'Paper Trails: Re-reading Robert Beale as Clerk to the Privy
Council', Ph.D., dissertation, University of London, 1998

Merton, Charlotte Isabelle, 'The women who served Queen Mary and Queen Elizabeth:
Ladies, gentlewomen and maids of the Privy Chamber, 1553–1603', Ph.D.,
dissertation, University of Cambridge, 1992

Index

Index

employs PS in Germany, 94,
100–1; friendship with PS,
57–8; negotiates to marry
daughter to PS, 58–61
Challoner, Sir Thomas, 24, 39
Chapman, George, 226
Charles of Hapsburg, Archduke,
suitor to Elizabeth, 26–30
Charles of Styria, Archduke, 34
Charles V, Holy Roman
Emperor, 284
Charles IX, King of France, 33,
68–9, 75, 76, 77, 78, 79–86,
90, 93, 102, 219; makes PS
gentleman of his
bedchamber, 81–2, 130; death
of, 128
Charlotte de Bourbon, wife of
William of Orange, 183
Cheke, John, 16, 42
Christopher, Prince Palatine, 116
Churchyard, Thomas, 37
Cicero, Marcus Tullius, 54; *De
amicitia*, 124; *De officiis*, 45, 110,
150; letters of, 45, 108
Ciceronianism, 54–5
Clanrickarde, Earl of, 159, 199
Clark, 285
Clifford, Christopher, 133
Clifton, Sir Gervais, 281
Clinton, Edward Fiennes de,
Earl of Lincoln: embassy to
France, 69, 70, 72, 73, 75–6,
77, 167, 170
Clowes, William, 314
Cobham, Lord, ambassador in
Paris, 209, 246, 258
Cockeram, John, 39, 143–4
Coligny, Admiral Gaspard de,
69, 75, 76, 77, 79, 80–1;
assassination attempt, 84–5;
murder of, 86, 88–9
Colshill, Robert, 166
Condé, Prince of, 85
Coningsby, Thomas, 104
Constable, Henry, 240
Contarini: *Il Stato di Vinegia*, 108
Cooke, Sir Anthony, 16
Cooper, Dr Thomas, 53–4;
*Thesavrvs Lingvæ Romanæ et
Britannicæ*, 53
Copernicus, Nicholas, 253
*Copy of a Letter . . . [Leicester's
Commonwealth]*, 260–1
Corbett, Sir Andrew, 50
Corbett, Robert, 120–1, 125
Corbett, Vincent, 120
Corbett family, 42
Cornwallis, Sir Thomas, 26, 242

Council of Trent, 31
Coventry and Lichfield, Bishop
of, 42
Cox, Richard, 16
Crato von Crafftheim, Johannes,
104, 166, 245
Crescia, Captain George, 312
Cressy, Gervase, 170
Croft, Sir James, 26
Crowley, Robert, 53
Culverwell, Mr, 99

Dalrymple, David, 180
Daneau, Lambert: *Geographiæ
Poeticæ*, 188, 247
Daniel, Samuel, 226
Dannewitz, secretary to
Matthias of Austria, 222
Danus, Johannes Laurentius, 116
Darcy, Lady Elizabeth, 26
d'Avigna, Antonio, 246
Davison, William, 202–3, 213,
237, 264, 276, 280–1, 285–6,
288–90, 294, 306
Day, Thomas, 54
de Banos, Théophile, 78, 127,
136, 139–41, 154, 247
de Bacqueville, Sieur, 209
de Bèze, Théodore, 255
de Brii, Derick Theodor, 2
de Coligny, Louise, wife of
William of Orange, 240, 244
de Foix, Paul, 130
de Fremyn, Charles, 246
de Glaubourg, Jean, 136
de Guaras, Antonio, 122–3, 158,
185
de Harlay, Charles, 136
de Lansac, 130
de l'Écluse, Charles, 104, 147–8,
173, 175, 274
del Vasco, Marques, 311–12
de Marne, Claude, 97
de Mount, Canullo, 302
de Morvillier, M., 89
de Niort, M., minister at La
Rochelle, 255
de Quadra, bishop of Aquila,
26–9
de Serres, Jean, 83
De Sidne, William, 15
de Slavata, Albert
de Slavata, Michael, 116, 120, 123,
155–6
de Stolberg, Juliana, 117
de Sydenie, John, 15
de Tamars, Comte, 191
de Thou, Jacques-Auguste, 81–2,
107

de Vere, Edward, seventeenth
Earl of Oxford, 59–60, 132,
207, 234, 236; quarrel with PS,
215–18, 220
de Villiers, Loiseleur, 212, 244
de Viçose, Alfaranti, Sieur
d'Alfeyran, 246
de Vulcob, Jean, Sieur de Sassy,
104, 126
Dee, John, 40, 55, 66–7, 169–70,
253–4, 266–7; *General and Rare
Memorial*, 156; *Monas
hieroglyphica*, 111
Delius, Matthaeus, 118
Denbigh, Robert Lord, son of
Leicester, 235, 247, 261
Denny, Edward, 109–10, 169,
248, 262
Derby, Earl of, 61
Derricke, John: *The Image of
Irelande*, on HS and PS, 64–5,
247
Dethick, a goldsmith, 211
Devereux, Dorothy, 238, 248
Devereux, Lettice, née Knollys,
158, 214–15, 235, 288
Devereux, Penelope: see Rich,
Penelope
Devereux, Robert, second Earl
of Essex, 4, 162–3, 255, 258,
281, 321
Devereux, Walter, Viscount
Hereford, Earl of Essex, 50,
141, 157–8, 161–4, 238
Diego de Mendoza, Don, 17, 18
Dietrichstein, counsellor to
Rudolf II, 175
Digges, Leonard, 252
Digges, Thomas, 252, 278, 295
Dohna, Fabian, baron and
burgrave of, 120, 123
Dormer, Lady Jane, 17
Dormer, Jane, Countess of
Feria, 17–18, 22, 30
Dorsett, Robert, 150
Douglas, Archibald, 262–3
Dousa, Janus, 190, 246, 296, 317
Dowe, Robert, 134
Doyley, Thomas, 302, 305
Drake, Lady Elizabeth, 272
Drake, Sir Francis, 241, 256;
planned voyage with PS, 265,
269–73
Drake, Richard, 273
Drake, Thomas, 271
Drant, Thomas: *Praesul*, 223–4
Drayton, Michael, 226
Drummond, William, 127
Drury, Drue, 26